KT-464-159

BIG BROTHER 2

THE OFFICIAL UNSEEN STORY

Jean Ritchie

First published 2001 by Channel 4 Books
an imprint of Pan Macmillan Ltd
20 New Wharf Road, London N1 9RR
Basingstoke and Oxford

Associated companies throughout the world

www.panmacmillan.com

ISBN 07522 6173 8

Copyright © Jean Ritchie 2001

The right of Jean Ritchie to be identified as the author of this work has been asserted by her in accordance with the Copyright, Designs and Patents Act 1988.

BIG BROTHER © ENDEMOL Entertainment International B.V. 2000
Licensed by ENDEMOL Entertainment International B.V.
Big Brother is a trademark of John de Mol Produkties B.V. and is used under licence.

Photographs © Channel 4 Television
Photographs on plate 16 by Peter Aitchison

All rights reserved. No part of this publication may be reproduced, stored in or introduced into a retrieval system, or transmitted, in any form, or by any means (electronic, mechanical, photocopying, recording or otherwise) without the prior written permission of the publisher. Any person who does any unauthorized act in relation to this publication may be liable to criminal prosecution and civil claims for damages.

1 3 5 7 9 8 6 4 2

A CIP catalogue record for this book is available from the British Library.

Designed and typeset by seagulls

Printed and bound by Mackays of Chatham, plc, Chatham, Kent

This book is sold subject to the condition that it shall not, by way of trade or otherwise, be lent, re-sold, hired out, or otherwise circulated without the publisher's prior consent in any form of binding or cover other than that in which it is published and without a similar condition including this condition being imposed on the subsequent purchaser.

This book accompanies the television series *Big Brother*
made by Bazal for Channel 4.
Executive Producer: Ruth Wrigley
Series Executive Producer: Conrad Green

CONTENTS

ACKNOWLEDGEMENTS

The author would like to thank all the production team, the web team, the Outside Organisation, Henry's House and the Channel 4 press office for their help. Particular thanks to (in alphabetical order, like the nominations):

Julian Alexander, Rachael Barnes, Julian Bellamy, Billy Buddle, Debbie Choat, Toni Cox, Philip Edgar Jones, Isabel Forte, Jonny Francis, Petrina Good, Conrad Green, Helen Hawken, Julian Henry, Morgan Holt, Tony Hussein, Paul Osborne, Adam Page, Colin Pigott, Chrissy Robinson, Chris Short, Julian Stockton, Liz Warner, Gemma Wickes, Verity Willcocks, Ruth Wrigley.

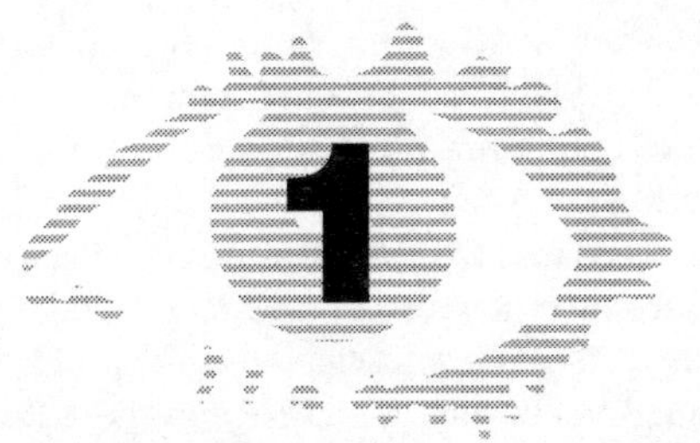

CABIN FEVER

At 9.33 a.m. on Friday, 25 May 2001, a twenty-four-year-old man with a hat jammed on his head and a suitcase in his hand crossed the metal bridge over the River Lea at Bromley-by-Bow in East London, walked along the shiny, blue side of a bizarre-looking building, and went in through a sliding door. He was, briefly, on his own. Within the next forty minutes, nine other people, all strangers to each other, joined him in the house that was to be their home for at least two weeks, and possibly nine.

The madness had begun again. *Big Brother* was back, and it was bigger, tougher and more exciting than ever. Weeks of preparation and a five-month complete re-vamp of the house were at an end: the production staff were once again handing over the scripting, plotting and acting of a massive TV series to a bunch of people with no background or training for the task – people whose only job was to be themselves (under twenty-four-hour scrutiny) for as long as they were in the show.

The huge difference between the second series of *Big Brother* and the first, which had had the whole of Britain riveted during the summer of 2000, was that this time the contestants and the viewers knew what they were in for. Or did they? The main thrust of the show was the same: a group of people living in a controlled environment, with no contact with the outside world. Every week the housemates nominated two of their own number for eviction. The two with the most nominations were then put to the public vote, with the television viewers deciding who would leave the house and who would be granted a reprieve. The prize for being the last one in the house was the same – £70,000 – while those who were evicted along the way got nothing – except a brief moment of celebrity.

However, within the basic *Big Brother* framework, the second series had many surprises in store that the contestants did not expect and for which they could not prepare. Most of all, the people were different: a new mix of personalities whose interactions with each other would astonish the viewers, the programme-makers and especially the contestants themselves.

Everyone involved in making the programme knew they had to build in surprises. Liz Warner, Commissioning Editor for Channel 4, described it as 'turning up the thermostat'. Ruth Wrigley, Controller of Entertainment for Endemol UK, the company that makes the *Big Brother* programmes, called it 'upping the ante'. Conrad Green, Executive Producer for the daily Channel 4 shows, said it was 'wrong footing the contestants'. What they all meant was that, although the *Big Brother* experience alone made compelling viewing, there had to be some major variations on the theme which would stamp the second series with originality.

That's why the team decided that there would be eleven housemates this time, which was the single biggest change from the original format. Ruth explained, 'We wanted eleven because it solves the problem of the final week, which could be incredibly boring, with three people sitting around just waiting to get out. They disengage from the game show, and it's like a long, slow death. Having four left in the final week meant that we could have an eviction on Thursday, so that on the final Friday evening we were left with three, like last year.

'We'd done all the planning for eleven people going in from the start when we realized we couldn't do it, because the website was designed to take ten pictures and names, and it couldn't be changed. As a programme maker I was furious about this rigidity but because this is a multi-media programme, and as the website is even more important this year that it was last year, we had to come up with another scheme; that's when we decided to put the eleventh person in after the first eviction. In the end, what seemed like a problem worked out well, because it gave us the chance to let viewers decide who it should be, and that meant there was more viewer participation in the first week. The public were able to decide who they wanted to add to the mix.

'The other great thing about not putting that final person in until the first eviction was that it kept the other ten in suspense. They didn't know what was happening, all they had was the message pinned to the rag doll.'

The element of surprise was not the only thing built into the structure of the show to prevent the contestants from feeling too at ease. The production team also decided that the tasks set for the contestants would be more demanding for the second series. 'For example,' said Ruth, 'we got them to learn first aid. Last year they would simply have been given a test on it, using one of those dolls you practise resuscitation on. This year, they got up to find that a meteorite had crashed in the garden injuring four people – they had to deal with it.' The disembodied Big Brother was also harsher and less accommodating towards the second set of housemates, who soon discovered that pleading and wheedling in the Diary Room wouldn't get them anywhere.

It was written into the rules that the contestants could not talk about the first series or the celebrity series. 'We wanted it to be their experience,' said Conrad. 'We did not want them defining everything by comparing it with what happened last year, or what happened with the celebrities. That's why the house was revamped, so that it would feel unique to them.'

One of the biggest surprises, for contestants and viewers alike, was the house itself. The original *Big Brother* house, with its pastel-coloured, curved walls and spartan furniture, had become familiar to the millions who tuned in to watch the first series. When the week-long *Celebrity Big Brother* was run in aid of Comic Relief, only eleven weeks before the second series was launched, the place looked unchanged. Jack Dee, Claire Sweeney, Vanessa Feltz, Anthea Turner, Chris Eubank and Keith Duffy found themselves confined to the same

BIG BROTHER TECHNICAL TRIVIA

1. Five manned Hitachi broadcast cameras moved around the camera run, following the contestants from behind the one-way mirrors.
2. Another thirteen remote-control cameras were operated by the producers.
3. Thirteen more fixed cameras kept every area of the house and garden under surveillance.
4. More than forty microphones were positioned around the house.
5. The housemates had to wear their radio microphones, costing £3,000 each, at all times, except when asleep in bed or in the shower.
6. The voice of Big Brother was relayed through the house by a tannoy system. The voice belonged to the producer on duty.
7. The control room contained thirty-five monitors, watched over round the clock by teams of producers, directors, loggers (who keep a record of what happens in the house) and vision mixers.
8. Two thousand radio microphone batteries were needed for the whole series. The contestants renewed their batteries twice a day.
9. Nine thousand hours of tape were recorded.
10. A total of 150 producers, directors, editors, production staff and members of the web team worked on *Big Brother*, with a team of sixty working on each programme. Even through the night there were always three producers, two directors and twenty-two other crew members on duty.

rooms that had been home to Mel, Anna, Craig, Nick, Nichola, Caroline, Andrew, Sada, Tom, Darren and Claire the previous summer.

But behind the cameras, the house was already changing with as many as fifty people working on it at any one time. The hammering and sawing was put on temporary hold for *Celebrity Big Brother*, but work was well under way to transform the house into the bigger, more luxurious, more chic home that was unveiled first to Bubble, then to Amma and Helen, then to Dean, Stuart and Narinder, and finally to Penny, Elizabeth, Brian and Paul on that Friday morning when they left their lives behind to take part in the most fascinating game show ever invented.

The £200,000 makeover was the work of Colin Pigott, the man responsible for the original house. Although the second house looks completely different, it is, in fact, an extended and refurbished version of the first. The sitting room and the bedrooms are all bigger, one of the bedrooms has a huge three-seater jacuzzi en-suite, and there is twenty-five per cent more garden than there was last year. But it is the increase in the comfort and stylishness of the house that is most striking – Colin's style for the first house was nicknamed 'penal chic'; this year it's base camp meets cabin fever, after the Scandinavian wood cabin feel of the place.

The theme of the design is 'natural', with plenty of wood and stone used throughout. The kitchen has purpose-built units of waxed oak, with curved lines and no sharp corners; wood and cork line the walls, and bright rugs and comfortable seating are arranged around a large coffee table. Double doors lead on to a decked patio, so that the garden can be used whatever the weather. Continuing the natural, environmentally-friendly theme, there are comfortable lounging seats made from recycled tyres in the conservatory area. It is much more homely than the original house.

One major innovation is the addition of natural light in the bedrooms, with real windows allowing daylight into the rooms. Colin resisted attempts to have blinds put up at the windows, so the contestants grew used to sleeping

PETS: CHICKENS AND FISH

The chickens were not neglected in the re-design and re-building of the *Big Brother* house. Their state-of-the-art hen house even had a 'bedroom' upstairs for them to roost in at night.

During the first series, the hens were all Rhode Island Reds, but this time round they were a mixture of different breeds. The cockerel and two of the hens were Rhode Island Reds, there were two black Bovans Nera hens, and two pretty White Star hens, hybrid Leghorns. Colin Pigott's deputy, Chrissy Robinson, was again in charge of providing the hens for the programme.

'They are not the same hens, but for everybody who keeps asking, Marjorie is alive and well and living happily at the farm in Essex where she came from,' she said. 'The hens moved in two weeks before the programme started. But they'd already been living together to get to know one another. They are not such good layers as the ones we had last year – the Rhode Island Reds provided us with eggs the day after they arrived, but the others are more easily upset by change, and it took them a while to settle down. I called the cockerel Harry – the one they had for Comic Relief was called Colin. But this lot of contestants have named them after the Spice Girls, including the cockerel who is known as 'Scary'. It was really important that the contestants put the hens to bed and locked them in at night, because there are several foxes prowling the area. When we were working here in the winter and there was snow on the ground we saw several sets of prints. I watched carefully to make sure they were locked in at night – not that I could have done anything if they hadn't been. But I was worried about them.'

The hens were not the only living creatures the housemates had to care for. This time there were also two large, fantail goldfish, nicknamed Joseph and Tara by the crew. The fish promptly became Darth Vader and Dinky when the contestants took over their care. The fish had lived in a pet shop and are used to people – they swam up to greet Bubble as soon as he entered the house. Looking after the fish caused the housemates lots of problems and endless visits to the Diary Room: they were either overfeeding them or underfeeding them, and at one point Darth Vader looked listless and the contestants were worried that he was ill as the other fish was eating all the fish food. But he too survived his time in the *Big Brother* house.

through the dawn. The wooden beds (four singles and one double to each bedroom) were custom built, and the walls were painted in rich reds, yellows and oranges. They purposely made sure that neither bedroom looked like a boy's room or a girl's room so that the contestants didn't feel it was one room for the boys and another for the girls.

The en-suite bathroom can be entered from the hall as well as from the bedroom. The frosting on the glass door had to be increased because it was letting too much light from the constantly lit bathroom into the bedroom, which would have disturbed the girls' sleep. The problem was discovered only two weeks before the contestants went in, when a group of 'guinea pigs' spent a week in the house to give the production staff the chance to look for any possible snags.

Despite the addition of an extra bathroom, there was still only one loo for the housemates to share. It is painted in bright red and, in Colin's words, looks 'like something out of *The Shining*'. The shower was also re-vamped, with a stone floor and frosted-glass wall.

But not all of the plans turned out as Colin and his team had hoped, they had also installed a specially built open fire where the coffee table is now, around which they hoped the housemates would share intimate chats. It had the opposite effect – the guinea pigs instead became mesmerized by the fire and stopped talking. It also obscured too many camera angles and they decided to remove it.

For viewers, two of the most obvious changes to the house are in the approach to the entrance and in the Diary Room. The shiny, blue external wall is actually £100,000-worth of solar panels, the longest solar wall in Britain. Although it was not able to supply all the electricity used in the house (with cameras running twenty-four hours a day and lights permanently switched on, the demand for electricity is exceptionally high), the solar-panelled wall made a considerable contribution to the power supply, as well as giving a surreal, space-age feel to the building's exterior.

The Diary Room overhaul was not just cosmetic. After the mini-disaster in the first series, when the other contestants heard Darren making his nominations, the room was soundproofed and given a nine-inch thick door. The famous chair was upholstered in black, grey and white, so that the people sitting on it provided the colour.

Outside, the garden was redesigned to include two more unexpected discoveries for the housemates. The first was a den, which is made entirely of cedar wood and rammed earth. Inside, the theme is oriental, with a Japanese *titami* mat (a thinner version of a futon) covered with plump cushions. The den (nicknamed the 'woo-den' by the crew) provided a place for housemates to get away from each other – or get away together for some privacy – sharing their time in there with nobody except millions of television viewers. It's a favourite place to sleep – Dean, Bubble, and Elizabeth have all dozed off in there and it was in the den that Elizabeth took off her top for the boys while posing for the BB calendar! Next to the den is an outdoor shower.

The second big surprise was the concealed hot tub in the garden. When the housemates arrived, all they could see was a rockery feature in the middle

FENG SHUI IN THE *BIG BROTHER* HOUSE

Feng Shui Doctor Paul Darby went round the house before the contestants entered it. He takes us on a guided tour:

'Winston Churchill said buildings affect the people in them more than the people affect the buildings. The energies within the *Big Brother* house are very important: they have influenced the housemates' behaviour.

'The front door, the Min Tang, is excellent for fame, reputation and passion, which is good for all the housemates. As we enter the house, we are in the area of the South East, which means fortunate blessings and wealth. The wooden walls and floors are both very good Feng Shui.

'There are serious problems in the kitchen area, where there is a clash of fire and water. The open plan for the kitchen is not good. The fire and water problem – from the cooker and the sink – exists in all kitchens, but they can be positioned much better than this. The fish would be good Feng Shui if there was one more goldfish: two goldfishes and one black one bring good luck. The mirror above the sink is extremely bad Feng Shui, as it reflects death: dead meat, dead fish. Worst of all are the knives on display. Naked blades spell trouble – backstabbing, vicious insults and jibes.

'The dining room is full of wood, which is excellent for health, growth and ambition. But there are two big problems in this area: the blue wall and the terracotta wall, both with straight edges pointing at the seat on the outside of the dining table. Both walls are shooting poison arrows of energy at this seat, and anyone who sits here will feel stressed, picked on, on edge. (Fortunately, the housemates did not have regular seats, so nobody sat in the 'bad' seat all the time.)

'In the lounge area, the curves of the walls and the furniture encourage the movement of Chi energy, which is excellent. This is in the area of the North East, which means self-realization, inner growth, spirituality and finding out about yourself.

'The bedrooms have too many vivid colours, too many mirrors. The beds in the girls' room are all in the East, which is good for sleeping. In the boys' room, almost all of the beds are in the East. Bubble's bed, however, is in the North East, symbolising inner growth, learning and ancient wisdom. This is an excellent place for redirecting your life (if Bubble had been so inclined, the *Big Brother* house could have been a good place to give up smoking!). But this is a terrible place to sleep because the energies are far too active and disturbing – leading to stress, depression and nightmares. If Bubble had moved his bed he might have enjoyed a better night's sleep.

'The Diary Room is situated on the border between the South East (which brings wealth) and the South – an area that symbolises fame, passion, and public reputation.

'The garden is in the West – a place for pleasure, relaxation and creativity. The metal and terracotta containers are excellent Feng Shui, so are the cobbles. But there are too many plants, too much wood which can bring unpredictability to the surface.' Sure enough, the garden would witness more than its fair share of arguments

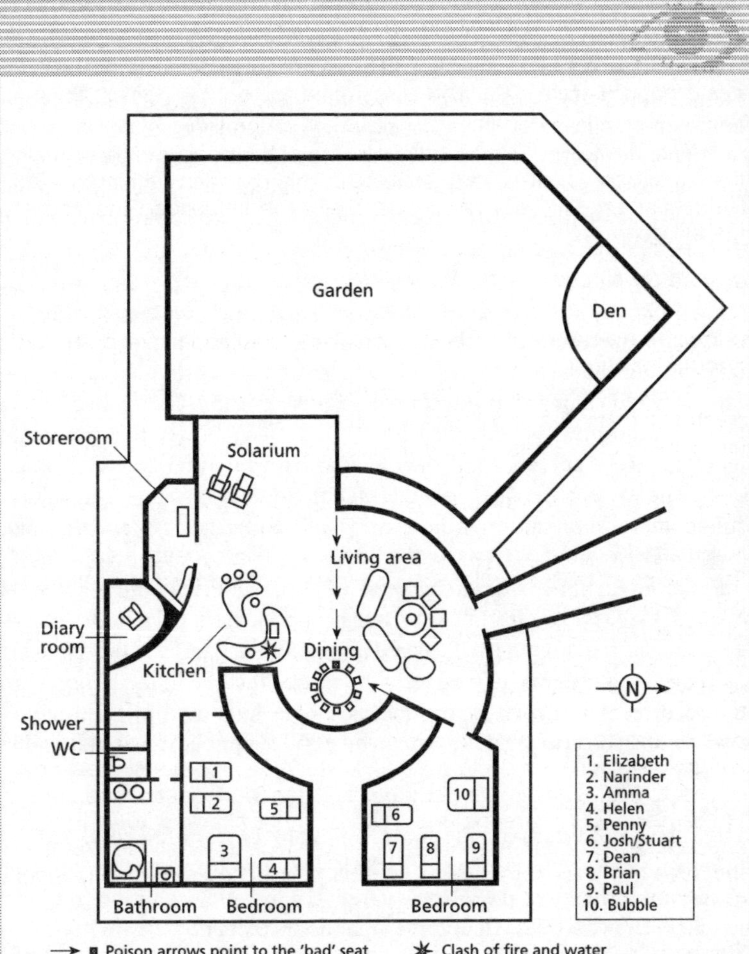

between the housemates as is shown by the heated exchanges between Stuart and Penny, Amma and Stuart, and Brian and Josh. The table outside is in the South West which is a good area for relationships. Having the fire there was very beneficial in helping people get to know one another. The building in the garden is in the North West which is a good area for networking (Helen and Paul often came here to be on their own). The interior with its rounded shapes and Buddha statue is perfect for thought, protection and recharging spiritual batteries. It often provided a sanctuary for the contestants, including Elizabeth who spent a lot of time here.

'The only area missing from the house is the North, symbolising progress in life and career.' Many of the show's psychologists would comment on the sense of dislocation felt by the contestants as they tried to adapt to being removed from their normal routines and adjust to life in the *Big Brother* house.

of the garden. It was not until the third week and the arrival of Josh that the tub was revealed.

In the first series, the walls of the house were left blank (until the housemates decorated them). But this time round there were eight striking and colourful paintings to brighten the place up, all provided by an art project being run at the nearby St John at Hackney community centre. The artists who go to the project are drug addicts, alcoholics and homeless people who have discovered a new enthusiasm for life through art. Chrissy Robinson went along to the centre after reading about it in *Big Issue* magazine, and was struck by how good the paintings were. 'We hope the artists enjoyed spotting their work on television, and that it helps them sell some paintings,' says Colin Pigott.

Most of the technical problems of making a fast and part-live series such as *Big Brother* had been ironed out on the first series, but there were still plenty of headaches for Production Executive Petrina Good. Because the camera run around the extended house was much bigger this time, more cameramen were needed, 'and they had to be a bit fitter to move around faster'. The extra coverage – on the digital channel E4 and on the web – required more staff, more equipment, and meant that, potentially, more things could go wrong.

Philip Edgar Jones was in charge of Channel 4's Friday-night live shows presented by Davina McCall, who is as much a part of the *Big Brother* experience as the house itself. These programmes featured the incredible Travelling Diary Room chair, an exact replica of the one in the house, which travelled around the country on the back of a lorry and allowed anyone, crowd-pulling celebrity or unknown member of the public, to sit in it and tell all to Big Brother.

Phil was also the Executive Producer of E4's *Big Brother's Little Brother* – a light-hearted, fun magazine show fronted by Dermot O'Leary, with lots of phone-ins, competitions and behind-the-scenes revelations. Every Sunday, the programme featured the interview from the live show with the contestant who had been evicted less than forty-eight hours earlier.

The live coverage of the house on E4 ran throughout the night and most of the day, stopping only when scheduled programmes were shown in the evenings. An astonishing 50,000 people were watching at 5 a.m. on the first night on which the live coverage was broadcast.

The level of coverage proved they had no secrets: 'What other television programme allows you to see everything?' said Conrad Green.

When the live coverage was not available on E4, it could be seen on the web – along with lots more news, gossip, games and competitions than last year. It was altogether a more sophisticated website, but at the same time was much easier to get into and navigate. Because it had more than double the capacity of the first *Big Brother* website, as many as 17,000 users could be logged on at any time. Chris Short, Director of New Media for Endemol and the man in charge of a twenty-five-strong web team, knew that last year's *Big Brother* website introduced lots of viewers to the internet for the first time.

'We wanted to make it simple for them, giving them what they were looking for quickly and easily. For more sophisticated web-users there was

GIRL FRIDAY: DAVINA

She's as much a part of *Big Brother* as the chickens or the Diary Room chair. When that frantic rush of house music begins, and Davina McCall bounds excitedly on to the screen, everyone knows they're in for another adrenalin-packed dose of *Big Brother Live*.

Every Friday night, the housemates look forward to hearing her disembodied voice coming over their tannoy system. Apart from the stilted tones of Big Brother, Davina is the contestants' only contact with the outside world during the time they are in the house, and she becomes part of their folklore. In the first series of *Big Brother*, Anna told Claire, who was joking about going out for the night, that they always stayed in on Fridays, 'because Davina comes round'. In the second series, the rag doll was nicknamed Davina. The contestants treat Davina as an honorary housemate.

The perfect choice of presenter for *Big Brother*, Davina's chatty and exciteable, she loves all the gossip and really gets into the goings-on inside the house. When she's not on the set, she rings in for updates on the housemates' antics.

'She's as fascinated by them as the rest of us, and she reacts just like a viewer – that's the magic of having her as the presenter,' says Ruth Wrigley. 'She's ideal. Young and fab-looking, but down-to-earth and really, really into the programme. Her involvement and her excitement come over on screen, which is great.'

With her first baby due in September, Davina, who is married to TV presenter Matthew Robertson, had to take things a little bit more slowly for the second series – she didn't run over the bridge and up and down the walk of shame as much as she did in the first year. But that doesn't mean she was any less enthusiastic about the programme. The contestants returned the compliment: 'Hearing Davina's voice live is as exciting as being told I was picked to come into the house,' said Brian.

lots more on the site – you could peel away layers like an onion skin and find other things.'

Web-users were able to get the latest *Big Brother* news. 'We were putting stories on the web within minutes of them happening in the house,' said Chris, who had a team of journalists monitoring the activities of the housemates twenty-four hours a day.

Through the website, it was also possible for users to pick up masses of information about individual *Big Brother* contestants, play interactive games and watch live pictures from the house at any time of the day or night. They could also go on a video tour of the house that allowed users to focus in on any part they wished. Perhaps the most amazing innovation of all was that viewers could control some of the cameras themselves. In the middle of the dining table, housed under an unobtrusive perspex dome, was a camera with a panoramic view of everyone sitting round the ten-sided table. Web-watchers could choose who to bring up on to their screens, virtually producing and

THE OTHER BROTHERS

Big Brother isn't just a British phenomenon – this year it is running in seventeen other countries around the world, with a total TV audience of two billion. Although every country puts its stamp on the show, they all have the same essential ingredients: a group of interesting people, all strangers, spending time together in a house cut off from the rest of the world.

Many of the other brothers are raunchier than their British counterpart, with couplings between men and women and (in Sweden, naturally) between two women. One girl in Belgium was happy to put her head under a housemate's duvet to give him some relief, but in the same series there was a real romance, with love notes and flowers left on pillows. In Portugal, one couple got married a week after one of them got out. And our very own *Big Brother* had its own romance (albeit after the series was over) between Claire and Tom who are now expecting their first baby. In Switzerland one couple retired to make love sitting on the loo – perhaps forgetting that even the loo is on camera. Their antics caused a few problems for other housemates who needed to get in there for different reasons.

There's usually lots of nudity, with the boys in Switzerland performing a Full Monty for the girls, strip shows in several other countries, and always lots of romping in the hot tub.

There's also, occasionally, more violence than we are used to here in Britain, where words may get heated but blows are not exchanged. In Portugal one of the girls insulted the mother of one of the boys, who lost his rag and kicked out at her – the other boys had to hold him back. Both were removed from the house and new contestants installed.

In France, there was a tendency to take the whole thing too seriously, with protesters picketing the television company and eco-warriors storming the compound in a bid to release the contestants – but the general public roared its approval with huge ratings figures. The French version also had a twist: the winner and the runner-up are awarded a house as a prize, on condition that they live in it for six months under scrutiny of round-the-clock cameras.

In Argentina the twist was a visit to the housemates from Diego Maradona, who played football with them. And in Australia the *Big Brother* theme has been taken further: there's now a *Big Brother* theme park. In Switzerland, the next series will have a really different shape, as the twelve housemates will run a bar where members of the public can come in and drink with them.

Pets are one thing all the other brothers have in common. Although our housemates only have the chickens and the goldfish, in Italy and Spain the housemates looked after a parrot, in Sweden a rabbit, in Belgium and Holland a dog, in Portugal a puppy, and in Germany a cat.

editing their own, personalized *Big Brother* programme. There was also a 'fan cam': every day, an internet poll would decide who was the favourite contestant, and that person would be on camera all day.

Fans of the second *Big Brother* could register to receive e-mails containing news from the house. They could also watch *Big Brother Confidential*, a magazine programme just for internet users, featuring interviews with contestants' friends and families, reactions to the show from famous people and video clips of bits that had not gone out on television.

Chris believes that the introduction of interactive television this year on E4 will mean that eventually pictures on the internet will become obsolete, because the quality is so much better on a television screen. During the second series of *Big Brother*, digital TV viewers who were able to interact with E4 could choose whether to watch the house live (with a ten-minute editorial delay to make sure that nothing too risqué was broadcast during daytime hours) or whether to watch it with a two- or four-hour delay – which meant that if anything very exciting happened, the viewer could re-play it in full several hours later. They could also enter competitions to win instant cash prizes, with the ultimate winner getting a tour of the house after the end of the show.

The growth in the number of WAP phones (WAP stands for Wireless Application Protocol, and means that they are mobile phones which can connect to the internet) meant that this year, many more people were able to follow the goings-on in the house when they were away from their computers and television screens. But you didn't need to have a WAP phone to keep abreast of the contestants' activities: anyone with a mobile phone could register to receive regular text messages containing *Big Brother* news. You could even give *Big Brother* as a present – £4.99 bought a BT voucher entitling the recipient to a four-week supply of text messages from the show. There was no excuse for not knowing the latest goings-on inside those famous walls!

SELECTION PROCESS

The surreal *Big Brother* experience began two days early for the ten contestants who went into the house in May 2001. A leak to the press of several of their names and addresses meant that, to protect the secrecy and security of the show, *Big Brother* executives whisked the future housemates away from their homes on Wednesday and hid them in two London hotels until they were taken to the Three Mills Studio complex, the home of *Big Brother*, early on the morning of Friday, 25 May.

The contestants were chauffeured away from their homes in a fleet of black BMWs, their heads covered with jackets and blankets to prevent any of the loitering photographers from getting a picture: it was a first taste of celebrity. Although they didn't meet, five of the contestants spent the next two nights at one hotel, and the other five at another. Each contestant was chaperoned by a member of the production team who had not been involved in the selection process and had never met any of the other housemates. The contestants' phones were confiscated, and the televisions in their hotel rooms were disconnected. Although they were not yet in the house, their contact with the outside world was already almost over.

On Thursday, the contestants were driven separately to the studio complex, where they had final photographs taken and an interview with each of them was filmed. They also handed over their suitcases to be searched: no forbidden contraband was found. They were given a final talk by Conrad Green, the Executive Producer, and Jeremy Phillips, the Series Editor. The contestants were then briefed on how to look after their radio microphones, and seven of the ten filled in postal-vote applications to allow them to vote in the general election. They also met the team of people who would be looking after them when their stay in the house ended. That night they were allowed out for a final night of freedom with their friends and family – the *Big Brother* team had to co-ordinate all the plans to make sure that the ten farewell parties did not bump into each other. Afterwards, the contestants were given their phones back for one hour, to allow them to say their goodbyes to their loved ones – some of whom still had the press camped outside their homes. Those who were married or in a long-term relationship spent a last night with their partners.

At the studio complex early on Friday morning, the housemates were given a final briefing by Senior Producer Helen Hawken, who had been in

BIG BROTHER SAYS

- Contestants will have no contact with the outside world. Phones, televisions, radios, music and newspapers are banned. Contestants may bring in two books and two magazines.
- Electrical equipment is not allowed.*
- No writing implements must be brought into the house. Big Brother will provide these for specific purposes, such as ordering shopping.
- Contestants must wear their radio microphones at all times except when asleep or in the shower.
- Contestants must not have private conversations that cannot be recorded.**
- Contestants may take in only one item of each beauty product: one shampoo, one moisturizer, one mascara, one lipstick. More may be purchased from the weekly shopping.
- Contestants must not discuss the nominations.
- Contestants must not discuss the first series of *Big Brother* or *Celebrity Big Brother*.
- Big Brother is watching, twenty-four hours a day; what Big Brother says, goes.

*An exception was made for Dean's battery-operated hair clippers, as he has a sensitive scalp.

** Although, inevitably they tried.

charge of the selection procedure. The contestants were then frisked, and put through a metal detector, before walking away from friends and family waving them goodbye, through a bank of press photographers and into the house. Although they walked in together, the contestants were forbidden to speak to each other until they were inside the house. Paul, Brian, Penny and Elizabeth's arrival was delayed until 10.10 a.m. because Elizabeth's attempt to smuggle in more than one lipstick had been discovered.

The final ten contestants – plus Josh, Anne and Natasha, the three who stood for election as the eleventh housemate – had all gone through a long and rigorous vetting procedure to win their places in the house. The selection process had begun five months earlier. On 23 December 2000, Channel 4 screened a special *Big Brother* night, which included a documentary about the original eleven housemates and how they were coping with fame. Interspersed between the programmes was a trailer telling anyone who wanted to take part in the second series to phone for an application form, or download one from the internet. Fifty thousand forms were sent out.

The initial application form was ten pages long, and included a series of questions about the applicant's life, career, hobbies, family and medical history, as well as asking them to describe their idea of a perfect day and their greatest achievements. Importantly, every applicant also had to send a two-minute home video of themselves. This streamlined the process: for the first series, only those applicants whose forms looked interesting had been invited to send in videos.

'The whole idea was to put people off,' said Helen. 'If they couldn't be bothered to make a video, they wouldn't stick nine weeks in the house. We were amazed at how many we got, and we were scrupulously fair and looked at every single one.'

The team received slightly more applications from men than from women, and about a third of the male applicants were gay. There were lots of applications from disabled people, three of whom got on to the final shortlist. Many of the five thousand tapes sent in were bizarre. Some were very short with tongue-tied applicants failing to fill two minutes. There were lots of *Blairwitch Project* impressions and many of the applicants, aware that they could be filmed naked or on the loo, sent in videos of themselves sitting naked on the toilet. One applicant dressed as a gorilla, strolled into a barber's shop and asked for a haircut. There were women dressed as fairies and men in drag. Some told touching stories about themselves. Others sent presents – knickers, sweets, cuddly toys, towels, even a lifesize cutout of themselves. One man sent in six applications, each with a different name and with different handwriting, but the production team sussed him. Some weren't too careful about the other contents on the tape – sending in clips from their home porn movies as well as their two-minute clip by mistake. One man told the team he was so confident that he was going to be taking up residence chez *Big Brother* that he had sold his house. There were lots from prison officers (who may have thought doing time in the *Big Brother* house would be a doddle compared to the real thing). And several applicants phoned up in tears because they had missed the deadline.

The five thousand videos were whittled down to nine hundred very quickly. 'It's a bit harsh, but if they don't grab you in two minutes, they're not going to be interesting enough to keep the viewers tuned in,' said Helen Hawken. All of the nine hundred applicants were invited to attend auditions, which were held during February and March in London, Manchester, Bristol, Birmingham, Newcastle, Glasgow and Belfast. The auditions lasted for two and a half hours, and groups of fifteen applicants were seen together. They were given warm-up activities to get them to relax, and then asked to perform tasks as a group.

'We wanted to see who took on the leadership role, how they reacted to each other immediately, how they performed as one of a team, who were the artistic, creative or imaginative ones,' explained Helen. Afterwards, applicants took part in one-to-one interviews. Everything they did was filmed. They were also given much longer, twenty-five-page forms to fill in, which, like the initial one, had been compiled by Helen in collaboration with Brett Kahr, Senior Lecturer in Psychotherapy at Regent's College, who formed a vital part of the *Big Brother* team.

After the main auditions, the production teams would gather together and argue about the people they had seen. The views of all the *Big Brother* staff at the auditions, whether they were producers, researchers or runners, were given equal weight. The teams rated everyone they saw as a 'yes', a 'maybe' or a 'no'. They then drew up a shortlist of one hundred from the list of applicants who had been marked 'yes' or 'maybe'.

'The yeses had that X factor that made you want to watch them, they stood out,' said Helen. 'The maybes weren't dominant members of the group, but they were people with interesting personalities who could work with others.'

With Helen's input, the list of one hundred applicants was whittled down to about eighty, all of whom were invited to London to meet Conrad Green and Jeremy Phillips, and to have personal psychotherapeutic assessment interviews with Brett Kahr. These meetings were originally being held at the London offices of Endemol, the company that makes the *Big Brother* programmes. But there was consternation when it was discovered that one of the applicants who had made it this far through the selection process this far was actually a journalist from the *Sun* newspaper. She had filled in the second application form with information that was slightly different from that on her first form, and these discrepancies, combined with her preoccupation with asking about the possibility of contestants having sex in the house were enough to arouse suspicions.

'After that, we had to set up the rest of the interviews at secret venues all over London,' said Helen. 'We were contacting applicants and meeting them outside shops or theatres, in cafes and taking them to hotels – it was all a bit like being in a James Bond movie!'

Brett Kahr interviewed each of the potential contestants at least twice and also involved a fellow psychologist in these interviews. 'I had a very strong concern that, because the first programme had been so successful, the second series might attract more needy, psychologically vulnerable people,' he said. 'But my fear was not at all vindicated, partly because the intensity of the initial rounds of the selection procedure was increased.

'When we were devising both of the forms, we tried to make them as much like an honorary camera as possible, using them to see into the most private parts of the applicants' lives. Anyone who goes into the house is observed in the most intimate physical and emotional contexts, so the form was a first template of what the cameras and the nation would see.

'We made sure the applicants needed to give long, written answers to a lot of the questions. I also asked them to draw a picture of themselves, which is a technique psychologists have been using since the 1920s and which reveals a lot about a person. It has got nothing to do with how good at drawing they are. It provides a rough and ready way of seeing who are the more integrated and coherent personalities. Also, just the fact of asking them to draw themselves as a person is another way of asking them to expose themselves for bodily examination, and again it must have helped to keep unsuitable people at bay.

'So, all in all, by the time the short-listed applicants reached me they were a much, much more robust sample than last time ... This group were a rich, multi-layered, verbally fluent group. Of course, they had a better sense of what they were getting into than the first contestants, and I think this encouraged the sort of people who are more confident. The ones we chose might have, of course, their vulnerabilities, but they would have mastered them. They've had all kinds of experiences, but I was looking for how well they dealt with them and what sources of support they found. In the end, the group contained some really strong survivors.' All this meant that it was even harder to finalise the shortlist this year – as Brett says there was 'an embarrassment of riches'.

Brett, like Conrad, Jeremy and Ruth, went to great lengths to stress the down side of the *Big Brother* experience to the applicants. 'I could see, as the

LIFE IN THE HOUSE

Cameras watched the contestants all the time, through two-way mirrors that reflected back to the housemates, but allowed anyone on the other side, including a camera lens, to see through. A total of thirty-seven cameras and forty microphones made sure that nothing, not even a whispered conversation, was missed. Private moments in the shower and the loo were filmed, to make sure that the contestants didn't use them as secret places to meet away from the cameras. Before they went in the contestants were reassured that the loo films would not be broadcast.

Basic provisions of flour, pasta, rice and a small amount of fish and meat were provided but the housemates had to order the rest of their supplies through Big Brother, with an allowance of £1 each per day – 50p less than last year! As well as their shopping list and basic supplies, they had eggs laid by the hens and vegetables (potatoes, broccoli, cauliflowers, cabbages, lettuces) and salad from the garden. Each day they had to bake their own bread. Every week, the contestants were offered the chance to gamble a percentage of their allowance – up to ninety per cent – on their ability to fulfil the weekly task. If they failed, the money was deducted from their total and they had to live on short rations for the week. The contestants were also set other, shorter, daily tasks that earned them bonuses and treats.

The Diary Room was a place of sanctuary for the housemates at any time – Big Brother was always available to talk to the contestants. If they were really upset, they could request a private talk with the psychotherapist, which would not be filmed or recorded.

There were no rules about how well the contestants looked after the house – it was up to them whether they kept it clean and washed their bedlinen and clothes. Hot water was supplied for one hour every morning, between 9.30 and 10.30 a.m. A separate tank supplied the water to the jacuzzi, which meant that Big Brother could reward the housemates with hot water at any time. The bedrooms were not designated: they could have had mixed-sex rooms.

With the exception of the first week, each Friday evening one housemate was evicted. The contestants would each nominate two people for eviction and the two with the largest number of votes were put up for public vote, with the audience ultimately deciding who had to pack their bags and go. Nominations were made on Mondays, except in the first week, when they were made on Friday live to the nation (although the housemates did not know this). In the final week, the public began voting for a winner from the final four. The one with the least amount of votes was evicted on Thursday, with the winner being announced on the Friday.

first series unfolded, that being offered a place in the house would be very seductive. There was the sense of being chosen out of thousands of other hopefuls, and there was all the tabloid-newspaper hype about becoming celebrities, making money. I wanted to be sure that these contestants had lots of time to give genuine, informed consent, and that's why I felt it important to see them more than once. I gave each of them a tailor-made set of concerns about their private lives, suggesting that they talk to their parents, partners or whoever about certain problems, and that they work out how they would feel about particular aspects of their lives being exposed on television. Conrad and Jeremy were able to warn them, from real stories of what had happened to last year's contestants, of what might be in store for them. Not all of the public would react with pleasure towards them. Brett also stressed that when they left the *Big Brother* house they would be met by cheers and applause, but that may be the only time in their lives when they would experience such a reaction. He wanted to make sure that they could cope with that and the contrast of ordinary life.

'Quite a few of them said they wanted to launch a career in show business from their *Big Brother* exposure, and although I could tell them it was possible for this to happen, I pointed out that they should not be pinning their hopes on a television programme. They should be exploring their own inner resources to see how they could achieve their ambitions and develop their talents and abilities... I wanted them to accept *Big Brother* as a more ordinary episode in their lives, rather than something that would make or break their lives.'

Brett's involvement in the selection process was only part of his responsibility to the programme. At any time while they were in the house, the contestants were allowed to request a private talk with him, from the Diary Room. This was the only time they were not filmed or recorded, and everything they said to Brett was strictly confidential. Throughout the show he was on twenty-four hour call and could be called in to the house if any of the production team felt a contestant needed help. He gave the senior members a seminar on how to differentiate between situations when he should be called in and those where the contestants could draw on their own intelligence and resources, and that of the other housemates, to help them through.

Brett was also involved in an extended programme of aftercare provided by the *Big Brother* team for contestants who had left the house.

'They had been in this *Big Brother* cocoon for weeks, they needed a bit of time to recover, to still feel that they were being looked after by *Big Brother*,' said Ruth Wrigley. 'It's a bit like a diver going into decompression. Although it seems natural to reunite them with their family and friends straightaway, that could actually cause problems. They might have a brother, mum or girlfriend telling them that they are bigger than Robbie Williams, that they are going to earn millions – it's all too much too soon, and it's not realistic. This year they were in our care afterwards for up to a week, getting balanced professional advice from a specialist agency and they had several sessions with the psychotherapist.'

When Brett was satisfied with the candidates for selection, responsibility for the final choice passed back to the production team. The juggling began. There were a couple of people everyone agreed were right, but it was a matter of getting the whole mix worked out, and hours were spent discussing the possible combinations.

'The standard was so high this time that we all agreed we could have filled the house several times over,' enthused Helen Hawken. 'So with all that choice, of course we ended up with brilliant people. We felt this time we wanted people with lots of dimensions, and that's what we got – people who have interesting, intelligent, contradictory, thoughtful areas to their character.'

When the final list was agreed, with a reserve list of another fifteen, all the contestants were given what the production staff call 'the talk of doom' by Conrad, Jeremy and Ruth.

'We were aware that, because they knew what they were going into, it might be different this time, so we stressed the importance of taking it seriously,' said Ruth. 'We explained that they were free to leave at any time, but we would be very disappointed if they did, and that if they had any doubts at all they should say so before they went in. We told them that at some point each of them would, inevitably, have a period of feeling down and perhaps want to leave, but that they should all help each other, and that it was their duty to try to stop any other contestant from walking.'

'We also felt it was important to have a big reserve list, so that if necessary we could replace them all. In some countries the contestants have rebelled. In Spain they refused to nominate each other, so all the evictions

SAMPLE APPLICATION FORM QUESTIONS

- Describe your personality in no more than thirty words.
- What things – not people – will you miss most if you go into the house?
- Write the headline you would least like to see about yourself if you were in the house.
- What is your favourite childhood memory?
- Describe your perfect day.
- What do you think are your best qualities?
- When did you last lose your temper, and why?
- Who in your family are you closest to, and who do you not get on with?
- Have you ever had your heart broken? What happened and when?
- Are you happy with your current relationship, or lack of it?
- Where would you like to be in ten years?
- Who do you get on better with, imaginative people or realistic people?
- Have you ever shared a bedroom? Who with?
- In your quieter moments, what do you dream about?
- Which famous person do you most admire, and why?

were done by public vote. In Denmark they all climbed over a wall, and they were allowed a visit by a friend or partner to soothe them. We made it clear to them that we would not cave in to demands, there would be no trade-offs. After all, this is a game show and they didn't have to do it.

'We also played down the fame that they might get at the end of the programme. We stressed that this was the second series, it may not work at all for the public, and they should not go into the house thinking it was a route to a career in television or the media. Conrad also stressed that if they or anyone close to them blabbed to the press, they would certainly not be going in.

Inevitably, as soon as *Big Brother* launched on television, the press latched on to any behaviour by the contestants that could be interpreted as risqué – in particular Penny's cuddles with Paul in the first week. The programme was accused of being sex mad, and of having chosen the contestants purely with the aim of creating sexual chemistry.

'If that was the case, would we have put two married people, a gay man, and two others who are in long-standing relationships in there?' asked Conrad Green. 'Of course there will be sexual tensions whenever you put a group of people together, but we hardly cast it with that in mind. We chose them because we felt they would all have something interesting to say to one another.'

And they did. For nine, compelling weeks.

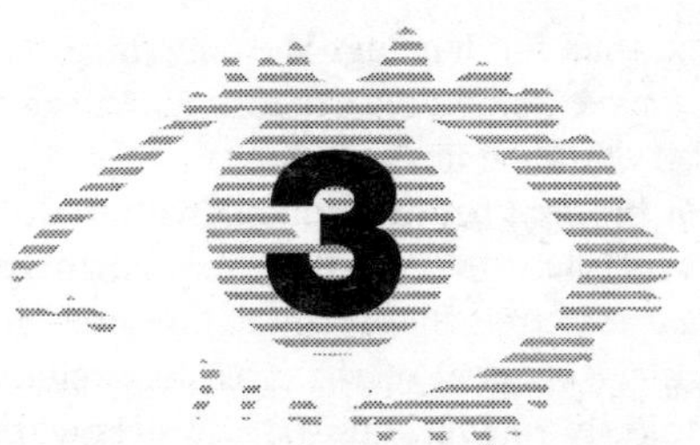

THE HOUSEMATES

AMMA

Full name: Amma Antwi

Nickname: Isis

Age: 23

Marital status: Single

Star sign: Pisces

Height: 5 feet 7 inches

Weight: 8½ stone

Dress size: 8

Piercings and tattoos:
Pierced belly button

Favourite food:
Love everything – too many to list

Ambition: To be happy. To be filthy rich wouldn't be bad, either!

What's in her suitcase?
Grommit hot water bottle; two bottles of wine; cigarettes; a book on stretching and a book on survival. She forgot her photos.

Beautiful Amma stunned the other housemates when they discovered she is a professional table dancer in a London club. It didn't cause her any problems with the other housemates – they were fascinated. Her mum, who comes from Ghana and brought Amma up in a strictly religious household, found it harder to cope with: Amma had to tell her what she does for a living before she went into the *Big Brother* house. She also had to confess to her mum that she smokes about ten cigarettes a day.

Amma was happy enough to let the viewers know about her work because she says she wanted to show Britain that not all strippers are 'the *Jerry Springer* stereotype'. When Bubble asked her about her work, she explained that she loves dancing for men she doesn't like, enjoying getting them worked up and in a sweat.

She reckons her job was good preparation for being filmed twenty-four hours a day in the house. 'A large proportion of the male population of Britain has seen my bits and bobs already, so what's a few million more?'

Amma really wanted the dancing job – she has been doing it for three years, and really enjoys it. 'My time is spent drinking, talking, smoking, and the odd dance thrown in for good measure. I make money doing all these things, actually more than for dancing. The only thing I have to do is perform on stage a couple of times a night. I work for myself, and going back to working for someone else would be fairly difficult.'

Amma's job has brought her into contact with lots of other dancers, and when she was asked what she would take as her specialist subject on *Mastermind*, Amma answered 'breast implants'. Not because she has had them, but because sixty per cent of the girls she works with have, and they talk about them endlessly. She reckons she knows how much breast implants cost in different countries, and all about the various materials used in them.

Amma says she's also interested in serial killers, because she's amazed that 'we all start off more or less the same, but some go so wrong'. She studied psychology, sociology and media studies for her 'A' levels, so she's obviously interested in what makes people tick. She hasn't really formulated her ambitions, but thinks that she would like to either work in entertainment or in some way exploring the human mind, watching how people interact with each other.

The one thing Amma reckons she could not live without is conversation, which is lucky because there was plenty of that going in the *Big Brother* house. But she really missed her cat Cheyenne, who shares her flat in a converted matchbox factory in London.

Amma describes herself as selfless, approachable, loyal, honest, empathetic, confident, bubbly, and very chilled. She's also very polite, never forgets to feed the cat, and has a fantastic memory for conversations. On the down side, she says she's stubborn, blunt and not very politically correct. Others have told her that she can be bossy, annoyingly persistent, critical, a bit manipulative, that she talks too much and that she burps and farts in public.

What makes Amma happy is making others happy, sunshine in the morning, amazing food and meeting great new people. Her heroes are her mother (who brought Amma up alone after her father died when she was five), Martin Luther King and Nelson Mandela for their peaceful fight against prejudice, and Lara Croft 'because she's bad, beautiful, British and she's got some really big guns'.

Amma's job keeps her fit, but she also goes in-line skating five times a week – and is proud to boast that she once knocked over a moving motorbike. Apart from enjoying karaoke, her greatest pleasure is going out with mates and just talking and drinking.

She's single, but she would love to meet the right man.

BRIAN

Full name: Brian Dowling
Nickname: Bambie
Age: 23
Marital status: Single
Star sign: Gemini
Height: 5 feet 10½ inches
Weight: 12 stone
Piercings and tattoos: None
Favourite food: Junk foods and foods that aren't good for me!
Ambition: To be happy and successful.
What's in his suitcase: Two bottles of wine; Mr Cow and Mr Bear; Twister; photographs of family and friends; *Posh & Becks* by Andrew Morton; *Captain Corelli's Mandolin* by Louis de Bernieres.

Brian is a cabin-crew supervisor for an airline, which means he's in charge of the cabin crew, passenger safety, the bar and stock control, but he's happy to describe himself as 'a trolley dolly'. He always wanted a job in flying, but after three years with the airline, he now thinks he would prefer to work in public relations or media. Because the job involves him keeping a smile on his face all day and being nice to people who are sometimes rude and unappreciative, he likes to relax with close friends, watching television, going to the cinema or going dancing, without having to impress anyone.

Brian has lived in Bishop's Stortford, Hertfordshire, for three years, but originally comes from Co. Kildare, Ireland. He's open about being gay. He first completely admitted it to himself four years ago, when he went on holiday with some friends and met his first boyfriend. Being gay gave him lots of special privileges with the girls in the *Big Brother* house. They were happy to share their bathroom with him, and when Elizabeth wanted to remove her bikini top for the calendar photoshoot, Brian was allowed to help her. He also moved into the girls' bedroom – at their invitation – when Josh first arrived! The men in the house joked that he was probably just pretending to be gay, but when it came to the truth game and he was asked which housemate he would sleep with, he plumped for Dean.

As the only boy in a family of seven, Brian reckons he was thoroughly spoiled and has lots of happy childhood memories. His proudest achievement is having packed his bags and moved alone to live in England, establishing his own life.

He's a cleanliness freak – it's appropriate that he chose to have his calendar picture taken under the shower – and he reckons he knows so much about soap that he would choose it for his specialist subject on *Mastermind*. He describes himself as 'a vain git' and says his toiletries are the one thing he could not live without. But he's certainly not a health freak: he does no exercise, hates eating healthy food like vegetables (although he ate veg. every day in the *Big Brother* house – smothered in lashings of ketchup), and includes junk food as one of the things he most missed in the house (along with music, his mobile phone, his own bed and TV soaps).

Brian is a real romantic, says he cries easily, and dreams about meeting his soulmate, falling head over heels in love and settling down and having his own family, even if it's just a dog. His idea of a perfect day is: 'Waking up in a big, warm bed next to the man of my dreams. He'd be an average, down-to-earth guy, nothing special really, except that he'd love me, even my bad points. Living in a nice house, going to a job that I enjoy, then coming home after a hard day to a bubble bath and a piping-hot shepherd's pie with loads of tomato ketchup, then cuddling up on the sofa in each other's arms until he falls asleep. I look, I listen, I realize I'm so happy.' Unfortunately for Brian, he says this ideal has so far only been a dream.

Brian reckons his best qualities are that he is fun to be with, he's honest, trustworthy and a good all-round team player. He's tidy, always laughing and joking, and not afraid to get his hands dirty. He admits he can be loud and a bit over the top at times, and that other people can be irritated by his brutal honesty and his vanity.

His hero is his mum, because he says that in bringing up him and his six younger sisters, 'She gave up all her own goals and gave us everything. She's never denied us anything. What she gave us and still does is priceless.' If he had to have a famous person as a parent, he would pick Joan Collins, because 'she's chic, lean, mean and she kicks ass.'

Brian worries a great deal about how he looks and how other people see him, and reckons that going under the *Big Brother* microscope has helped him deal with his constant fear of not being liked. Before he went into the house, he said that what he wanted most from the experience was to walk out completely self-confident, happy with how he looked and how he portrayed himself.

BUBBLE

Full name: Paul Ferguson

Nicknames: Bubble, Hat, Fergie

Age: 25

Marital status: Single

Star sign: Gemini

Height: 5 feet 7 inches

Weight: 11 stone

Piercings and tattoos: Nipple pierced

Favourite food: Chicken curry, my mum's pasta, cold Heinz spaghetti hoops, beef and noodles in black-bean sauce, crème caramel, fish and chips.

Ambition: To get to the top in whatever I do.

What's in his suitcase? Little pink ring from daughter Bryony; sponge football; ball game; *The Beano* (because Bryony loves Dennis the Menace); two bottles of wine; 200 cigarettes; ten hats; lots of photos; two books: *Excession* by Iain M. Banks and a trivia compendium.

Bubble is a real likely lad – as he explained to Helen and Amma as soon as they joined him in the house, he got his nickname by farting down a straw into a pint of beer and making bubbles. But there's a great deal more to Bubble than his brash, jack-the-lad image. He has a three-year-old daughter, Bryony, who is the light of his life, and he's a real hands-on dad, looking after her at the weekends. He also surprised the housemates by revealing that he likes writing poetry, loves cooking and enjoys learning new things.

Bubble has done lots of jobs – before going into the house he was working for an insurance company. Since he split from Bryony's mother, he has given up working in pubs and nightclubs, so that he can be around at weekends for his daughter. He lives in Surbiton, Surrey, the area where he grew up with his Scottish father and Italian mother.

Bubble had a girlfriend while he was in the house, but happily told the housemates that he reckons he has bedded more than one hundred women in his lifetime. If he were to take part in *Mastermind*, his specialist subject would be 'how to laugh a woman's knickers off' – he reckons there's nothing he doesn't know about this subject. His ideal relationship would be with a 'fun-loving girl, full of life, who doesn't want to change me, someone I can grow old with'. But any woman who wants a place in Bubble's life will have to get on with his daughter, who is the person he missed most while in the house and whose laughter, he says, is the main thing that makes him happy. He also feels pretty good if Chelsea wins, Manchester United loses, and he's got a pepperoni pizza and a good video to watch.

He says he was happy to be filmed twenty-four hours a day, 'Because there are so many unlucky people in this world who have never had the pleasure of me putting a smile on their faces, so it could be awesome.' Shy, Bubble ain't. But he realized the *Big Brother* experience would not be easy. 'But if it was,' he says, 'I wouldn't have wanted to do it.' He doesn't reckon going into the house changed him. 'I haven't changed since I developed the character I have, and I don't intend to. I like me, people like me, I wouldn't let it change me.'

Bubble's own description of himself is 'a charismatic clown with a heart of gold, whose only wish in life is to make people smile'.

Hats are Bubble's trademark and he feels naked without one – the cameras managed to get the odd peek at his hair, but he even wore a hat – a bobble hat with a teddy-bear motif – in bed.

Bubble doesn't make a big effort to keep fit, but does do a few press-ups every night. He reckons he gets exercise from chasing around after Bryony and her hamster Pookie Baby (which keeps him awake at night rattling around in its cage).

He's a season-ticket holder at Chelsea, but doesn't get to go to the games unless they are midweek, because he looks after Bryony at the weekend. The main down side to being in the *Big Brother* house was missing watching England play on telly.

Bubble's perfect day has already happened – it was Christmas Day and his dad dressed up as Santa to bring presents to Bryony. 'The whole day is a blur, all I remember is her face as she opened the parcels.'

DEAN

Full name: Dean O'Loughlin

Nicknames: Stan, Uncle Dog

Age: 37

Marital status: In a long-term relationship

Star sign: Aquarius

Height: 6 feet

Weight: 12 stone 7lb

Piercings and tattoos: None

Favourite food: Fish, chicken, pasta, Italian, Thai and Mexican

Ambition: Happiness

What's in his suitcase? Weights; two bottles of wine; hair clippers; Birmingham City scarf; two wooden bats and a ball; vitamins, including his special herbal mixture; essential oils; sheet music; guitar. Two books: *Me Talk Pretty One Day* by David Sedaris, and a Tai Chi instruction book.

Dean – the tall, dark, handsome one – is self-employed and runs his own newly-formed internet company. He was the oldest of the housemates, and was relieved when he discovered that Stuart was in the same age bracket – he says he was afraid he would find himself surrounded by 'Ibiza kids', all being noisy and silly. Not that Dean doesn't like a bit of silliness – he reckons his ability to laugh at life is his greatest asset, and he says he laughs out loud at least once every day.

He's a real lad at heart: he ranks football and having sex as joint top of his list of things he enjoys.

His mother is Irish and his late father was Jamaican. Dean lives in Birmingham with his stewardess girlfriend Vanessa – they have been together for ten years and he calls her his soul mate. They share their home with a cat called Baldrick. The most exciting job Dean has ever had was when the band he was in was signed up by a record company for three years. Unfortunately, after one tour of America, their contract was terminated and Dean's first attempt at achieving fame and fortune was over. But he thinks *Big Brother* will give him another chance! Other jobs he has done include being a builder, a carpenter, a youth-project worker and a sound engineer. The weirdest job he ever did was as a clerk at Birmingham Crown Court – he lasted one day.

Dean is a talented artist and studied art after leaving school. He uses his building skills in his spare time to renovate the house in which he and Vanessa live. He likes to have a serious relationship, he has never been one for playing the field. He married at nineteen, but split up with his wife after five years, although they didn't get divorced for nine. He reckons the longest he has ever been without a girlfriend was six months. The best relationship he has ever had is with Vanessa. He describes his ideal partner as 'clever, sexy, kind, funny, honest, open, committed but also free and exciting, and a friend first before a lover'.

Dean is football mad, and took his Birmingham City scarf into the house in his suitcase. He's not just a spectator: he turns out twice a week to train and play with a local team, and he also works out twice a week at a gym. He thinks it is important to keep fit. He also loves listening to music (he likes jazz, Indie, pop, reggae and especially soul, but he doesn't like manufactured groups and is not keen on most of the stuff in the charts), playing his guitar, surfing the net, playing computer games, watching movies, drinking wine and whisky, and reading and dreaming. His perfect day, which would start with breakfast in bed in a smart hotel, would be spent on a hot beach. Then there would be wine, talk, good food and great sex – with Vanessa, of course.

Dean is a man with principles: he's a member of Greenpeace and Amnesty International, is concerned about the way politicians are 'messing up the world', and doesn't value material possessions. In ten years' time he would like to be in a position to 'help others or do something significantly "good"'. The things that make him happy are Vanessa, toddlers, sunsets and sunrises, good food, sex and laughter. His greatest achievement so far, he says, is finding Vanessa, and she's the one thing he missed from the very start of his time in the house. On another level, he's also very proud of the night he took part in an open-mic night in New York and brought the house down.

Dean expected to get on well with the women in the house because he was brought up surrounded by sisters – he has four, as well as one half-brother. He loved his childhood, his happiest memory of which is the goal he scored for the school team when they played against the teachers and parents.

He thinks his best qualities are that he is kind and amusing. He describes himself as, 'A tryer up to a point, then I become a realist. I split from one career choice to another because things bore me once I've mastered them.' He says he is also 'charming, domineering, sensitive, impatient, opinionated, affectionate, a good listener, a good talker, witty, extrovert, melancholy, creative'. The skills he took into the house include being artistic and good with his hands, being athletic, playing the guitar, juggling (but only with three things, not four!) and being able to tell good stories.

Before he went into the house, Dean realized there would be times when he wouldn't like it. 'I truly don't know how it will affect me. Half of me thinks it will be a positive experience, the other half is wary of the unknown. I'll get really pissed off when I need to be alone and there are always cameras there.' But he was looking forward to being isolated from the outside world, even though he knew he would miss TV and music.

'It will make everything more interesting when I get out. And, although it won't change me, it may change how people see me and their attitude towards me. I might leave the house wiser, having discovered something about myself.'

ELIZABETH

Full name: Elizabeth Woodcock

Nicknames: Biba, Bibs, Libby, Elli, Lizzie, Eliza, Bessie, Bizzie

Age: 27

Marital status: In a long-term relationship

Star sign: Cancer

Height: 5 feet 4 inches

Weight: 9 stone

Dress size: 10/12

Tattoos and piercings: None

Favourite food: Baked fish in brown sugar, avocados, fruit

Ambition: To run the Omsk Ice Marathon in Siberia.

What's in her suitcase? Wire, which was used as a washing line and to mend the basketball hoop; a roll of elastic, used as the volleyball net in the early weeks; Pritt stick; the big green exercise ball; Playdough; Twister; joss sticks; marbles; bubble blowing kit; dominoes; Cluedo; a sewing kit; two bottles of wine; Danish blue cheese and oatcakes; a cookery book; a compendium of Bill Bryson travel books; two magazines: *Bizarre*, and a geographical magazine.

Elizabeth was the quietest housemate at first – so much so that Brian nominated her at the end of the first week, simply because he said he did not know her. But she soon warmed up, although she was never one of the noisy ones. Her image was cool and cerebral: if she had to choose an actress to play her in a film about her life it would be Emma Thompson, whom she resembles, not just in looks, but in her self-contained personality.

There's a wild streak behind the calm, slightly restrained exterior: Liz once shaved her head for a laugh. And she's physically strong: she ran in the 2001 London Marathon, finishing in four hours and thirty-eight minutes. She also spent three months travelling alone around India, making friends and hooking up with other travellers on the way.

Elizabeth describes herself as 'flexible, fun, open-minded, honest, loyal, independent, idealist, energetic', and says she smiles a lot. But she admits that her curiosity and stubbornness sometimes irritate other people.

The things that make her happy are sunshine, interesting people, animals, nice surprises, love, sex and friends. The things she missed most during her time in the house were her niece Amy, her dog Billy – a Yorkshire Terrier–Jack Russell cross (who she says makes her laugh every day) – and other animals, freedom, open spaces, the beach, healthy food and good wine. She also missed long phone calls with friends.

Originally from Cumbria, Elizabeth now lives in Edinburgh with her partner Steve, who is twenty-seven years older than her. She studied Politics with European Studies at Durham University, and then went to Spain to study at Salamanca University.

Elizabeth describes her perfect day as waking up with her partner, friends and family in a rough and ready, traditional home next to a wild coastline. The weather would be crisp and cold, with snow on the ground, and the day would be spent skiing, sledging, walking and riding, before returning home to a real fire and a big meal. A trip to the pub to meet the locals would round off the day.

She says the worst thing that could happen to her would be to end up doing a dreary, nine-to-five office job. Before she went into the house, Elizabeth was working on an emergency foot-and-mouth programme in South Wales, and her dream job would involve working outdoors with animals, and preferably using her fluent Spanish.

Elizabeth spends her free time cycling, swimming, writing, drawing, painting, eating, cooking and chatting. She cycles and swims every day, goes riding whenever she can and goes sailing in the summer. She says the best holiday she has ever had was two months before she went into the house and was spent cycling across southern Spain with her brother, sleeping outside. It was a 250-mile ride, and it took them a week.

Elizabeth's motto is to live in the present and enjoy it. She says that it was her love of new things and adventures that made her rise to the *Big Brother* challenge. She had to wait a year for her chance as she was originally selected as a standby for the first *Big Brother*, but didn't make it into the house. She recognized that her stay in the house would be a test of her relationship with Steve, but they both agreed that if the relationship was meant to last it would.

HELEN

Full name: Helen Adams

Nicknames: Hilda, Helena, Lolo, Buffet

Age: 23

Marital status: Single

Star sign: Gemini

Height: 5 feet 3 inches

Weight: 9 stone 7 pounds

Dress size: 12

Tattoos and piercings: Ears pierced

Favourite food: Chips, chocolate, jacket potatoes, rice

Ambition: To be the new girl in *Friends*; to go shopping in New York; to have a walk-in wardrobe.

What's in her suitcase? Hair colour; hotbrush; lip gloss; photographs; two bottles of wine; cookery book; *Bridget Jones Diary* by Helen Fielding; *Hello* magazine

Helen, who comes from Cwmbran in South Wales, stunned the housemates by slipping effortlessly into the splits for her calendar pose. It was no trouble at all for the girl who works as a hairdresser during the day but teaches dance four evenings a week. She has been dancing from a very early age, and the biggest achievement her life so far was winning the Eurodance competition at Brean Sands in 1996 with her dance team.

She lives at home with her mum Liz, who is one of her closest friends, although they do have occasional spats about Helen's lack of enthusiasm for household chores. Helen says cleaning the bathroom and emptying the bin are the worst jobs she has ever had to do, but she reckoned she would do her share of the cleaning in the *Big Brother* house, and that she might even learn a few domestic skills in there.

Helen is a real girlie girl. She cares a great deal about her appearance – her worst fears in life are losing her hair and getting acne, and what she most wants to achieve is 'supreme glam deluxe'. She would even take 'glitz and glam' as her specialist subject on *Mastermind*. She must have been delighted with all the mirrors around the *Big Brother* house, as the one thing she says she could not live without is a mirror. She says her family would describe her as 'big hair, big mouth, big arse'. Helen loves shoes, but turned down her dream Gucci shoes and handbag in favour of a party for the other contestants when she celebrated her birthday in the house. However, she has not given up hope of getting hold of her designer-label treats – Helen says her ideal man would be 'someone who can buy me a Gucci bag and shoes'.

While the other contestants all listed phones and televisions as the sort of things they would miss while in the house, Helen said she would miss *Hello* magazine, high heels, glitter and handbags. Her perfect day would be spent getting up late, having a long bath, blow-drying her hair and covering herself in glitter and fluff, which is exactly how she spends most Sundays. She wowed the other girls in the house with her leopard-print dressing gown and slippers.

Helen loves her job as a senior stylist at Classy Cutz in Newport, where she has worked since she was fifteen. If she could choose her perfect job, she would be a celebrity hairdresser to the stars. If she can't quite make that, she would like to live in Florida and work as a hairdresser there.

Her heroine is Madonna, partly because she has done a lot with her life, but also because she's always changing her appearance. Helen describes herself as enthusiastic, chatty and with good communication skills, but she admits, 'I put my mouth into gear before my brain'. The house was the ideal environment for Helen, because there's nothing she likes more than a good chat, and she rates not being chatty as the most irritating characteristic anyone can have. Her favourite way to relax is catching up with the gossip from her friends at her favourite nightclub in Cardiff.

Helen is soppy about her one-year-old Dalmatian puppy Ruby (who was born in the back of her car). When she went into the house she had a boyfriend Big G, but he ended their relationship while she was in the house because of her flirtation with Paul.

Despite all the girlie fluff, Helen has a strong streak of determination. She has battled all her life to overcome dyslexia, and reckons it was her dancing that gave her a sense of achievement and pride in herself when she was a child. She pays tribute to her mum, who fought to make sure Helen could read and write, and drove her all over the country for her dancing competitions.

JOSH

Full name: Joshua Rafter

Nicknames: Josh, Bellies

Age: 32

Marital status: Single

Star sign: Virgo

Height: 6 feet

Weight: 12½ stone

Tattoos and piercings: Borneo earth sign tattooed between shoulder blades

Favourite food: Fresh baked bread, cheese, yogurt, plums, raspberries, English breakfasts, liver and bacon, steak and mushrooms, mangetout, broccoli, asparagus.

Ambition: To own and run a chain of tapas bars. To learn another language. To live for half the year somewhere hot and sunny. To write a book.

What's in his suitcase? Volley ball, reclining Buddha (a present from a friend to 'stop you going mad'); a shot glass and an American dime for drinking games; backgammon set and lots of other games; two magazines: *Wallpaper*, *Arena*; two books: *Lord of the Rings* by J.R.R. Tolkien and *The Painted House* by John Grisham; six cans of Stella Artois (consumed by housemates in first ten minutes); cigarettes for the smokers; teddy bear called Scruffy, a present from his friend, Simon; a framed photo of his dog, Bailey, and an album of pictures of his friends and family.

Josh was the viewers' choice, the late entry who joined the housemates at the end of their second week of the *Big Brother* experience. He describes himself as an effervescent character, always happy, with boundless energy, a good listener, generous, gentle, kind and forever smiling. He admits his energy can irritate other people, as can his competitiveness. He, in turn, is irritated by people who are negative and pessimistic.

He's known to his family as Paul, which is his real name and would have made him the third Paul in the house. But all his mates call him Josh, after the U2 album *The Joshua Tree*. 'They started calling me Posh Josh because at the time I had my own business and a smart car. Then it stuck, and now everyone knows me as Josh.' His other nickname, Bellies, is a result of his mates winding him up about his dread of getting fat, calling him Five Bellies, or Bellies.

In his manifesto, Josh told the TV audience that he had 'made a million and lost a million': he was referring to running his own promotions company for eight years. His biggest achievement in life came when, as part of that job, he organized an array of festivals and events, including an annual VW Beetle festival, which in seven years grew to be the biggest specialist car rally in Europe. He went bust when England got through to the European Cup quarter-finals and the attendance at that year's Beetle rally dropped by 10,000 because everyone stayed home to watch the match. He now runs a property company specializing in finding accommodation for gay men and women, and is hoping soon to become a partner in the business. His dream job, however, would be to be an international tennis player, travelling the world playing a game that he loves and earning lots of money for doing it.

If he was a contestant on *Mastermind*, Josh would choose London's bars and pubs as his specialist subject, as there's nothing he likes better than spending hours chatting with friends over a pint or two. But don't be deceived by this unhealthy pursuit: Josh is actually a fitness fanatic who has a well-used gym membership, and says his fitness instructor has had the biggest influence on his life so far. Josh also plays badminton, squash, tennis, yoga and volleyball and enjoys gardening and travel. A trip to India for a friend's wedding was one of the most beautiful and spiritual experiences he has ever had, and Josh now wants to spend three months trekking around the country.

Although he had girlfriends when he was younger and was once engaged, Josh is openly gay. He has loads of friends, belonging to an informal club called the Global Disco Family, which is a group of like-minded, fun-loving music fanatics from across the globe, who have their own sign, stickers and a keyring. He's promised to initiate disco queen, Helen.

While he was in the house, Josh missed keeping up with the news – but he didn't miss his monthly mobile-phone bill! The worst thing about going into the house was leaving behind his dog Bailey, a 'devilishly handsome mutt' he rescued from Battersea Dogs' Home four years ago.

He originally comes from Surrey, although his mum and dad now live in Spain. But he has close ties to his old family home, because his brother and sister-in-law live there, and Josh is a regular visitor to see his baby niece Saffron and his eighty-nine-year-old grandmother, who lives next door.

Before he went into the house, Josh did not expect the *Big Brother* experience to change him, saying 'I am confident and happy with who I am'.

NARINDER

Full name: Narinder Kaur

Nickname: None, although some of the housemates called her Naz

Age: 28

Marital status: Married

Star sign: Virgo

Height: 5 feet 2 inches

Weight: 8 stone

Dress size: 8 or 10

Tattoos and piercings: None

Favourite food: Anything spicy, Chinese food, chips, egg sandwiches

Ambition: To be successful.

What's in her suitcase? Two bottles of wine; two magazines; two letters, one from a friend and one from husband Jat; family photos; two books, *The God of Small Things* by Arundhati Roy and *Ladder of Years* by Anne Tyler.

Narinder stirred up a lot of interest in the house when she told the others that she had had a part in a Bollywood movie – but she moaned that she hadn't been seduced on the casting couch. She was cast in the part after appearing on an Asian television programme, and spent six weeks in Bombay filming. But she was disturbed by the poverty she saw there. On top of that she's not sure the film-makers knew what to do with a Geordie Asian.

A bright girl with a law degree, Narinder was working as a medical rep before she joined *Big Brother*, travelling in the area around her Leicester home to see doctors on behalf of a drug company, and working part time as an actress. But what she really wanted, she says, was the opportunity to entertain Britain. 'I want to give my all in the house – guts, sweat, the lot.' She's a Geordie and proud of it. She's also proud of being Asian, and hopes that she can become a role model for Asian women.

It is very important to Narinder to do well in life – she says she wants to give her grandchildren something to aspire to. Her greatest ambition is to become an influential and respected person in Britain, and to help other people, and her biggest fear is that she will never make a name for herself. 'I want to fulfil my dreams of at least contributing something towards racial peace and harmony,' she says, admitting that her favourite daydream involves making her Oscar acceptance speech. She was the only Asian girl at the school she attended, and although it was tough at the time, and she was called names, she thinks the experience made her stronger. Her hero is her older brother, who once made one of the name-callers kiss her feet.

One of the two married people in the house, Narinder grew up in a traditional Asian family. She met her husband Jatinder on her second day at university. They have a volatile relationship, but Narinder believes he's the man she wants to grow old with.

She describes herself as wild, cheeky, fun and says she is a big softie who cries easily, but at the same time she is a strong person who can stand up for herself. One of her greatest qualities, she thinks, is that she is not false, and her emotions are upfront: she doesn't bottle up her anger, her tears or her laughter. Narinder is generous, forgiving and says, 'I carry and distribute happiness'. On the down side, she reckons she can be a bit too intense, too sharp and can expect too much from others. She calls herself 'the bitch with the itch' – a reference to the fact that she has an irritating habit of scratching her scalp. She's also impatient: she hates slow walkers, slow thinkers and slow entertainment. She adores her mum, her brothers and sister, and her nephews and nieces, who she says 'have truly brought laughter into my life'.

Narinder is a real homemaker, priding herself on her sparkling crockery and glassware and her clean toilets. She enjoys painting and decorating, and cooking Indian food, which she really missed in the house. She also missed reading newspapers, listening to Chris Moyles on Radio One, and the smell of hotdog stands.

Her perfect day would involve getting up at 10.30 a.m. to watch *Good Morning with Richard and Judy* while eating salmon and scrambled eggs, followed by a frenzied shopping spree, buying lots of new clothes and shoes, then going home for a nap before an evening out.

Narinder's main fear about her *Big Brother* exposure was that she might never get chatted up again (although she admits that when she goes clubbing she spends a lot of time telling guys where to go), and that when she watched the videos of herself in the house she would think, 'You stupid, dumb, inconsiderate cow.'

Narinder puts herself down a lot, usually flippantly. She reckons her legs are chubby, and that women all over Britain will identify with her cellulite problem. Despite her criticism of her body, Narinder works at keeping it in trim, doing boxercise four times a week, going to the gym and running.

PAUL

Full Name: Paul Clarke

Nicknames: Clarky, Posh (because he once referred to Twickenham as 'Twickers')

Age: 25

Marital status: Single

Star sign: Aries

Height: 6 feet 1 inch

Weight: 13 stone 5 pounds

Tattoos and piercings: None

Favourite food: Cheese, warm bread, pasta, rice, chicken, bacon bits, iced doughnuts, bananas, oranges, seedless grapes, ham and eggs.

Ambition: To make a difference.

What's in his suitcase? Eight Crunchie bars; skipping rope; four packets of cigarettes; five bottles of beer – including one with a special '*Big Brother* emergency booze' label made by his sister; a picture frame full of snaps of friends and family; two books: *The Negotiator* by Frederick Forsyth and *Glamorama* by Brett Easton Ellis; two magazines and, most important of all, a Maltese cross and chain given to him by his father, and a gold disk with 'I Love You' inscribed on it, a gift from his mother to his father.

All the girls in the house agreed Paul has a pretty face – but at first they accused him of being boring. Although Penny described him as a 'bit of rough', Paul is a well-educated bloke with a good job. He works as a computer-aided designer in the automotive industry, a job he started when he left university and has been doing ever since, for various employers. It takes him to different countries, and he loves the travel and design parts of the job. Paul comes from Reading and lives there with his parents, but works in Cologne, Germany.

Paul, who has had two long, serious relationships but lots of other short-term girlfriends, says that before he went into the house his ideal woman would have been about five feet eight inches tall, slim, brunette and pretty (and she wouldn't have massive breasts). Not exactly a blueprint for Helen, but he admits it was her personality, not her looks, that he fell for. She would have a bubbly personality, would be outgoing, adventurous, educated, romantic and touchy-feely, and would get on well with his mum – and if that's not enough she would also have to enjoy playing men's games like pool.

He's in no particular hurry, but he does want to settle down and have a family one day. 'I want children really badly, but not yet. My life wouldn't be complete without a family. I hope in ten years time I have done well with my life and have a family who are proud of me.'

He reckons that the one ingredient in life without which he couldn't survive is fun: 'Life is about so much more than work and worry,' he says. But he still wants to do well at work, and says he always sets himself goals.

Paul has travelled a lot, which he thinks makes him interesting and gives him plenty to talk about. He is generous, adventurous, reckless, clean and gets on well with people. He says he is also laidback, really cares about others and speaks his mind, so that people know where they stand with him. But he recognizes that his directness can annoy others, especially if he doesn't think before he speaks and hurts their feelings. He also knows that some people feel he is boasting when he tells tales of all the experiences he has had. 'They may see me as cocky – but there's a nice person here,' he says. The things Paul finds annoying in other people are selfishness, creeping, a lack of manners and not having any get up and go.

He's a mad-keen film buff, mainly because his father works in films, and if he had to choose a specialist subject on *Mastermind* it would be the movie industry. He won a prize for his university thesis, which was on the use of computer-generated humans in films.

Paul says he loves a challenge, whether it's sport or chatting up a girl. Exercise is important to him – he feels happy when he has been to the gym for a good workout, and he hates it when he doesn't feel fit. His idea of complete happiness is lying on a hot beach drinking a cocktail, with a beautiful woman massaging him.

Sharing a bedroom with strangers in the house didn't phase Paul at all – he says he has woken up hundreds of times with raging hangovers in all sorts of houses, sometimes with people he has no memory of meeting. 'I'll sleep with anyone, anywhere, stuff like that just does not bother me,' he says.

Paul could rival Brian in the cleanliness stakes: he says his friends are always amazed at how many bathroom products he has, and the thing he could least live without is his moisturizer.

PENNY

Full name: Penny Ellis

Nickname: Sometimes called Lisa

Age: 33

Marital status: Single

Star sign: Libra

Height: 5 feet 11 inches

Weight: 11 stone

Dress size: 12

Piercings and tattoos: Japanese symbol tattooed on ankle

Favourite foods: Any vegan food.

Ambition: To finish seeing the world; to put my play on; to keep writing.

What's in her suitcase? A disco ball; juggling balls; nail decorating kits; a huge scrapbook of photos of the girls in her class at school.

Penny is an English and Drama teacher who seemed to find it hard to remember that the housemates weren't her teenage pupils. In the first few days in the house, she cooked all the meals, made the bread, and cleaned out the chickens, until the others mutinied and insisted on a turn at the cooker. They didn't seem quite so keen to take over the cleaning for her, though …

Penny admits to being naive at times, and says she knows it annoys people when she becomes quiet and withdrawn when she's upset, instead of having it out. On the plus side, she can always see the best in everything, she is a good friend who listens for hours on the phone, and she sends her friends cards and poems to let them know she cares. She says she's patient, kind, energetic, a bit manic, comic, girlie, shrewd, analytical and full of common sense. It's ironic, considering that some of the housemates regarded Penny as domineering, that the qualities she most dislikes in others are having very strong opinions and being domineering.

For the last ten years, as well as teaching in a girls' secondary school, Penny has spent her spare time working with a theatre project for teenagers. Seeing many young people's lives changed for the better through the project has been her greatest source of satisfaction. Apart from her work, the things that make Penny happy are snow, skiing and nice surprises. Her perfect day would start with an early-morning swim, followed by listening to the radio, drinking proper coffee and reading the newspapers. She would then make two or three long phone calls to catch up with friends, go to see a theatre matinee show and spend the evening in a bar with friends. It's not a dream – she says she does it regularly.

She has had one long relationship, and admits she is looking for her dream man – there are times, she says, when she gets sad living on her own, and would love to be in a relationship. She went into the house open to the idea of a bit of romantic action: 'Who knows? Anything could happen.'

Penny had no worries about being on camera all the time, because as a teacher she has kids staring at her all day. She didn't expect the *Big Brother* experience to change her life much: in ten years' time she would like to be travelling, writing and laughing a lot.

In the house, Penny was usually the first up, which is hardly surprising – at home she gets out of bed at 5.30 a.m. to do her exercises and say her prayers. Penny is a born-again Christian. 'Some people have drugs,' she says, 'I have Jesus and a bottle of wine.' She goes to church on Sundays, and spends Wednesday evenings helping out in the church kitchens. Although she prayed while she was in the *Big Brother* house, she stressed, 'I don't impose my views on anyone, and I make fun of myself all the time.'

Penny is the only culture vulture among the contestants, enjoying trips to theatres and art galleries, poetry readings, jazz and classical music concerts, as well as the cinema, dinner parties, travelling and watching videos. She can also juggle, do the splits, tap dance and sing.

She keeps in trim by swimming twice a week all year round, and playing tennis in the summer. She follows a strict diet: she takes lots of vitamins, and although she drinks milk and eats goat's products and some fish, the rest of her diet is vegan.

She was born in Singapore and spent part of her childhood in Cyprus as her father worked in the RAF, and has happy memories of days spent on the beach, the sand so hot it burned her feet, picking pomegranates and riding donkeys. But she also remembers fleeing the island under gunfire, with bombs going off around the car. When the family moved to Scotland, the contrast amazed her: she could not believe that washing froze on the line. She had some unhappy times as a child, and became anorexic, but she has now fully recovered. Having her breasts enlarged at thirty has boosted her confidence.

STUART

Fullname: Stuart Hosking

Nickname: Stu

Age: 36

Marital status: Married

Star sign: Aquarius

Height: 5 feet 10½ inches

Weight: 13 stone

Tattoos and piercings: Pierced left ear

Favourite food: Snails, hot foie gras, spicy Indian curry, buffalo wings, duck.

Ambition: To be happy.

What's in his suitcase? Two bottles of wine; nine cans of Red Bull; dice game; two bags of sweets; two packets of chewing gum; loads of photos; wedding anniversary card from Sian; trick contact lenses; three pairs of sunglasses and as much suntan cream as he was allowed; two books: *Captain Corelli's Mandolin* by Louis de Bernieres and *Lord of the Rings* by J.R.R. Tolkien. Oh, and a mascara of Sian's which got in there by mistake.

Stuart has a taste for the finer things in life. But he also has a steady drain on his finances: his children six-year-old Isabelle, four-year-old Madeleine and

Rory, who celebrated his second birthday while Stuart was in the house. Stuart has been married to Sian for seven years and they live in Oxfordshire. He describes his role in the family as taxi driver, banker and fun master. He adores his family, and says his biggest fear in life is not being able to protect them – but occasionally he likes to escape from them for a round of golf.

Stuart reckons he gets on well with all sorts of different people, and that he has good sense of humour, is a good listener and is not judgemental. He's generous, and goes out of his way to help people. He often finds people asking him for advice. However, he knows that he can at times be too direct and too stubborn, and he thinks he's 'Mr Perfect' – which drives his wife nuts. He admits he's a complete poseur, and that his entire wardrobe is made up of designer labels. The worst headline he could imagine being written about him is 'Contestant caught dressed in Marks & Spencer T-shirt', because his friends would never let him live it down. For his specialist subject on *Mastermind* he would choose 'the perfect sun tan'. He and his friend Charlie are in permanent competition to get the best tan, and have developed techniques for the best sunbed position, the right factor of lotion, 'and many other sad facts, even avoiding white marks on the webs of our hands'. Stuart continued his sun worship in the house, and the others believed he was jealous of Josh's tan!

A self-made man, Stuart left school with a few GCSEs, but took evening classes in Maths, English and Computer Studies. All his jobs have been in sales, and he has worked his way up to being his own boss, running the European, Middle Eastern and African arm of an American telecommunications firm. Immediately before going into the house, he was embarking on a career change and resigned from his job to take part in *Big Brother*.

He says his life is so good that every day is fairly perfect, although he admits there are some bad times as a boss when he has to sack someone. Despite having such a happy work and family life, Stuart wanted to go into the *Big Brother* house 'to escape from reality for a while' and to learn about himself in a strange environment. He felt his experience as a parent, husband, friend and boss would be useful qualities to bring to the house, and that he would provide a stable influence.

He didn't claim to be an asset in the kitchen, his wife, Sian is an excellent cook, which has made him lazy. But he surprised everyone, including Sian, by becoming the best bread maker in the house. He reckoned his guitar playing would be popular. Sian's food, Red Bull, music and Indian takeaways were the things he most expected to miss, apart from Sian and the kids, of course.

The peak experiences in Stuart's life have been the births of his three children, and he describes seeing their tiny faces for the first time with one word: 'Wow'. His main aim in life is to make enough money to secure their futures. He describes his ideal woman as 'Sian', and says she is his best friend as well as his wife.

Viewers saw him doing his sit-ups and press-ups: Stuart says he needs to take some exercise every day, and if nothing else is available he'll do a few floor exercises. At home he goes to the gym every week. He loves skiing of any sort, on snow or on water, and also enjoys ice-skating and roller-blading.

CHINESE HOROSCOPES

AMMA, HELEN, BRIAN

Amma is a horse, as are Helen and Brian. Horses are popular, amiable and pleasant. But they can hold bitterness and have the capacity to be wilful and stubborn, often wanting to get his/her own way. Horses are very image-conscious and dress well. Horses do not enjoy asking for help.

AMMA, BRIAN, HELEN
Get on with: Elizabeth
Friction with: Josh, Narinder, Stuart, Bubble, Paul

Famous horses: Samuel Beckett, Neil Armstrong, Paul McCartney, Janis Joplin.

BUBBLE, STUART, PAUL

Bubble is a dragon and so are Stuart and Paul. Dragons like giving orders. They do not like weaklings. They enjoy and need compliments. They have the capacity to be selfish, strong-willed, sensible, straight-thinking and silver-tongued. But they can also be sad and sentimental and have a 'take it or leave it' attitude to others. Sometimes vindictive and resentful, they can make bad enemies. They enjoy glitter and clothes, and keep in shape, liking to stand out from the crowd. With good instincts, they regard newcomers with suspicion. They are lucky hustlers who enjoy making partnerships and alliances. They like to be the centre of attention!

BUBBLE
Gets on with: Josh, Narinder, Elizabeth
Friction with: Stuart, Paul

PAUL
Gets on with: Josh, Narinder, Elizabeth
Friction with: Bubble, Stuart

STUART
Gets on with: Josh, Narinder, Elizabeth
Friction with: Bubble, Paul

Famous dragons: Che Guevara, James Coburn, John Lennon, Al Pacino.

DEAN

Dean is a rabbit. Rabbits can win through by being in the background, taking compromise and getting on with everyone – generally being the nice guy! Rabbits are adaptable, romantic and sympathetic. They like harmony, and are thin-skinned and sensitive, picking up on people's feelings and avoiding conflict. They can be over-indulgent. Innovative and open-minded, they are very artistic and enjoy singing and dancing. They don't like change and will avoid confrontation. Rabbits can be stand-offish for a while when getting to know people. They have real compassion, are cautious and need security. They like to be casually well-groomed, favouring loose-fitting clothes for comfort.

DEAN
Gets on with: Josh, Helen, Amma, Brian
Friction with: Stuart, Bubble, Paul, Elizabeth

Famous rabbits: Fidel Castro, Ali McGraw, David Frost, Albert Einstein.

ELIZABETH

Elizabeth is a tiger. Tigers usually win! They have beauty, intelligence, shrewdness, cunning, charm – and claws if necessary! Tigers are capable of having torrid affairs and have no problems attracting the opposite sex. They are very beguiling with a great capacity for achievement and getting what he/she wants. They are lucky, foolhardy and passionate but can be self-destructive. Tigers have a natural calm authority and can be ruthless.

ELIZABETH
Gets on with: Helen, Amma, Brian, Stuart, Bubble, Paul
Friction with: Josh, Dean

Famous tigers: The Queen, Hugh Hefner, Germaine Greer, Evel Knievel.

JOSH

Josh is a monkey. Monkeys are bright, quick-witted, sociable, youthful-looking and make good companions to people they want something from! Clever, lucid and inventive, monkeys thrive on fantasy and ulterior motives. Monkeys are very sexual. Under too much pressure, monkeys may crack.

JOSH
Gets on with: Narinder, Stuart, Bubble, Paul
Friction with: Helen, Amma, Brian

Famous monkeys: Elizabeth Taylor, Yul Bryner, F. Scott Fitzgerald.

NARINDER

Narinder is a rat. Rats need to be loved. When cornered, rats can be aggressive. They can be uneasy about their image, and may fall for anyone who flatters them – they should avoid monkeys! Rats lean on their mates, and like to be dominant in a relationship. Honest and shrewd, rats are good communicators both publicly and privately. They like to impress and can be very persuasive and sensual. They are charming but can have a temper and never consider themselves to be wrong. Rats can be inclined to complain and can be dissatisfied with the efforts of others.

NARINDER
Gets on with: Josh, Stuart, Bubble, Paul
Friction with: Helen, Amma, Brian

Famous rats: Marlon Brando, Richard Nixon, James Taylor, Yves Saint Laurent.

PENNY

Penny is a goat. Goats do not like rules or authority, are creative and inventive and are often involved in the arts. They can have a tendency to speak first, and then think and may find themselves having to apologize for their words and actions. Sometimes scatty, goats float in and out of situations; they ramble and daydream. Goats can be eccentric, sensitive, seductive and sensual.

PENNY
Gets on with: Josh, Dean
Friction with: Elizabeth

Famous goats: Mick Jagger, Pete Seeger, Joni Mitchell.

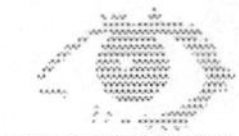

WHO GOES, WHO STAYS?

	Prediction	Result
1	Elizabeth	Brian
2	Dean	Helen
3	Brian	Dean
4	Josh	Elizabeth
5	Bubble	Paul
6	Amma	Josh
7	Paul	Amma
8	Stuart	Bubble
9	Narinder	Narinder
10	Helen	Stuart
11	Penny	Penny

(1 = winner, 11 = first to leave the house)

Horoscopes supplied by Feng Shui Doctor Paul Darby

WEEK ONE

'I'm glad I'm big and old 'cos you can get away with stuff.'
Penny

When the final four contestants enter the house at 10.10 a.m. on Friday, 25 May 2001, the door is electronically locked behind them and the disembodied voice of Big Brother announces that it will not be opened again until the first eviction in two weeks' time. Now it's real. They have put their lives on hold for this, some of them have given up their jobs, some have left families behind. Amid the handshaking and hugging, they look around at the environment that is now their home, and at the nine strangers with whom they are going to have to live. It feels weird for all of them, but there are so many introductions to be made that the ice is soon broken.

Bubble's name gives rise to a few questions, and he has to explain more than once that he was given it for farting through a straw into a pint glass. *Big Brother* has allowed him to use his nickname to avoid confusion because there is another Paul in the house. As the housemates know absolutely nothing about each other, they start by exchanging information about their ages and their jobs – the other girls are amazed to discover that Amma is a table dancer, and delighted to find that Helen is a hairdresser.

The girls immediately take over the bedroom with the en-suite bathroom, and Bubble bags the double bed in the boys' room before any of the others realize it's up for grabs. When the boys realize there is no bathroom attached to their room Paul is unhappy about the girls claiming it. They agree they should toss for it – then they remember that they have no coins to toss. Dean settles the matter by gallantly saying that a bathroom means more to the girls than it does to the boys, and although Paul and Brian may not agree with him about that, they graciously give way.

Penny admits to Brian that she's feeling so nervous, 'I think I'll fall over and pass out'. Brian says he's feeling OK, because his main fear was that the other housemates would not be nice, but they are. Penny hugs him, and warns him that she's a hugger and a groper.

'Hugging's OK, it's cool,' says Brian, 'And grope away!'

Soon afterwards, in a conversation with Narinder and Elizabeth, Brian admits he is gay, and says that he is worried that the boys won't accept him, and that he'll be nominated first. Narinder reassures him.

'I wanted a gay bloke in the house. Lots of my mates are gay. My fear is that I'm the only Indian. Everyone's got their little fears. But rest assured that [being gay] is so not a fear.'

She and Elizabeth are both delighted to chat with him, and when he says 'Girls, I really want to pee but I don't want to be the first one to go,' Narinder's instant reaction is, 'I'll give you a hand.'

An alliance is formed between Bubble and Amma when they discover they are the only smokers in the house, and that the others would prefer it if they smoked outside. Bubble's not happy and he and Amma share a cigarette and commiserate.

The girls are still fascinated by Amma's job, especially when she admits she only told her mother a week ago what she did for a living. She also had to break it to her mother, who is a committed churchgoer, that not only is she a stripper, she is also a smoker, and she's worried that 'the people at her church will give her hell'.

Elizabeth says she wanted to be a lap dancer until she met one who was 'six feet tall and had big tits'. Amma, who is only five feet seven, says it would be boring if they were all the same.

WHAT THE EXPERTS SAY

FIRST IMPRESSIONS

'As the housemates get to know each other and their new environment, they become noticeably more relaxed, in marked contrast to when they first arrived and met for the first time. Bubble was the first to arrive, and his greetings for Amma and Helen are actually rather formal, almost cool: Bubble offers his hand, shakes hands, says "nice to meet you" and gives each a single kiss. Helen and Amma shake hands. The whole tone changes when the next group arrive on the scene. Again, most greetings are handshakes, but there are more intimate exchanges. Narinder hugs first Amma and then Helen. After Narinder has kissed Helen she turns away. As she does so, Helen's expression changes immediately. Look at her surveying Narinder, trying to gauge how attractive she is and if she represents a threat. Helen follows Narinder and repeatedly tries to engage her, eventually successfully. The two have a girlie exchange, with lots of submissive bobbing up and down, mutual touching and gesturing mimicry. When the final four enter the house, all hell breaks loose. There's lots of screaming and enthusiastic kissing and hugging – greetings we normally only perform with close friends. This assumed familiarity breaks the ice and establishes early bonds. Whether they are positive or negative, such bonds are very difficult to dislodge.'

Dr Peter Collett, Experimental Psychologist

'I know a lot of people think it's sleazy,' says Amma, 'but it's OK to walk about on a beach with your tits out, or run around on a nudist beach, that's fine. That's not considered lowly. But if you use your body to your advantage ... '

'I think it's something to do with money,' suggests Elizabeth. 'If you're on a beach, nobody's paying you.'

'The prejudice comes from the fact that it is a sexual thing,' says Amma.

'I think having the bottle to do it, to be so at one with your body, and to be able to move and love yourself, that's a really good thing,' says Elizabeth.

The boys, in the meantime, have got down to the really serious stuff. They're having a 'name your favourite Abba song' session, with Narinder joining in.

It doesn't take long for character traits to come to the fore. Penny is very soon in control of the food situation. She has already inspected the chicken coop and brought several eggs into the kitchen. Now the storeroom is opened to let them collect their supplies, and Penny calls a meeting to discuss food. She takes over to such an extent that Brian mutters, 'Now we know who Big Brother is – it's Penny. She's a plant.'

One of the rituals of the house is making bread every day, and Penny and Elizabeth have the first go, with Penny firing instructions at Elizabeth to bring her the ingredients. Meanwhile, Amma and Narinder unpack their clothes. Amma is worried to find that there is a strange smell in her suitcase: she eventually realizes that her cat, Cheyenne, has peed on a pair of her trousers and the smell has permeated through all her clothes. As she stomps off to find a bucket to soak them in, she announces that she is going to kill her moggie when she gets out. Narinder, who is allergic to cats, is concerned enough to tell her to clean out the bucket afterwards with disinfectant.

In the boys' bedroom, Brian and Bubble are developing a teasing relationship. But there's a serious moment when Bubble explains how much he misses his daughter during the week, because he only sees her at weekends.

'It's excessively hard, but life is hard,' he says. Stuart says that his wife and three kids have been very supportive, and without their agreement he would not have come into the house. He sticks photographs of them on the wall above his bed, using plasticine that Big Brother has thoughtfully provided. Having unpacked, the boys lounge around in deckchairs in the garden and discuss the girls. They agree that Amma is wild and Elizabeth is quiet. Bubble, who is rapidly becoming the group clown, tries to skip with a skipping rope. He's so hopeless at it that the others are soon in fits of laughter watching him.

Dean and Paul decide to try to construct a sundial in the garden: all their watches and clocks were confiscated before they came in and they now have to rely on their body clocks and daylight to determine when to eat and when to sleep. They put a stick in the ground and try to work out the time from it – they're pretty good, only half an hour out.

Brian says, in mock disgust: 'Save me from these people. They're making a watch. The whole point is that Big Brother takes away what you are used to.'

At 1.30 p.m. the first meal in the *Big Brother* house is served. It is pasta with garlic, bacon and herbs, accompanied by a salad. The contestants open a couple of bottles of wine and drink a toast to being in the house. Penny goes round the table clinking glasses with everyone, and then asks everyone to sit down and not wander off during the meal.

After lunch it's Narinder's turn to amaze the other girls. She tells them she has acted in a Bollywood movie although she's disappointed that she didn't get the casting-couch experience. She was cast in the film, which was called *Dillagi*, after appearing on an Asian TV programme. But after six weeks spent filming in Bombay, she was glad to return to Britain, upset by the poverty of India.

Dean and Stuart, aged thirty-seven and thirty-six respectively, are the two oldest housemates, and they have already been probed by Bubble and Brian about whether or not they feel old, and whether or not they thought they would feel old in their mid-thirties when they were in their twenties. Now Dean expresses his relief to Stuart that there is another older guy in the house.

Brian and Bubble are getting on famously. As Stuart, Dean and Paul expose their trim bodies to the sun, Brian and Bubble compare bellies in the kitchen. Bubble's is the larger, and Brian offers to be his fitness advisor for the next few weeks. Bubble says if he was going to have a fitness advisor he would choose someone who knew about it – to which Brian insists that he does work out.

'Really? Well you don't do it very well,' says Bubble.

Brian, Narinder, Helen and Penny inspect the chickens, and decide to name them all after the Spice Girls. (Dean jokes that this will make it easier to kill them.)

Later in the afternoon, it is the turn of the two fish to be the subject of concern. Narinder is worried that the big one, which they have called Darth Vader, is eating all the food and leaving the little one, Dinky, to starve. She goes to the Diary Room to share her worries with Big Brother.

A flirtation is beginning to develop between Penny and Paul. He winds her up by making up a story, and she playfully flicks him with a towel. Penny tells the other girls that she is a born-again Christian, and Elizabeth says she wants to talk to her and find out more about her beliefs. Narinder, who is a Sikh, is relieved that someone else is religious. Elizabeth is even more fascinated, and Narinder promises to tell her about Sikhism.

Although the housemates discovered the den in the garden – which they have already nicknamed 'the shagging pad' – as soon as they arrived, they are only allowed into it at 9 p.m., when Big Brother releases the electronic lock on the door. They all run to it. They have already spotted a strange figure in there: they now discover it is a rag doll with a note on its lap. Brian reads it out:

'I am the eleventh housemate. I will be joining you in the *Big Brother* house after the first housemate is evicted.'

The contestants initially suspect the doll is a reference to Davina McCall, but Helen and Paul take the dummy to the Diary Room to find out. With the dummy in the black and white chair, Paul plays ventriloquist, giving the doll a Southern drawl.

'In two weeks' time, is someone new coming in or do I come alive? I'm really concerned about what's going on. Why have I got no eyes?'

Big Brother reminds them that they were told to expect the unexpected, and that this is their first surprise.

After a late meal, the whole group question Brian about being gay, although some of them are chastened when he points out he would never dream of asking them about their sexuality. Under questioning from Narinder, he says he has never had sex with a woman. He says he did not tell his mother he was gay, but let his sister tell her. His mother said, 'Are you trying to be fashionable?'

'She was completely shattered. I mean, I think it's obvious, but why would your mother think it?'

Although Brian has two teddy bears with him, he's not so keen on the rag doll, and says it will have to be tied down overnight. When he comes back from having a shower – with cold water – he squeals in mock horror when he finds Bubble has put the doll in his bed.

The housemates all sleep peacefully on their first night in the *Big Brother* house. But Penny is up early – at 6.15 a.m. – and goes out in her pyjamas to talk to the chickens. Bubble wears a woollen bobble hat with a teddy-bear motif to sleep in – he later tells the girls that the only time he takes his hat off is to have sex, so if they want to see him without it they know what to do. Bubble is the only one of the housemates who doesn't start the day with a few exercises. The other boys have their own routines: Stuart does sit-ups, Paul

WHAT THE EXPERTS SAY

SMILING

'During the first twenty-four hours in the house, the most common facial expression is the smile. Smiles are very effective social signals. By smiling a lot, the housemates are trying to create as favourable an impression as possible, and to form bonds with others. But the smile is also one of the most common masks people use in everyday interaction. It can reflect positive emotions, like happiness, but it can also be used to cover more negative ones. When the housemates first met, many of their smiles covered initial responses to each other and their environment – they were false smiles, what we commonly call nervous smiles. We can distinguish real smiles from false smiles on the basis of a number of behavioural clues. Real smiles involve the muscles around the eyes in a way that false smiles do not. It is much easier to fake a false smile in the mouth region than the eyes. False smiles fade abruptly for most people. In the first half hour in the house, two thirds of all smiles were these false smiles. As the housemates become more familiar with each other, the smile remains the dominant expression, but it doesn't necessarily mean people are entirely comfortable with each other. Some housemates have quite specific strategies of smiling. These smiling strategies may have an important role to play in the weeks to come.'

Professor Geoffrey Beattie, Experimental Psychologist

does press-ups and Dean lifts weights. Brian joins the girls for stretching exercises in the living room. Then Elizabeth demonstrates how the skipping rope should be used, before a flash of inspiration turns the rope into a makeshift limbo pole. Helen wiggles under comfortably. Paul falls over but is successful on his second attempt.

Although it's only the second day in the house, thoughts of home are starting to creep in. Dean tells Penny he misses his girlfriend. Penny confides that she would love to have children. Narinder is missing her husband, and goes to the Diary Room to wish him a happy sixth anniversary. She tells Big Brother how she is getting on:

'Hilda, [Helen's nickname] Miss Joan Collins, keeps staring at me, which is a bit worrying. Penny is a bit mumsy. It's all a bit scary. People are not being dead honest yet.'

She says Bubble can't look her in the eye when he speaks to her. But she reckons she is fitting in OK, and says she's trying.

Dean follows Narinder into the Diary Room, not to bare his soul about the other housemates, but to plead for the chance to watch the England–Greece football match in ten days' time. No luck.

Big Brother gives Stuart the details of the housemates' first task. They have to light a fire before noon, and then keep it alight until Thursday – a total of five days. The catch is that the fire has to be attended by two people at all times. The contestants argue about how much of their weekly shopping budget to wager, but eventually settle on thirty per cent. This means that if they win, they will have £91 to spend, but if they lose they will have to survive a week on £49. They have just enough wood for the task, and have to be careful not to burn it too quickly. They get the fire going easily enough, but it goes out almost immediately as they argue about the rota for watching it round the clock.

Penny's boobs are intriguing the others. Narinder says they look lovely, and Brian says he would like a feel. Penny says she'll put her bikini top on, but that's all. When she's giving Paul a massage he asks her about them, and she tells him they are size 36C. She ignores a question about whether or not she has had a boob job, and Paul comments that they look normal and natural to him. Penny tells Paul that if he had a posh accent he would be very attractive, and he laughs and tells her that his nickname at work is Posh.

Penny has become the house masseuse. She says she doesn't want to be labelled 'the one who feels up the boys', and to prove her point she gives the girls a turn.

Elizabeth is the first person to use the den: she curls up there for an afternoon nap, and later tells the others that it was like being in a little nest. As she sleeps, the others sunbathe and talk about sex. Amma challenges any of the boys to say they wouldn't react if a naked girl walked into their room. Brian chips in with 'I wouldn't!' but later says that he would like to kiss a girl. Helen volunteers Penny, but Penny says that she couldn't snog anyone called Brian, because that's her dad's name.

Amma tells Paul that she prefers dancing for men she doesn't like, because she enjoys getting them worked up.

WHAT THE EXPERTS SAY

STUART, AT THE DISCUSSION ON HOW MUCH TO BET ON THE FIRE TASK

'As the group settles into this week's task, Stuart settles into his role here. Stuart was called to the Diary Room to be given the instructions, and thus has an arbitrary advantage, which he capitalizes on. He strategically arranges the group in a large arc around him so that he can maintain eye contact with each and every member, but they can't maintain eye contact with those immediately adjacent to them. Think of a conductor in an orchestra: this is how he has positioned himself, and it gives him an enormous advantage in controlling the flow of the conversation. The effectiveness of this can be seen in the fact that the rest of the group restrict their responses to appropriate junctures in his speech – they do not overlap with his talk. It's as if he was directing them to respond only in certain places, like a conductor telling musicians when to play. After he gets to the end of the instructions, there is genuine and widespread competition for the floor. Stuart leaves them to it: he doesn't want to compete on level terms. However, eventually a suggestion is made that he likes, and he allows that view to be spread among the group. The motion is carried, but see whose hand goes up first, [Stuart's] indicating this is a particular view he agrees with. He has controlled the whole sequence, but not appeared to be overbearing. He knows when to step back and let others fight it out.'

Professor Geoffrey Beattie, Experimental Psychologist

'I want to see that rise in your pants, I want to make you sweat. If you upset me, then I will give you hell. I'm a bitch, I'm a hard woman. I don't suffer fools gladly.'

Later on, one of the girls asks Amma if she ever gets propositioned by men and how much she has been offered. She says the highest offer was £25,000 for one night, but she has never accepted.

Penny and Narinder have a long chat while Penny gives her housemate a manicure. The two girls decide to have an escort evening, during which the boys will have to pick a girl and entertain her for the evening. At the end the girls will mark the boys out of ten. Paul thinks it's a brilliant idea, as long as the following night the roles are reversed and the girls have to look after the boys.

The fire is already causing friction: Stuart and Dean are not happy with Helen, who runs inside when she is supposed to be on the rota with Stuart. Because Dean is outside they are covered, but the two older men can see problems brewing. They discuss it again later, and Dean comments that, 'It's one thing being crap at something, it's another thing being lazy.'

In the kitchen, the flirtation between Penny and Paul continues, and Brian joins them in a game of throwing bread dough around.

During the evening meal, the contestants drink a toast to Narinder's wedding anniversary. But after the meal, she goes into the Diary Room again to confess that she's unhappy with the way the other housemates get her name wrong.

'It's constant. Lorinda, Serena, Serinda, Narina, Uranda. From everyone apart from Stuart, who's a sweetheart, and Dean. Have they never met an Asian person before? I'm getting their names right, for God's sake.'

She admits she's being sensitive about it, and says that apart from this she's getting on alright.

Narinder is followed into the Diary Room by one of the boys, this time Bubble. It's a silly request: he wants to know whether the rag doll can do fire duty. Big Brother points out that the doll is not a human being and cannot supervise the fire.

The doll, which was originally nicknamed Davina, is now 'Paul', and is dressed in Paul's clothes.

It isn't only the girls who while away the hours talking about their beauty routines. The day draws to a close with Paul, Stuart and Brian discussing skin care. Paul and Brian both admit to having body hair waxed – Brian on his back and Paul on his chest. To Brian's amazement, Paul says he also waxed off an eyebrow once as a joke, and had to wait five months for it to grow back.

The fire task means that some of the team are up all night. Bubble isn't on duty, but stays up with the others. He only goes to bed for three hours.

The girls, especially Narinder and Elizabeth, are put out to discover that Dean has been allowed to bring hair clippers into the house: they have been forbidden to bring hairdryers, and Narinder has had to bring her hair straighteners (she says without them she looks 'like the Lion King') as one of her three luxuries. Dean says he produced a doctor's note to say that he had to have his hair short for medical reasons, although he jokes that it's because he needs to look cool.

It is Sunday, the day on which the housemates have to produce their shopping list, and Penny takes charge. 'I feel like God here,' she says. The others are not so sure. Narinder stays in the girls' room praying. Dean has walked away to clean up the kitchen, where he is joined by Brian and Stuart who joke about how stressed Penny is getting. She takes the list into the Diary Room but Bubble interrupts, trying to change the wine they have ordered to cider, which is cheaper. Penny is flustered and cross with him, apologizes to Big Brother, and is told it is too late to change the list. As soon as they have given it in, Helen realizes they forgot to ask for washing-up liquid. More importantly, they have forgotten to order yeast for the bread. Penny says they will have to eat pasta for breakfast, but Stuart suggests flat bread. Luckily, they have miscalculated the total cost of the list and Big Brother tells them they have enough money left over for yeast.

Discussing the shopping-list fiasco, Stuart and Amma agree that it will have to be done better next time, and that they should all contribute more and not let one person be responsible. Amma says she can already see some personality clashes in the house, because she has been 'sitting back and watching'.

'Yes, you are a bit of a watcher, like me,' comments Stuart.

Penny and Paul are still flirting heavily. During their night shift by the fire, he asked her whether she had a boyfriend, and she told him not to be afraid, because she hasn't. She later tells him she had expected the group to be 'a load of goers', and when Paul says he is gutted because they aren't, she embarrasses him by saying that he can count on lots of women 'out there wanting to give you one when you get out'.

Narinder and Brian sit with Paul and Penny in the garden, and Narinder says she thinks Paul and Penny are going to shag each other. When they protest, Brian says 'Well, somebody has to, for the ratings'. When Penny gives Paul a kiss on the mouth, the other two look delighted and give each other high fives. But then Penny blows raspberries on Paul's neck, which he says 'does not get me horny'. She says that she doesn't want to get him horny, but Narinder and Brian look disbelieving.

Dean goes to the Diary Room about a broken radio microphone, and Big Brother takes the chance to discuss with him how he's feeling. 'Knackered,' is the reply from Dean, who says it feels as though they have been in the house for longer than three days. He says that the contestants are pairing off with the people they get on with, and in his case he's really able to relate to Penny, Brian and Stuart. But there's nobody in the group he does not get on with.

The contestants spend a lazy Sunday afternoon discussing their most embarrassing moments. Stuart tells a story of getting it on with his wife in a lift at a works do. They thought the lift was stopped between floors, and were so carried away they did not notice it slowly descending and the doors opening to a crowd of people waiting to get in. Stuart was frantically hitting the buttons to close the doors while desperately saying, 'We are married, you know.'

Helen's story is about one of her dance tops coming down and exposing her boobs while she was performing. She didn't realize what had happened, and thought all the cheers of encouragement were because she was dancing so well.

Stuart's story reminds Paul of the time when he went out in fancy dress, dressed as a woman, and got it on with a girl wearing a rubber nurse's outfit. This tale prompts Helen to ask him how many girls he has slept with. She guesses it must be about twenty, and Paul agrees. Bubble boasts that his total is in treble figures and Stuart settles for fifty. Narinder admits she has only slept with one man – her husband.

Bubble explains he has a fairly basic approach to these things: 'The game is, women say you can or can't have it, men just want it.'

After two hours in the kitchen, Penny serves a meal of beef chilli. She has cooked every meal so far and the others are beginning to rebel. They try to stop her washing up, but she says she wants to.

'I'll feel a lot better if you don't,' says Bubble, 'I feel a bit uncomfortable about it. You've done more than anyone else in this house.'

Eventually, reluctantly, Penny agrees to give up the kitchen.

In the early hours of the morning, on fire watch, Bubble decides to give up smoking, because he says it will be easier to succeed while he is in the house than outside. He lasts for three hours before lighting up again. Paul, who said he was a non-smoker, has been seen having the odd cigarette: the house is definitely not an easy place in which to try to kick the weed.

Penny and Paul are on the daytime fire shift together. They have a long chat about their jobs, and Penny tells Paul all about her relationships, the kids she teaches and her love of poetry. She's already worrying about how people outside the house will see her. 'People might spit on me, they might shout and flick bogies at me,' she says.

After Paul is called away to deal with a spider emergency in the girls' room, Narinder, Brian and Stuart join Penny by the fire. Brian talks wistfully

WHAT THE EXPERTS SAY

STUART, NARINDER AND BUBBLE

'Throughout the first weekend, clothes have been very important for the housemates. It is one way we have of controlling and influencing the way others see us. The outfits are chosen with care from the start, in the knowledge that the signals they send out will be read by the other housemates and the viewers.

Stuart's flamboyant choice (the suit he arrives in) demands our attention. He's working on the principle that it is better to be looked over than overlooked. Later, he joins the others wearing shorts, and the next day he is relaxed again, but on his own terms. The bright orange top ensures everyone notices him. Stuart likes attention.

Narinder is less comfortable with being watched. She takes extreme care of her grooming so that she looks good, so that she does herself justice. Often, she seeks endorsement from the others. While most of the others change their clothes, she sticks with it. The only thing she checks is her makeup. This is someone who believes that to get it right you have to pay attention to detail.

Detail is important to Bubble, too. After only a day, the other housemates realize that the hats have a function – they signal Bubble's mood. (Brian observes that the black hat "is a serious hat", while the burgundy hat "is really happy". Dean says that the "little baseball, Norman Wisdom hat is out of control".)

The rest of Bubble's clothes are chosen with equal care. The high-contrast colours – black and blue with white – send a strong signal, usually implying authority. But it is also an uncomplicated, easy way of ensuring you're always co-ordinated. Bubble has streamlined his wardrobe. This man is organized. If he had a motto, it would be "be prepared". From the hat down, the systems he has developed allow him to manage his image and his life.

Within a few days in the house we see some changes in the way the housemates dress. However flamboyant the first outfits, we see a degree of conformity – this is a very basic tribal instinct. Most people don't like to single themselves out as being different from a group – and being different could be dangerous in a game like this.'

Penny Holman, Image Consultant

about wanting children, but not knowing what to do about this longing. Stuart tells the story of how he proposed to his wife Sian, including how he formally asked her father for permission in a Pimlico toilet. The talk of home seems to unsettle him, and he spends an hour or so on his own in the kitchen, making bread.

Out in the garden, Penny and Paul have another close encounter. She calls him 'my little lovely, my one and only' and kisses him. Paul tells her she's 'a big old girl'. Penny retorts that she is proud of her bigness and oldness. 'I've been around a lot you know,' she tells him, 'I'm glad I'm big and old because you can get away with stuff.' Paul says he has undying respect for her, and she cuddles up to him as they lie in the sun.

Under instruction from Penny, Helen makes brioche (a sweet bread). It turns out badly, and both Penny and Helen are upset when the others criticize. Penny seems to take it harder than Helen, and goes off into the garden alone. The others discuss her, affectionately mocking her obliging behaviour. Brian says, 'You could beat her senseless, mug her, take all her clothes and leave her at the side of the road and the next day say "sorry" and Penny would say, "That's OK. I love you"'.

Dean jokes that she's a plant, and after two or three weeks of supreme niceness, she'll turn on the housemates. It's not just Penny's niceness that bothers Narinder: once again, she brings the discussion round to the subject of Penny's breasts, and the possibility of her having had a boob job. She suggests the others hug Penny and 'feel her tits'. The boys offer to squeeze them. Penny, now back from the garden, seems upset, but then hugs Narinder and Bubble, and Narinder says to him, 'Now you know what I mean.'

It is only their fourth day in the house, but sex, and the lack of it, is beginning to pre-occupy the housemates. Brian suggests that the *Big Brother* ratings will go through the roof if they have an orgy in the jacuzzi, one of the girls gets pregnant, and they have to work out who is responsible. They discuss group sex, and Dean says he would agree to a threesome if his girlfriend Vanessa was willing. He says he wouldn't mind whether the third party was a man or a woman – Narinder and Amma agree that this is commendable.

The contestants are given another mini-task by Big Brother: they have to take photographs of one another for a calendar. Paul is appointed chief cameraman, and the rest of the afternoon is spent taking pictures. Helen does a *Charlie's Angels*-style pose, with a gun, but eventually the others prefer a picture of her doing the splits. Bubble pretends to steal a chicken, Dean poses with his guitar, and Elizabeth is snapped reading a magazine in the den. Brian helps her to take her bikini top off and arrange a scarf over her breasts. Paul reckons Brian has been lying and he's really straight, but is pretending to be gay to get close to the girls.

After the photoshoot, Paul trips over a ball in the garden and falls heavily on his ankle, which swells up impressively. The others make him lie down, and Dean tells Big Brother they are worried about it. Big Brother gives Paul some frozen peas to put on his ankle (he later asks Big Brother for choc ices instead) and tells him to rest it. That evening he sees the doctor in the Diary

Room. He is told to use crutches for a couple of days, and Big Brother promises to supply them.

Although Paul's injury is the most spectacular medical problem, the others are beginning to suffer from all kinds of minor ailments. Both Stuart and Liz have asked for medication for bunged-up noses and sore throats, and Narinder and Bubble are complaining of skin problems.

In the Diary Room, Penny tells Big Brother she is trying her best to prevent the others from discussing nominations. 'It's hard to stop it without sounding like a party pooper. Earlier I was shouting a bit.' She says she is enjoying being in the house. 'I felt a bit anxious today, I want to make sure there's some kind of structure going on. Dean's done all the cleaning, they're all pulling their weight and getting into a routine, which I thought wouldn't happen. I enjoy looking after everyone and I know I've got to hold back a bit ... I was concerned for Narinder being upset about her name. I get upset for other people, I want her to feel supported.'

Penny complains that whenever the group have a discussion, the other housemates jump from one subject to the next. 'They're very excitable, it's quite endearing.'

Penny has taken on the role of Big Brother's spokesperson among the housemates: when, in the early evening, they are all told to go into the boys' room while security men search the garden because someone has been trying to throw something over the wall, Brian tries to incite Narinder to break the curfew and go into the lounge, where they can hear someone moving around. It is Penny who firmly stops her, reminding her that she will be evicted for disobedience.

Liz is getting close to the other girls: she has a chat with Helen in the bedroom about how she once had her head shaved which, she says, made her look like 'a fat lesbian'. Then she looks at the pictures Narinder has brought into the house of her family. Narinder is missing life outside, particularly the food. She is constipated, because her normal diet is much spicier, and she misses vodka. She and Amma compare notes on how much they drink, and agree that it takes at least seven vodkas to get them going – Narinder admits to having been barred from a couple of pubs after all-evening vodka sessions.

After a dinner cooked by Amma, and spiced up with green chillis to help Narinder's problem, the contestants have their first house meeting. Helen says she thinks she is being treated like the dumb blonde and that nobody takes her seriously. She moans that they all laughed at her bread. Dean, rapidly becoming the elder statesman, explains: 'The reason people laughed at your bread was because it was rubbish bread. But you had a go. My bread would be rubbish too. Bubble made bread with no yeast, and that was as much use as a chocolate teapot. So don't knock yourself out over that.'

Narinder says she thinks it is pathetic that the housemates, Helen in particular, are still failing to get her name right.

They discuss how some of them are feeling marginalized by more dominant members of the group. Amma admits she is one of the dominant people, but says she knows it is her own fault.

'My mouth is big and my voice is loud and I should shout. But everyone should make a little bit more of an effort to listen to people you know don't say a great deal all the time.'

Bubble, in a not-very-veiled reference to Penny, says it is not just talking over people that is upsetting him, but 'doing over people'. He explains he would love to get into the kitchen to cook (Bubble prides himself on his cooking) but never gets the chance.

Penny seems upset, and says she feels threatened. 'It's making me feel guilty for just being myself.'

The discussion broadens to include the housemates' relationship with Big Brother. Narinder is frank: she regards the Diary Room as a confessional where she can open up. She thinks that is better than pretending to be 'all lovey-dovey' with each other. The others disagree: they regard Big Brother as the enemy, to be outwitted.

After the heavy-duty meeting, the night ends in hilarity. The boys squeeze the doll inside Bubble's clothes. He lies down in the lounge, and Narinder screams when the 'doll' appears to get up and move.

The boys have solved the problem of remembering Narinder's name: they are calling her Naz.

Paul, Amma, Bubble and Stuart are on the graveyard shift, tending the fire. Amma and Bubble pass the time by discussing whether they would have sex in the house. Amma says she would only go as far as a snog. But Bubble, the man who has boasted of more than one hundred lovers, says, 'If the opportunity is there you have to take it. I don't get offered it a lot, so you've got to take it while it's there.' Despite their discussion, the hours drag, and at 3 a.m. they decide to mow the lawn and water the plants.

Penny, Brian and Dean are on the 6 a.m. fire-duty shift. Penny tells the other two that she was weepy after the house meeting the previous evening. 'I felt I had to justify the fact that I had just been trying to help out … God, have I just become this kitchen woman?' Brian repeats the essence of what Amma said at the meeting – that everyone else in the group should be able to stand up for themselves when they want to cook.

The big drama of the morning comes when Helen drops Penny's comb through the slatted decking as she cuts Penny's hair. Bubble manages to retrieve it, to applause from the girls. Helen has a premonition that she's going to be one of the first to be nominated, and says she won't mind being the first to leave the house. Liz tells her not to be paranoid, but admits that she has her own doubts about staying the course now she has seen how strong the opposition is.

It's another sunny day, and the housemates are all lounging around the garden. Brian dances in front of Narinder, and Amma tells him how, if he were a table dancer, he should handle a customer who groped him. Narinder obligingly rubs Brian's legs, and Amma tells him how to grab her where it hurts – except that Narinder is a woman, so it wouldn't work. But Amma still warns Brian to make sure he gets the money first, and he demands £50 from Narinder.

No-one knows whether it is as a result of seeing Brian dancing, or the chillis in last night's meal, but halfway through their fifth day in the house, Narinder finally does a poo. She announces her success to all the others, but doesn't discuss it with Big Brother when she goes into the Diary Room. Instead, she delivers a rundown on her opinion of her fellow housemates:

'Helen is still getting my name wrong, and if she's still doing it by the end of the week, I'll blow. I'm bonding with Brian, we can have a laugh and we don't take offence. I was very wary of Penny at first, but I'm beginning to think she's alright, she means well. The kitchen seems to be her comfort zone, she's quiet when she's out of it. I thought I'd never get on with Bubble but I like him, I don't mind his little comments. I thought he would be exactly like the kids who picked on me at school, but we've got over that barrier and I prefer him to most of them. Paul is the most boring man I've ever met. Such a pretty face, but there's nothing there. I thought Dean was a great bloke but he can be a bit controlly sometimes. He thought me, Penny and Brian weren't very responsible over the fire task. Liz is lovely. I was a bit worried about Amma, but she's nice ... Everyone is getting to know each other better, not pretending any more. At first everyone was a bit false and pretending to like each other – now they are more themselves. I was nervous for the first couple of days, but now I think if they don't like me, they don't like me. If they do, that's great.'

Brian goes to talk to Big Brother after Narinder and takes the chance to talk about how he's getting on with the others.

'Some people need a lot of reassuring and some can be over-sensitive. Helen can be over-sensitive. I think she misses her boyfriend – I don't want to sound as though I'm backbiting her. Naz can be a bit over-sensitive. I know she's joking but if you didn't, you might think she seems on edge. Myself and Penny get on well, plus me and Naz, we have a laugh and a joke. Dean's a really nice guy, I wasn't talking to him much at first. I don't know Liz well. As a whole I think we're getting on well, but then again I'm the sort of person that says something if they've got a problem … Yesterday I felt bad talking about people – I'll find it difficult when we make nominations. If I was nominated, I'd be upset, and if I was to nominate someone and they left, I'd be gutted.'

But he reverts to his usual flippancy when he tells Big Brother, 'I've got a tan and a red nose so I'm quite chuffed at the moment.'

Brian has also had a heart-to-heart with Liz in the garden, about his sexuality. He says he would love to have children, but doesn't think it would be fair on them, 'having a daddy one and a daddy two'. He talks about his one long relationship, and how his boyfriend's friends didn't really like him. Liz asks whether they will get back together, and Brian says he will go to the Diary Room to wish his ex a happy birthday on the right day.

It's a day for talking to Big Brother, and next up is Dean. He says he likes everyone in different ways for different reasons. 'I'm getting on particularly well with Bubble, he's down to earth. There's something mysterious and interesting about Elizabeth, and there still seems to be something vulnerable about Penny. I've tried harder with Helen because I think I upset her because I was blunt about things. I think she got the impression that I think she's not really good enough to be here. I've tried to make her feel better, and that she is as important as anyone else.'

He's relieved to report that he has had his first good night's sleep since

PET HATES

Amma: Telling lies; Jamie Oliver; strangers who touch me; anything on people's faces that should not be there (like food in facial hair, bogeys, cold sores).
Brian: People with bad personal hygiene; people who smoke huge amounts; ignorance.
Bubble: The door being left open; ice in an ashtray; people who wave money at me when I'm behind the bar; spitting.
Dean: Bad drivers.
Elizabeth: Bureaucrats; smokers; rude people.
Helen: Bald men with comb-overs.
Josh: Finding at breakfast that someone has used the last of the milk; dirty ashtrays in the dishwasher.
Narinder: Cleaning the bins out; Hoovering; paperwork (paying bills).
Paul: People who think they are better than you; girls who are impressed by blokes with expensive clothes; people who pick their noses at traffic lights (although I probably do).
Penny: People who snuffle instead of blowing their noses; people who think they can use me.
Stuart: Anne Robinson.

coming into the house. And he can't leave the Diary Room without another plea for the chance to watch the England–Greece football match: he and Bubble have been keeping up a sustained attack on Big Brother about their football deprivation.

When Dean comes out, Liz goes into the Diary Room. She says she thinks everything is 'very nice'.

'The chat last night was good. I think Penny just wanted a role, she needs to be busy all the time … Hilda [Helen] surprised me, she felt she was being treated like a dumb blonde. People's insecurities surprise me ... Bubble and Brian are really funny all the time, and Dean's a real wit.'

Next it's Helen's turn. She tells Big Brother that she is finding it hard because she's missing everybody, but that she's getting stronger each day.

Although she says Dean is 'pretty cool', she claims she does not fancy any of the men.

'There's not one I find attractive. Does that sound bitchy? They're all like brothers. I think Penny wants to mother me. It is nice, but it can be a bit overpowering. At first I thought she thinks I'm just a cutie little thing. She's worldly, she knows so much. Narinder does my head in with her singing and all that. But I probably do her head in with little things I do. The more you talk to Elizabeth the more she shocks you. Amma's cool – I thought she'd be in love with herself but no, she's really cool.'

Helen says she sometimes wonders why she was picked, and she hopes one of the tasks will be a dance routine.

Bubble goes in after Helen and says the house is 'like a prison, I'm locked up in a luxurious prison and I have to do ridiculous things'. He is pleased to have learned to juggle, and admits he finds it awkward talking to the disembodied Big Brother.

Stuart, who has been one of the quiet members of the household, becomes a bit more forthright today. He criticizes Penny's schoolmarmish attitude: 'We are not school kids. The raised voice is a bit unnecessary. She's left that environment behind,' he tells the others.

Liz and Stuart have been chummy since the beginning, and they spend part of the afternoon playing a makeshift game of tennis with two bats and a ball brought into the house by Dean. In the kitchen, Liz asks Stuart whether he would have a romance in the house. He says he wouldn't even consider it, although he wouldn't be boring if everyone took their clothes off. They rejoin the group in the garden, where everyone is being beaten at tennis by Brian. This leaves the men on a mission: Dean pleads with Stuart to have a go, saying, 'He's got to be beaten by a heterosexual male, or God knows ...' But Stuart fails, and Brian wiggles his hips as he scores another victory. Stuart doesn't give up, and eventually beats him, although Brian insists he let him win out of pity.

At seven o'clock in the evening there is a crisis. Helen dashes into the house to bring out one of her dance dresses and leaves Elizabeth on her own with the fire, which is against the rules of the task. When they realize what has happened Helen is devastated, and is comforted by Dean. Big Brother refuses to tell Paul whether or not they have failed the task, and they agree they will have to keep the fire-watching rota going until Thursday, which is two days away. The contestants are upset on Helen's behalf, and Liz threatens to physically hurt anyone who blames her. Lucky, then, that she doesn't hear Narinder bitching in the kitchen about their blonde housemate.

Helen isn't the only one the housemates are worried about. The black goldfish, Darth Vader, has lost his appetite and Stuart, Brian and Narinder decide he looks sickly, moping at the bottom of the bowl while Dinky swims around happily. After cleaning out the tank, the big fish seems to recover his spirits, and Penny collects more fish food from the Diary Room.

She tells Big Brother that she feels she is not contributing enough to the conversations in the house. 'They are all playful and young. I thought I might be the stupid one, but I'm really sensible. I'm a bit worried about all our swearing. It's still all a bit bewildering ... I hope we can all stay safe and well. They're so full of it, we could have major accidents.'

In the evening, the peace of the house is disturbed by noises of shouting from across the fence. A bunch of schoolchildren are dispersed by the security men. Penny thinks that they are kids from her school, calling her name. Bubble later moans about them to Big Brother because they failed to shout out the football scores.

Penny also goes into the Diary Room, and sends a message to her pupils: 'I have lots of your photos with me and lots of memories and I am missing you a lot, but it is important that we don't hear anything from the outside ... I am really glad of your support, but if you could stop shouting, that would be great.'

Bubble reveals an unexpected side of himself when he confesses he writes poetry. Penny follows his admission with questions about which famous poets he has read, and Bubble says he doesn't read much. Maybe he's just trying to avoid a discussion with Penny, because his favourite subject at school was English Literature and he has read a lot of the classics. Narinder thinks Bubble is winding them up about his poetic leanings, but he insists he's not.

There is a growing pattern to the end of each day, as Bubble and Brian try to find new tricks to play on each other. Tonight Bubble pretends to throw Brian's skincare products on the fire, to a great deal of shrieking from Brian and laughter from the others.

Bubble and Amma are on fire duty together again, although Bubble can't see a lot of point in carrying on with a task they feel sure they have lost. But it gives him another opportunity to chat up Amma, telling her she will eventually give in and sleep with him. She says she's prepared to bet £70,000 – the prize money they are competing for – that she won't.

In the early morning, before the others are awake, Penny and Stuart have a quiet chat. She tells him of her dreams of being an actress, and of her fears that the kids from her school will mob the place when she is evicted. She tells Stuart that she may not go back to teaching, and she also tells him how devastated she was when a long-term romance broke up: despite not being Penny's greatest fan, Stuart seems visibly moved by her tale.

It's Helen's birthday on the sixth day in the house, and she wakes up feeling a bit miffed and half-hearted about it all. Brian also gets up and is not too pleased about Penny kissing and hugging him from behind. Later in the morning she gets very kissy with him again, and again he seems uncomfortable with it.

Amma and Liz discuss snogging girls. Liz has done it once but Amma has done it quite a lot. Liz says she didn't enjoy it because the girl's lips were too big. Amma is surprised, because in her experience girls are better snoggers than blokes, who 'have to be coaxed into doing the right things'. She claims it is not just friendship that has made her kiss girls – she's prepared to be experimental. Liz has been fascinated by Amma's life and job since day one, and now she is again agog to know more. She says it's fashionable to believe that you are not a true woman until you have experienced sleeping with another woman. Stuart interrupts them.

The hot weather is making Penny and Paul frisky, and Narinder catches them sharing a kiss. Helen asks them to do it again, but Paul says the moment has to be right. Narinder says she won't introduce Penny to her husband, because 'you'll have him in five minutes'. But it's Paul who is on Penny's mind, and within seconds they are tickling each other and flirting again. 'She's so gagging for it,' Narinder announces.

Narinder also spots a potential romance between Stuart and Elizabeth, who are having another long game of tennis together, and she tells Dean she thinks they will be the first to have sex in the house.

Bubble has been washing clothes in a bucket – he's the first housemate to do washing; as the house doesn't have a washing machine, they have to do it the old-fashioned way. Afterwards, he joins Amma and Penny in the girls' room to wrap presents for Helen. Penny senses that the other two like being alone together, and leaves. The flirtatious probing that has developed between Bubble and Amma continues. When Amma asks Bubble if he really believes he could get any woman to sleep with him he says no, just ninety-nine per cent of them. He teases Amma that she wants him, but she says she thinks he would just make a wicked friend. They agree that Penny is driving them crazy: Bubble says she is patronizing him in the same way his school teachers did.

The housemates talk about dreams, and Helen is persuaded to tell them about one she had in which Paul locked her in the bedroom. Dean says he once dreamt he was married to his sister, which was horrible, especially as it was the day after his wedding. The dream questions stop immediately, as everyone turns the spotlight on Dean's marriage. He tells them he married at nineteen, split up at twenty-four, but didn't divorce until nine years later, because he 'couldn't be arsed'.

Out of boredom, Dean and Paul decide to paint their toenails. This leads to much speculation about them from Bubble, but he is promptly silenced by the girls, who are happy to see some of the men getting in touch with their feminine sides. Stuart is with Bubble on this one: 'I would rather stick hot, steaming pokers in my eyes than have my toenails painted,' he says. Paul, whose ankle is still bandaged, says that a week ago he would not have believed he would be on crutches with his toenails painted. When the conversation turns to cross dressing, Bubble gets even more alarmed, and says he won't be able to have a serious conversation with Dean again. 'We haven't had one yet anyway,' remarks Dean.

The arrival of the calendar, made from the photographs they shot, causes a big stir, and there are many ooohs and aaahs as Paul holds up each page.

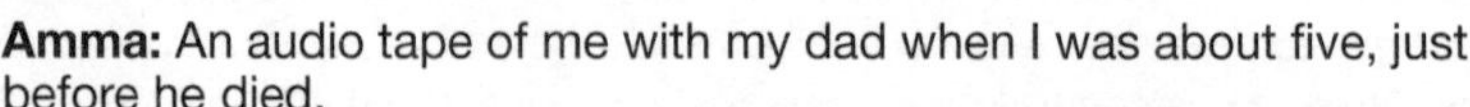

MOST TREASURED POSSESSION

Amma: An audio tape of me with my dad when I was about five, just before he died.
Brian: My two teddy bears, which I've had since I was six months old. They've been with me always and know the real me – thank God they can't talk.
Bubble: My dad's army hat: it's cool, trendy, comfy and has always brought me luck.
Dean: I haven't got a single possession I value above all others.
Elizabeth: My bicycle – I can go where I want, when I want (well, nearly).
Helen: My lipstick case – wait till you see it!
Josh: My friends and my personality.
Narinder: My home, it's beautiful.
Paul: A Maltese cross. My dad bought it for me when I was conceived, and gave it to me when I left home.
Penny: My writing.
Stuart: A Lamborghini Diablo that I used to own.

An hour later, Helen is called to the Diary Room and offered a choice of two presents. The first is in a box in front of her – a pair of Gucci shoes and a Gucci handbag. It's everything the Welsh lass has ever wanted, and her eyes gleam. The second present is a party for the housemates, with takeaway food, six bottles of champagne and a box of party treats. Big Brother tells her to take as long as she wants, but she only hesitates for two seconds.

'I love the shoes and handbag, and this would be the best birthday present I could ever want, but I think everybody else could do with a big nosh, a good booze-up and a party,' she says. She rushes outside to tell the others, who reward her with hugs and kisses, while the girls want to hear all about the shoes and bag. The boys discuss whether they would have been so philanthropic, and Bubble comments that if he had been offered the choice of seeing the England game or a party, he would have taken the England game and would simply not have told the others there was another option.

The girls get dressed up and look very glamorous. Penny is tearful, because she has managed to break her microphone and drop it down the loo. As she has lectured the other housemates on the importance of not getting their microphones wet, there's a certain amount of *schadenfreude* among the others, who laugh about her not practising what she preaches.

Stuart causes even more laughter – and terror – when he turns up at the party wearing dark glasses which he whips off to reveal some bizarre cat-eye contact lenses that make his eyes look frighteningly feline. There is tension between him and Penny: they are talking about each other to the other contestants. Narinder and Penny discuss Paul, agreeing that he fancies Helen. Penny says her flirtation with him was just a joke, and that he reminds her of her friends. Narinder, who thinks Paul is boring, says she expected Penny to have more interesting friends than him.

Despite Brian whingeing that he would rather have Coke than champagne, the booze goes down well at the party. Helen's mum has had a huge birthday cake delivered for her – a chocolate cake made by Helen's Auntie Shelley to her favourite recipe. It has a huge picture of Helen on top. Amma goes to the Diary Room to collect it, and then lights all the candles with Brian's help.

The party atmosphere turns sour as the housemates settle down at half past ten to play the truth game. They are each asked in turn who they would sleep with. Paul says Helen; Bubble says Amma (if he can't have all five girls together); Penny says Brian; Brian says Dean; Narinder says Bubble; Dean says Liz; Amma says Liz. Stuart is next in the game, and prevaricates. He tries to avoid answering, but, pushed into a corner by the other housemates, he says he would have a foursome. Helen asks him which of the girls he would not sleep with, to which he replies, 'I wouldn't sleep with Penny, but I'd go with the rest of you.'

Wounded, Penny mutters 'Fuck you, arsehole' under her breath. Paul questions Stuart as to why he wouldn't sleep with Penny, and Stuart lightens his remark by saying it is because 'Paul is already going with her'. Penny tells him that she and Paul have a good rapport and that Stuart should not give him a bad time over this.

Stuart then reveals that he heard Penny's earlier comment.

'Would you like to repeat your "Fuck you, arsehole" comment Penny?' he asks. Penny says it was a joke, but Stuart is not letting her off so easily. He says he does not understand 'Fuck you, arsehole' jokes, and tells her: 'Defend it, explain it or take it back.' Penny, desperate to end this angry confrontation, immediately says she will take it back. But Stuart, who has had a lot to drink, will not give up.

'You can't just come out and say "Fuck you, arsehole", because I'm the type of character who doesn't accept that. I'm offended by that type of comment. It's offensive to me.'

Paul intercedes on Penny's behalf, explaining that she had felt rejected when Stuart didn't choose her, and she uttered the phrase now causing all the trouble because she was upset. Penny agrees, and again asks Stuart if she can take it back.

He retorts, 'No, I am completely offended. You have shown yourself out to be quite shallow. Sorry.'

This is the most serious row in the house so far, and the repercussions rumble on into the night and the next day. Amma tells Stuart she would have been upset too, if her name had been excluded, but adds 'I'd have given you shit'. Narinder, Brian and Bubble try to comfort a tearful Penny. Bubble says, 'I'll sleep with you, Penny. You've said you're sorry, you can do no more. Put a smile on your face – think of me naked.' Narinder, who has to stretch up to cuddle the much taller Penny, tells her she has done everything for everyone.

But Penny will not be comforted. 'He won't forgive me,' she sobs. She goes to the Diary Room to talk to Big Brother.

'I didn't mean it horribly, but he's offended and won't accept my apology. I'm trying to pull everyone together, to see where I could fit in, sorting out stuff, encouraging people, being part of the group. He's knocked me back a few times, but I've just let it go. Tonight we were all just mucking about. I sensed he's not got the best rapport with me. I didn't mean it, but he's really offended.'

Big Brother asks what prompted her angry comment. 'I've got close to Paul in a muck-about sort of way,' she replies. 'I've got lots of boyfriends but I'm not girlie-girlie. Me and Paul know where the boundary is. Stuart made a comment and I thought, "No, don't start that now". So I just said it. I didn't mean it. I'm not hard – I would cry if the fish died. I would say the same to Brian and it would be alright. I'm worried that he [Stuart] is not going to forget it. I should have gone to bed.'

Big Brother tells her that tensions build up easily, and that it would be best to try to sort it out.

Penny, who is fighting back her tears, says: 'It's been a vulnerable day. I'm upset with myself. No way will he forgive. I'll try to sort it out. It's been a nightmare day ... I feel sad he took it like that. I'll try and sort it. Everyone in the group is special.'

The postmortems on the row continue through the night. Elizabeth is very drunk, and falls asleep in the garden, while Amma and Narinder, both the worse for wear, discuss the others. Narinder says the two she has least bonded with are Helen and Paul. At 1 a.m., Big Brother calls everyone into the house because fireworks are being let off outside. The housemates lounge around the living room discussing two of their favourite topics: football and sex. Having got nowhere with Amma, Bubble tries it on with Narinder, but she isn't having any of it. Then Brian accidentally flashes his assets, and Narinder runs behind a chair shouting, 'I've never seen a white one before'. Brian laughs and spreads his legs to give her another eyeful. Narinder says she didn't know they were so 'wrinkly or foldy', but Amma reassures her that Brian's is pretty normal. Eventually, all but the fire-watchers retire to bed, Dean complaining of feeling sick.

Bubble, who has had the most erratic sleep pattern of all the housemates, stays up chatting, and again he and Amma end up talking about sex. Narinder tells them they are 'well on your way to a shag', and Bubble says he hopes so. Then he has a serious thought: he has a video he forgot to return before coming into the house, and he's dreading the bill.

It's a quiet morning, with the other housemates trying to pour oil on the troubled waters around Stuart and Penny. Paul offers some words of wisdom:

'Don't worry about it, it was something that was going to happen. At the end of the day we know why. It just got out of hand. It has been such a big change for all of us, it's all happened too quickly, we've been here for nearly a week. I'm totally cool about it. Nobody's going to offend me in here, not unless you went mental. None of us know each other, none of us know how we'll react in certain circumstances, because we've never experienced each other before.'

Helen looks bemused by all the talk: she slept through the entire row. When Stuart comes into the garden, he gives Penny a restrained hug, all the while winking to Paul behind her back. Elizabeth crawls out of bed with a hangover at 11 a.m., just one hour before the group are officially told they failed the task. Bubble wants to argue, and goes to the Diary Room against the advice of the others. He is told that they failed the task for several reasons.

Stuart tells them all that they have done well as a team, but they are all worrying about the prospect of only having £49 to spend on food for a week. Dean says that wouldn't be enough for him alone. One good thing comes of the task: the housemates were given a small clock to help them organize fire-watching rotas, and Big Brother allows them to keep it, on the advice of the psychologist, who says it will help them regulate their sleeping patterns.

There's another row brewing: Bubble is angry when Amma tells him that Paul twice neglected the fire before Helen did. 'I feel so sorry about Helen beating herself up so badly,' says Amma. Bubble says that in one way it makes life easier – he is referring to the nominations.

Narinder and Penny have another heart-to-heart about Paul, and Penny admits she has had a crush on him, but she's over it now.

'I've realized he's not in my league. He's not sophisticated enough,' she says. 'So many of the men I fall for have this fixation with young, girlie types. I knew he didn't fancy me. But to actually go for Helen? That's what men want – the illusion, not the reality.'

On a roll, Penny goes on to describes Stuart as a poser, and Narinder agrees.

The relative calm of the day is shattered when Bubble is given a message from Big Brother to tell the contestants that they will be making their nominations tomorrow, on Friday, instead of on Monday. They are all disconcerted. Dean says he thought the first round would be easy, because there were bound to be two people he didn't like. But in fact he likes everyone, and it won't be easy. Amma, who has already decided, says it is not because she dislikes anyone but that there are eight people she would rather be with than the two she has chosen. Later, she tells Narinder, 'My main bitch is that my mind is changing about people, and who's to say how much more it might change'.

Helen reminds them that if she goes, the cake goes. Flippantly, she says the biggest problem she has is what to wear: should she wear her best clothes now, because if she is evicted the nation will not have another chance to see them? Seriously, she is convinced that she will be nominated because she lost them the fire task. Most of the rest of the housemates admit that they have at least one nomination clear in their minds already. Brian stays unusually quiet throughout the discussion.

Bubble takes it to heart, and goes to the Diary Room to explain to Big Brother that nominating someone feels like betraying a friend. It is harder than he thought it would be before he came into the house. 'I don't like offending people,' he says. 'If ever I've upset someone, it's been by drunken stupidity or accident. Now I have to come in here and give you a reason, a valid point. The reality, now it's here, is tough.'

As usual, Brian lightens the tone. Narinder is singing and says she wonders which top male celebrities are watching the television and falling in love with her. Brian offers 'Stevie Wonder'.

Stuart is called to the Diary Room, where Big Brother questions him about the row. Stuart is very guarded, saying that he does not prejudge people, and that the group is getting along fine. Penny, who follows him into the Diary Room, is a lot more unbuttoned:

'It was really hard, it really got to me. This morning was cool, he gave me a hug. I still feel slightly paranoid. It's a big drama that's happened here, and it's going to be around in people's memories for a while. That's the last thing I wanted. I'm disappointed in myself, I feel I let myself down. You shouldn't swear at anyone – I tell the kids at school that. But I do believe that if someone begs you to forgive them in the context of being in a house together … I really believed they would be people who would forgive. Now I'm a bit wary of how I approach people here. I do find egos get injured quite quickly. I'm not used to being around people like that. I feel a bit older than them. It doesn't worry me. I feel I can face it now. I've got it in my head: just be strong, just face it.'

However, when she leaves the Diary Room, she can't resist giving cooking instructions to Amma, who is roasting a chicken for the evening meal. Amma politely but firmly tells Penny she knows how to cook chicken. So Penny joins in a ball game with Brian and Narinder, but gets irritated when the other two fool around instead of playing. She walks away, and they don't even notice.

Bubble and Narinder have both been complaining of skin rashes – Bubble's on his feet and Narinder's on her arms. They both see the doctor. Narinder comes out from her appointment in the Diary Room surgery to tell the other girls that the doctor is shy but quite sexy, and that she had to strip to her G-string. Helen gets excited at the thought of another male ('I like shy') and tries to peek at him when Bubble goes in. Bubble tries to persuade the off-camera doctor to give him a hand signal to tell him the football results, but he fails to understand whether the doctor responds or not. Big Brother has to remind Bubble that he can be expelled for trying to make contact with the outside world. Narinder pleads for the chance to have a bath to ease her rash, and Big Brother capitulates and turns on the hot water for the bath, which has its own hot-water tank. A few hours later, when most of the housemates are in bed, Brian, too, goes into the Diary Room complaining of blotches on his skin.

Again, the evening ends with an argument, although it is rather more contained than the previous one. Amma and Bubble confront Paul about the fact that he neglected the fire, but has allowed Helen to shoulder the blame. Amma says he did it twice, and that she told him about it. Paul denies doing it on purpose. Amma agrees that he didn't neglect the fire deliberately, but that he knew afterwards that he had done it, and so he should have owned up to Helen.

Narinder and Brian watch the encounter with amused detachment, Narinder commenting that she doesn't know who is fighting who, and Brian adding that it's like being on the set of *Jerry Springer*.

After Paul has gone to bed, Amma tells Bubble that she doesn't believe Paul was telling the truth. Bubble says he's done his bit by asking the question, and Amma says she is not very angry, but that she thinks Paul was wrong.

With the fire-watching task over, there's no need for anyone to stay up all night, but Bubble and Amma can't seem to kick the habit. It is 3 a.m. when they finally decide to turn in. Bubble, who doesn't appear to be able to sleep for long, is one of the first up, just five hours later. He helps Dean clean the living area: they sweep the circular, brown rug that surrounds the coffee table, because they think this might be the cause of the rashes and blotches that are affecting them.

Big Brother is also worried about the skin complaints, and tells the housemates they must all wash their bedding in non-biological powder. They struggle – none of them seem to have much idea how to use a mangle, and Bubble sees the down side of having the double bed: bigger sheets to wash. They overload the washing line, which collapses, and Bubble (the practical one) again comes to the rescue. Later, a shower forces them to rush outside and gather up the sheets, amid lots of complaints that they won't be dry for bedtime. They are asked to go into the boys' room while Big Brother fixes the line properly. Stuart and Bubble, the only fathers in the house, swap stories about their children, while Dean and Elizabeth tell altogether different tales: ghost stories.

Once the group has been released from the bedroom, Dean collects together a pile of stones and writes the initials VJ in the garden, for his girlfriend Vanessa. Narinder copies the idea, writing JAT, her husband's name. She gets angry with Bubble who can't remember what these letters stand for: Narinder is very touchy about people remembering names. Helen joins in the initial game, writing BG for her boyfriend Gavin, who is known as Big G. Big

WHO NOMINATES WHO

Amma nominates Paul and Penny
Brian nominates Helen and Elizabeth
Bubble nominates Paul and Penny
Dean nominates Narinder and Penny
Elizabeth nominates Penny and Helen
Helen nominates Bubble and Narinder
Narinder nominates Helen and Bubble
Paul nominates Amma and Helen
Penny nominates Helen and Amma
Stuart nominates Penny and Narinder

Amma	Brian	Bubble	Dean	Elizabeth	Helen	Narinder	Paul	Penny	Stuart
					Penny				
					Paul			Stuart	
					Narinder	Stuart		Dean	
Penny		Narinder			Elizabeth	Helen	Bubble	Bubble	
Elizabeth		Helen		Brian	Brian	Dean	Amma	Amma	
2	0	2	0	1	5	3	2	5	0

Week 1 nominees: Helen and Penny with five nominations each.

Reasons

Amma on Penny: 'She tends to talk to us like we're children. She can be patronizing, and over a long period of time it would irritate.'

Brian on Elizabeth: 'It's unlucky for her, she is the only person I haven't got to know well over the week. It's pure unlucky.'

Narinder on Helen: 'I find she can be very offensive. She didn't put one hundred per cent into the task and she constantly gives me hacky looks.'

Brother intervenes and reminds them they are to have no contact with the outside world.

Liz is called to the Diary Room by Big Brother, and tells him that there are five people in the house that she gels with, and four that need more work. She gets on with Dean, Bubble, Helen, Narinder and Stuart, although feels Stuart is 'being a bit weird at the moment'. She says she likes Brian, but thinks that he regards her as too serious.

'Everyone is having a different experience to me. Today we are all quite sensitive, because of the nomination thing. You catch someone looking at you – it's general paranoia. I think I take one of the quieter roles in the house. I'm not here for entertainment. I think I've got to let down a few more barriers, but I'm not sure what those barriers are.'

Paul has been moaning for days about his ankle, and the girls share a wry look when he tells them that he hasn't been complaining because he didn't like to make a fuss.

The impending nominations dominate the day. It is the group's first taste of the worst aspect of life in the *Big Brother* house. The girls seem to be more resilient than the boys: Narinder is positively looking forward to it, and Amma has no problems with it. Brian threatens not to participate, until the others tell him he will be expelled. Penny says she will be upset when there is an empty bed, and wonders what it would be like to be the last girl, with empty beds all around the room. Helen decides to do her hair, so that she will look good for her Diary Room trip to make her nominations. She has already spent part of the afternoon practising her eviction run, which seems to involve a lot of giggling and screaming. Bubble says he's in the house to win the money, and when the others all deny that they care about the prize money he tells them to let him win, because £70,000 would make a big difference to his life. He later tells Stuart that he felt they all looked at him 'like scum' because he was honest about wanting the cash.

Penny stays remote from the rest of the group for much of the afternoon and early evening. She twice tries to kiss and cuddle Brian who, without being rude, shows that he doesn't want the display of affection. She goes for a sleep.

Eventually, there is so much discussion of nominations that Big Brother reminds the housemates that this topic is off-limits, and they must not talk about it any more. Finally at 10 p.m., after a long and tense day, the nominations procedure begins. The contestants sing their own version of the Beatles song 'Ob-La-Di, Ob-La-Da' as each of them goes in, with a separate line for each housemate.

After the nominations, Penny again keeps her distance from the group, and starts cleaning the kitchen. Brian asks if she is thinking that this will be their last week together and she says, 'The way people are looking at me, I think this is my last week.' He hugs her. The others talk about the whole process, Amma warning them it will get harder as the weeks go by. Elizabeth said she suffered pangs of regret as soon as she said the names.

The housemates know that they must wait until Monday to hear the results of the nomination vote, and this depresses them. What they don't

WEEK ONE FACT FILE

Main task: To keep a fire burning from Sunday until Thursday, with two people on duty at all times.

PASS ☐ **FAIL** ☒

Mini-task: To take photographs of each other for a calendar.

Treats: Helen's birthday party, with six bottles of champagne, a Chinese takeaway, party treats and a chocolate cake.

Bets are on!
To win: Dean is favourite with odds of 20/1 against him being evicted. Amma and Brian are both up with him as potential winners.
To walk: Bubble is favourite for first eviction, with odds of 2/1, closely followed by Penny, at 3/1.

know is that viewers saw the nominations live, although Brian, who has shown himself to be more aware of the televisual element of life in the house than most, suspects it. It's an early night for Bubble, who goes to bed before midnight for the first time. He is feeling low, because outside the house on Friday evenings he would be preparing to look after his daughter Bryony for the weekend. In the girls' room tension is high: they don't know it, but out of the ten nominations they made between the five of them, seven were for other girls. There is certainly no suggestion of a girl–boy divide, as there was among the first *Big Brother* housemates.

After she has been in bed for a while, Elizabeth gets up and goes to talk to Big Brother. Although the housemates don't know it yet, Penny and Helen are the two up for eviction – and Liz is the only one who nominated them both. Liz seems to feel a need to vindicate her choices, and talks to the Diary Room camera as if she were addressing both Penny and Helen, when they see videos of the programme:

'Penny comes too much into my personal space. She bores into you. If you make eye contact she takes it as an invitation for her touchy-feely ways. Choosing Helen was so difficult. She is so sparkly and pink – she has great humour. But she sleeps a lot and sunbathes – I don't mind that, but I have to have reasons. I was really going between Paul and Helen. I originally went for Paul, but I have talked to him since and he at least contributes. So it was Helen.

'Helen, when you see this, I love you and really want you to do my hair. Penny, I could get on with you, but it would take a while to get close to you.

'It has been very difficult.'

WEEK TWO

'I don't know what the fuss is about, I could have nominated six people.'
Narinder

After the drama of nomination night, the housemates are probably expecting a quiet time on Saturday. The day certainly starts peacefully enough. There are a few trips to the Diary Room, as the contestants share their thoughts and feelings about the process. The housemates are all preoccupied with the issue of who is going to be up for eviction – although the viewers already know, the housemates will not be told until Monday. Dean is the first to confide in Big Brother.

'Some people have taken the nomination thing to heart, and it's causing a fair bit of mistrust and paranoia. It's doing interesting things to the group, making people think about other people in a way they hadn't … The majority of people have got their heads round it. If you start taking it too personally you could mess your head up. It's difficult when I'm on my own, I start thinking about my other life and my girlfriend, so I have to immerse myself in it. If I don't try, I think it's only a game and I could walk out the door any minute.'

He adds that as people have come out of their shells he has changed his opinion of them.

'I get on with Bubble, Brian and Liz best, but as Amma has started to speak more, I'm getting on with her. People I thought didn't have much to offer have come alive and proved me wrong. I put people into roles where they probably didn't go, as time moved on it turned out they weren't suited to that role or it was a front … Liz didn't really say much, but she's become a very stable influence in here that everyone has appreciated, but it could be construed as non-input.

'I thought Penny was the maternal figure who got a lot of things done, which was good, because they're things I'm not good at. But perhaps the other girls didn't see that as a good thing, they saw it as her being domineering. It was only a few days ago that I realized there was resentment: Bubble told her to step back, then there was the altercation with Stu. He was extremely tactless, but her reaction let her down. I think that caused uncomfortable feelings in the group. I think she's well meaning, and I'd be happy to spend weeks in here with Penny, but I think it would be probably better for the rest of the group if she wasn't here.'

Brian is then called into the Diary Room for adjustments to his radio microphone. He tells Big Brother that he was very stressed during the nominations.

'I'm sure as the weeks go by it is going to get tougher saying goodbye to friends. The people I get on best with are those I can have a laugh with, people I have something in common with. It's pointless being in the house if you can't talk to someone, if you ask advice and they can't give it to you. I want to be with people I can have a laugh with and remain friends with afterwards. I'm getting on well with Penny, Narinder, Bubble, Dean and Stuart.'

He adds that he has found life in the house easier than he expected, although he gets homesick and has had difficulty sleeping. 'I thought they might have a problem with the fact that I'm gay, and I wasn't going to advertise the fact, just be myself. But on the first or second night one of the girls asked, and I was so relieved to find it wasn't a problem. Now we laugh and joke together about silly things, like the amount of toner and moisturizer I use, and it's funny and OK.'

Bubble finds a good way of passing an hour or so in the garden. After his success at retrieving the lost comb that had fallen through the slats in the decking, he has decided to go treasure-hunting down there. He finds a cigarette and some screws, and spies some mugs and a staple gun, which he can't reach.

Narinder goes to the Diary Room to talk about the nominations. She's not impressed by the emotional way in which some of the others reacted.

'Yesterday was too much. They knew they had to vote. Why was it such a big deal? I don't think they're being true to themselves. They're acting like they're all each other's best mates. Bubble was doing my head in, they all were. I did feel certain people were sucking up to each other yesterday. Amma was really creeping a lot. I don't like that. Why pretend we're the bestest pals in the world when we're not? We do have friendships and some of us have got close, but it's false.

'I could have nominated about six people. For the first few days, it was going to be Helen and Paul. I chose Bubble because he talks over people and he's self-important. Everyone is het up and overwhelmed by it all, but it's just part of *Big Brother*. Monday is going to be horrendous.

'Everyone has got their little groups. We do mix, but we've got comfortable with certain people. I get on with Brian and Liz. Liz gets on with everybody. The guys have their guy talk and they feel threatened by us women. Dean and Bubble don't give me the time of day. Guys feel intimidated by a young girl with an opinion.'

Dean and Brian are still making up lyrics for their version of 'Ob-La-Di, Ob-La-Da'. Brian makes up a verse about Bubble's hats, and they sing it to Dean's accompaniment on the guitar.

At noon, the housemates are given their new task. Over the next four days they have to learn some basic first-aid techniques. They will be issued with a new booklet each day covering various aspects of first aid – the first booklet is about resuscitation procedures.

Brian, who reads out the instructions, is in his element. He has learned first aid as part of his job, and he's confident they will all pick it up. Helen looks worried, but despite her reservations the group decides to wager sixty per cent of the shopping budget on passing the task. They are all fired up and determined: they have learned the lesson that they cannot afford to lose their money.

Helen tells the rest of the group that she is dyslexic, and will have trouble reading the booklets. The other housemates reassure her. Brian, who has taken control, helps her to learn the abbreviations she needs by translating them into dance moves for her.

In the afternoon, Bubble goes to the Diary Room. He wants to know how they will be tested on the first-aid task, but Big Brother evades the question, telling Bubble he will get back to them. Bubble admits that he found last night very hard, because he was thinking about his daughter.

'But that's part and parcel of it. I miss other things, things like the England game, cans of Coke – you don't realize how much you enjoy them until they're not there. I get on well with Brian and Dean especially, Stuart and Amma too. They take me for what I am … There's a lot more to me than meets the eye. I like to have fun. I might act the fool, but I'm not a fool. Some people don't get my humour, some do. When you come in here, you think it will be like a holiday. But it's not easy. You can't be up-front with people, and

WHAT THE EXPERTS SAY

BRIAN

'Brian, who has been one of the clowns of the group, takes a pivotal role in the teaching of the task because of his prior knowledge of first aid as an air steward. This means there are two potentially conflicting sides to Brian's character. In his role as a teacher, he displays particular types of non-verbal behaviour with his willing pupil Penny: he maintains high levels of eye contact, and keeps her focussed on the task by firing questions at her. His facial expression is serious: this is Brian in the role of teacher and he's very effective at it. He responds to Bubble's constant interruptions – at time he ignores him, but he's forced to engage with Bubble. To do so he has to break free from his teacher role, and the more familiar Brian re-emerges, Brian the clown.

'We've already seen much evidence of Brian's wit, but perhaps even more striking is the way he regularly uses humour in the group to diffuse difficult or tense situations. This is a critical role, and one that only Brian seems confident enough to play. In his clown role, he often uses exaggerated facial expressions, and it is this exaggeration that tells Bubble he is not to be taken seriously.

'It is very important for Brian to show that he can effectively manage more than one role at a time. Survival in the ever-changing Big Brother household depends to some extent on adaptability.'

Professor Geoffrey Beattie, Psychologist

you worry about how people on the outside will see you. Not being able to talk about the nominations creates a tension. You are playing mind games with us, Big Brother.'

After Bubble has added that the housemates are dividing into cliques and there's lots of gossip, Big Brother asks him if there is anything else he wants to talk about. 'I didn't want to talk about that lot, but you kept asking me questions,' replies Bubble.

Later in the afternoon, Liz is in the Diary Room collecting more chicken feed, and she talks again about the problems she has relating to Penny.

'I need to make more effort with her. I just need to get on with her. The more I draw away from her, the more she's going to try. I feel OK with her, but I'm still going to keep my distance,' she says.

After dinner, all the worries about the nominations become trivial. Big Brother sets the contestants a discussion topic: they must share with each other their life-changing experiences. The task is not necessarily intended to make the contestants open up about their innermost secrets – passing an exam or landing a job could be a life-changing event. But the housemates take the discussion very seriously and really unburden themselves.

Dean starts them off with a story about visiting a friend in New York, and a nightmare drug trip that unbalanced him for several months afterwards, giving him 'panic attacks and weird paranoia'. He says the experience changed his whole personality, making him less arrogant and much more humble.

Helen tells the others about her dyslexia, and how her mother helped her struggle with it. She also talks about having a boyfriend who was sent to prison, and her visits to him. Stuart also gives two examples of life-changing experiences: first he cites the births of his three children, all of which he witnessed, and second the death of his grandmother. He tells the others that, after his parents divorced, he was mainly brought up by his grandmother. When she died, 'it was like taking away my mother and father in one fell swoop'.

Paul is next. He explains how he was born with 'really sticky-out ears and other kids really took the piss'. As a teenager he had an operation to pin them back, and the bullying and teasing stopped at once. What's more, he found himself suddenly attractive to girls.

'I hadn't changed in myself – I was still the same person, but their attitudes to me changed.'

He doesn't regret the rough ride he had as a kid. 'There are things that make you stronger in life, and I think when we've all told our stories you will realize why we're all here, because we have all got interesting pasts.'

Brian tells of his first big romance: he fell head-over-heels in love with a man he met on holiday. It was his first gay relationship. They caught each other's eye on the beach, and then the man placed a note in a bottle and dropped it near where Brian was sitting. It was the start of an affair, although Brian felt 'physically sick' when he woke the next morning and thought about the fact that he had kissed a man. Eventually the relationship turned sour, but Brian has no regrets about it.

Liz's story is about falling and damaging her back badly when she was trekking through India. She was temporarily paralyzed, and she was staying in a remote village with no medical help for miles around. She later had more problems with her back when she was doing a lot of sport at university, and the whole experience has made her value her health and appreciate her body.

Penny is next: 'My story is about body image, and it explains why I have such a relationship with teenagers and the girls I work with.' She mentions that she had severe problems, including anorexia, which started when she was very young, in the years between the ages of nine and eleven. She had medical problems and her breasts didn't grow.

'I didn't have lots of the hormones I should have had, but when I tried to talk about it, it was just "Come on, get on with it".' She gained confidence and happiness through her involvement with the theatre, because on stage she could be the person she wanted to be. Then, at the age of thirty, she decided she was going to have breast implants.

'I've found a new confidence. I still struggle with my body image, with trying to build a new relationship, but I've got myself sussed. It's hard, but I can be quite self sufficient now.'

Bubble starts to tell his tale: 'It's about the day my little girl opened my heart. I wasn't particularly nice when I was younger, I did bad things and I wasn't a great dad, but when we split it was hard and I was bitter … '

Bubble can't hold back the tears any longer, and with his hands to his face he asks the group if he can take a break. They're all very concerned about him. While he is recovering, Narinder tells her story, which she says is similar to Paul's.

'I was one of the very few Asian or coloured people in my school, and I got "Paki this" and "Paki that" all the time. When I was about twelve or thirteen, I realized all my girlfriends were going out with boys and nobody ever asked me out. I really fancied one guy, but he said he wouldn't go out with me because I was a Paki. He said he would get labelled a Paki-lover. And I could see that he would, and I felt sorry for him, I really loved him … Another guy said, "You would be so pretty if you were white". So all my life, all I wanted was to be white. Then, when I was fifteen or sixteen, I realized I would never be accepted by these guys, and I started getting more into my own culture, being me.'

Bubble resumes his story. He is slightly calmer, although still fighting back the tears: 'There was a horrible side to me. I wanted to get to the top as quickly as possible, and if that means tripping people up, so be it. I was not the best dad in the world. When my relationship split, I was bitter, angry, and still not a good dad. I started drinking, I did things I'm not proud of. I saw my little girl at weekends, but I never paid her enough attention. One day I went to stick a video on to occupy her and she said, "I don't want a video. I want to play with you, Daddy." That's the first time I opened up and let her in. And since that day, no matter what you throw at me, it doesn't matter. What I've done in the past doesn't matter. I have something no-one can take away. You are so proud of every little thing they do, it's unconditional love that you can't compare to anything in the world.'

Amma tells her story last. She took up table dancing, she says, 'because I was insecure and needed others to tell me I was good'. All the others are subdued and visibly moved by the intensity of the stories they have heard. Brian, who is clearly deeply affected, jokingly asks if he can change his nominations (he chose Helen and Elizabeth).

After their difficult time, the housemates are more united than they have ever been. They play a game of volleyball, and for the first time every one of them joins in. Big Brother calls Amma to the Diary Room, and tells her that the purpose of the task was for the members of the group to get to know each other better. Amma, who leans against the side of the huge chair as if for protection, says she felt the timing was not appropriate, with a bit more time she would have thought of something more positive. Big Brother thanks her for her honesty, and asks her to thank all the others on his behalf.

Helen also goes to the Diary Room, and says that she is worried because Paul has told her she is not very tactful. She wants to change. She says she wants people to like her and she doesn't want to come across as bad. The discussion has helped her look at the others in different ways. She says she thinks there is a division in the group, caused by Brian, Narinder and Penny, who want to spend a lot of time together, but she is getting on well with everyone.

Despite revealing such a different side of himself during the discussion, before bedtime Bubble reverts to his role as the clown, putting the resuscitation doll they have been given for the task into Brian's bed. The day ends, like so many others, with Brian screaming at Bubble.

In the girls' room, Narinder and Liz discuss the stories they have heard. They are feeling more sympathetic towards Helen. Narinder says she prefers the new, sensitive Bubble they have now seen. It's 2 a.m. before Amma goes to bed, and Liz, who can't sleep, climbs into the double bed with her and they talk

WHAT THE EXPERTS SAY

ELIZABETH

'Elizabeth didn't register on the radar for the first few days, but things have started to change. She is busy forming alliances with several of the housemates, most of them based on her sexuality. In the kitchen with Stuart, she raised the possibility of romance. The topic is highly suggestive, and so is her body language. She sends out several flirtatious signals: she arches her back, a primitive sexual signal used by females to convey a message of availability. We have also seen her in action with Dean, but she doesn't confine her attentions to the males. She uses a lot of loving and touching to develop her relationship with Amma.

Whether or not she's aware of it, sexuality plays an important part in the development of Elizabeth's relationships. She has become popular and powerful, and has managed to do it with subtlety.'

Dr Peter Collett, Experimental Psychologist

into the night, eventually getting up to eat cake in the kitchen. Amma doesn't rate Paul, but Liz says that as time goes on she is beginning to have respect for him. They both agree that Bubble is a real asset, and they love the constant funny bickering between him and Brian. Liz feels she has yet to make a connection with Dean, but Amma is enthusiastic about him, describing him as 'a wicked person'. Amma feels she has a lot in common with Narinder, but that the Geordie has a much shorter fuse than she does. They both agree that Helen brings out motherly instincts in them – even though Amma is only two months older than the Welsh housemate. At 4 a.m., the household is finally asleep.

Sunday begins quietly, with only Liz up early. She's worried they will not get their shopping list done on time. They do, but it is a pathetically short list as they only have £49. Stuart takes it into the Diary Room, and Bubble, ever hopeful, scrawls 'Can we watch the England game?' on the back.

Aware of how much it means to them financially if they fail, all the housemates work hard on the first-aid task, with Brian taking on the role of teacher. In the middle of the afternoon, Bubble goes to the Diary Room and talks about how difficult the previous evening's discussion was for him. 'I got so choked up, I couldn't explain as well as I would have liked to.'

At seven o'clock in the evening, Big Brother gives the group a nice surprise. Several large crates of grapes are delivered, and the contestants are told to crush them into grape juice with their feet. For every three bottles of juice they produce, they can have a bottle of wine. The housemates set to work with enthusiasm, to a chorus of jokes about sweaty feet, corns and verrucas. They make eighteen bottles, and are rewarded with six bottles of wine. As a bonus, they are told they can keep the grape juice, which they label Chateau Foot. Saving the wine for later, they drink the grape juice with their evening meal, although Stuart refuses it.

After the meal, the contestants knock back five bottles of wine and lose a few inhibitions. Penny gets very excited, and gives a loud rendition of 'Big Spender', which causes the others to share a few knowing looks. Stuart irritates Amma, who makes an exasperated and disbelieving face when he says that he is a graceful loser. He boasts about spending money on clothes: he once bought a jumper for £3,500, much to Bubble's horror. When the hour slips past midnight, Stuart opens a wedding-anniversary card from his wife, and is confused to find she describes it as their eighth – he believes it is their seventh. (Sian, his wife, later explains that she did it deliberately, to prevent him having the seven-year itch while in the house.) Narinder says she cannot read her husband's card or she will cry. Later, in the dark, in bed, she takes the card out and silently weeps.

Penny tells them a funny but poignant story about how she has been mistaken for a transvestite at least three times 'because I am so tall'.

The sexual tension between Bubble and Amma continues, and there is a lot of banter. Amma is not used to the amount of alcohol she consumes in the house: she is so drunk she falls over, and then goes into the Diary Room to drunkenly send messages to everyone, including her cat. Liz follows her in there and talks about the division in the house, with Brian, Narinder and

Penny on one side and Stu, Dean, Bubble and Helen on the other. Liz sees herself and Amma floating in between these two groups.

She and Amma are getting on really well, and the night ends with them sharing a huge giggling fit as they search for Liz's toothbrush.

Paul talks in his sleep, a fact that the other boys are by now well aware of, as it's loud enough to wake them. He's worried that he may have been discussing the nominations, and tells the others how he once said the wrong girl's name aloud. He apologizes to the other boys for waking them up.

Monday morning is spent practising first aid. The housemates have all been trying hard not to think or talk about the impending nominations, but at just after one o'clock, Big Brother announces that they will hear the results in an hour. Helen bets twenty pounds that her name will be one of them, and says, 'Everyone is emphasizing too much the first person to leave. Even if you are the first person, you've done so well just to get here.'

To break the tension, Brian and Narinder lapse into one of their song-and-dance routines, imitating Janet Jackson. Helen joins them. Penny copes with the wait by flirting mercilessly with Paul, telling him that he's 'cute', that she's 'desperate', and at one stage pinning him to his chair.

When the nominations finally come there is a moment of stunned silence. Then Amma takes Helen onto her knee for a cuddle, and Brian, Narinder and Paul swoop on Penny to hug her. Helen seems genuinely cheerful, and reiterates that she was expecting it. Penny says she is 'a tough old bird' and will be alright.

Narinder and Brian talk to Penny, who keeps telling them she is alright, which begins to irk Narinder.

'Every time I try to show my support you cut me off, so forget it. I'm one of those supporting you in this group and there are others who are obviously not. The last thing you need is for me not to be supporting you. And I'm supporting you a lot and I just get cut off.'

Penny apologizes, and Narinder concedes that she too would be snappy if she had been nominated.

When Penny eventually runs weeping to the girls' room, it is Bubble who follows her and comforts her, telling her that she is 'talented, sensational and clever'. When Penny says she is scared, he says, 'You should be so proud you even got here. You are not gone yet – you could be nominated every week and the public could fucking love you, that mad woman in the kitchen. People haven't nominated you because they don't like you, they just had to nominate someone. Put a smile on your face ... It's just a game and you're still in with a chance of winning it. Fuck the £70,000 – you got to meet me! That's the clincher. How many people in this world have never met me? I feel for them.'

Penny is smiling by now, and Bubble tells her to come to him if she needs a hug. She says 'What about a grope?' and makes to grab him, but Bubble leaves the room saying, 'Easy, tiger'.

It is Bubble's turn to be a little upset when Brian quizzes him about his hats. Brian wants to know whether Bubble's girlfriend wakes up and screams, 'Why do you wear those fucking hats in bed?' Bubble says he only sleeps in a hat if he's not in his own bed. This makes Brian roar with laughter at the prospect of

Bubble taking a collection of hats along with him for a one-night stand. Bubble has a go at him, suggesting that Brian doesn't know what a one-night stand is.

For a few seconds, the two – who have been such good mates until now – are in a stand-off. Brian had not expected Bubble to be so prickly. Bubble explains: 'We're very different. If I feel comfortable wearing a hat in bed in a house I don't know and that makes me feel at ease, then I don't care what you or anyone else thinks … You use your toner, and that's cool. In all fairness, if that makes you feel better, then you use it. I wouldn't use it, but I don't mock you for using it.'

Narinder tactfully rescues them from this unexpectedly serious exchange by insisting they get on with practising bandaging.

Over a dinner of pizza, the housemates toast Stuart's wedding anniversary. He is wearing a customized black T-shirt, with handwritten messages from his children and friends scrawled all over it.

Penny spends a full half-hour in the Diary Room talking about how she feels. She says she is dazed. She admits that she finds Amma, Liz and Stuart a bit formal, and worries about Helen being evicted, because she nominated her. She also tells Big Brother that she is worried about the reaction of the pupils at her school. Teenagers, she says, 'can be very cruel'.

When she leaves the Diary Room, she tells the others what a good chat she has had, which prompts Helen to go in. She tells Big Brother she isn't shocked to be nominated, and still thinks she will be the first to leave the house. She believes some of the girls may have voted to get the two blondes out of the house to give themselves a better chance.

The next morning, Stuart and Elizabeth are the first up. Although Stuart does not enjoy cooking – and has yet to cook a meal – he's a dab hand with the bread-making, and he's happy to join in the cleaning routines. He and Elizabeth discuss Penny: they think she is calmer since her long session with Big Brother, but Elizabeth cynically suggests that she was warned not to be too despondent because it would make viewers vote for her.

All the housemates are determined to do well in the first-aid test, and spend the day revising and practising. Big Brother calls Penny to the Diary Room in the middle of a first-aid session.

'I'm feeling more positive. It's been such a nice day, we're really cramming. It feels like being back at uni. I've chatted more with Liz and Stuart … I like Dean a lot, he's able to mix in with everybody. He makes people laugh, he listens, he is really grounded. I wouldn't be surprised if he won … I'm worried about Bubble going to sleep all the time. I think he's exhausted after the nominations. But he's a chirpy thing when he gets up.'

During the day the conversation turns to ways of getting revenge, and Amma tells the others the apocryphal tale of the jilted girlfriend who stuck several prawns inside her ex-lover's curtain pole, the smell maturing nicely over the next few days. Elizabeth said someone she knew at agricultural college injected some pig semen into an ex's toothpaste. Just when you thought the conversation couldn't go any lower, Paul started talking about freezing poo and then hurling it through someone's window, and waiting for it to thaw. They stress that none of them has actually carried out these dire acts of vengeance…

Bubble has two major preoccupations: one is the England-versus-Greece football match, and the second is his shortage of cigarettes. He gives Liz some of his last forty cigarettes to hide. Big Brother has refused to allow him to have nicotine patches unless they are on the shopping list, and, as Bubble points out, they're more expensive than tobacco. Liz makes sure Bubble will not find his emergency ration – she hides them in a tampon box.

The first-aid testing carries on through the evening, with Brian supervising everyone's revision. At one point, Brian goes to the Diary Room to talk about progress with the task. He says everyone is giving one hundred per cent, driven by the fact that they are all hungry. He adds that he can sense that some people in the house have their own agendas.

At midnight, Big Brother asks for all the first-aid instruction manuals to be delivered back to the Diary Room. Penny takes them in, and tells Big Brother that she is still feeling a bit weepy, and she is scared that she is going to be the one to be voted out.

The boys have been plotting all day, trying to come up with a good trick to play on the girls. Stuart suggests a handful of peas under each mattress. They don't have peas, so in the end they agree on stones from the garden, which Dean sneaks in while the others are having a late-night chat. The prank gets a predictable reaction.

That's not the only trouble in the girls' room. Amma, who tends to stay up longer than anyone else in the house, is brushing her hair in the dark shortly after climbing into bed. The sound disturbs Penny, who has a go at her, telling her to go into the living room if she wants to make noise.

Bubble, Dean and Stuart chat late into the night. Bubble asks if either of the others wants to go home, and Dean says he wants to go so much he'd be happy to go to Bubble's home. They discuss the eviction, and Stuart and Dean agree that Penny will be voted out, because viewers will have seen the way she is, and Helen comes across as a bright, bubbly character. Brian asks Paul what he thinks he will get the most stick for when he leaves the house, and Paul replies unhesitatingly 'kissing Penny'.

Paul is still talking in his sleep, and he seems to have the first-aid task on his mind. At quarter to four in the morning he says, very loudly and clearly: 'Be prepared. Be really, really prepared.'

And, boy, do they need to be prepared. While the housemates are all still sound asleep at 7 a.m., a team of *Big Brother* staff sneak into the garden. At 7.24 a.m., the housemates are woken by the sound of banging and whistles. Then comes Big Brother's voice, telling them that a meteor has crashed in the garden and they have two minutes to dress and assemble in the kitchen.

Taped to the patio window are some instructions, which Dean reads out to the others. Their garden is a disaster zone, with four casualties strewn around it – life-size dummies with labels attached to them stating the type, extent and severity of their injuries. The housemates are to attend to them until the emergency services arrive, and if any of the injured 'die', the housemates

BAD HABITS

Amma: Farting and burping in public, messy, talkative, smoking in bed, not punctual.
Brian: Biting nails, hogging the bathroom, stealing flatmates' clothes, playing love songs at half past four in the morning.
Bubble: Biting nails, being horrible when first woken up, picking nose, smoking, drinking, swearing, telling white lies, farting, belching, talking loudly, slamming doors.
Dean: Biting nails, slurping tea, eating noisily, untidy.
Elizabeth: Untidy, blunt, bad in the mornings.
Helen: Going from one bump in the car to another ... and another ... and another, scraping my dinner plate, not emptying the bin.
Josh: Untidy, leaving lights on, forgetting birthdays.
Narinder: Leaving dishes in the sink for yonks, scratching my scalp and everywhere else on my body, picking dirt from my nails, forgetting birthdays.
Paul: Putting hand down trousers, walking around with one sock on, picking nose, looking in the mirror a lot.
Penny: Nervous and anxious at times, low self-esteem.
Stuart: Stubborn, a bit of a control freak, picking nose.

will have failed the task. A siren gives them the go-ahead, and they all rush into the garden. Dean assumes control and assigns them all to different tasks, giving Brian the most seriously injured casualty to deal with. Helen, without any prompting, goes to the phone box and calls the emergency services.

After ten frantic minutes, the housemates hear the sirens of the ambulance, and Big Brother tells them to go into the boys' room to allow the 'meteor', the phone box and the dummies to be removed. Dean is amazed at how well they all did, and is sure they must have passed. Helen says she feels sick, it was so realistic.

They all go back to bed, and while they sleep the task is marked. First-aid expert Brian Cassin, who helped devise and set up the task, is one of the judges. Although the housemates delayed the treatment to the burns victim, and one of the resuscitation dolls had its stomach compressed instead of its chest, he says the contestants did really well:

'Dean was calm throughout and really good, taking charge. Stuart was good, he showed authority and calmed things down, took them through it step by step. Bubble was moving from one scenario to another, offering good advice. Narinder and Brian worked well as a team, very co-ordinated, almost a dance, willing each other on. And Helen, of course – all the first-aid skills in the world are useless if nobody calls an ambulance. They were brilliant!'

The housemates don't know this, though. They are left on tenterhooks until 12.30 p.m.

Penny's late-night spat with Amma leads to a day of back-biting among the girls. Amma tells Helen, 'She hates my guts because I won't lick her arse and I can do anything she can.' Later on, Narinder and Amma agree that Penny can rub people up the wrong way. Amma describes her as 'petty and childish' and complains that Penny gives more food to the boys which really annoys Narinder. She asks Amma how she will cope if Penny survives the eviction.

'I'll have to deal with it. Once I've established that Penny doesn't like me, fine. I'll stay out of her way, talk to her only when I need to.'

Narinder comments that that is the kind of relationship she has with Helen, but Amma disagrees with her, saying that while Narinder and Helen are getting on better, the relationship between herself and Penny is getting worse.

When the housemates are told that they have passed the first-aid test they are jubilant, cheering, hugging each other and jumping up and down. They now have £112 to spend on next week's shopping – a huge relief after this week's short rations.

Bubble believes the increased budget means he can have cigarettes on the shopping list. After all, he is teetotal nowadays, and the others will order alcohol. But they all try to persuade him to stick to his resolve to give up smoking. Part-time smoker Paul has given up completely, and even Amma, who is Bubble's trusty smoking companion, is giving up for three days. She says if it goes well, she will use her time in the house to give up completely. But Bubble is afraid that the other housemates and viewers will see him being tetchy and snappy if he goes cold turkey.

'If you want to win this game, you need to be yourself,' he says.

While Penny is very emotional about the impending eviction vote, Helen affects to be unconcerned. She's mostly worried, she tells the others, about catching her heel in the metal grille they have to walk over when they leave the house. She's already planning how she'll do her hair and what she'll wear.

Helen's hairdressing skills are called upon when Bubble asks her to shave a union jack into his hair, to show his support for the England football team. But he is disappointed with her efforts, and in the end settles for Dean cutting a large cross of St George into his hair. When that doesn't please him, he decides to go for the full skinhead look, but halfway through he agrees to a 'David Beckham', in tribute to the England captain.

Helen is on happier turf doing Liz's hair, while Narinder and Amma do Liz's make-up. Liz looks different, unusually glamorous, and the other girls admire the way she looks.

The world outside impinges on the *Big Brother* house today – and not just because Dean and Bubble are talking unremittingly about the football they are missing. It is the day of the general election, and seven of the housemates are voting. Stuart cast his vote by proxy and the others, Penny, Helen, Elizabeth, Paul, Narinder and Bubble, all cast postal votes, filling in their forms in the Diary Room.

Brian starts a discussion by asking Amma if she would sleep with Tony Blair for a million pounds. She says she would 'because he's quite cute'. Narinder would do it for a tenner. Paul says he would snog a man, but not sleep with one.

Later, Big Brother asks them how they have voted. Helen blithely admits she has voted Labour, 'because so far they've done alright and the

Conservatives are all stuck up'. She later panics and goes into the Diary Room to confess her fear that now all the Tories will vote for her eviction. Halfway through expressing her fears, she decides that maybe it's alright after all – because all the Labour supporters will be voting for her. She doesn't know that Penny has also voted Labour.

Bubble and Dean stage a vigil in the garden, wrapped in blankets, for the duration of the England game that they are missing.

Late at night, Penny and Helen discuss their beauty preparations for eviction night, and agree that they will coat themselves with fake tan. At midnight the group, with the exception of Penny who is in bed, sing 'Happy Birthday' to Bubble, who is twenty-five on Thursday. Afterwards, they sit around while the rain pours down outside, telling each other scary stories. Helen is so spooked, she goes into the Diary Room and tells Big Brother that the boys have been winding her up.

'They say a man is going to get in here, and it won't be Big Brother because you'll all be dead. But it won't happen will it, because we're quite safe here aren't we? Are there security guards outside?' Big Brother assures her that she is being watched at all times, and that she is safe. As she walks out, she encounters Bubble plastered in fake blood, and screams in terror.

After more practical jokes – this time they remove the slats from Brian's and Paul's beds – the boys settle down and quietly talk about Penny. Paul grumbles that since the nomination she has said some rude things to him. Brian, her friend, puts her point of view:

'I think it's a form of rejection. I think she feels it is happening all over again.'

Stuart says that if Penny can't take rejection, she should never have volunteered for a game of which rejection is a fundamental part. The others agree. Dean and Paul say they are sure they already know which of the two girls will be leaving the house on Friday night.

The girls stay up later than the boys. Elizabeth is baking some special bread as a present for Bubble, and they talk about him while it is in the oven. Helen

WHAT THE EXPERTS SAY

PENNY

'If you look at Penny on paper, she is not naturally a person you think of as insecure: she's older, she's a teacher, which is a responsible job, she's religious, and she seems to be well supported. Yet she does not seem to have fared well in the house, but that's largely to do with the way that the others are treating her. She has been scapegoated to quite a large degree. It could have been a completely different situation if she had been more supported. There are lots of insecurities in her life, and her experience in the house resonates with them and brings them to the fore.'

Dr Sandra Scott, Psychiatrist

says she thinks he is weird, but Elizabeth says he is simply having a problem with nicotine withdrawal. Amma sympathizes – her pledge to give up smoking was broken earlier in the evening when she puffed away at half a cigarette.

They all get up slowly the next day. Sitting in the garden, Dean and Stuart discuss their lives and their ambitions. They agree that, because they are older, they have more realistic expectations of life after *Big Brother* than some of the younger housemates. They talk about age, and when Stuart goes to wake Bubble, he tells the shaven-headed football fanatic, 'Twenty-five – you're getting old!' Even half asleep, Bubble is up for it: 'I'll never be as old as you,' he retorts. But he seems low, and soon goes into the Diary Room to send messages to his daughter, his mum, his dad and anyone who shares the same birthday as him.

Penny is having a big grooming day. Helen touches up her roots for her, Paul gives her a manicure, and Brian gives her a pedicure before rubbing instant tan all over her.

At lunchtime, Bubble gets his best birthday present: a journalist with a megaphone shouts the results of the England–Greece match (which England won 2–0) over the fence. Dean hears it before the housemates are ordered in from the garden by Big Brother. Bubble is ecstatic, although not entirely sure that Dean isn't winding him up.

The girls are impressed when the boys talk of the romantic gestures they have made for their girlfriends. Dean once filled a fridge with flowers for his girl; Bubble drove to Manchester to deliver a box of chocolates, and Paul gave a girl twenty-five presents to open, one for each day in the build-up to Christmas. Brian decides that flowers in the fridge is the most romantic of them all, but Paul gets the sympathy vote when he tells how he was dumped by a girlfriend on Christmas Eve.

The girls go to their room to work on a song they have been composing specially for Bubble, which they sing to the tune of 'Stuck in the Middle With You'. When Brian walks in, he makes a faux pas by asking Elizabeth if the photograph on her wall is of her father. She tells him it is her boyfriend, and Brian screams apologetically. Shortly afterwards, Elizabeth tells the other girls how she met her partner, who is much older than her. She says her parents were worried at first, but they were fine about it as soon as they met him.

The boys are still playing tricks on each other, moving all Brian's bedding out into the den. To retaliate, Brian hides Bubble's hats. Bubble bursts noisily into the girls' room, where Penny and Narinder are talking, and demands to know where his hats are. When he has gone, Penny's overwrought behaviour shows how emotionally she is dealing with what she believes the other housemates think of her:

'Why do they think I'm a neurotic weirdo, how about Bubble and his fucking hats?'

Penny has already told Narinder that she thinks Elizabeth 'wouldn't be my chosen friend because she's always about number one'. Now she doesn't hold back in revealing her feelings about the others:

'How about Stuart with his no-lip sparrow head, only knowing one fucking song on his guitar? Why don't they pick up the guitar and improvize?

They will have a boring programme if this continues.'

She reprises the row she had with Amma: 'It was like a railway station with the noise, and then she's in the bed and was scraping her hair like a horse. I'm like, "Can you be quiet?" and she says, "Just go to bed," and I'm like, "I'm *in* bed."'

With Narinder prompting her with the occasional question, Penny lets off more steam and launches into a rant:

'Elizabeth will put on a turban and smoke a joint and snog Amma on the bed. On the magic carpet are Brian and Dean, and hanging on for dear life is Stuart smothered in suntan lotion. And at one end is Bubble and his hats and his fucking neurotic football and fucking psycho-ness because he's not smoking and his fucking fat gut ... '

Brian appears and Narinder, who has been convulsed with laughter, tells him how funny Penny has been. Penny is now almost hysterical, and is screaming about leaving the house tomorrow. She says (wrongly) that seven people have voted her out.

The noise of her outburst brings Amma and Helen tiptoeing to the door, just as Penny is reliving her argument with Amma the other night. When Amma walks into the room, Brian deftly changes the subject.

At seven o'clock, Big Brother tells the housemates the Store Room is unlocked. Inside, they find boxes of blue props for turning the house into Chelsea heaven for Bubble's birthday. Among the boxes is a game of table football and a 1970s Chelsea shirt. As Bubble paints faces blue and white (and Dean, as a Birmingham City fan, has a crisis of conscience), Amma and Helen dress as cheerleaders and chant Bubble's name. The Store Room is opened again, and this time the surprise is a takeaway curry, blue lemonade (Bubble doesn't drink) and a birthday cake. Unknown to the housemates, a splendid cake provided by Bubble's family has not been allowed in. Helen was allowed hers, but since then Stuart's wife has been caught trying to smuggle a note in with some food that was being delivered to the house, and Big Brother has toughened up.

The housemates agree is it the best curry they have ever tasted. For Brian, it is the first curry he has ever tasted, and all he can say is that he's 'hot'. Bubble makes a speech, and they all toast Helen and Penny, the two who are up for eviction. After the meal, the girls perform their song for Bubble and the musical tribute doesn't end there. Big Brother surprises Bubble by playing a medley of Chelsea songs into the house. The whole group drape themselves in blue material and do a conga through the house.

Bubble, who is thrilled with his party, goes to the Diary Room to thank Big Brother and to send messages of love to his parents and his daughter.

Penny goes into the Diary Room next and appears philosophical about the prospect of eviction. But her calmness soon dissipates. Over a game of table football with Paul, she is supercharged, dancing and shouting in near-hysteria. Paul is worried about her, and afterwards tells some of the others, 'She's not handling it at all. She's talking to herself, dancing around, she's just not with it.'

He talks quietly to Penny, trying to calm her down. She tells him that she is just getting used to the house:

'I'm letting go a bit more of my manicness, I'm having a laugh. It's been quite frightening for the last two weeks.' She confesses she is scared about tomorrow, and Paul tells her that if she stays in, she should 'just chill', adding, 'And if you go, go out in style, do yourself justice.'

In contrast to Penny, Helen is very laid back about the impending eviction. 'What is there to be nervous about? You've got to enjoy moments like this.' The others serenade her with a chorus of 'Che Sera, Sera (What Will Be, Will Be)'.

Friday is eviction day, and there is tension in the house all day, most of it emanating from Penny. She is assuming – as are most of the housemates, with the exception of Helen – that she is definitely going to leave this evening. She has a long talk with Liz, who says she would like to get to know Penny on the outside, in a normal environment. Dean, too, says he wants to meet her again, and tells her he will invite her to his wedding.

In the girls' room, Helen tells Narinder and Amma that she thinks Penny sees her as a rival. She says she can't lose tonight: if she leaves, she sees her family and boyfriend, and if she stays she's still in the game. Narinder, who, along with Brian, has been Penny's closest ally, tells the others that Penny has been snapping at her. Helen remarks pertinently that she doesn't think any of them really know Penny. Then Amma and Narinder, who have been wary of each other, open up and Amma apologizes if she has seemed stressed, blaming the lack of cigarettes.

The housemates decide to have a good clean up, so that the house will look its best for Davina. Helen is designated the task of cleaning the mirrors, which means she spends most of the time checking her hair. Bubble sleeps through the cleaning, to the annoyance of some of the others.

Helen tells Paul she is excited about tonight and says she will be upset if she doesn't go. Then she worries about her mother and Big G, travelling all the way from Wales. 'What if I get nominated every week and don't go? They will be so pissed off with that.'

Brian gives both the nominated girls another coat of fake tan, so that they will look their best for the outside world. Helen discreetly keeps her towel in place, but Penny cheerfully bares all.

In the afternoon, Penny has an eviction dress rehearsal, trying on her spangly dress and practising walking with her suitcase in tow. Brian and Liz both reassure her that she looks great, and Liz says, 'Remember, Penny: dignity, grace, smile and be calm.'

Penny agrees: 'No manicness.'

But that's Penny's pledge for tonight. In the meantime, she's more manic than ever. Interrupting Brian and Narinder's chat about some of the others, she gives an impromptu, over-the-top rendition of 'Big Spender', which involves lots of wild dancing, and culminates in her raising her skirt and flashing her bum at the camera. She remains on a high, snapping at the others and reading out the eviction procedure in an exaggeratedly school-teacherish fashion. Then she calms down, sitting quietly with the rag doll clutched to her.

VOTING

More than a million viewers cast their votes in the first *Big Brother* eviction. A total of 624,788 votes (fifty-eight per cent of all those cast) were to evict Penny, while 447,337 (forty-two per cent) of the voters wanted to see Helen leave the house. For the first time, many viewers were able to cast votes via their TV screens, and 373,128 (or thirty-five per cent of the total) voted this way in the biggest ever interactive-TV vote.

Up to half a million people at a time watched the live transmission of *Big Brother* on the digital channel E4 – an astonishing 50,000 viewers were tuned in at 3 a.m. on the first morning of transmission. On the internet, there were an average of 1.2 million downloads of live video streaming, and the website became the UK's number-one entertainment site.

Television-viewing figures were up by more than a million on the first *Big Brother* series, with an average of four million tuned in during the second week. *Big Brother's Little Brother*, the magazine programme on E4, attracted an average of 317,300 viewers, peaking at 524,000.

The boys discuss her mental state. Brian says her exaggerated behaviour is just her way of coping.

Called to the Diary Room, Penny tells Big Brother she knows she has been a bit hyper because the whole experience has been so scary. She says that if she is not evicted she will try to become more normal and less stressed. She promises to help Helen, and says she will 'make her feel as sweet and pretty as we can'. She says that she feels quite similar to Helen, despite not being twenty-three and cute. 'We both put our feet in it, and that's maybe why we have been nominated.' Then she reiterates the pledge she made to Liz: 'I will be very gracious and completely professional tonight, not swearing or saying anything naff.'

But outside, she immediately pounces on Bubble, giving him lots of hugs and kisses which obviously make him feel uncomfortable. Soon afterwards it is Paul's turn, and she lies on top of him, kissing him all over his face. He doesn't protest at first, calling her 'a child', but after continued attempts to free himself he eventually says, 'Get off me – go and pack your stuff.'

Helen is called to the Diary Room, and is a complete contrast to Penny. She says she's excited about the evening – 'it's going to be cool' – but she does not seem phased. She says she enjoyed yesterday more than today, because she did her nails, her roots and her legs.

The housemates are nearing the end of their week of short rations, and even though Big Brother has today re-stocked their fortnightly supplies of basics, they are not able to have a gourmet dinner for eviction night. Dean and Bubble cook some form of sausage-meat concoction, and they only have water to drink.

Over the meal, the others demand speeches from the two evictees.

'I've had a nice time – and whoever voted for me, watch your back when you get out!' jokes Helen.

Penny says: 'It's been the most terrifying experience of my life, being with you all and trying to adapt to that. You have seen the worst side of me, the most neurotic, most manic, insecure side. So it would be really lovely to see you in the real world, a normal environment, to see how your lives are moving on. So thanks very much.'

They all hold hands round the table as Davina announces the results, milking the suspense with a long pause before giving them Penny's name. The housemates all get up and crowd round Penny, hugging her. As she hugs Amma, Penny says she knows they have been horrible to each other. 'I wish we'd had the chance to get to know you better,' Amma replies.

Penny spends her last hour and a half in the house saying personal goodbyes to everyone. She tells her mates Brian and Narinder that they are really special, and she thanks Paul for letting her grope him: 'I'm so insecure and I needed someone to grab hold of. Thank you for letting me grab your bollocks loads.'

Helen is worried that Narinder will blame her for Penny's departure, but both Paul and Bubble persuade her to put her fears to one side until after Penny has gone.

Big Brother plays music into the house while they wait for Penny to leave, and they all enjoy dancing, especially Stuart.

Then it's time for Penny to go. The others form a guard of honour, with their hands linked over her head, as she walks through the front door, dragging her suitcase and carrying her high-heeled sandals in her hand, in case they stick in the grating.

The mood in the house is subdued. Helen is upset, and goes to talk to Big Brother, explaining how she feels bad about dragging her friends down from Wales.

'When you're in this situation and you're missing your friends it's big-time tough. I suppose I should see it as a good thing that people voted for me to stay in here. It's just a bit sad, knowing they're out there, and hearing people's voices, and Davina's voice, it brought home the reality of it. I hope Penny has a fab time, because Penny is amazing. It will be difficult in the morning, because there will be nobody to make porridge. In the living room just now, it felt like there was a big gap. She will be missed.'

Liz bakes scones, which everybody scoffs hungrily, talking about the food they are going to order. After everyone else is in bed, Amma goes to the Diary Room. She wants to make a pact with Big Brother to be less 'moany'.

'I have been blessed with spending time with unique, wonderful people that I would never otherwise have met. It's been strange. I've felt emotions I never knew that I would. I didn't think that today would move me. I want to apologize to Penny, to say that I was unfair to her because these are weird surroundings and none of us is themselves. In the last hour I really liked you, Penny. In small doses I would really enjoy your company.'

She says the atmosphere is lighter after Penny's departure, and that she would like to have known her outside the *Big Brother* house, but comments, 'She would have cracked soon, she was fraying at the edges.'

Amma bets Big Brother fifty pounds that she won't be in the house at this time next week.

'I don't think anyone hates my guts, but I don't see myself as necessary to the group dynamic. It has been a good experience, and I don't want to feel like I haven't made the most of it. If I leave next week, I don't mind: I have done something that thousands of people wanted to do. I wish I had never had my disagreement with Penny in the night. I was very sharp. I wish I had not given in and started smoking again. I wish I ignored more things, I wish I opened my mouth and spoke out more. I have never been so quiet in my life, or so serious. I have no sense of humour in here. I have lost my ability to talk to anyone about anything, which to me is the weirdest thing. For my job I can sit and talk to strange men about anything and sound witty and charming and full of life. In here I sound as dull as ditch-water.'

PENNY LOOKS BACK: THE EXCLUSIVE INTERVIEW

Penny on the housemates

Paul: 'My friendship with him was never going to become anything more. It may look, on camera, as though it was a sexual thing, but in fact it was always only fun. It was a friendship, and all that grab, tickle and laugh was just a jest, we didn't do it in a turn-on way. He let me know when he called me a 'big old girl' that I wasn't his bag, but that meant we could have a laugh. And he was lonely, too. At the moment Paul is young and a bit shallow, but I think by the time he's thirty he'll be a great catch for some girl. He's easily influenced. The minute Stuart started showing the top of his boxers under his shorts, Paul started doing it too. He got more cocky towards the end of my time there. He fancies the pants off Helen, but he's very defensive about it.'

Stuart and Elizabeth: 'I didn't get close to understanding Stuart and Elizabeth. I was horrified to see Liz suggesting that I went to kiss her in a lesbian sort of way. As far as I was concerned, we'd had a nice, girlie chat, and I took her a cup of tea when she had chronic wind. The kiss was just a friendship thing, but she saw it as something else. I just don't live in that mind set, to me it was so obviously innocent.

'Being with those two was like being in a maze, because I just didn't know how to find my way round them. They did not get me at all. They are too quiet. I like quiet people, but they are quiet for the wrong reasons. It's an eerie quiet, they're thinking and watching. Stuart is either looking at himself in the mirror or staring at someone else.'

Bubble: 'Bubble is crass and crude, but cute. I think he could flip out, he's controlling himself.'

Brian: 'Brian is terrific, so talented, fantastic company. He doesn't realize how gifted he is. His main aim in life is to work for a different airline: he should be setting his sights higher than that. He has a lovely naivety and innocence: he had never had an Indian meal, didn't know how to make a bed. I hope he stays the same, that the *Big Brother* experience doesn't change him.'

Narinder: 'Naz is very up-front: what you see is what you get. She has a permanent negativeness about her, and I got caught up with that. I wanted to talk about happy things, but she wanted to unburden on me. That's why I had that bitching session: it was me bitching, but she set the mood. Then I got paranoid, wondering if she was really my friend or whether she was deliberately drawing this stuff out of me. You get paranoid in there: when Bubble comforted me when I was crying, half of me was really glad, and the other half wondered if he was doing it in order to look good on television.'

Dean: 'Dean is all things to all of them, he's so chilled. But there is a real intensity there, like when he was so bossy during the first-aid test. He told me that he was so stressed about being there that he was relieved to spot the fire escape, to know that there was always a way out.'

Amma: 'Amma got completely the wrong impression of me, thinking I was being patronizing and sarcastic, when what I said, praising her, was truly meant. She's selfish: she's made her life the way she wants it. But there's a lot of vulnerability there, and I didn't find any way of getting close to her. She's like one of the girls at school who just don't like me. She's a stroppy girl. There was venom and ugliness in the way she spoke to me.'

Helen: 'I got Helen wrong at first. I thought she was a sarky bitch, but she's actually a nice girl. She's not tactful and she's got a lot of confidence, which can give her an abrasive edge. She's ignorant, innocent, naive and at times a bit nasty. She's as beautiful as a rainbow, and just like a rainbow, all the colours of her personality are part of her. You can see it all, and you have to accept it.'

Penny on life in the house

'There's a little bit of me left in the house – I gave Paul and Narinder my blue and white crystal bracelets before I left. A friend gave them to me when I went

PEOPLE ON PENNY

Penny's friend, Pete: 'When you really get to know Penny you have to love her. She's a very natural person, loved by everyone. She's very touchy-feely. I knew nothing would happen with Paul – she goes for more sophisticated types. She was picked on big time in the house, she wasn't supported by the rest of the household. I think some of the girls felt jealous and threatened by her.'

Susan, a waitress: 'I love Penny, she's just part of the show, she makes it brilliant. She's really fun-loving, she likes everyone, and tries to be everyone's friend and I think she really is.'

Josie D'arby, TV Presenter: 'Aaaaaaargh!'

in, and told me to wear them whenever I wanted my friends to pray for me – so I was wearing them a lot towards the end.

'I also left my henna nail-decorating kits for Brian, for his birthday, which is coming up. We've already had two birthdays while I was in there. I gave Helen a glittery disco ball, which you stick to a mirror – it was the perfect present for her. And I gave Bubble my juggling balls. He learnt to juggle with them since he's been in there, and it helps distract him when he runs out of cigarettes. I learnt to juggle when I was ten, so I've told him to teach his daughter when she reaches ten. The balls were very useful in the house. We had a game where we sat in a circle and threw them to one another. It got quite hard and vicious, but it released a few tensions.'

Penny found herself in the *Big Brother* house almost by accident. She telephoned what she thought was the number for the *Big Breakfast*, because she wanted to ask whether some of her pupils could take part in a programme. She found she had dialled the *Big Brother* hotline, so she left her name and address and the application form duly arrived.

'I delayed filling it in – at one point I even put it in the bin. But I loved the vibe of the first *Big Brother*, I loved the fun and the tongue-in-cheek feel of it. I knew how much my girls at school were into it, so I thought it would be great for them if I could be in there – it would give me the opportunity to be closer to them.'

Penny has been teaching the same group of girls for four years, and took a large scrapbook about them into the house with her.

She describes the atmosphere in the house as 'quite brutal at times'. 'There was so much friction,' she says, 'It was like sandpaper rubbing on sandpaper. I thought the girls would be jovial and friendly, but there's a hard core to all of them. It scared me, reminded me of previous unhappiness in my life. So I retreated into doing the cooking, looking after the chickens, which was seen as mumsy and boring, which I'm not.'

Penny says Brian and Narinder are the two whose friendship she thought was genuine during her two weeks in the house – although she was upset to see tapes showing Narinder criticizing her for giving the boys too much food.

'I don't know why she didn't say it to my face. I did give the boys more, because they need more – Dean has lost so much weight, I'm worried about him. And although I was criticized for being bossy and taking control, nothing would have got done if I hadn't. The chickens would not have been looked after – more than once I found them without any water. When I suggested a rota they all said I was bossy – but in the end that's exactly what they did.'

Penny on Penny

She describes her time in the house as 'the most terrifying thing I have ever done'.

'The person you saw in there was me, but she was the most extreme, neurotic, frightened version of me, the five-year-old me, having to cope with all sorts of emotions. I think I gave the programme an edge, made it

WEEK TWO FACT FILE

Main task: Learn first aid and treat casualties at the scene of a meteor crash.

PASS ☑ **FAIL** ☐

Mini-task: Crush grapes with their feet.

Treats: Six bottles of wine for the grape treading. Bubble's blue birthday party.

Bets are on!
To win: Brian is favourite to win with odds of 3/1, with Dean not far behind on 7/2. For those who like a risk, Josh, who has not yet entered the house, is 6/1.
To walk: Helen may have survived the eviction process once, but she's still favourite, at 2/1, to be the next out. Narinder is second favourite at 3/1.
Evictee's tip: Penny says: 'Brian will win. The last four will be Brian, Dean, Bubble and Narinder, or maybe Josh. The next to be evicted will be Amma or Stuart.'

interesting: after all, if you believe everything the papers say, I've dropped my towel, almost shagged a bloke and I may be a lesbian.

'I don't remember dropping my towel, it was totally accidental and the sort of thing that happens all the time – it's just that it went out live on TV. As for shagging, I was never going to do that, even if there had been anybody worth doing it with. And the lesbian bit just can't be serious. Luckily, I don't take myself seriously.

'The most difficult thing in there is just being yourself. The sad thing is that if I had been there longer I'd have come out of being bossy and mumsy and would have become this secure person the others could turn to for advice. I'd have liked the others to see me as I am, the real me, the outside me.

'The whole experience has helped me realize that a lot of my life I have been controlled by others, and I'm now going to do something about that. *Big Brother* has lifted me, made me feel more confident. I know I can do whatever I want. I am so glad I did it.'

▲ Liz, Penny, Paul and Brian make their way down the path during their last minutes of freedom.

▲ Bubble is first in the house.

▲ Josh goes through the security checks.

▲ Getting to know you – the housemates introduce themselves.

▲ Settling into the house – and the garden.

▲ Paul and Helen synchronise their moves.

▲ After the romantic date, Helen and Paul can't let go of each other.

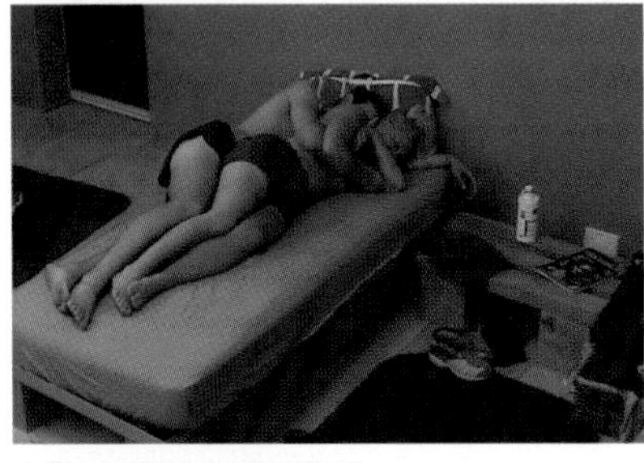

▲ Spooning on the bed.

▲ Paul enjoyed the fun and games in the house.

▲ Paul carries Helen to the bed in the den.

▲ 'I have lived my adult life like an international pop star.'

▲ Dinner in the Big Brother house was an informal affair.

▲ Paul and Helen's romantic meal.

▲ Dancing Queen – Helen takes the stage with Narinder.

▲ Helen resolves to improve her hula-hooping after Paul teases her that good hula-hoopers are good in bed.

▲ Helen reckoned her model of Dean made him look like Mick Jagger, he thought he looked more like the Wild Man.

▲ Helen said she didn't mind what she wore for the Ascot task as long as it was pink and glittery – Josh took her at her word.

▲ **Bubble takes a tumble.**

▲ **Chelsea boy and Chelsea girl.**

▲ **Bubble writes a birthday poem for Liz.**

▲ **Brian succeeds in persuading Bubble to have a face pack.**

▲ **Bubble with Davina in the exciting moments after his eviction.**

▲ **Bubble was never without one of his ten hats.**

▲ Amma, dressed to kill, chops wood for the fire task.

▲ Amma and Stuart come to verbal blows in the hot tub.

▲ Amma's habit of wrapping food in tin foil meant that a tin foil dress and hat was the natural choice for her Ascot outfit.

▲ Amma is comforted by Dean and Liz in the den after the confrontation with Stuart.

▲ Amma, Liz, and Helen sent temperatures rising with their jacuzzi antics.

▲ **Brian's antics kept the rest of the house, and the viewers, in stitches.**

▲ **Brian dressed as Josh, with Liz dressed as Amma during the soap opera task.**

▲ **Brian's bum is exposed as Josh pulls his trunks off.**

▲ **Brian and Narinder doing a dance routine.**

▲ **Brian and Josh romping.**

▲ **Brian tells Paul and Helen he can see them getting married one day.**

▲ **Narinder does her 'Paul' face.**

▲ **Narinder and her husband, Jatinder, on her eviction night.**

▲ **Narinder and Brian share confidences in the bathroom.**

◀ **Narinder loved to make her feelings known in the Diary Room.**

▲ **Narinder plays one of her B-movie characters.**

▲ **Narinder at prayer.**

▲ **Dean and Liz share a date.**

▲ **At times, Dean resented the ever-present Big Brother.**

▲ **Dean was rarely seen without his guitar.**

▲ **Dean, dressed as Narinder, and Josh, dressed as Brian, show off their moves in the soap opera.**

▲ **Dean and Liz put the world to rights while wrapped in those regulation orange blankets.**

▲ **Dean, the world record-breaker.**

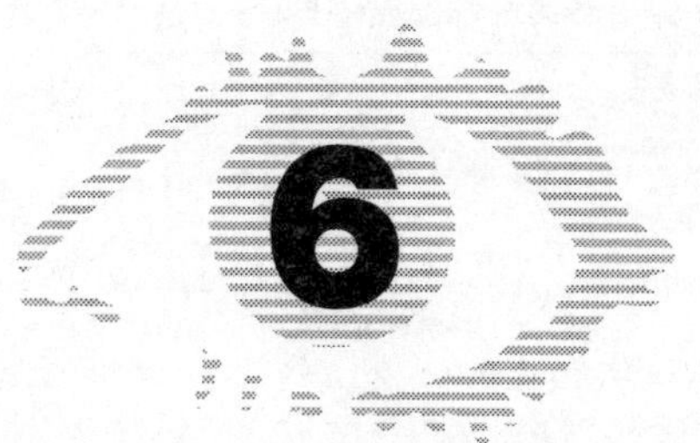

WEEK THREE

'I hope the whole fucking country votes him out on Friday.'
Amma

The excitement of the first eviction has exhausted all the housemates, and Saturday starts slowly and leisurely. Stuart gets up at half past eight, but after reading for a while goes back to sleep in a deckchair outside. The others stir when the hot water comes on. Bubble takes over Penny's porridge-making duties, and Stuart makes bread.

Dean takes the batteries to the Diary Room, and stays for a chat.

'I felt bad yesterday, because I nominated Penny and she was going. Yesterday was quite boring until the eviction. I lost sight of what I was here for and didn't really enjoy it at all. Later I felt kinda jealous that Penny was going, that someone was leaving. She was getting back to normality, and the underlying feeling in here is that we would all like some normal life.

'Everyone got very upset by the eviction. It was a strange, emotional experience. While I thought Penny had to go for herself, I didn't feel particularly good having nominated and having to be nice to her and help her cope with being nominated. I don't like doing that, it's not the sort of thing I would do on the outside. But it was right that she went, because she was finding it difficult to relax and be herself.'

Outside in the garden, Bubble announces confidently that the eleventh housemate will be a girl. Dean tells the others about his brush with fame, when he was in a band with a recording contract. He says he was 'gutted' when the record label dropped them. Meanwhile, in the kitchen, Brian, Narinder and Amma are discussing Stuart. Narinder says he doesn't have a personality, but Amma thinks he has a strong personality, which he hides behind an obsession with his appearance.

At 1.23 p.m., Big Brother asks for someone to take the eleventh housemate, the rag doll, to the Diary Room. Narinder obliges. There is now an air of great anticipation. Behind the scenes, new boy Josh has been security cleared and has been led, blindfold, into the Diary Room. Five minutes after the doll is given in, Josh emerges into the house to a chorus of screams and

THE ELEVENTH HOUSEMATE

While the housemates were having fun getting to know each other during their first week in the house, viewers were also having fun deciding who would join them as the eleventh housemate. It was a choice of one from three, and the candidates stated their cases in short video-clips at the end of the programmes.

The contenders were Anne, a forty-five-year-old grandmother; Josh, a thirty-two-year-old property consultant; and Natasha, a twenty-six-year-old part-time model. All three of them had made it through every round of the auditions and were on the reserve list for going into the house. Natasha even spent five days in there as one of the 'guinea pigs', taking part in a trial run to make sure that all the systems were working properly.

The voting was intense but in the end Josh was the winner. For the week of the vote, all three were whisked away by Big Brother to Portugal, where they had the time of their lives. Josh was kept abroad for the next week, until it was time for him to carry his suitcase into the house, because it was important that he didn't see any of the programmes.

Both Natasha and Anne agreed that their week together in exile was almost as good as being in the house – and they were both devoted Josh fans, rooting for him to be the overall winner.

shrieks from the housemates. Narinder is thrilled to see that he's good looking. Paul and Bubble are thrilled he has brought lager and cigarettes in with him. Helen is so thrilled she vies with Narinder to show Josh the house. When, under a barrage of questions from the girls, he says he is single and unattached, both girls cheer.

Narinder is so excited she makes a trip to the Diary Room to thank Big Brother for Josh.

'Hi, I just wanted to say "Whoaaaa!" You should see the look on the guys' faces.' She giggles. 'I just want to say thank you – not because I think he's good looking, because I don't – but he's just another person who has brought some extra energy into the house. They were all so content with themselves, sitting in the garden, having a little lounge, having their little lives. Then he came in and they all pulled these faces.' She shows a long face to the camera.

Ten minutes later, when Brian comments that it is going to be hard accepting a new member of the household, Narinder disagrees:

'We've been here two weeks and we hate each other. It's brought it home to me how boring everyone else is, and I want them out. Bubble has been acting really peculiar, like when he first came in, he's well annoyed. And Dean's in a bit of a mood.'

When Josh collects his suitcase from the Store Room, he finds with it a letter from Big Brother. Not only have they discovered a new housemate, they are about to discover a hot tub, which has been hidden under the rockery in the garden. The tub will not be ready for them to use until tomorrow afternoon (the water has to be purified), but it increases the level of excitement in the house yet further.

But there's an even bigger surprise in store. Over lunch, as they quiz Josh about his fortnight in exile in Portugal, Helen asks him whether he shagged either of his competitors for the eleventh place, Anne and Natasha. He says no, adding, 'I bat for his team,' and nodding in the direction of Brian. The girls are astonished. 'Bloody hell, I need a lie-down,' says Helen. Bubble reckons Josh is not really gay, but has come in with a game plan that will allow him to get very close to the girls.

Ever since Josh arrived, the housemates have been discussing how to accommodate him. There are no spare beds in the boys' room. Brian was invited to move in with the girls as soon as Penny left, but spent last night in his usual bed. Now he announces that he will join the girls, because he thinks he should, rather than because he wants to.

Brian is probably more shaken by the news that Josh is gay than the girls, and he admits as he moves into their room that he is feeling uncomfortable. He says he feels weird – not because he is jealous, but because he thinks the viewers will be watching to see how the two gay men react to each other. Liz advises him not to go into his shell, but to treat Josh like a straight bloke. When he has left the room the girls agree that they think Brian fancies Josh. They also reckon that Stuart's nose is out of joint because Josh is more tanned, trendier and better looking than him.

Stuart seems even more put out when he realizes that Josh not only runs a very successful business in Soho, but also has a better – and even more expensive – collection of clothes than he has. As Helen models Josh's £800 leather jacket – which Bubble comments cost more than his entire wardrobe – Stuart asks his rival in the sartorial stakes what his most expensive buy was. Josh tells him that it was a pair of trousers, hand-embroidered in red, for which he paid £2,500. He has brought them with him, for the night he leaves the house.

Brian goes to the Diary Room to share his fears with Big Brother. He says he was under the impression that he would be the only gay housemate, and predicts that he will be teased both inside and outside the house about fancying Josh. He also tells Big Brother that the other guys are inwardly raging over Josh's arrival, as they think the girls will give him more attention. Despite having failed to persuade Big Brother to play a Celine Dion track to calm him down, Brian emerges from the Diary Room his old, cheerful self.

Over dinner, the tension that has been simmering since Josh's arrival erupts into a huge fight between Helen and Narinder, who have not hit it off since their arrival in the house. The row starts when Josh describes having his haircut at Faro airport for £3.50, with a stylist who couldn't speak any English and one of the airport cleaners doing the shampooing. Narinder comments that Helen 'works in one of them'. Helen thinks she hears Narinder describe her hairdressing salon as 'crap', and when she challenges her, refuses to believe that Narinder didn't say that. Narinder claims she said 'classic' (the name of Helen's salon is Classy Cutz) but Bubble fans the flames by insisting he heard Narinder say 'crap', upon which Narinder swears violently at him.

The meal, of Brian's favourite comfort food, shepherd's pie, is over more quickly than most, and the two girls disappear in opposite directions. In the bedroom, with Brian and Paul, Narinder cries and sounds off about Helen:

'I hated her from the start but I thought I would give her the benefit of the doubt. I tried and tried to be nice to her ... She's mincemeat if she comes near me. I'm not going to give her another chance.'

Brian counsels her not to do anything that will jeopardize her stay in the house, to which Narinder retorts: 'I don't care, nobody's going to piss on me like that.'

In the meantime, Helen is in the garden, also seething with rage.

'He said he'd had a haircut in a dodgy place and she said, "Well Helen works in a place like that". I could smack her one. I could drag her out of this house by the hair.'

Stuart calms her down and she makes the first move to heal the breach, going into the bedroom to talk to Narinder, who at first seems reluctant to make peace.

'I'm sorry about earlier, but I get the impression from you all the time that you don't like me,' Helen says.

Narinder, after initially shrugging away from the idea of discussing it, answers:

'That is so wrong. I've been making such an effort all the time, being really nice. So if you got that impression, you're wrong. But maybe that's my fault as well, not your fault. But I've been making an effort, thinking "She's a lovely, lovely girl". This was all a misunderstanding.'

Helen concedes that she must have misheard her, but reiterates that she feels Narinder doesn't like her.

'We did have our little problems to start off with,' admits Narinder, 'but I gave you the benefit of the doubt.'

Helen replies: 'When you first walked in, I thought you were alright, then I got the impression you thought I was a stupid cow. We're too much alike.'

Narinder vehemently rejects the idea that she is like Helen, but they have managed a rapprochement, and they are both upset that they should have had their public spat in front of Josh.

'He's probably thinking he's glad he's gay,' says Helen.

Soon afterwards, Narinder is in the Diary Room explaining herself to Big Brother. She says Helen gets away with things because she is sweet and innocent, but it was not right for her to go on like that. The other housemates let Helen get away with it, she reckons, because they see Narinder as a stronger person and feel sorry for Helen, which is unfair. 'She has thrown my friendship back in my face.' She tells Big Brother she regards Josh as a guest in the house for the first day, and she's ashamed the quarrel happened. But from now on, she says, she will go with her instinct that she and Helen just don't get on. She hadn't been planning to nominate Helen again, but now she's back in the running.

As soon as Narinder leaves the Diary Room, Helen goes in:

'I don't want people to think I am a cow – it was a misunderstanding ...

I don't think the others understand how bad it is being up for nomination. I thought Naz was taking the piss out of me for being a crap hairdresser.'

She says that, although they have talked, Narinder is still the person she gets on least well with in the house. She hopes viewers don't perceive her as bitchy and nasty, because she would not be like this in the real world. She says the tension of having been part of the eviction vote is what has made her snappy and distant all day, the *Big Brother* experience has been harder for her than she thought it would be. She ends by saying she doesn't hate Narinder, because 'life is too short to hate people'.

Josh's presence has certainly unsettled Stuart, who seems to feel the need to let the newcomer know his status. In a discussion with Josh about how hard it must be coming into the house two weeks after everyone else, Stuart lets the younger man know that he is enjoying the stress-free environment of the house, because: 'Normally I work in a hierarchical structure, and I can say "You do this" and "You do that" and get it done. But in this situation I didn't want to take control.'

Brian goes back to the Diary Room and lets Big Brother know that he is no longer worried about what the outside world thinks of him. He discusses his gum disease, and asks to see a dentist, preferably one who is 'six feet two inches tall, dark and handsome'.

Brian's prediction that he will be teased about fancying Josh comes true almost immediately, courtesy of Bubble. Bubble, playing matchmaker, tells Brian that Josh fancies him. Brian retorts that he does not fancy Josh, but Bubble won't have it. Brian gets the better of him by teasing, 'Don't you fancy me Bubble?' and leaning over to plant a kiss on Bubble's cheek. Bubble steps back to avoid it, warning, 'Never do that again, I nearly had a heart attack.'

Before going to bed, Brian and Narinder talk about the others. Narinder describes Stuart as 'dangerous'.

'Not dangerous as in evil, but he's got this plan,' she says. Narinder finds Paul 'boring', Elizabeth 'anal sometimes', Dean 'too quiet' and Josh 'up himself'. In contrast, Brian describes Bubble as 'honest and sweet', Paul as 'sweet' and Dean as 'honest'.

When Josh goes to bed, Paul, Bubble and Amma discuss him. Although Bubble is horrified at anyone spending so much money on a pair of trousers, he says that Josh has earned the right to be friendly with the housemates: if he had been the one coming in after two weeks he would have wanted to be given a fair chance.

Sunday morning is dominated by the usual haggling over the shopping list. Even with a massive £112 in the kitty, there isn't enough money to buy everything everybody wants, and there are heated discussions. The contestants settle on twenty litres of cider as the cheapest route to a hangover.

At noon they are given their task: over the next three days they must memorise the other housemates' answers to fifteen questions about themselves. They decide to wager 40% of their shopping total on it. They give their answers in, and then test each other, immediately regretting not betting a higher stake. When he goes into the Diary Room to hand in his answers,

COOK THE BIG BROTHER WAY

Did your mouth water at the sight of the treats the housemates cooked up during their nine weeks in the house? If so, here's three of the very best recipes so you can recreate the magic of the *Big Brother* kitchen.

ELIZABETH'S SARDINE QUICHE

Serves: 4–6

for the pastry:
225g (8oz) plain flour
pinch salt
100g (4oz) butter

for the filling:
2 x 120g cans of sardines in oil or brine, drained
3 medium eggs
30ml (¼pt) milk
salt and freshly ground black pepper
100g (4oz) mature Cheddar cheese, grated

1. Tie your hair back and roll up your sleeves.
2. Place the flour and salt in a mixing bowl, then rub in the butter to form fine breadcrumbs, add a little cold water to form a firm dough. Nothing better than getting your hands dirty. Knead lightly on a floured surface and roll out.
3. Open a bottle of cider whilst you try to remember how you made your last quiche that went down so well last summer. Use the pastry to line a 20cm (8") loose bottomed flan dish. Chill for 15 minutes.
4. Burp loudly to get rid of your greedy housemates sniffing around your cooking.
5. Arrange the sardines over the pastry base, sprinkle with the cheese, then beat together the eggs, milk and seasoning. Pour over the sardines while reminiscing about the Cumbrian Fells.
6. Place on a baking sheet and cook in a preheated oven, 190C, gas mark 5 for 35–40 minutes, until the filling is set and lightly golden.
7. Once baked, serve to ravenous housemates who will want you to cook again.

NARINDER'S CAULIFLOWER CHEESE

Serves: 1

225g (8oz) medium sized cauliflower florets
15g (½oz) butter
15g (½oz) plain flour
150ml (⅓pt) milk
salt and freshly ground black pepper
50g (2oz) Cheddar cheese, grated
Extra grated cheese for topping

1. Your housemates decide to cook a meaty meal, so it's another night of dinner for one.
2. Pick the smallest cauliflowers possible, hand-selected by stingy Big Brother – value for money, huh! Cook the diminutive cauliflower florets in lightly salted boiling water for 3–4 minutes until tender. Drain.

3. Meanwhile, in a small saucepan place the butter, flour, milk and seasoning and whisk continuously over a low heat to form a smooth glossy sauce, all the while muttering under your breath that you are feeling left out. Stir in the cheese and cook until melted.
4. Shout at Amma as she wanders through the kitchen snacking, unable to resist the smell of your cooking.
5. Place the cauliflower florets in an ovenproof dish and pour over the cheese sauce. Top with a little grated cheese and place under a preheated grill until golden. Eat in the lounge on your own. Remember to call Brian 'ugly' every now and again to really give him a complex.

BRIAN'S WINDY SHEPHERD'S PIE

Serves: 4–6

900g (2lb) potatoes, peeled and chopped
15ml (1 tbsp) oil
1 large onion, chopped
1 clove garlic, crushed
450g (1lb) minced beef
15ml (1 tbsp) plain flour
2 medium carrots, peeled and chopped
150g (5oz) small cauliflower florets
400g can chopped tomatoes
150ml (⅓pt) beef stock
10ml (2 tsp) dried mixed herbs
salt and freshly ground black pepper
50g (2oz) Cheddar cheese, grated

1. Get all your pots and pans ready – noisily banging them together before you start the preparation to inform your housemates you are in the kitchen. Cook potatoes in a large pan of lightly salted boiling water, until tender and drain.
2. Enlist the help of Helen as your kitchen assistant.
3. Chop and fry the onions and garlic – this will make you cry. Blame Josh for your tears. Meanwhile heat the oil and cook the onion and garlic until softened.
4. Brown the mince, then stir in the flour. Add the tomatoes, stock and herbs, then add the vegetables. Simmer, uncovered, for approximately 10 minutes or until the sauce is reduced. While you are waiting, do a little dance to keep yourself amused.
5. Tell Helen to chop the vegetables faster and add them to your meat mix.
6. Once boiled, mash the potatoes with a knob of butter, a little milk and seasoning, resisting the temptation to flick it at Josh.
7. Put mixture in a baking dish and spoon over the mash and cheese topping.
8. Bake at 200°C/gas mark 6 for thirty minutes or as long as it takes to scream 'evil demons' at least 100 times.
9. Once served, attach a clothes peg to your nose in preparation for the windy after-effects from your housemates!

Stuart is questioned about Josh by Big Brother. Stuart rarely chats in the Diary Room, and now answers politely but succinctly:

'It's going OK. The group dynamic has changed with the departure of Penny. It's a lot easier, if I'm honest. Everyone is quite excited by the concept of getting to know Josh. He's a strong character and he's doing well.'

The hot tub is ready, and the girls race to put their bikinis on and plunge in. Within minutes, all except Bubble and Dean are in the tub. They play word games, and the forfeit is to duck under the water. As Brian gets out, Narinder pulls his shorts down, which makes Amma laugh. Brian gets his revenge by pulling both girls' tops off.

Bubble decides he's fed up with his Mohican hairstyle, and Dean obligingly shaves off the remaining strip, leaving Bubble completely bald. He says that his mum will kill him, but as he quickly clamps a familiar hat on his head, it is unlikely that either the housemates or the viewers will notice the difference.

In the early evening, under probing from Narinder, Josh tells them all about his first gay experience. Unlike Brian, he has had girlfriends, and Narinder wants to know whether he liked sleeping with them. He says it didn't feel right, but it also felt weird when he was first kissed by a man. He was in a gay club with his business partner when a man leaned over and kissed him. Later, when Josh was drunk, it happened again, and he ended up giving the guy a lift home.

'He became my first boyfriend, for a month, until he broke my heart. It did my head in, because I couldn't tell anyone. I was living at home.'

He says he then went on to put an advert for partners in a magazine – as a result, he made ninety-four phone calls and went on six blind dates. He said that telling his father – who did not know for long that his son was gay before he went into the house – was hard, but that his father told him, 'You're not how I wanted you to turn out, but I still love you.'

Josh says that he wants to have children, and that he has a girl who is willing to help him, when he feels settled enough. Helen asks if he would have sex with her, or do it the other way.

'With a turkey baster?' asks Josh. 'I'd like it to be natural, but it's difficult.'

Helen comments that this must mean that he is really 'quite bi'.

Under pressure, Josh tells them that he fancies 'Spanish-looking men', prompting Helen to suggest that Brian put some fake tan on. Brian laughs, and then shares with them all the worries he expressed earlier: that everyone will be expecting something to happen because they are both gay.

'Don't worry, babes, I won't be snogging you,' says Josh.

Helen can't hide her disappointment, and says she would really like to see two blokes kissing. Paul says it would be 'wicked' to see two girls smooching. Instantly Helen and Amma fall into each other's arms, but stop short of a snog.

'I can't do it,' Amma says. 'She's my mate. I have kissed girls, but she's my mate and I don't fancy her.'

Helen tells Paul, 'The only person who would have enjoyed that would have been you, Paul, and we don't want you enjoying yourself in this house, do we?'

Josh goes to the Diary Room and tells Big Brother how he is getting on.

'Today has been a really good day. Yesterday was tough for me, but I have enjoyed myself. For me, getting to know everybody and trying to get in with everybody has been hard. Yesterday was difficult as hell. What I have enjoyed most is that they have all been friendly and let me in quite quickly – and I'm enjoying the food. The group is quite mixed. I relate more to people like Stuart and Liz, and I quite like Paul, because he's outgoing and friendly. Bubble's great, really funny. The girls are sweet, especially Amma, who is sarcastic. Yesterday I went to bed thinking it would be really hard. I didn't know what to expect coming in here.'

At bedtime, the girls and their room mate Brian have a good old bitch about the boys. Amma leads it with her thoughts on Paul. 'He is probably a bright boy, but his common sense is lacking. He only has one topic of conversation: girls and going out.' They decide that Stuart is smug and competitive. Helen says she thinks Stuart has a problem with gay men, and Liz, who was once his closest ally, describes him as being like a concrete wall that absorbs nothing. Brian and Narinder argue that Stuart feels threatened because Josh is a lot younger and has a better body. Helen delivers the final condemnation of Stuart: 'He tries to be fatherly towards me. He looks a bit like my dad as well.'

'Josh is cool, confident, outgoing, charming and they're all vying for top dog,' adds Liz.

The goodnight routine in the boys' room is altogether more wholesome. Bubble is wearing his sleeping hat again – he's been without it for a few nights. When Josh questions him, he explains he wears it when he feels uncomfortable. 'I don't know you yet Josh – in a few days it will come off. It's nothing against you.'

The boys have developed a round of goodnights based on the old TV programme *The Waltons*, and they settle down to a chorus of 'Goodnight, John boy' and 'Goodnight, Mary Lou'.

When everyone else is asleep, Bubble goes to the Diary Room. He says he is finding life in the house hard, and that he is missing and worrying about his little girl. Then he tells Big Brother about his gran, which seems to cheer him up.

Stuart is up first on Monday morning, as usual. He has accepted that his competition with Josh for the best tan is a household joke, and even manages to make fun of himself for it. He's still trying to impress Josh, and goes into a lot of detail about travelling to and from New York.

A conversation about dangerous experiences has the boys, particularly Paul, vying for the most hair-raising tale. Liz and Narinder go into the bedroom and have their own discussion about Paul. They've both noticed how he always tries to outdo every story anyone else tells.

For today's memory task, each person has to describe a dream, confess their greatest fear and reveal which of their fellow housemates' habits most annoy them. Amma picks Paul's 'one-upmanship', and has to explain to him what she means. He argues that it is not one of his characteristics, and later in the kitchen he asks Narinder whether she thinks it is. Despite her earlier chat with Liz, Narinder says no. Paul is also chosen by Liz, who hates his spitting.

WHO NOMINATES WHO

Amma nominates Paul and Stuart
Brian nominates Stuart and Helen
Bubble nominates Paul and Helen
Dean nominates Narinder and Paul
Liz nominates Paul and Stuart
Helen nominates Narinder and Bubble
Narinder nominates Stuart and Helen
Paul nominates Amma and Bubble
Stuart nominates Amma and Narinder

Housemate	Nominations	Nominated by
Amma	2	Paul, Stuart
Brian	0	
Bubble	2	Helen, Paul
Dean	0	
Elizabeth	0	
Helen	3	Brian, Bubble, Narinder
Narinder	3	Dean, Helen, Stuart
Paul	4	Amma, Bubble, Dean, Elizabeth
Stuart	4	Amma, Brian, Elizabeth, Narinder

Week 3 nominees: Paul and Stuart with four nominations each.

Analysis
Narinder has exactly the same nominations as last week. Brian remains unnominated for the second week running. Amma and Elizabeth have voted for both nominees. She voted for last week's nominees also. From having no votes at all in the first week, Stuart has got four nominations.

Reasons
Brian on Helen: 'At times she requires a lot of reassuring regarding tasks and daily things.'
Liz on Paul: 'I am not on the same wavelength as him, and he also spits a lot, which I don't like.'
Narinder on Stuart: 'I feel like getting rid of some of the boring blokes in here. I'm starting with Stuart. His main focus is getting a tan.'

Stuart is annoyed by Josh's tan. Bubble is branded the most annoying housemate: Brian chooses him 'for being Bubble', Narinder and Paul choose him 'for being loud' and Helen picks him 'for being himself'. Josh tries to avoid the question, saying he has not know the others long enough. But Big Brother insists on a reply, so he, too, opts for the Bubble noise factor.

The new boy is excused the worst job of the day – nominations. Like all new housemates, Josh cannot nominate or be nominated for his first week in the house. Big Brother tells the other housemates they will get the results of their nominations later in the week.

Before she starts cooking one of her, by now, famous, curries, Narinder joins Brian in a Janet Jackson routine, much to the amusement of Josh, who has never seen their double act before. Outside in the garden, Dean and Elizabeth spend a long time together, doing Tai Chi and then just sitting talking. They think they have been cast in the roles of mother and father to the group, and find they agree on their assessments of most of the others.

As the evening progresses, the housemates hit the cider. Brian, who has never had cider before, has eight glasses and gets quite drunk. They dance to a song that Dean has written, and Helen does the splits. They then insist that Josh tell them which female housemate he would sleep with. He's reluctant, but they tell him they have answered this. He chooses Amma, to the unconcealed astonishment of both Helen and Narinder.

All somewhat the worse for wear, the housemates then plunge into the hot tub, where Brian instigates a kissing game in which the contestants have to guess who is kissing their back. Brian says he would like to snog a girl, which causes consternation from Helen, who asks: 'Brian, are you really gay? You've seen my fanny!'

Narinder goes to the Diary Room and cries as she tells Big Brother how much she is missing her husband. 'The past two days have been really hard. The hardest thing is having to get on with people. In the real world, you can walk away from it, that's how you deal with it. Here you have to get on with people. And you don't have the people who know you and don't mind your bad points. Here, your bad points are noted, put away, and brought out to be accounted for, because your bad points get accounted for on nominations day.'

Later, Amma and Helen go into the Diary Room together to thank Big Brother for a brilliant day. Amma stays to chat. She says she has had a really good three days because she has decided not to stop smoking, and also has relaxed and been herself more. She has not enjoyed the nominations process, because there is nobody within the group she doesn't like. Helen and Elizabeth are the two housemates with whom she gets on best.

'Helen because she's open, honest, very youthful, naive, fresh, wide-eyed. Liz because she's honest, laid-back and pretty low-key, and that's pleasant because I'm low-key, too. She's a good listener and she communicates with everyone in the group.'

The cider has overcome Brian's inhibitions. He admits to Narinder and Amma that before he came into the house, he had never had a conversation with an Asian or black person. The others are shocked, but Brian points out that he is young and naive. Narinder asks Bubble if he has any Asian friends, and he says he has.

When everyone else has gone to bed, Bubble and Amma stay up, smoking and talking. He tells Amma all about his daughter, the things they do together, and the ways in which he spoils her. He's worried that his absence might affect her.

'It's just harder than I thought it would be. But it's not alright for me to get upset – I put myself here,' he says. Amma disagrees: 'You should never, ever tell yourself it's not alright to be upset if you are.'

Bubble says his justification for his absence is that he thought he could win. If he doesn't win, it will all have been for nothing. 'Would I have rather met you people, or had twenty days with my little girl?' he asks, rhetorically. He and Amma exchange stories of their childhood, and Amma talks about the time she has spent in Ghana. Bubble discusses how he was ill as a child, and how it affected the way his parents treated him.

Paul also talks late into the night, but in his sleep. He clearly says, 'I'm up for eviction already' – a prophetic observation, for the housemates do not yet know who has been nominated.

The big event of the day is the announcement in the afternoon of the nomination results: Paul and Stuart are up for eviction. They both profess to be 'cool', but Stuart is visibly shocked.

Paul says he does not feel rejected. He would feel rejected if his mates were not there to greet him when he came out, but not because people he doesn't really know don't like him. He thinks the experience will make him stronger.

The housemates spend most of the afternoon practising for the task. In the Diary Room, Liz says she feels there are two camps in the house, with the girls and Brian in one, the rest of the boys in the other, and herself in the middle.

Before dinner, we see the first boy-to-boy flirting in the house, as Brian and Josh relax together. They're having one of Brian's familiar teasing sessions – all the housemates are the butt of his wit from time to time – and Josh reacts by grabbing him around the neck. They mock-struggle and then punch each other affectionately a few times.

Helen sparks a discussion about how long is it since they each had sex by announcing it will be three weeks tomorrow for her. Josh says he hasn't had any bedroom action for a month; Paul admits to two months; Narinder to a month; and Amma and Stuart, like Helen, say they last had sex the day before they came into the house. Brian hasn't slept with anyone for two years and claims he doesn't miss it. 'I'm a born-again virgin,' he says.

He entertains the others by using an oven glove as a puppet, and squatting behind the sofa putting on a squeaky voice. But he soon becomes tired, and announces that as he is twenty-three tomorrow there can be no more silly games after tonight.

After a dinner of spaghetti cooked by Bubble, Paul is called to the Diary Room.

'When it came round I knew my name would come up. It's a bit of a shock, but at the end of the day we'll see what happens on Friday. I don't feel rejected. Everyone's gonna come up at some point. There are quite a few natural leaders out there. We're all individually strong people.'

Next in is Dean, who, after saying how much he is missing his girlfriend, goes on to tell Big Brother that he is surprised by Stuart's nomination, as he feels Stuart does a lot for the group. 'He may not be the best laugh. But he's a very good, steady influence, and he's been getting a lot done. Maybe people don't appreciate what he does, and they're going for much more personal reasons. I wasn't aware that he'd upset anyone. I'm going to stop trying to guess what people are thinking. I think he feels hurt, but he's grown up and can handle it.'

Stuart is called to the Diary Room as soon as Dean leaves. Earlier he had joked with the housemates about taking revenge for nominating him: 'Fuck being nice to you lot... Next time you get a sweet, I'll have pissed on it. When I make bread, I'll stick my cock in it...' Now more serious, he describes being nominated as 'part of the process', and reckons he knows who voted for him.

'People need to be very careful with their body language. I've worked in business long enough, I've got a fair indication of who has nominated me. They've got their reasons and I don't feel aggrieved by it. I've always tried to be myself, I've not tried to impose myself on anyone, I'm putting one hundred percent into it. I don't think I've put out any personality traits indicating that I'm exceptionally arrogant or exceptionally disliked out there. Before I came in, a friend gave me some advice – he told me that I like to be in control but that I shouldn't do that in here. So I've been holding back in taking control. I've tried to influence where I can, tried to motivate. I want to lead, but don't want to be OTT.

'I've talked with Bubble, because the preconception about me is "he's got everything", and I wanted to make it clear that the position I'm in, nothing has been easy, I've always had to work hard. This is probably the first real break I've ever had. There's no-one in here I am best friends with, but there's no-one I dislike.'

He says he is worried about the reaction he will get when he leaves the house, but says he is taking things one step at a time. Asked how he will feel if he stays in, Stuart pauses for a long, long time before replying:

'If I don't go, I will be sad because Sian and my family are outside. But if I stay I'll be pleased in a perverse way, because it means I will be going a little bit further in this experience.'

As midnight comes, the housemates break into a ragged chorus of 'Happy Birthday to You' for Brian, who seems to be genuinely overcome with emotion. Bubble presents him with a customized T-shirt: he has spent much of the day cutting the figures two and three into the back, but when Brian models it, they simply look like two big holes.

Brian goes to bed early, in preparation for his big day, and Narinder goes with him. They discuss how upset Stuart is.

'Even if he stays, it will stick out in my mind that he's been nasty, that he can't take defeat,' says Brian. 'If he goes he won't be happy and if he stays he'll be a bastard.'

When Helen joins them the girls agree that Bubble would stab someone in the back to get the £70,000 prize money, but Brian adamantly disagrees. Helen asks Narinder if she would sleep with Josh, to which Narinder replies, 'He is probably too good in bed for me.' Helen then asks Brian whether he fancies Josh. Brian – who is touchingly insecure – replies that Josh is not the kind of person he would talk to in a bar: 'Look at me, compared to him I am nothing.'

In the Diary Room, Bubble expresses his shock at Stuart's nomination. 'I just thought Stuart pulled his weight and did everything and got on with everyone except Penny. I thought he was one of the popular people I want to be with at the end. It's made me realize I'm not noticing what's going on around me.' He says he has trouble sleeping, and that the house is completely different to anything he had expected: 'It's like a luxurious prison. I thought it would be a walk in the park.' He adds that he is really missing his little girl – and the footie results.

Up late chatting, Amma and Elizabeth discuss Narinder. They agree that she feels threatened by Helen. And Amma is irritated by her, saying that she makes jokes about others, but doesn't like it when people do the same to her.

The next morning, all the housemates are preoccupied with the looming memory test. Paul is in a reflective mood, and tells Helen that he feels sad at the prospect of leaving on Friday.

'It could be the end of an era, and I've enjoyed it. It makes you realize what you've got here, and in a funny kind of way it's cool, there's a good atmosphere.'

Josh cooks tortilla for lunch, which wins him the accolade Man of The House from Narinder. Brian, who is still feeling insecure and missing his friends on his birthday, is found to be the source of the bad smell in the girls' bedroom, and his trainers are unceremoniously relegated to the garden.

Each housemate is called to the Diary Room to answer two questions from the 150 they have memorized about the whole group. They are allowed only one mistake. They go in alphabetical order, and there is ecstatic cheering and punching of the air when Helen, who has been so worried about the test, answers her two questions correctly. Astonishingly, Josh, who seems so confident, gets one answer wrong. Luckily the rest get theirs right, and when Stuart completes the task there is a great deal of excitement.

For his birthday celebration Brian is offered two parties. One is a teddy bear's picnic, and the second is a roast-beef dinner with champagne and wine. There is only one catch: he has to hand over to Big Brother's safekeeping his two faithful companions, Mr Bear and Mr Cow, the stuffed toys he has slept with since he was six months old. It's a close call, but he surrenders them eventually, with much encouragement from the others. Josh and Liz bake Brian a cake, which does not turn out very successfully, and Amma makes him biscuits in the shape of the figures two and three, which are presented to him covered in candles.

The housemates are each issued with a teddy bear that growls, and lots of picnic goodies, including a cake with pink icing. Brian and Bubble have a cream fight, splattering each other with it. They use the teddies as puppets, a

WHAT THE CLOTHES SAY

'AMMA's shower cap makes her look aggressive. What is she hiding under it? Horns? She dresses like Raquel Welch in *Journey to the Centre of the Earth* and then wears a blanket over it.'

'LIZ has the worst item in the house – the cerise jumper. Where did she get it from? It looks like a home-knit. She wears a huge hat, dark glasses, covers her head – and then wears hot pants. Or she wears a huge jumper with bare legs. She dresses like a nudist, like someone not used to wearing clothing.'

'HELEN's nightwear is a surprise. She's the kind of chick you would think would have a sexy, boudoir thing going on. But her night clothes say middle-aged mother of four.'

'JOSH's trousers (the £2,000 pair) are very Ronan Keating, David Furnish, a bit of Venga Boys. He's got the body to carry them off.'

'PENNY's exit outfit was a real disappointment. She's got a good body, but she made herself look middle aged.'

'BUBBLE wears clothes you would dress a four year old in. If you scaled him down, he would look like a little kid.'

'BRIAN looks good, he's got a good little body and everything looks good on him. He doesn't spend much money, but he accessorizes well, with his white belt for instance.'

'STUART dresses like an estate agent.'

'NARINDER is the best dresser. She likes bright colours and she's got crazy tops. She looked a complete fox on her eviction night.'

Angela Buttolph, Fashion guru

game which disintegrates when Bubble's bear humps his leg and Brian uses his to impersonate Paul trying to get away from Penny's clutches.

The girls are in party mood. They do Liz's hair and makeup for her, and Amma lends her a dress. The boys submit to Helen 'glittering' their faces. Stuart wears an exotic zebra-print shirt, to Helen's amused consternation, as she is also wearing a tight-fitting zebra-print top: Narinder says they look like Mr and Mrs. Narinder is miffed because Liz has hidden the alcohol so that they can drink it with their meal – Narinder thinks she is being bossy and taking over. When Narinder has left the room, Amma comments that if Josh had hidden it, Narinder would have thought it was a great idea.

Before dinner, Stuart goes to the Diary Room to pass a birthday greeting to his little boy, Rory, who will be two tomorrow. 'Daddy loves you to bits. Look after Mummy and the girls for me, and I'll see you soon,' he says.

Dean reveals that he nearly took a job as a male escort. Having passed three interviews, he was lined up to escort a gay woman who had to go to social events through her work. She cancelled, however, and Dean didn't try to get any more work.

Over the meal, the contestants drink six bottles of wine, four of champagne and one of cider, after which they are all – with the exception of the teetotal Bubble – much the worse for wear. A drunken Helen goes to the Diary Room to say how much she loves being in the house, and how she hopes she doesn't sound too Welsh. She propositions Bubble, who reminds her that he is happy with his girlfriend, and she tells Dean that she can see four of him. A glass breaks and she cuts her finger – the others wash it and put a plaster on it. As Helen becomes increasingly loud Elizabeth takes her to one side and suggests she drink more slowly. In a flash of prophetic insight, Paul tells Dean he is worried that something will 'kick off'.

Josh introduces the others to a drinking game, boys versus girls. The forfeit for failure is to give up an item of clothing, and Brian is soon down to his underpants. Eventually, these are ripped off and Paul sets fire to them in the garden, while Brian runs around screaming. Bubble puts the fire out with the garden hose.

While the boys are fooling around with Brian's pants, Helen is in the Diary Room for more than half an hour, pouring her heart out to Big Brother about missing her boyfriend, her family and her friends. She emerges in floods of tears to be comforted first by Amma and then Paul. Eventually, after she has been sick (in the sink), Narinder and Paul get her to bed.

Which means that for the second time, Helen misses the big event of the night (she slept through the Stuart–Penny fight). Tonight's row is even more spectacular. The first bout on the card is between Brian and Josh. The group are in the hot tub, playing a truth game in which everyone has to speak about their most difficult experience since being in the house. Brian says it was moving to the girls' bedroom to accommodate Josh, and he recalls that he had to move his things on his own, because everyone was making such a fuss of the new boy.

'I had been here for two weeks and I got respect from four straight men, I had bonded with the guys, I was settling in. When you walked in I felt this high,' he says, holding his thumb and forefinger together.

Josh and he are having a heated discussion, with the boys all listening open-mouthed, when Amma says something to Narinder. They all tell her it is not her turn to talk: there is a structure to the truth game. But Amma carries on.

There has been a row brewing between Stuart and Amma all evening, with Stuart accusing her of having a shallow mind, and announcing that she is 'so bad at body language' that he knows she nominated him (she did). Amma tells him he is 'a smug, insecure person who feels they need to be better than everyone else around them'. Stuart calls her 'childish', but she comes back with: 'Says the man who gets upset with another man with a better tan.'

Now the sniping becomes open warfare, as Stuart tells her repeatedly to be quiet. 'You are not in this conversation. We don't want to hear what you are saying.'

WHAT THE EXPERTS SAY

STUART'S WINKS

'Stuart has been one of the central authority figures in the house. Like all of the housemates, he's had to work hard at establishing control. But Stuart has his own unique, covert strategy for doing this: the wink.'

Professor Geoffrey Beattie, Psychologist

'Stuart is the biggest winker in the house. His winks convey several messages, but all include some people and exclude others, sometimes at their expense. Stuart is noticeably detached during one discussion when Amma is holding forth. He looks around for a kindred spirit. He spots Narinder and winks at her. This wink is inclusive, it says, "We both know, we're together on this." But it is also at Amma's expense, because it suggests she is not sufficiently interesting to hold the others' attention. There is a similar thing the morning after his row with Penny. He comes into the garden, approaches Penny, and gives her what appears to be a conciliatory kiss on the cheek. He winks at Paul, which is an act of collusion, drawing Paul into a temporary conspiracy. At the same time as including Paul, it excludes Penny. Any affection in the hug is cancelled out by the wink. Paul knows it, but Penny doesn't.'

Dr Peter Collett, Psychologist

'The wink places Stuart firmly in control. There's a dangerous paradox at play here. While Stuart is in control, that wink is accepted and taken at face value. But should any mistrust of his motives creep in, that wink will be seen to have a rather different value, and will be seen as him being two-faced. It could easily backfire on him.'

Professor Geoffrey Beattie, Psychologist

Amma loses her rag and begins shouting at him, and Stuart becomes cold and angry. 'I do not tolerate people shouting at me,' he growls. Amma storms out of the hot tub and goes into the house. Brian bursts into tears, and Josh gives him a hug before following Amma inside and holding her in his arms as she sobs bitterly. Bubble and Narinder tell Stuart that Amma is crying, but he makes no gesture towards her.

In the bedroom, with Helen, Josh, Liz and Narinder around her, Amma snaps and shouts out loud: 'I'm sick of him. Friday, hurry up and come. Just leave. I wish he'd go. He's a fucking shit. Smug shit, I hate you.'

She tells the others that Stuart said he didn't approve of where she came from or how she lives her life. 'Well, fuck you! How dare he tell me that? I hope the whole fucking country votes him out on Friday.'

Dean says that things have to be calmed down, but jokingly vetoes Bubble's offer to try. Dean then takes Amma to the den and wraps her in a blanket. He and Liz talk to her quietly. She is embarrassed by the whole scene, and says that, much as she enjoys the comfort of the den, she doesn't want 'to sit in here moaning and whining and crying and shouting'.

Stuart comes in, in an attempt to make amends, but Amma politely and calmly tells him that she does not want to talk it all through until the morning. Stuart, as is his habit, persists. He begins, 'None of us have had an easy background ...', but before he can get any further both Dean and Liz tell him to leave it for now. He tries again, and again they gently rebuff him. Then he says, 'I don't want to be misrepresented', obviously concerned that Amma's views are going to be aired to the general public, who are voting on his future in the house.

After Amma has calmed down, Liz's next mission is to comfort Brian, whose problems have been totally eclipsed by the Amma–Stuart drama. She gently explains to him how difficult it has been for Josh, having to bond with nine other people who have known each other for two weeks.

The Diary Room does brisk business, with the housemates practically queuing to tell all to Big Brother. Paul rushes in during the row, to ask whether the camera on the hot tub is working 'because it's a blinder'. Having felt depressed earlier on, his mood has improved, 'It's been quite funny watching everything come to a head,' he says. Half an hour later, however, he is back in the Diary Room in more sombre mood:

'People are falling apart at the seams. People just don't realize that alcohol is the worst drug known to man. You've probably got three more hours' filming, because they're not going to bed. I think they need to go to bed, and if there's more conversations to take place it should be in the cold light of day. From what's happening tonight the only person with normality is Dean, because everyone else is popping at each other.'

Next in is Narinder, closely followed by Bubble, who admits he regrets not doing more to ease the tension 'as the only sober person'. 'It's mental out there, absolute mayhem. I ask you not to give them any more alcohol at any stage.'

Outside in the seating area, Dean and Narinder are helping Josh and Brian talk through the problem. Dean comments that it is weird that the four

PHOBIAS

Amma: Slight fear of open water.
Brian: Rats and snakes.
Bubble: Heights.
Dean: Losing control of my sanity.
Elizabeth: Rock climbing.
Helen: Weak tea and spiders.
Josh: None that I know of.
Narinder: Total darkness.
Paul: I'm not scared of heights, but when I'm on a balcony I think how easy it would be to jump off.
Penny: None.
Stuart: Don't like heights (but did a 145-foot bungee jump!).

straight guys in the house have no problem with either Brian or Josh being gay, but that Brian has a problem with Josh because of it.

Josh is puzzled as to why Brian won't accept him. Narinder points out that to Brian, Josh appears so much older, more experienced and more sophisticated. Josh remarks that it is very strange for him, having accepted he is gay and being comfortable with it for the first time in his life, to feel that another gay man is judging him badly because of it.

It is Amma's turn in the Diary Room. She describes the evening's events as, 'Stupid things, stupid misunderstandings, a situation where people speak out of turn when they shouldn't, where people are not communicating properly, and not leaving a situation alone when they should.' She says she feels awful. Big Brother advises her to talk to the others tomorrow, and she agrees. 'It hasn't surprised me, because it was all simmering and I saw it coming. I wish that everything that came out tonight could have been said when people were sober. I apologize for my outburst.'

Dean goes in as she comes out. He's surprised by the evening's events, 'The group feels very fragile… it seems like there's a loose fabric of politeness holding this together and the slightest tension tears it.'

Josh is next up for a chat with Big Brother. He tries to make sense of the evening's events. 'I thought I'd get some animosity to me being a stranger, but the last person I thought I'd get it from was Brian, because he's gay. But tonight he said it's him or me. I don't understand why, I don't understand the reasons. I feel a little hurt, because I thought we had something in common. I tried to speak to him, told him he was drunk. I really hope in the morning it's all a lot clearer. For some reason he wants me out. Alcohol always brings out your true feelings, and he's adamant that I am out of here before him. If he dislikes me, that's fine, but if he dislikes me because I'm gay, that's wrong.'

Then it is Brian's turn to visit the Diary Room, and he's very upset, crying at times:

'Emotions are very high tonight, to be honest. I think I've been an absolute bastard to Josh, I was completely out of order. I don't know what I said. It's really weird. Coming in here was hard enough. I was twenty-two. I lied to everybody, including you, Big Brother, about how long everyone had known I was gay – my parents only knew for three days before. I found that hard. Then, just when I bonded with everyone, he walked in, confident. I just feel really, really bad. I'm not a bad person. I'd like to say to Josh I'm sorry, I'm being really foolish. I had too much to drink and don't mean what I said. But he's thirty-two, though. I'm so stupid.'

He breaks down in tears. 'I feel so shit right now. I never thought I'd feel like this. I miss my mum, my friends and my family and my goddamn teddy bears. Talking to the group is hard because people expect me to laugh and joke all the time. We're going to have a big argument tomorrow, fur is going to fly.'

Amma, Josh, Bubble and Elizabeth stay up talking. Elizabeth eventually goes to sleep in the den, but Bubble stays up all night. Amma and Josh have a heart-to-heart, and she attempts to make sense of Brian's reaction to him.

'One thing that bothers him indirectly is that Narinder gets on really well with you and so does everybody else. He's twenty-three going on fifteen. He's very young for his age, he's had very little experience of life.'

Josh says he feels sure he will be nominated next week, 'because I'm the easy vote'.

Stuart has only been in bed for three hours, but the row is preying on his mind, and at half past six in the morning he makes another attempt to apologize to Amma. She brushes him off politely, saying they need to talk, but not until she has had some sleep.

The following day is a day of recriminations, reparations, forgiveness – and cleaning up the mess. In the Diary Room for the second time that day, Bubble confesses he has had his worst day so far in the house. 'I'm shocked, confused, gutted. It affects everyone. One gay guy being threatened by another seems bizarre enough. I don't understand Brian's problem, but hopefully he will realize he's been an idiot himself. Josh is big enough to forget about it and move on. I feel responsible for Stuart and Amma, because I could have stopped it but I chose not to. Amma's a lot more upset than Stuart realizes.'

Amma and Brian are the last two to wake up, and in the privacy of the girls' bedroom compare notes about their behaviour last night. Amma can barely remember what her row with Stuart was about. Brian is mortified when he thinks about the things he said.

Just after 1 p.m., the group call a house meeting, which opens with Stuart making a fulsome apology to Amma. 'I wouldn't let you say what you wanted to say. I had no right to basically stifle your opinion. I got to a point where I wasn't letting you speak, and I apologize for that. On the second part, what I was most concerned about was the reaction to a comment I made. What I said to Amma was that none of our backgrounds have been easy, and she took it personally. It was not intended the way you thought.'

Amma accepts Stuart's apology and says she also owes him one. 'I said a lot of things I didn't mean. You were talking to me as if I was eleven. I don't like authority, and nobody in here has authority over me. I can accept that I may have misheard it. But I thought I heard you say "I know your background and I know about you and I don't agree with it". That's why I left. I actually really like you. It was an argument that didn't need to happen and it was over nothing.'

Stuart says the whole experience has been an education for him. 'One thing I've learnt is how to walk away from arguments. That's been a lesson for me to take out of here.'

They agree to move on, and give each other a hug. Brian makes a hurried apology to Josh, explaining that he was over-emotional because it was his birthday, and he was missing his friends and family. Josh accepts his apology. Dean, who is effectively chairing the meeting, thinks they need to talk more about the cause of Brian's outburst. They all get involved: Bubble is accused by Narinder of 'shit stirring', Amma says she was trying to calm things down, and Paul sums the whole evening up from the point of view of someone who was not directly involved in any of the fights. 'It was heavy duty. It's very embarrassing watching people break down and crying.'

Narinder points out that they don't have to like each other. She reminds them that they are in competition with each other, and the game is not about getting on. Amma disagrees: she thinks they do have to get on to survive in the house. Stuart ends the meeting by reminding them of Big Brother's famous words to them: 'Expect the unexpected.'

In the kitchen after the discussion, Brian and Josh talk. Brian, who cannot remember most of what happened, was horrified when Narinder and Amma told him some of the things he said to Josh.

'I'm hated,' Brian groans. 'I'm the most hated man in Britain.'

Josh jokes: 'No, only Old Compton Street' – a reference to the gay area of London's Soho.

Brian carries on: 'I am spoilt, arrogant, self-absorbed, up my own arse. Once I say something, I won't say sorry straight away.'

He hopes Josh didn't take him seriously, but Josh remarks that it seemed serious last night and he was scared. He really thought Brian disliked him. They end up laughing, but Josh says he's never going to go out drinking with Brian.

Lunch is a restrained affair, with Narinder, Brian and Josh eating separately from the others, and Stuart becoming the first housemate to eat alone, out in the garden.

The afternoon and evening pass lethargically. The housemates sleep, play board games, read and chat. Liz reveals to Dean that she wants to win. She cannot understand housemates who say they will be happy to get through to the fifth or sixth week.

Paul and Josh cook the evening meal together, and joke about it being the last supper, as tomorrow one of them must leave the house. Just before 10 p.m., Stuart goes to the Diary Room. He still has mixed emotions about the prospect of going home, and he is low because he has missed his son Rory's second birthday.

'Today we have been patching things up from last night. It was based on people's emotions, people are moving on, the mood is fine. It needed this morning to sort it out, and I wanted it sorted out. No-one was being malicious. Probably from the outside, being in here looks like a walk in the park, but it's not, because outside you can walk away ... The air has been cleared and there are no grudges held now.'

Despite the lack of sleep from the night before, it is 2 a.m. before the last of the housemates staggers to bed.

On Friday, Paul finally gets his chance to dress up as a woman – he has suggested doing it for a joke more than once before, but now Josh is insisting on it as a forfeit from the drinking game. Narinder lends him a dress. Elizabeth gives him a thong. Helen is in her element doing his makeup, and Amma gives him lessons in how to walk and sit like a woman.

Because it's eviction day, the contestants clean up the house. After lunch, Paul goes to the Diary Room, and seems very relaxed about the impending vote results. He says he would be happy to stay in the house, as he now feels he is getting on better with the girls.

VOTING

The public vote for Stuart to be evicted was more than decisive: he polled a massive eighty-six per cent of the total votes cast. More than a million people registered their choice, with 899,788 going for Stuart and 143,170 for Paul. More than a third of the votes were cast through interactive television screens. Viewing figures rose to an average of 4.35 million – an increase of nearly half a million over the previous week. The website recorded a high of almost four million page views on Thursday, the day after the Amma–Stuart row.

Brian follows him into the Diary Room and explains that he has been feeling unsettled for the past few days, partly because one of his sisters is pregnant, partly because he came out to his parents so recently, and partly because he is missing friends. He believes he let himself down in his attack on Josh. He apologizes to whoever was in the Big Brother seat last night and saw him crying.

The suitcases are delivered back to Paul and Stuart in readiness for one of them leaving. Paul is still wearing his dress, and Helen touches up his makeup. Paul insists that he will be taking his drag off as soon as the results are announced, but the others joke that, if he is evicted, he should leave the house wearing the dress.

When the results are finally announced, Stuart leaps in the air and shouts, 'Yes! I'm coming home! Excellent!' He changes into a Gucci sweater – which draws approving comments from Josh – and then gives away all the goodies he has left: his sweets and his cans of Red Bull. Then he tells all the housemates that he has just bought a nine-acre farm, and that they will all be invited there for a party in the summer – but he'll only be serving dried-up pasta and cider. As Stuart packs up alone, Brian helps Paul take off his dress. Paul comments on how surreal it all is: he's being stripped out of women's clothes by a gay man on national television. 'Everything's normal, then,' laughs Brian.

The housemates discuss the perils of drinking too much. Bubble tells them how he lost his driving licence, but has now given up drinking completely so that he can be a better father to his daughter.

Stuart leaves, under the arch of arms that has become another house tradition. When he has gone, Paul, in a quiet moment with Elizabeth, says that the experience of being nominated has been good for him. He feels he has been given a second chance, and he has now made the effort to chat with some of the housemates who may not have known him well, and might have judged him without realizing there was another side to him.

Before bed, Bubble spends ages in the girls' bedroom teasing Brian. Amma comments that their relationship is one of the nicest in the house. As usual, as the week draws to a close, Bubble is last to go to bed.

STUART LOOKS BACK: THE EXCLUSIVE INTERVIEW

Stuart on the housemates

Helen: 'She's a lovely, bubbly girl, quite young for her age. I really admired her when she explained how she'd battled against her dyslexia. We heard about her boyfriend, Big G, every day. He must be the most famous boyfriend in Britain. I felt so sorry for her when she felt she had failed the fire challenge, and I was really, really pleased that, led by me, we went on to finish the task even though we felt we would lose. I don't have a lot in common with Helen, so I don't think we'll be great friends outside the house, but I really like her.'

Narinder: 'I thought she made too much of an issue about people remembering her name. The first week, I felt she was a lovely girl, but after that she changed and started complaining about her allergy rash and her problem going to the toilet, which she discussed endlessly. She became miserable. I felt she could have put more effort into the house, and I also saw the way she was going around to different people, making allies.'

Amma: 'Despite our row, I really liked Amma. She's got a great smile, it lights up a room. She's prickly and sensitive, and she was a bore in the kitchen, always wrapping up bits of food in tinfoil. I think professionally, as a table dancer, she is very much in control of the men she meets, and she felt she couldn't control the men in the house, which she found a bit threatening. I think she's got an issue with men. But she's got a lot of spirit. We put our argument behind us, and although we come from very different backgrounds, I'll always be happy if she wants to ring up for a chat some time.'

Elizabeth: 'She came over as quiet, demure, almost shy, and then she'd say something really shocking, like telling us how she ran around a field naked. She brought a magazine into the house which was really raunchy – everyone assumed it was Bubble's. I didn't notice her flirting with me, and I would have done if it had been heavy. Elizabeth was someone you could have a good conversation with, although I tried to steer clear of having real buddies.'

Penny: 'Penny was very hysterical, particularly near the end, although I now understand what it's like living under the strain of being nominated. But she was too bossy and teacherish. We had one meeting when she told us off for not putting our hands up before we spoke. The house was calmer and easier after she left. She was constantly challenging me, which I didn't understand. I made a great effort to get to know her, and had a long talk in which she told me all about her religion, about her early life and her ex-boyfriends. I thought we got on really well, but that evening she called me "a fucking arsehole".'

Dean: 'He's a cracking guy, and I hope I'll see him when he's out. I've already phoned his girlfriend – he gave me his home phone number by pointing to numbers on the contents page of a magazine. We had a lot in common: we were about the same age, he was missing Vanessa as much as I was missing Sian, and we both played the guitar. He was a really cool guy to talk to, and the other people in the house really like him.'

Paul: 'Paul's very genuine. He reminds me of the way I was at his age, a real lad. He doesn't think about what he's saying. I know some of the girls complained that he always outdid them with stories, but it wasn't in an "I'm better than you" kind of way. He's accident prone, and lots of things have happened to him. Because we were nominated together, I felt a real connection with him.'

Josh: 'Despite what everybody seems to think, I never saw Josh as a threat. My competitiveness about suntans is a joke, as all my mates know. If Josh and I competed, it was never malicious. We have things in common: we are both into keeping fit, we're both good fun in a group. Although I don't have any gay friends, I had no problem with him being gay. I told him and Brian "Just don't kiss in front of me".'

Brian: 'He's so funny, he's wasted in his job with the airline. He's very camp, and very naive, although that might be a bit of a game. I saw how mature he can be when we got the first-aid task. When Josh came in, he changed almost instantly. He felt challenged. I kept telling him off, about the way he was avoiding eye contact with Josh. I think one of them needs to leave the house, otherwise the tension between them might become too much. It was great the way he bonded with all the straight guys in the house before Josh came in: we had so much banter in the bedroom at night that my sides would actually be aching from laughing.'

Bubble: 'He's a character. He thought I was from another planet because I had designer clothes, and he was always asking me the price of everything. I wanted him to know that beneath my poser exterior I'm a genuine bloke. I tried not to rub their faces in the fact that I probably have more money than any of them – that's why I only told them about my farm in my final speech. Bubble and I had a link, because he was missing his daughter and I was missing my children. The weekends were particularly hard for him, because that's when he would have been with her, and I always made a point of speaking to him when I saw he was low. He's in it for the money. He was honest about that, and I'd like him to win. On nominations day I noticed he was wearing a certain hat, and I said "That's your lucky hat, isn't it?" He said that in a couple of weeks I knew him better than many of his mates who have known him for years.'

Stuart on life in the house

'Nobody can prepare you for what it is like in there, and nobody can describe it properly. I was completely out of my comfort zone, which was an important part of the experience. For me, it was a very stress-free environment: I didn't have the normal high pressure of work. And because I've got young children, all the noise and silliness didn't bother me as much as it did some of the others. I was shocked by the manners in there: they're appalling. Meal times were embarrassing. There were no napkins, and half of them just don't know how to eat. Helen's birthday food disappeared like it was being devoured by locusts. And all the burping, farting and talking about their loo habits that goes on, even at the dinner table. Elizabeth burps like a bloke, and Amma farts noisily.

PEOPLE ON STUART

Stuart's wife, Sian: 'I can't believe he made bread and did a shopping list – he's got a phobia about supermarkets. On the very first day, one of my friends rang up and told me to switch the TV on because Stuart was doing the washing up. He doesn't do anything domestic at home! I got a bit upset, because I think the programmes have made him out to be someone he's not, and there was nothing I could do to defend him. They portrayed him as flash, but in fact he's generous and never pre-judges people. I think the girls turned against him, possibly because they unburdened themselves to him – people find it easy to talk to Stuart. But then they felt vulnerable, and turned on him. Stuart adores women, all my female friends love him. He's just a great guy, as all our friends and family know. I'm very proud of him.'

Stuart's friend Darren: 'He's a highly competitive person, and that's why he's got to a high level at work. I think he approached being in the house more like a business – I just wish he'd relaxed and let everyone see the Stuart we know.'

Nemone, Radio One DJ: 'Hey Stuart, less of those exercises, less of the sleaze and smarm factor. Just chill.'

'We all had a problem getting used to living without hot water. There were one or two days when the hot water was left on by mistake, and we developed a code for it so that we could tell each other without alerting Big Brother: we'd say "It's hot outside today".

'The worst thing was missing my children and Sian, but I coped by making a little shrine to them, with photographs and drawings that the children did, and I kissed their pictures every night. On Rory's birthday, I carried a photo of him round with me all day.

'My first few days in there I was very nervous, like a scared rabbit trapped in a car's headlights. I didn't use the Diary Room much because I'm not the sort of person who feels the need to unload my feelings. If I have a problem, I sort it out myself. Amma said I was insecure, but I think I was the least insecure person there. And besides, getting into the Diary Room would have been a problem – Bubble, Amma and Narinder were always in there, and it was the Brian show as well.'

Stuart on Stuart

'I've learned a lot about myself. I am a nice guy, believe it or not, but I know I'm going to have to work hard to change the way the public sees me, because I'm now known as a man who argues with women and makes them cry. That's just not me – I get on really well with women.

'I'm happy to admit I'm a poser. All my friends tease me about it. But I think it's very unfair that I've been labelled the new Nasty Nick, because

WEEK THREE FACT FILE

Main task: Memorize fifteen facts about each housemate.

PASS ☑ **FAIL** ☐

Treats: Brian's birthday, with a teddy bears' picnic and a roast-beef dinner.

Bets are on!
To win: Brian is still the hot favourite to win, despite his row with Josh. Only Dean has now joined him at 2/1.
To walk: Narinder is tipped as the next to leave, with odds of 7/4.
Evictee's tip: Stuart says Brian or Josh for the next evictee or perhaps Narinder. Bubble or Dean to win.

although I'm competitive, I'm not Machiavellian. What you see with me is what you get, and I admit I can be too direct, and that I don't suffer fools gladly. But I was surprised by the way Amma took our row – I thought it was just a heated discussion and that it would blow over. I was really surprised when Bubble said she was crying.

'I was desperate not to be the father figure in the house. Although I'm older and more mature than most of them, I'm mentally aged about twenty-five, and I was up for all the fun that was going on. I laughed the whole time – I can't remember three weeks in my life when I have laughed as much. At times my sides hurt from laughing. I loved it. I didn't want it to be like work, or serious. I wanted to let down what little hair I've got.

'I applied to go into the house because I love a challenge. I've worked all my life, very hard, and I wanted to do something different. This was a once-in-a-lifetime opportunity, a chance to really find out about myself. It lived up to all my expectations. Three weeks may not sound very long, but it is in there. I never forgot where I was. I got used to the cameras, but I never forgot I was on camera, which some of the others seemed to.

'I didn't handle myself very well, especially with the two rows. I'm used to settling things: Sian and I have a rule that we will never go to bed on an argument. So that's why I seemed to press Amma too hard to talk about it. I've learned there are times when you have to back off. In retrospect, I should have let both the rows go, just shrugged my shoulders.

'I was pleased with myself for not taking control. The last words one of my friends said to me were, "Don't take control, Stuart, because you know you can, so just don't do it." And I didn't, though there were lots of times when I would have liked to organize everything better.

'I was very flattered to be chosen to go into the house, and that alone has done a lot for my self-esteem. I took the whole experience for what it was worth. I've met some people I would never normally have met, I've made some friends. And I've got a great tan!'

WEEK FOUR

**'Let me out of this house,
it's driving me mad.'**
Bubble

There is always a slump in morale on the day after an eviction, but this week the endless hours of rain didn't help. But there is a new task to take the housemates' minds off Stuart's departure.

A strange, white podium has arrived in the garden overnight, and Bubble immediately guesses that they are all going to be asked to dance. He's right – for five days, they are told, at irregular intervals between 8 a.m. and 2 a.m., music will be piped into the house in short bursts. Each contestant has to choose a dance style, and after their blast of music is announced, they will have twenty seconds to grab a partner and get to the podium. During their one-minute dance, they must perform a special move three times.

They wager only ten per cent of their weekly shopping budget on the task. One reason for keeping the wager low is, as Dean points out, the problem of trying to rouse a sleeping Bubble.

Their dance styles are: Dean, punk; Josh, hard house; Helen, disco; Brian, waltz; Liz, salsa; Bubble, robotics; Paul, country and western; Narinder, rock and roll; and Amma, bump and grind. From time to time, when the conga is announced, all the housemates must take part. This time they have thirty seconds to get to the podium.

There are high points of comedy over the next few days, as Brian waltzes dreamily with unlikely partners such as Bubble and Dean. Paul really gets into dancing with his hands on Amma's bum, which makes Bubble envious. There is one moment of pure tension, when Narinder has a go at Helen for always rushing up to be first on stage. Helen, who teaches dancing, has been very enthusiastic about the task from the beginning. She was blamed when the group failed the fire task, and she struggled valiantly with the memory test, but this one seems designed just for her, and she wants to show the others how hard she's trying. After Narinder's jibe about letting others have a turn, Helen goes to the Diary Room to complain to Big Brother.

'I don't think I'm doing anything wrong by running up. But Narinder thinks I shouldn't be running up all the time. I think you've gotta run up, just in case nobody else does. She does like to have a go about it, and I've been trying to be really nice to her, but I think she can't stand me. I don't want to be on stage all the time. I'm just trying to put a bit of effort into the task. But obviously she's got some problem with me, and I've been going out of my way to be really nice to her. I'm not going to row with her, because she wants that so I look bad. I'm going to rise above it and be a mature adult in this situation. I love the task, it's the best task we've had.'

Paul also visits Big Brother, and says he's had a good night's sleep and is feeling very happy to still be in the house. He thinks, wrongly, that the vote between him and Stuart was probably very close. He says the bad weather is affecting the mood in the house, with all the contestants feeling like caged animals.

Trapped indoors, the housemates play another round of the truth game, initiated by Josh. Brian and Josh both admit to peeing in the shower. Dean, Josh and Amma own up to biting their toe nails, and Elizabeth, Amma, Brian, Josh and Paul reveal they have eaten dog food. Narinder is the only person to have fantasized about a housemate (Brian). Bubble, Narinder and Brian all stand up to admit they have lied since being in the house, but no amount of interrogation by the others will make them reveal any details.

Josh has now been in the house for one week, and is called to the Diary Room to assess how he feels. 'Bloody excellent, fantastic ... great fun, they're a great gang, I've had a lot of laughs,' is his verdict. He says he likes Elizabeth because of her calming influence on the 'erratic and loud' people in the group. And while he appreciates Narinder's and Brian's double-act patter, he isn't always sure that it's a joke.

Brian moves back into the boys' room, reclaiming his old bed from Josh, who moves into the one vacated by Stuart. Paul and Dean welcome Brian home, but the girls say they will miss him.

Bubble and the girls stay up talking: Helen confesses to Narinder her fear that Big G will find another girlfriend while she is in the house. Amma, Liz and Bubble agree that the house has lost its innocence, and that they cannot be fully themselves for fear of upsetting other housemates. Bubble claims the house has sucked all humour out of him.

Dean is up first on Sunday morning, but finds he's not the only inhabitant of the house who's awake. A tiny wren has been trapped in the living room all night, and is happily pecking at crumbs on the coffee table. Dean catches the bird in a towel and very gently carries it outside.

All the contestants' regular activities – washing, shaving, compiling the shopping list, making bread, preparing lunch – are punctuated by wild bursts of dancing on the podium. Bubble staggers out of bed at 1 p.m. to do the conga, and then staggers back into it again. He has managed to sleep for twelve hours. Josh, who has turned himself into the group's games master, is organizing a tennis tournament, and is busy cutting letters out of magazines to spell out 'Strong Cider Three Mills Tennis Tournament' on the wall. Bubble says he won't take part in any competition with alcohol sponsorship, even if it is imaginary alcohol.

Narinder is feeling unwell, and spends a couple of hours curled up under a blanket in the living area. Brian lies with her and they share a horrified realization that one of them may be evicted on Friday. Narinder says Brian will die if she goes, and she will cry because she is leaving him. Brian retorts that he will become best friends with Amma. He says it to wind Narinder up, and it works. 'I would kill you if you did that,' she says.

In the afternoon, Liz is called to the Diary Room to give a report on how the group are coping. 'People are bored, they're finding it hard to occupy themselves,' she says. However, she denies that she is bored herself, saying, 'I don't think you should use the "b" word. When it gets like this, you've got to occupy yourself, use your own mind, and the worse thing you can do is sit down and be bored.' She says she was saddened by Stuart's departure, but not surprised after the row with Amma. Paul, like Helen, seems to have relaxed since being nominated. She says the other girls are tetchy because they are all having or about to have their periods.

'Narinder is finding it quite difficult at the moment. She's short-tempered and has a short fuse, and from what other people have told me they think she gives out a lot but can't take it.'

She says Bubble is coping with the boredom by sleeping. Of all the people there, Dean is the one she gets on with best, although she also likes Amma when they are on their own.

Outside in the kitchen, Narinder is bitching to Brian and Bubble, but manages to avoid naming the other housemates. She pulls faces to identify different housemates by characteristics she believes they have, she thinks that Paul is stupid (Narinder confirmed that this face was meant to signify Paul, rather than Helen), that Amma has a false smile, and she nicknames Josh 'Mr Motivator' or 'Mr Creator of Dreams'. Brian adds his own name for him, 'Mr Tennis Tournament'. Bubble laughs at her, but suggests she goes and sorts her feelings out in the Diary Room.

She does, telling Big Brother that she has been feeling weepy for the past few days.

'Some people are really getting on my nerves. I'm trying to control myself and I have succeeded today, because I was ready to burst. Amma's been irritating me all the time: her laziness, the way she just sits there and picks at things, and has to argue about everything. She has to have a disagreement with everybody.'

Narinder claims that she sat separately at lunch to prevent herself 'having words' with Amma over the way she let Bubble have a biscuit but wouldn't let her have one. She says her feelings could just fester but might explode, and the bad feeling will go on until one of them leaves the house. Narinder says she would like to warn Amma to keep out of her way, and says she's feeling very detached from the group.

The rain has eased, and while Paul and Dean are doing weight-lifting exercises, Bubble has his own spectacular burst of energy, running round the garden screaming, 'Let me out of this house, it's driving me mad.' Dean suggests that Bubble should walk out, and then come back and throw things

WHAT THE EXPERTS SAY

NARINDER PULLING FACES AND BITCHING WITH BRIAN AND BUBBLE

'Brian and Narinder have let Bubble inside their circle, sharing with him the secret code of how they refer to their housemates. It's a very effective code because it reduces the complexity and subtlety of a human being to one single aspect: Helen is stupid, Amma is false and her smile should not be trusted, Josh is a dreamer full of big ideas. This is mind control, like finding a brand name for a product. They're saying: think Helen, think stupid. But there's a second code in operation here. Bubble is being made to think about who he could be living with in the final weeks, and what the implications of that are. At the same time, he's being welcomed into a very tight alliance, so close that it has its own private language. It's a powerful way of focussing the mind the day before nominations. It is against the rules of *Big Brother* to discuss nominations, but it's not against the rules to bitch.'

Professor Geoffrey Beattie, Psychologist

over the fence for the others, but Bubble tells him that once he gets away from the *Big Brother* house, he has no intention of ever coming near it again.

After dinner, Narinder is bitching to Brian again about one of the girls: this time it is Helen. She says Helen keeps giving her nasty looks. Brian tells her the tension between the two of them is wearing him down. Unlike everybody else in the house, Narinder positively relishes the prospect of making nominations.

Bubble is unhappy. While Josh has been cutting out a sign for the tennis tournament, Bubble has decided to put up his own letters and numbers on the wall. He puts up his daughter Bryony's initials and her date of birth, but Big Brother deems this to be an attempt to communicate with the outside world, and orders him to take them down.

A dreary day in the house ends with a pillow fight, with Josh, Paul and Brian storming in to attack the girls as they prepare for bed. But, despite being surprised, the girls soon recover and launch themselves into the boys. Helen soon has Brian screaming for mercy. As the boys limp away to regroup they agree that Amma was 'like a raging animal' and decide against staging another offensive. The girls, in the meantime, plot their revenge, aiming to kidnap the boys' most prized possessions: Josh's teddy, Paul's hair wax, Brian's toner and Bubble's hats.

The high point of Monday morning is the arrival of the food (and the tobacco for Bubble and Amma) in the Store Room. Narinder later tells Amma that she is a different person now that she has had a cigarette, and that when she's not smoking she is 'not nice'. Amma agrees, and points out that for the last few days she has also been suffering from PMS and severe chocolate deprivation, as well as nicotine-withdrawal symptoms. The shopping list takes care of the chocolate cravings as well – a yard of chocolate is delivered, which causes great excitement, particularly from Helen. She feels very aggrieved two hours later when the chocolate is being distributed and she reckons some people are getting more than her – she compares it with being nominated for eviction.

Helen gets a lot of attention from the boys today. Paul has been following her around and flirting with her for a few days. The others have teased him that he calls out her name in his sleep and, according to Liz, Helen spoke about Paul while she was asleep last night, clearly saying 'Paul, you are off your head'. Bubble also teases and flirts with Helen after she tells him he's got lovely soft hands when he adjusts her bra.

The tennis tournament is now in full swing, with Paul seeded the highest and Amma (who has never even seen tennis being played) the lowest. Narinder goes to the Diary Room to complain about Amma's smoking, and also tells Big Brother she thinks the tennis will end in tears. She comments on how much she enjoys nominations. In the girls' bedroom a little while later, however, Narinder agrees with Liz that the housemates are all so nice, it is difficult to pick who to nominate.

The main event of the whole day is, of course, the nominations. Although Amma and Narinder seem to have had a rapprochement, they nominate each other. Helen also goes for Narinder, who is very high on the house hit list – three quarters of the other housemates vote for her, with Paul and, of course, Brian her only allies. It is the highest number of nominations anyone has received. Paul is chosen by the same four who picked him last week – his campaign to talk more and make more friends has obviously not worked.

WHAT THE EXPERTS SAY

BUBBLE

'Bubble took the order to remove the letters above his bed really badly. Earlier on the same day we saw a typical example of how Bubble usually copes with different situations in the house (when he ran around shouting about wanting to get out). Even though boredom and confinement are serious issues for the housemates, this is classic Bubble: loud, impulsive, funny, sociable. But hours later there is quite a difference: we find him alone in the bedroom, quietly cutting out letters, self-absorbed and serious. He has had a bad week. He reacted badly to all the arguments in the house last week, and he's lost Stuart, who was a source of emotional support to him. And Stuart was a father, too, and now he's back with his children and Bubble isn't.

'This apparent change in coping strategy could be very important. If he's no longer able to fall back on his old defence mechanisms, he could be vulnerable. He's already showing a sign of stress: disturbed sleep. Despite spending many hours in bed, there are bags under his eyes. In an environment like this, you have to have strong coping strategies. The old Bubble had them. Will we see them return?'

Dr Sandra Scott, Psychiatrist

Brian is visibly upset by the nomination procedure. He suspects (rightly) that Paul has nominated him, and asks Narinder if Paul hates him. She says yes, in much the same way that Amma hates her.

The tennis championship rumbles on all day, with Brian doing most of the umpiring. Narinder beats Amma, but behaves like John McEnroe, constantly questioning the umpire's decisions. Paul beats Helen, and it looks as though Narinder may have been right about the tournament causing problems when Helen refuses to shake Paul's hand when she loses.

Bubble is having a sleep when he is called to perform his robotics dance. Contradicting Dean's belief about how hard it is to wake him, he catapults out of the boys' bedroom so fast that he trips over the coffee table in the living area and injures his leg, to the consternation of the others. He misses his turn dancing, and hobbles into the Diary Room to plead the case for not failing the task. Big Brother tells him that from the moment he sustained his injury he is exempt from the task.

Shortly afterwards, Bubble returns to talk to Big Brother for twenty-five minutes. He won't say which of his housemates he likes best, but goes through them all outlining what he likes about them. He complains about the boredom in the house, and says the task – which he describes as 'poxy' – has not helped alleviate it.

'"Why am I here? Why have I voluntarily locked myself in a building with nine people I don't know and can't get away from, with the whole world scrutinizing?" You think that at times. And then you think, "I could clear that wall in five seconds."'

'Well, not right now I couldn't,' he adds, remembering his leg injury.

Narinder has cooked curry, which she serves up while muttering under her breath and calling Amma lazy for not helping. She then finds she has only dished up eight meals, leaving Amma out by mistake. Eventually, Paul gives Amma some of his meal.

Brian and Narinder chat, and lodge a couple of criticisms of one another: Narinder tells Brian he is becoming too possessive about her, and Brian tells Narinder she needs to stop snapping at people. In a serious moment, Brian tells his best friend how much he wants to be a father, but how he is worried that it will never happen. 'Once you take the gay road, you choose a lonely life. If I could change anything, I would like to be straight, to have a girlfriend and get engaged.'

Just before they all go to bed, the conga music strikes up and even Bubble, on crutches, hobbles into the line. The same music gets most of them up the next morning at half past nine – although Helen and Liz have already danced the salsa on the podium. Helen is putting a great deal more into this task than anyone else.

After praying in the bedroom, Narinder tells Amma that she has strong vibes about being nominated. Amma says she found the nominations particularly hard this week. The morning passes uneventfully, particularly for Bubble who, because he does not need to take part in the task, stays in bed until noon. An hour after he gets up he is summoned to the Diary Room to see a doctor, who examines his leg and prescribes several days of rest.

Afterwards, Bubble chats with Paul, whose crutches he is now using. They compare notes about their injuries, and Bubble confides that he is expecting to be nominated.

'I thought I had a good chance of going in the first week, because people judge me straightaway, and I'm too loud for some people. Then in the second week I thought I wouldn't go, because people would realize I wasn't a fucking idiot. Then this week I think they've seen the idiot, they've seen the other side of me, and now they just think I'm a pain in the ass.'

But when the nominations are announced at 3 p.m. it is Narinder and Paul who are up for eviction. They both take the news calmly, and neither of them seems surprised. Paul says he thinks it will be very funny to be nominated every week and yet not evicted by the public vote. For the third week running, Elizabeth has nominated both the possible evictees.

Amma and Brian talk to Narinder about her nomination. Amma suggests that Narinder was chosen because, although she is bubbly and funny, she moans a lot. Brian agrees she can be 'a bit narky'. Narinder, living up to the description, tells them that she only likes two people in the house and finds it hard being with the others. Amma is surprised that she dislikes so many of the other housemates. 'I'm hurt now. I know I'm included in that number,' she says. Narinder, ever direct, confirms this, but adds that when Amma has cigarettes she is a 'lovely person'.

Brian is worried about Narinder going, because it would make him feel 'so fucking alone'. Narinder reassures him that he will make other friends, but over the next hour or two if he gives her advice about how to win the vote, ranging from telling her to be nice to everyone to ordering her to 'get your tits out every day'. When she says that if she goes on Friday she will tell the others how boring she thinks they all are, he reminds her to be 'graceful'.

Despite Narinder's bullish attitude towards her nomination, in the evening she enjoys a few quiet moments in the girls' bedroom, looking at the photographs of her friends and family. Liz sits with her and advises her not to spend too much time on her own.

Before dinner, Paul is summoned to the Diary Room by Big Brother. He described the day as 'mad' and 'cool'.

'I'm not phased about being nominated. I'm up against someone different this week, we'll just see what happens, I'm sort of turned on about it in a way. It keeps the excitement going. The people in here are cool, great, but I'd never live with any of them in the real world. You can't get on with everybody, but I don't think anyone hates me.'

Afterwards he and Narinder, who have devised their own head-to-head dance, put their election manifestos to each other. Paul says he should stay because he is the backbone of the group, and doesn't have smelly feet or breath. Narinder reckons she should stay because she makes good food, wears good clothes and is beautiful. Paul says he only wants to go to stop his parents having to make constant visits to the studio on Friday nights, and Narinder replies she wants to go to see her husband.

WHO NOMINATES WHO

Amma nominates Narinder and Paul
Brian nominates Paul and Amma
Bubble nominates Narinder and Josh
Dean nominates Paul and Narinder
Elizabeth nominates Narinder and Paul
Helen nominates Brian and Narinder
Josh nominates Narinder and Bubble
Narinder nominates Amma and Bubble
Paul nominates Brian and Bubble

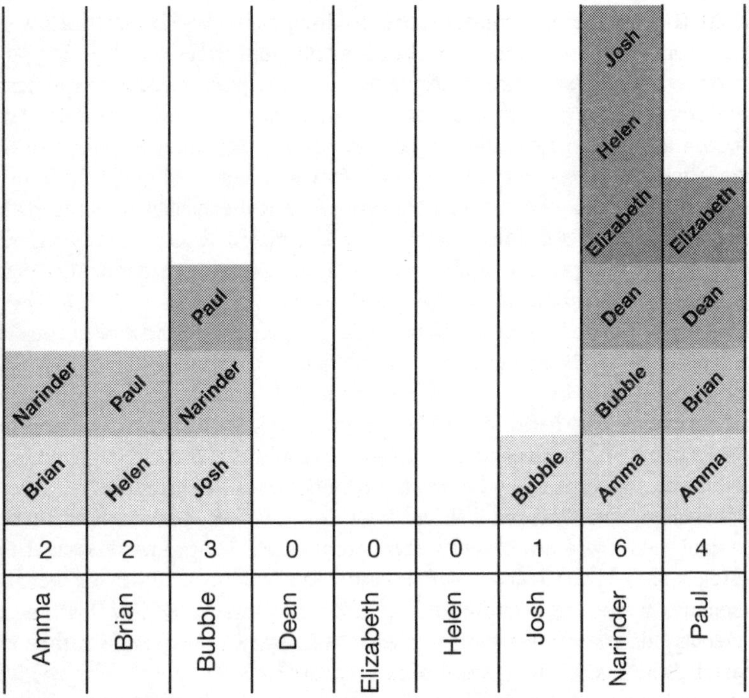

	Nominations	Nominated by
Amma	2	Brian, Narinder
Brian	2	Helen, Paul
Bubble	3	Josh, Narinder, Paul
Dean	0	
Elizabeth	0	
Helen	0	
Josh	1	Bubble
Narinder	6	Amma, Bubble, Dean, Elizabeth, Helen, Josh
Paul	4	Amma, Brian, Dean, Elizabeth

Week 4 nominees: Narinder with six nominations and Paul with four nominations.

Analysis

Helen seems to be receiving an ever-depleting number of nominations as weeks go by, from five in week one, in week four she has none. Bubble and Josh have nominated each other, as have Amma and Narinder, Brian and Paul, Narinder and Bubble. After Narinder and Paul, Bubble has the most nominations – a sign that he may be up for nomination next week.

Reasons

Amma on Narinder: 'She can be a bit selfish, she can't take what she dishes out.'

Bubble on Josh: 'I was brought up to say please and thank you and to ask permission before taking other people's things.'

Narinder on Bubble: 'There's a very thin line between when he's serious and when he thinks he's being funny. It's quite scary sometimes when he takes a fit and then says he's joking.'

At 10 p.m., the housemates gather to discuss a topic Big Brother has set them – each has to describe his or her proudest moment. Helen goes first, and relates how she won a dance trophy when she was eighteen. Bubble volunteers the moment his daughter gave away her sweets to her cousin, and also tells how he was 'choked' when the bar staff at one of the places where he worked wore black armbands on the day he was leaving.

Brian says he is proud of the way his younger sister is handling being pregnant. Liz is proud of finishing the London marathon. Josh tells the group how he was proud of being voted the best counsellor by the kids he was looking after at an American summer camp. He also speaks movingly about telling his family he was gay. His mother already knew, but he had to break it to his dad before he came into the house. His dad's supportive reaction meant a lot to Josh.

Narinder's proudest moment was her wedding day – or her two wedding days, as she had a traditional Indian wedding and a registry-office wedding. Amma says for her it was passing her GCSEs, having been told by her teachers that she would fail.

Paul tells a very emotional story, which reduces him to tears and results in Helen giving him a huge hug. He says that a month before he went to university, he and his grandfather had a big row. One week into his time at university, his grandfather died, and they had never had chance to resolve the quarrel. But he knew his grandfather was very proud of him, as he was the first member of the family to go to university, so he was determined to do well. When he felt like quitting, he thought of his grandfather, and in the end he won a design award and an award for the best dissertation in the country, and came close to getting a first.

Dean goes to the Diary Room and thanks Big Brother for setting them a discussion. He says that without the structure imposed by Big Brother, the group would only come together to eat.

'I think people are feeling a bit controlled in here, and people get lazy in here. When we sit down for a discussion, I learn something new about people. But without the forced discussion you would just gravitate to the people you get on with and not talk to the others.'

He says he has thought of initiating a discussion himself.

'But because I'm the oldest, I'm reluctant to take a leadership role. I don't want to sit people down and try to get them to join in. I'm more live and let live. I'm not very good at making people do things. I have a history of being that sort of person, organizing people, and I don't really want to be that person anymore.'

Next in the Diary Room is Narinder, who tells Big Brother that she is not at all surprised to be nominated. She says she does not feel she has had much support from the others in the group.

'They're probably relieved or excited. Amma's been a helluva lot happier today. Helen has been alright. Brian is Brian: it's "Oh my God what am I going to do without you?" He's not got a lot of faith in me staying. I think they'll all be so happy if I leave, apart from Brian.'

The evening ends with another pillow fight, but this time the only two protagonists are Brian and Josh. Brian accidentally catches a glimpse of Josh's willy, and jokes to the others that it is small and stumpy. Josh retaliates by dropping nail clippings on the screaming Brian, and then attacks him with a pillow. Narinder comes into the boys' room to save her friend, much to the amusement of Bubble and Dean. Bubble, as usual, is the last to bed, taking with him a bean bag to support his injured leg.

On Wednesday morning, the housemates are all roused from bed by the sound of the conga. As they rush to the podium, Josh darts back to the bedroom and grabs a T-shirt. He just fails to make it to the podium before the music starts, although none of the others seem to notice. As soon as they have sashayed sleepily around the garden for a minute, they all tumble back into bed. Bubble, who is excused from the task, is disturbed by them and gets up to have a cigarette and a quiet chat with Big Brother. He doesn't go into the Diary Room. Instead, he just talks into his radio microphone, revealing that he is beginning to go stir crazy:

'Big Brother, if you are listening, as soon as I come out of the shower I'm coming to you for painkillers. I slept with my leg up all night, and I think it's

OBSESSIONS

Amma: Food – eating it, cooking it, playing with it. Sex.
Brian: Myself, how I look and how people perceive me.
Bubble: Hats and sex.
Dean: Video films (he has thousands), football and sex.
Elizabeth: None – although thinks exercise is important.
Helen: Looking in the mirror.
Josh: Gym and fitness, healthy eating.
Narinder: To become something, to give my grandchildren great stories to listen to and something to aspire to.
Paul: Birds and success.
Penny: Checking the door is locked.
Stuart: Winning games.

a lot better. Thank you, over and out. P.S: Good morning, how are you? I hope the outside world is looking lovely. The thought of it is quite lovely: the facility to walk down the street or to a shop and buy a can of Coke. Fantastic!'

Helen is up next, helping Bubble make breakfast and then settling him outside with his leg on a bean bag. He says he could get used to her helping him. Helen is missing Stuart, who used to get up early and clear up the debris from the night before.

When the others are out of bed, they lounge around the garden talking about the brutality of life in a real prison. Brian, ever the innocent, is genuinely shocked.

Narinder still has a very strong feeling that she is the one who will be leaving. She says she wants to go to see her family, 'but I want to stay and be a bitch at the same time'. In the Diary Room, she admits it is the waiting that is hard.

'There are a few people I just don't get on with, and if I do stay I don't know how I will cope with that. It's just hard on my head. I'm thinking, thinking, thinking. I'm getting no support from the group, just Brian.'

At 1 p.m., and with another three hours to go on the dance task, Big Brother gives the housemates a mini-task. As it's Ascot week, they have to make hats and fans for each other, out of a supply of materials left in the Store Room. They must work in pairs, and they quickly team up: Elizabeth with Bubble, Narinder with Brian, Amma with Helen and Dean with Paul. Josh is the odd one out, but Amma and Helen willingly let him join them. He makes a hat for Helen, whose only instructions are that she doesn't want to look like a plonker and there must be lots of glitter.

In the middle of the millinery session the conga is called, and while they are all weaving around in a line the house lights go out, due to a power cut. This means they have to carry on with the task outside, as there is not enough light in the house. But it's windy, and the materials are blowing all over the place, so Brian goes to the Diary Room to complain. This is an unnerving experience, as the Diary Room is in complete darkness and he spills glitter everywhere. To make matters worse, Big Brother insists the housemates stay outside.

When the power cut is over, Big Brother summons Dean to the Diary Room and asks him how he is enjoying the task. He is making a hat for Paul, in the shape of a mortar board.

'Paul got upset last night and quite emotional, and I know it sounds ridiculous but it makes it easier to make the hat, because before last night we didn't know much about him.'

Paul has made Dean a hat with a football theme and a guitar-shaped fan, and Josh has turned Helen into a vision in pink. Helen has made not only a hat, but a whole outfit for Amma out of tinfoil (she's famous for wrapping portions of her food in tinfoil and putting it in the fridge for later). Amma's hat for Josh has a carnival theme. Narinder describes her straw hat for Brian as making him look like a country bumpkin, with cotton wool for clouds and brown balls 'for when he shat his pants a few years ago'. Brian has created a stylish, yellow-and-black hat for Narinder, with 'the black representing her dark, mysterious, sexy side and the yellow is like the sun, her happy side'. But he then went on to describe the colours as being those of the wasp and the bee: 'Like her, they have infectious stings that can kill,' he jokes.

Liz has made a pork-pie hat for Bubble, with a large smile on the crown, 'Because he's larger than life. The pink bits represent his little girl.' Bubble's hat for Liz is, he says, a BB hat – not for Big Brother, but for Betty Boo (the housemates are now calling her Betty).

Brian takes advantage of all the material that has come into the house for the hat-making, and dresses up as the murderer from *Scream* to terrify the others. It's hilarious, but some of the girls are really spooked. Narinder also livens things up by announcing that she's not wearing anything under her yellow dress. Brian looks up her skirt and confirms that she is telling the truth.

The last hour of the dance test sees all the music played in rapid succession, with the finale being a double conga. They're all exhausted, and collapse inside to discuss what their treat will be. Liz, who is so good at forecasting the nominations, guesses it will be Pimm's.

The girls settle down for an afternoon of full-scale bitching. First of all, it's Narinder, Amma and Brian (who after his stint in the girls' bedroom, is allowed in as an honorary girl). Amma says she thinks Narinder is angry.

'I'm not really angry about the nomination, but I'm angry about other things,' says Narinder. 'I think it's a bit unfair sometimes. Yesterday Helen said something that was really not nice. I felt someone should have said, "Helen, apologize". Everyone was waiting for me to attack back. Dean walked away. Brian signalled to me to bite my tongue.'

Amma points out, 'When someone says something to you, people are expecting you to make jokes, make light of it.'

Narinder replies that if she does say what she thinks the reaction is that she's a bitch. She says that some people don't make any effort with her, and Amma guesses that she's referring to Dean.

FAVOURITE BOOK

Amma: *Brother in the Land* by Robert Swindells
Brian: 'It's sad to say, but I've only read one book and that's Geri Halliwell's *If Only*.'
Bubble: *Consider Phlebas* by Iain M. Banks
Dean: *The Other Side of the Mountain* ('a book I read when I was ten')
Elizabeth: *One Flew Over the Cuckoo's Nest* by Ken Kesey
Helen: *Goodnight Mr Tom* by Michelle Magorian ('the only book I have ever read')
Josh: *Lord of the Rings* by J.R.R. Tolkien
Narinder: *Fools of Fortune* by William Trevor
Paul: *American Psycho* by Bret Easton Ellis
Penny: *Wild Swans* by Jung Chang
Stuart: Any book by Isaac Asimov

FAVOURITE FILM

Amma: *Good Will Hunting*
Brian: *Titanic*
Bubble: *Willy Wonka and the Chocolate Factory*
Dean: *The Third Man*
Elizabeth: *The Shawshank Redemption*
Helen: *Charlie's Angels*
Josh: *True Romance*
Narinder: *Dead Poets Society*
Paul: *Indiana Jones*
Penny: *Lovers of the Arctic Circle*
Stuart: *Arthur*

'He's a weird one,' she says, agreeing with Narinder that he doesn't go out of his way to talk to people, and that she finds him hard work. Brian says someone else always has to make the first move with Dean.

In the middle of their conversation, Helen walks into the bedroom to bring Amma her shoes and sunglasses. Brian, who is speaking as she enters, pauses for a moment until he sees who has come in, and then carries on. The pause is enough for the hypersensitive Helen to imagine they were talking about her, and she goes to the Diary Room to complain to Big Brother about them.

'I can see Narinder's a little bit upset because she's nominated, but that's what we're here for, you've just got to get on with it. Some of the looks I've been getting off her – if looks could kill I'd be dead. It's not my fault Josh had to make a hat for me. Or perhaps it's just me blowing everything up.'

In the kitchen, Brian tells Helen and Dean how upset Narinder is, and Dean suggests they all make a special effort to cheer her up this evening. Amma and Narinder are still talking about the others, dissing Dean and Bubble. The latter's comment that he is only interested in winning has cut deep with most of the other housemates, all of whom insist that they are just there to enjoy the experience. Helen joins in the chat, and so, eventually, does Liz who gives them something real to moan about: she and Amma believe that they have failed the dance task, thanks to Josh.

Liz was right about the Pimm's, which comes with strawberries and cream. Helen has never heard of Pimm's.

'It's twenty per cent alcoholic, that's all you need to know,' says Liz.

Narinder rates this her best moment so far in the Big Brother house. But the pleasure dissipates when the housemates learn that they have failed the dance task because of Josh. They are relieved that they have only lost ten per cent of their shopping money, and will still have £56.70 to spend. Josh later explains to Brian that he had to turn back for a T-shirt this morning (which cost them the task) because he had 'a huge stiffie'. The two compare notes about what they miss: for Brian it's chocolate, crisps and shopping. For the more worldly Josh it is his dog, his friends and sex.

Brian and Narinder give one of their best impromptu performances yet, acting out a melodramatic love story to fit the moody tune Dean is playing on his guitar. They play thwarted lovers.

'I want you so badly,' moans Brian

'But you never come to me anymore. I never see the footprints in the sand,' croaks Narinder, playing a sultry beauty she has named Signora Papparetto.

'That's because I have no feet since the accident,' retorts Brian.

'Time is running out, my dear. Signor Papparetto will be back. It is too late.'

And as the lovers turn away from each other, Narinder adds: 'One last thing – I have been sleeping with your best friend.'

'So have I – I am gay,' confesses Brian.

Amma goes to the Diary Room to ask for more Pimm's, promising the group will do a task to earn it. Big Brother says no, and asks her how she is getting on. Amma says that some days whizz past and others drag. She says she doesn't feel she knows the other housemates well, because it is a false situation. Despite nominating her, she says Narinder is one of her favourite people, but that she doesn't have the right personality for getting on in the house. Amma says she holds back on saying what she thinks a lot of the time, because you have to when you are living with other people.

'Narinder gets upset that people rally around others when they are upset but not around her. But you are afraid of the reaction you are going to get from Narinder, because she's harsh and scary.'

Amma admits she's restraining her own personality, and when Big Brother asks her which aspects are missing, she says 'It's probably my wilder, louder, silly side. I've had a sense of humour amputation in here. I can get jokes but I can't deliver them.'

Afterwards, she joins Dean trying to make cigarettes out of dried banana skin, but Big Brother intervenes to stop them, and confiscates the banana skins.

With the rest of the housemates in bed, Bubble tells Amma that, although Paul is a lovely bloke, having Narinder in the house is more lively and entertaining. Amma agrees, but says Narinder causes unnecessary friction. Bubble thinks it would be interesting if he was up against Brian in the eviction stakes, and Amma compares that to Bernard Manning against Graham Norton.

The next day, Narinder washes her hair and plucks her eyebrows in readiness for her eviction, which she is convinced will happen tomorrow.

Bubble's leg is still giving him trouble. He is wearing a brace on it, and the others have to measure it at regular intervals and report the size of the swelling to Big Brother. Bubble is also issued with a supply of painkillers.

The boys get up very late, with Josh, Brian and Dean not surfacing until after midday, although they have been awake for some time, chatting in bed. They probably wish they hadn't bothered to get up when they find themselves listening to Paul talking for fourteen minutes about the problems he has had driving around the M25. Liz and Amma then discuss which day is the summer solstice, Liz and Dean have a protracted discussion about why men like football. The only lively discussion is between Bubble and Brian, with Amma and Narinder weighing in on Brian's side. He says he would like there to be a gay man left in the house for the final week, and Bubble remarks that if he said he would like there to be only straight men left for the final week, he would be in trouble for not being politically correct. Amma and Narinder agree that they would like a woman and a black person in the final week. The heated argument about Bubble's stance ends when he is called to the Diary Room to have his leg checked.

It's still four days until the start of Wimbledon, but the house tennis tournament has reached its grand final, with Josh and Paul lining up to play. It's a fast and furious game, and there's lots of arguing about every point, but Brian proves to be quite a forceful umpire. Josh wins comfortably – nobody is very surprised, as the tournament was his idea. Later on, there's a close match between Dean and Paul to decide the runner up, with Dean eventually winning. Helen graciously hands out invisible trophies to the three of them.

Brian and Bubble have a comic five minutes, with Brian snatching Bubble's crutches, and the pair of them enacting a scene from the film *Misery*.

WHAT THE EXPERTS SAY

THE DIARY ROOM

'In the Diary Room there are only basic rules, and nobody knows how anybody else behaves. Therefore, it can be extremely revealing about the personalities, motives and strategies of the group. When Helen goes in to talk behind the others' backs, from the start her body language reveals the role she is adopting in relation to Big Brother. Her posture is open, her behaviour childlike in its tone, and when she talks about Narinder, her nervous fiddling betrays her discomfort. She's not hiding the fact that she wants support and comfort from Big Brother.

'But Elizabeth often approaches Big Brother in a different way. Her closed bodily posture signals her attitude to Big Brother. By locking her hands across her knees, she prevents them giving anything away of her inner thoughts. In the first week she nominates Penny and Helen, and says there will be more fun for Helen in Wales. Obviously this is not the whole story, there are other reasons for nominating Helen, which she is choosing to withhold. At the point of telling this half-truth, we see a high level of blinking, which indicates her discomfort, and a fixed, false smile, which fades slowly. She seems to resent being questioned by Big Brother. Yet Big Brother controls the Diary Room, deciding which questions to ask and when to ask them. This is the structure of an interrogation, but it does not have to feel like an interrogation unless you are withholding information. There is a power struggle going on with Elizabeth. She tries a number of strategies to disempower her interrogator (for example, asking Big Brother questions and saying she really wants to get to know Big Brother). She tries to personalize the voice of Big Brother, to know more about the personality who knows so much about her. Of course, she can't do that. It's against the rules. This may cause her to feel increasing resentment and frustration towards Big Brother.'

Professor Geoffrey Beattie, Psychologist

Josh intervenes, and ends up sitting on Brian, tickling him. But despite these distractions, Brian is preoccupied with the prospect of Narinder leaving: he seems to share her conviction that the eviction vote is a foregone conclusion. The two of them spend a quiet moment together in the girls' bedroom, reminiscing about the good times they have had, and pledging to meet when they are both out. The chat disintegrates into play, with Brian running around the house with a pair of Narinder's knickers on his head, and then leaping on her and blowing raspberries on her stomach.

After dinner, Josh throws water over Brian, drenching his microphone. It's meant to be fun, but there's an edge to it, and Brian is unhappy. Narinder comments that they are behaving like an old, married couple, and Elizabeth, Dean and Helen are worried that the scene is going to escalate into a nasty incident. But it blows over.

The day draws to a close with a series of late-night practical jokes. Using the ruse that she thinks the boys have stolen her Dalmatian stuffed toy and hidden it in Brian's bed Helen initiates a huge pillow fight. She leads a raid on the boys' room by girl warriors, emitting a piercing war cry as they attack. Everyone except Dean and the injured Bubble joins in the fight. Then Paul throws a beetle at Brian, who retaliates by filling Paul's bed with shaving foam. When the lights finally go out in the boys' room, Brian starts to scream hysterically. He thinks there are more beetles in his bed – it is another trick of Bubble's who has been throwing rice at Brian in the dark.

In the girls' room, things are more peaceful, but the room mates stay awake longer, discussing everyone in the house. First up is Brian, and they agree that Josh doesn't find Brian funny. Narinder then says she is not amused by Bubble, but Liz defends him and says he makes her laugh: 'Bubble's finding it very hard in here. I know it's not an excuse, but he's missing his daughter,' she says.

The longest time is spent discussing Amma. Liz says she thinks Amma has low self esteem, and for the next half hour they talk about this. Amma has more to say than anybody else.

'I don't think I'm really boring, I just don't think I'm a distinctive person. That's my opinion, it's not a self-esteem problem,' she says. Everyone is asleep by 3.30 a.m.

Friday is a day of preparation for the evening. Narinder paints her toenails, straightens her hair, and steams her face to make sure she's looking her best for the eviction. She tells the others she will be drinking Bacardi and Coke and eating smoked salmon this weekend. Everyone assumes she is going to be the one who goes.

The Diary Room has a busy day. Amma tells Big Brother that if Narinder leaves the house there will be a 'huge change of energies', but if Paul leaves the difference will be more subtle. She says Brian will bounce back, and Narinder's departure will 'remove a lot of negativity' from the house. Dean, visiting the Diary Room to complain about the ineffectual lawnmower, tells Big Brother that he would love Narinder to stay, but says she has placed barriers around herself. He says Brian will be sad to see her go, and this sentiment is echoed by Bubble when he goes in for a consultation about his injured leg.

VOTING

Sixty-two per cent of those who voted wanted to oust Narinder, while thirty-eight per cent voted for Paul. The total vote was 1,215,004, with sixty-five per cent of votes registered by phone and thirty-five per cent through interactive television. The average number of viewers for the week was 4.45 million – an increase of 0.35 million on the previous week, and more than a million up on week four of last year's *Big Brother*. The peak audience for watching the live streaming of life in the house was 480,000, and on Thursday the E4 magazine programme *Big Brother's Little Brother* was watched by a record 624,000 viewers.

The website remains the biggest entertainment site in the UK, with more than ninety-four million page views recorded so far, and more than ten million downloads of live action from the house.

Paul is also facing possible eviction, but his fears are marginalized in the concentration on Narinder. He and Helen are spending increasing amounts of time together, playing silly games and just chatting and sunbathing side by side for hours. Narinder observes that they are obsessed with each other, and Brian agrees, saying they have a lot in common.

Over dinner, Narinder reminds the group how to make lamb curry, collects any messages the others want delivering to friends and family, and tells the housemates she knows them better than she knows many of her friends in the outside world.

When Davina gets through to the house just before 9 p.m., Paul and Narinder sit head-to-head, facing each other. At the last moment, Narinder slips her hand behind her to grab Brian's hand. When the announcement comes, she jumps up and cheers. Paul looks very relieved, and while Narinder is whisked away to the girls' room to spend an hour and a half getting ready, he admits to Dean that he is glad the tension is over. He says the whole experience is 'not cool', which for Paul is as bad as it gets – his two favourite adjectives are 'wicked' and 'cool'.

The girls help Narinder primp and preen, and Brian fetches wads of toilet roll to stuff in her bra to increase her cleavage. She has promised all week that she will tell them all what she thinks of them before she leaves. Brian keeps urging her not to be vitriolic, but to leave with dignity. In the end, partly because of time pressure and partly because of his advice, she keeps her speech short:

'In all honesty, I was very bored here. You lot aren't the kind of people I would mix with. You did bore me.'

She says she and Helen did not really have a problem with each other, although she admits that she has had problems with all the housemates at some time. She tells them they have all done well, and implores them to look after Brian.

The others take it stoically, without defending themselves.

Privately, to Paul and Brian, Narinder pulls no punches, telling them that she wants to see Amma, Bubble, Dean, Helen and Josh out, leaving the two of them plus Elizabeth as the final three.

When the moment finally comes, Narinder passes under the arch of raised arms and through the door, only to pop back in twice in a routine she and Brian planned earlier. Then she's running along the metal grille into the arms of her husband, Jatinder. It's a highly emotional exit, with Narinder flinging herself enthusiastically at the banks of cheering fans. She has to be dragged away by security men to get her into the studio.

NARINDER LOOKS BACK: THE EXCLUSIVE INTERVIEW

Narinder on the housemates

Brian: 'He was my saviour, without him I would have survived, but I would have been really unhappy. We made it funny for ourselves. I don't think the others understood our humour – I had a discussion with the other girls on the last night and they said they found Brian's humour hard to deal with. And I know Josh was taken aback by us when he first came in. Brian is talented, great. We clicked the first day, standing by the chickens. My only fear is that

PEOPLE ON NARINDER

Narinder's husband, Jatinder: 'She's the girl with everything: looks, personality, she's a natural entertainer, just an amazing person. I think people felt threatened by her, particularly the other girls, because she has so much going for her. I'm very, very proud of her, the proudest man in Britain. I think she's brilliant. Now she's out I'm sure the ratings will go down, because the others are all so quiet and boring.'

Narinder's cousin, Serena: 'She's a nice girl, she's been a bit misrepresented. She's come across as loud and brutally honest, when she's just being herself, which the others in the house aren't. She gets a bit tetchy when she has PMT – it seems you can use that as a defence for murder but not for having a couple of rows in the Big Brother house. She doesn't look for arguments, they look for her. I think the others wanted to split her and Brian, because two people together are stronger than one, and they felt threatened.'

Gail Porter, TV presenter: 'Narinder really winds me up, totally gets on my tits. She goes from room to room saying she wants people to be upfront and tell it like it is, and then goes into another room and bitches about someone she's just been talking to.'

James, a banker: 'Narinder, I don't know what Brian is going to do without you. Who's going to be his best mate now?'

he will forget me now I'm not there with him. I told him to howl for forty-five minutes when I'd gone – I don't think he howled for forty-five seconds! We had such a good relationship, he could say anything to me: things that would sound racist from other people. He made me scream with laughter, because it was all said in such a funny, Brian way. For the last couple of days, he began to detach himself from me, because I told him to wean himself off me. But we've planned lots of meetings when he gets out.'

Penny: 'She's great. We had our arguments and she said nasty things, like how she didn't trust me anymore. But it was said in a moment of anger and I understood that, and we forgot it afterwards – if only some of the others could have dealt with anger the way we did, it would have been easier. The whole house was against Penny, apart from me and Brian. She needed support. I really missed her when she left the house, and although the others wouldn't admit it, they did too. She was a mother figure, cleaning, doing the food. When she went we were left in the lurch.'

Stuart: 'I thought we had something in common when we first met, because we were the only two of the housemates who are married, and I thought we could be allies in that. But, although he was very sweet, he was really boring. He was only there to get a tan. And to talk about clothes. Me and Brian couldn't believe that leopard-print thing he wore – I had to stuff my hand in my mouth to stop myself laughing. But I couldn't understand why the others criticized him for being too competitive – that's what we were there for. I didn't understand why he suddenly announced that he had bought a nine-acre farm, right at the end. I'd asked him about his home once or twice, and he'd brushed it off. But watching Dean's and Elizabeth's faces when he made the announcement was great – they were stunned.'

Helen: 'Everyone treats her like a child and she plays on it. When we had our fight, I burst out crying, but it was Helen they all ran after. She's like a seven year old. And she drove me mad in the first week, because she couldn't get my name right. She was fine when it was reduced to Naz, three letters – she could cope with three letters. But underneath our spats I like Helen, and I think I could really get on with her. She helped me with my hair before I went out, which made me feel closer to her.'

Amma: 'At first I thought I was going to get on with her, but she didn't like me. She has so many annoying habits. She farts and burps all the time – everyone does it now and again, but we were woken up every morning by Amma's loud farts. Also, she's forever wrapping bits of left-over food in tinfoil and putting it in the fridge. Brian and I joked about a trail of tinfoil leading to Amma. She'd pick at food – she ate raw bacon and raw mince. And I heard her in the kitchen when we were all in bed, and I guessed she was eating. She's so lazy. She'd cook occasionally, making biscuits or scones if she felt like it, but she wasn't keen on helping out the rest of the time. She earns a lot of money at her job, and all her clothes are designer label and really expensive. She's very uninhibited, probably because of what she does for a living: while the rest of us were nervous and coy about stripping off with cameras there, she would wander around naked. She'd sit around all day wrapped in a big, orange blanket, which really irritated me. But her worse fault is that she is false, she's working to a plan in there and so far the others haven't seen through her.'

Elizabeth: 'She's lovely, dead sweet. I admired her. She's intelligent, well balanced, and even though she sees people's bad points, she could also always see their good points. I think she's genuine. She wants to win: quite a lot of us were in there to have a laugh and enjoy the experience, but she's one of those who definitely wants to win. She's a dark horse. She's very sexy, and I think she quite fancies Amma.'

Bubble: 'I can't believe he's got so much support. I found him so irritating, his voice drove me mad. He thinks he's so funny and keeps telling everyone he's funny, but he's not. He's very calculating – he's voting tactically. If he thinks others are going to nominate someone, he'll add his vote. He's got a real temper, then he tries to pass it off that he was joking. He didn't know how to talk to me: it's not that he's racist, it's just that he's not sure what he can say and what he can't.'

Dean: 'He only makes an effort with some people, when he chooses to. He never made the effort to talk to me, and he judged me by things other people told him. He thinks he's a father figure, and some of the others treat him like that, asking for his permission to do things like opening a bottle of cider. He's boring. Every time he played his guitar, Brian and I would be yawning behind him. And he could walk away and play whenever he wanted to, but if one of the rest of us wanted time on our own, he'd say we were not being good housemates. He has a special herbal mixture he got made up before he went in, and he told us it is to suppress his sex drive.'

Paul: 'He's lovely, sweet, placid, such a nice guy. I once shouted at him because he was supposed to be helping me cook and he wasn't bothering, but he just said "Chill, Narinder". Some of the others would have over-reacted and we'd have ended up fighting. But Paul knew it was just me getting het up, and didn't worry about it. He's the cushion of the house – if you feel like crying, Paul will be there for you. And he doesn't take sides: even though he loves Helen to bits, when we had our big bust up he was one of the few who was there to support me afterwards. I don't mind losing to him, because I couldn't have been up against a better person. He's boring – but then, so are Dean, Elizabeth and Stuart, and at least Paul is nice with it.'

Josh: 'He said he was going to bring fun into the house, to spice things up. And what did he bring? Backgammon. That is such a boring game. He's not enjoying his time in there: he rolls his eyes and sighs a lot, then buries himself in a book or a game. Those are not his kind of people in there – his friends are much wilder. I was shocked to be nominated by him, because I really stood up for him when Brian was nasty to him. Josh looks great, but that's all there is to it.'

Narinder on life in the house

'It was hard. I was told before I went in by the production team that there would be high points and low points, but there were far more low points than high points. The worst time for me was the night of the big rows, when Brian rowed with Josh, and Stuart rowed with Amma. The discussions afterwards went on until about 5 a.m., and I was feeling exhausted and I really wanted to walk out.

'I missed good food and good wine. After our terrible starving week, when we had so little money for shopping, we had enough food, but it was boring food. Josh never experienced the starving week, so he was treating the food as if we had limitless supplies. He also wasn't as dedicated to the tasks as we were, which is why we failed the dance test and nearly failed the memory test. Those of us who had starved took the tasks very seriously.

'I didn't mind sharing a bedroom, although Amma was a nuisance when she came to bed so late and faffed around making a noise. The girls' bedroom was really good when Brian moved in.

'I missed Jatinder, my husband, and all my friends and family, people who just accept me for what I am. The people in there were a disappointment to me, they are just not the kind of people I like to hang out with. I thought they'd be more active, more up for fun. They were all too scared to put a foot wrong. They were trying to pretend it was *The Waltons*, not the *Big Brother* experience.

'There was tactical voting going on, and I did complain about it in the Diary Room. But it is very hard to prove. You don't have to actually say anything in words, you can do it with facial expressions. Brian and I were doing it, and I know the others were.

'When I was very low, I took myself off to the bedroom and read a card Jat wrote for me before I went in, which said: "Narinder, you've reached for the stars and now you hold them in your hand. I was dumbfounded by you, and so will everybody else be. See you in nine weeks." I also took in a letter a friend sent to me a couple of years ago, which reads: "Narinder, I suspect you are losing your dreams. Please keep a hold of them, because you will become a star." I read them both over and over again, to remind myself what I was doing there. I also read my horoscope in one of the magazines I took in. It said that I was in a phase of transition from being a nobody to becoming a somebody, which cheered me up.

'Coming out of the house was the biggest moment of my life. I've never known anything like it. I have no regrets at all about doing it. *Big Brother* was an amazing experience.'

Narinder on Narinder

For Narinder, her stay in the *Big Brother* house was her final bid for show-business stardom. She reckons she has made more than 600 applications for acting or presenting jobs, and she's hoping *Big Brother* will give her the break she has always wanted.

From the age of twelve, she has been a show-business wannabe, desperate to perform in public. But she would have passed up her big chance if her family had not been supportive.

'Jat was behind me from the word go, he always has been,' she says. 'But I didn't tell my mum and dad and my brothers and sister until a couple of

WEEK FOUR FACT FILE

Main task: Each housemate has a style of music to which they must dance for one minute whenever they are called. They have twenty seconds to get to the podium. Occasionally, when the conga is called, they all have to get there in thirty seconds. Fail, after Josh did not get to the podium in time for a conga.

PASS ☐ **FAIL** ☒

Mini-task: To make hats for each other.

PASS ☑ **FAIL** ☐

Treats: A jug of Pimm's, with strawberries and cream, for passing the hat task.

Bets are on!
To win: Brian is favourite, at 5/4, followed by Bubble at 11/4, with Dean and Elizabeth not far behind.
To walk: Amma is favourite for the next eviction, at 4/7, followed by Paul at 4/1.
Evictee's tip: Narinder says Brian will win. If it is not him then it will be Paul. She believes the next housemate to leave will be Amma.

weeks before I went in to the house. If they had said no, I wouldn't have done it. But they were amazingly supportive. I don't think my mum had a clue what it was about, but the others did. My sister had already guessed, because I kept going to London for auditions and I was buying new clothes. I hope they're proud of me.'

Narinder believes her feisty personality is the result of having to develop a thick skin when she was at school, when she and her cousin were the only Asians in the school, and some of the other pupils were, she believes, deeply racist.

'It made me tough, and I'm really grateful for that. It was "Paki this" and "Paki that", and one boy told me I'd be pretty if I was white. You either go under to that sort of stuff, or it makes you stronger – and I'm very strong. I think that some of the others in the house didn't know how to handle a strong woman.'

When she left her home in Newcastle for university in Derby, Narinder was determined to enjoy three years of fun and freedom. But on the third day she met Jatinder, her husband. 'So I got the fun but not the freedom,' she says. He is the only man she has ever slept with, and although over seven years of marriage they have had their ups and downs – even separating at one point – now they are very happy together.

'If I hadn't been accepted for *Big Brother*, I would have settled for a normal life and had a family. But now, although I still want to have children, I'm going to put it on hold for a while to see if I can make a career in television.'

WEEK FIVE

'I'm coming home, baby!'
Bubble

'Fewer people means less washing up,' Dean remarks on Saturday morning, as he and Josh clean up the debris from the eviction-night dinner. Helen joins them and comments that it is really weird sleeping in a bedroom with only two other girls.

Back in bed, Josh confides in Brian. He says he is having a bad day, because it has hit him how much he is missing his friends and the freedom to go out in London.

At midday, the housemates are given details of their next task. Big Brother wants them to break a world record and get their names into the *Guinness Book of Records*. They will have until Wednesday to practise the four potential records Big Brother has selected for them: eating three cream crackers in less than 1 minute 22.36 seconds; building a tower of sugar cubes more than 1.02 metres tall; blowing a bubble-gum bubble bigger than 58.4mm; and picking up and eating more than 169 sweetcorn kernels in one minute using a toothpick.

The housemates decide to wager the minimum of ten per cent of their food budget because, as Dean says, 'The pressure is off and we can have a laugh.' A supply of sugar cubes is delivered for the first part of the task.

Building the sugar-cube tower proves to be harder than the group first anticipated. Brian is excused from taking part, because he has sweaty hands and the others are afraid the sugar will melt in his hot grasp. Despite all the best male brains in the house being applied to the project, it takes Amma to come up with the engineering flair required: she tells them to build one layer straight and the next at an angle, to strengthen the structure. From now, the construction is known as Amma Tower.

Bubble goes to the Diary Room in the early evening to report on his leg, and tells Big Brother that the day has been 'rubbish'.

'I don't like Saturdays, because I want to be at home with my little girl,' he says, but refuses to elaborate. He does what Bubble usually does when he's feeling stressed: he goes to bed, even though it's only 7.30 p.m.

When the boys settle in bed, Helen and Amma go into their room to chat with them. Josh unwittingly exposes himself to Helen, who approvingly remarks, 'Nice lunchbox, Josh', and insists on Amma having an eye-full too.

Late at night in Amma's double bed, Amma and Helen discuss the other housemates until they are individually called to the Diary Room and ticked off for talking about nominations. One of her fellow contestants is on Helen's mind – in her sleep she calls out 'Hey, Paul'. It is the second time in recent nights that she has mentioned his name. She and Paul are still spending hours in each other's company. Only that day Brian has remarked on their friendship, saying, 'Supposing we meet in a year's time and you and Helen are engaged.'

Sunday morning is shopping-list time, and Josh, Bubble and Elizabeth take charge of spending the £56.70. Paul wanders around the house looking at himself in the mirrors – he looks in seven, in total – before joining the others sunbathing.

The sweetcorn arrives, and Bubble, at his first attempt, sets an unofficial world record. It doesn't count: the record attempts have to be made with an independent adjudicator watching. Following his example, both Josh and Liz manage to get above the target total.

In the garden the conversation takes a nosedive when Helen reveals that she caught sight of Brian's willy that morning.

'You know when you come out of the shower and it's all wrinkled? She's seen that' says Brian.

'It was like a wrinkled little shrimp,' says Helen.

Helen, Paul and Brian then enjoy a brief but, for Helen, enlightening conversation about the size of the average boy's willy, which he and Paul agree is about six- to six-and-a-half inches long. This is followed by a general discussion about going to Dean's wedding, an event the housemates have focussed on for a post-house reunion. Dean is undecided about having Brian at his stag night, unsure what his mates would make of his camp friend. 'Oooh, can you imagine me, I'd get so drunk and call you Treasure,' taunts Brian.

It's the hottest day of the year so far, and the contestants are all desperate to find a way of cooling down. Liz suggests an apple-bobbing competition, but they have no apples, and potatoes (her next suggestion), do not float. In the end, they have an orange-bobbing competition which dissolves into a water fight, with Bubble taking on the rest of the housemates.

In a discussion about what they are to eat, Helen asks 'Is there chicken in chickpeas?'

In the early evening, Bubble breaks the sweetcorn record again, leading to great confidence within the group about Wednesday's task.

Paul walks into the bathroom and catches sight of Helen topless. He claims he didn't do it on purpose, but Amma says that it is the third time it has happened. Helen asks him what he saw, and he tells her that he saw her breasts in the mirror and that they looked good. He adds that he likes her trousers, and she offers to de-fluff his shirt. Later, when he jokingly teases her about having saggy breasts, she asks him whether it was like seeing his sister naked. He replies that it wasn't like that at all.

Conversation in the garden is desultory, with the housemates sleeping, reading and playing backgammon. Paul and Helen talk about what would have happened if Penny had remained in the house. Paul says he would have put a stop to her flirting with him as she wasn't his type. When Helen says none of the girls in the house are his type, he looks at her and says some of them are.

Brian goes to the Diary Room, where he opens up about missing his mate Narinder. 'I'm lucky because I get on with everybody, but I was closer to her, so it seems a bit weird not having her around. I'm starting to read books, which isn't a good sign for me.' He adds that he is getting on surprisingly well with Josh, but doesn't really get on with Paul. Brian then admits that he didn't expect the *Big Brother* experience to be as hard as it is.

'I am shocked that I am still here halfway through. It has changed me. I don't think I will ever care what people think about me now. I think I have gained confidence.'

He also talks about the worries he has for his family. 'I felt bad telling my mum I was gay just before I came in here. I have never seen her as her gay son. Hopefully it will be fine. I hope my parents will realize that I have been chosen for being me, I just happen to be gay, and I hope my parents will accept that. I really think I will be up for nomination, and I will want to go. I want to meet my friends and do normal things.'

After dinner, the group talk about horror films, which terrify Brian. He

WHAT THE EXPERTS SAY

HELEN

'Helen and Paul are spending increasing amounts of time together. Their conversational topics and their bodily posture are both very intimate. But there are conflicting messages being sent out, and it all stems from Helen. On the one hand, she talks about Big G as her boyfriend. On the other hand, she asks Paul how his mother would feel if he took her home. Helen has a dilemma. She needs to feel Big G still wants her, and in order to do that she has to view herself as attractive. Her own self-worth is very bound up with how others respond to her as an attractive woman.

'When Josh was asked who he would sleep with, and he chose Amma, Helen's disappointment was written all over her face. But lately her whole body has been revealing her inner emotional state. When Paul says that if he took her home it would not be as his girlfriend, she's quite literally deflated by his response. Then, as Brian returns to a subject matter that allows her to think of herself as a sexually attractive person, we see her perk up again.

'Helen is welcoming anything other than outright rejection. By asking Paul to fetch her an apple, she is going even further. It forces a response from him. She's prepared to risk explicit rejection in her quest for the endorsement she craves.'

Professor Geoffrey Beattie, Psychologist

tells the others how, when he went to see *The Exorcist*, he tried to leave the cinema and the usher told him to act his age.

By the end of the evening, Josh has reverted to the theme of how he is not being himself in the house. He confesses that there are two people he would like to tell to 'fuck off', but he can't because it would create tension.

'It's just the noise. It's like, why don't you shut up for five minutes? I just wanted to be really me and I don't think I am,' he grumbles. He also complains about being sexually frustrated, and the other boys join in, discussing the difficulty of masturbating in the house.

'I give up as soon as I'm under the duvet and I hear the camera move. It ruins the mood.' Dean adds.

Cabin fever seems to have set in, with even Dean and Amma agreeing that if the boredom level gets much worse they will both consider walking out.

Bubble has made a fruit upside-down cake, which does not work out very successfully, but is still eaten enthusiastically. He takes some into the girls' room for Helen, but finds her upset. He assumes she's missing her boyfriend, but it transpires she's worried that she has said something to offend Josh. Bubble demonstrates his flair for comforting and calming distressed women – he was very good with Penny, and he now says exactly the right things to make Helen feel better.

The boys do not sleep well, because of the heat in their room, and they wake up with headaches and bad tempers. Paul says he is struggling to breathe, Dean suggests Big Brother take the £70,000 prize money and use it to install a ventilation system, and Bubble has a rant: 'It's too hot in the bedroom, the cola is shit, there's not enough tobacco .... '

The next part of the task arrives – a supply of bubble gum. They all practise blowing bubbles, and Brian (to his disgust and dismay) is clearly the best at it, so he's elected to go for the challenge on Wednesday.

Liz demonstrates what a great actress she is when she, Bubble and Josh play a practical joke on Paul, Helen and Brian. Dean and Amma know what's going on, and play along. Liz pretends to hypnotize Bubble and Josh, and she does it very convincingly. She tells them that when they come round, whenever they hear the word 'lush' Bubble will be very, very nice to Brian, and Josh 'will be afraid of everything. Like Brian, you will see demons in the mirrors and be terrified of the chickens'.

Bubble and Josh both perform their parts very convincingly, Bubble gently rubbing suntan cream into Brian and Josh simulating real fear of the mirrors and chickens. Poor Helen is very worried, and keeps telling Dean that she doesn't like it. They keep the deception going for two and a half hours, and Paul, Helen and Brian are convinced they have seen a true hypnotism. As Dean puts it, they have not just fallen for it 'hook, line and sinker, but rod and angler's arm – all that's left is a little seat on the river bank'.

Paul is teased by the others that he has been under Elizabeth's spell too and has told Helen that he loves her. Paul knows perfectly well that this is not true, but follows Helen into the girls' bedroom and, pretending to be hypnotized, tells her, 'I really fancy the pants off you, Helen.' He tries to climb on top of her, but Helen wriggles free and runs squealing out of the room, with Paul in hot pursuit shouting 'I love you'. It is all done in fun, but Helen makes it clear that his feelings are not reciprocated. She tells the others in the garden: 'He was all over me like a rash.'

Brian goes to the Diary Room under the misapprehension that Big Brother has ordered the housemates to stop hypnotizing each other (Josh has told him this). When he hears from Big Brother that there is no ban on hypnotism, he goes back to the others and says he is beginning to question his sanity.

At this point, Bubble suggests that Dean should call in all the others from the garden and reveal the truth about the spoof hypnotism. The three dupes shriek and yell, with Brian branding all his housemates 'bastards' and Helen tearing around after Amma, good-humouredly calling her a 'bloody bitch'. Paul is very impressed by the hoaxers, and describes it as 'the ultimate wind-up'.

As usual on Mondays, tension is running high as it is nominations day. Before they start, Josh is called to the Diary Room to pick up a tape measure to check on the swelling in Bubble's leg. Big Brother asks him how he is getting on.

'Yesterday was a bit of a low day for me. It just got to me – I was a bit irritable, tired, I'd had enough. The team were great, they made me cookies and milk, and I spoke to Liz in depth and Amma, and they gave me some support. The hardest thing for me, coming in late, is not knowing anyone in the depth I'd like to. I don't know when people are joking or when they are serious. I also think a lot of people are tiptoeing too lightly, it's not their true characters coming out. Sometimes I want to boil over and scream at someone, but, hey, they might think I'm a loony.'

After the nominations the housemates are, as usual, left in suspense. Paul has been nominated by everyone apart from Helen. Bubble will be Paul's running mate, having received one more vote than Amma and Brian.

The housemates have an energetic game of French cricket to help relieve nomination stress, and then they all relax in the hot tub. Afterwards, they concentrate on practising for the task, and Dean manages to build a record-breaking sugar-cube tower, which inspires Bubble, Josh and Liz to keep going with the sweetcorn challenge – all of them break the record.

Brian has developed a phobia of the chickens, although that day he tried to confront this by trying to pick one up, he only made it as far as the chicken run. Now he does an impression of them: 'They're like dinosaurs and their heads turn like this.' he says, struggling to swivel his neck around. Bubble tries to persuade him to touch a chicken – after much screaming and hollering, Brian stretches out a hand and gingerly strokes a hen. It doesn't break the spell though, and Brian starts yelling that the chickens have been sent from hell.

Dean is called to the Diary Room and complains about how hard the nominations procedure is, especially as the weeks roll on and there are fewer people to choose from.

'I have a process to deal with it. I think of a bus queue with the people I get on with best at the front, and the people I get on with less well at the back. It was confusing when Josh came in, because the natural thing was to put him at the back, but he has queue jumped.'

WHO NOMINATES WHO

Amma nominates Paul and Dean
Brian nominates Paul and Amma
Bubble nominates Paul and Josh
Dean nominates Paul and Helen
Elizabeth nominates Paul and Brian
Helen nominates Bubble and Brian
Josh nominates Paul and Bubble
Paul nominates Amma and Bubble

Nominee	Nominations	Nominated by
Amma	2	Paul, Brian
Brian	2	Helen, Elizabeth
Bubble	3	Paul, Josh, Helen
Dean	1	Amma
Elizabeth	0	
Helen	1	Dean
Josh	1	Bubble
Paul	6	Josh, Elizabeth, Dean, Bubble, Brian, Amma

Week 5 nominees: Paul with six nominations and Bubble with three nominations.

Analysis
Dean's clear run of zero nominations has now been broken with a nomination from Amma. Bubble and Josh have nominated each other as have Amma and Paul. Dean and Elizabeth have nominated Paul for the third week running.

Reasons
Amma on Paul: 'He's a bit over-excitable, a bit annoying.'
Bubble on Josh: 'He's over-domineering, always in the kitchen doing everything, a bit too nice for my liking.'
Elizabeth on Brian: 'This is probably unpopular, but Brian is very much a one-man show, you've got to get involved with his show and I'm just not that kind of person.'

He says life in the house is getting easier, and although he thinks about life outside, it is with less urgency now. He says the only thing that is worrying him is his girlfriend. Because they had to part in such a hurry, he did not have time to say goodbye properly, and he misses her very badly.

Talk in the garden turns mystical when Josh tells the others that before he came into the house he visited a clairvoyant in Portugal. His friends had asked him why he wanted to go into the house, sharing his private life with everyone. The mystic told him 'that it would cause great heartache and I would lose people close to me'. But he says he felt the opportunity was too good to miss.

Bubble then reveals that he went to a clairvoyant in Blackpool, who told Bubble he would only have one child. The clairvoyant also predicted a career move for Bubble which would involve unloading white vans, and that had come true.

Helen is the third housemate to have seen a fortune-teller, three years ago. The clairvoyant claimed to have a vision of Helen in a London television studio, looking sparkly.

Over the meal, Brian resolves to show the housemates his serious side, and announces that he will be serious all day on Thursday. To achieve this, he will assume an alter ego: he will become 'Scott', a gay man both older and harder than Brian. Dean tells him that this means he won't be able to scream, say 'demon', make his squeaky 'Sooty' noise, or sing and the others agree that he hasn't a chance of managing all this for twenty-four hours. (And, when Thursday dawns, he has forgotten all about it.)

Helen is called to the Diary Room, and gives Big Brother a rundown on what she likes and doesn't like about life in the house. The only thing she hates is the nomination procedure. She especially loves the birthday parties. Paul and Amma are the people she gets on with best, and to whom she would turn if she was upset, but she feels she could turn to anyone in the house.

At 1 a.m., the housemates start to drift off to bed, and Dean, Bubble and Paul decide to drag their mattresses out to the garden to escape the oppressive heat. Bubble turns down the chance to sleep in the girls' room. Eventually, the three boys sleep in the lounge.

The most exciting thing to happen on Tuesday morning is the visit from the dentist to check out Brian's bleeding gums. She tells him he has an infection called acute ulcerative gingivitis, and gives him antibiotics, mouthwash, a tiny toothbrush and a mirror to look inside his own mouth. He's thrilled, describing them as 'presents', but is less happy when he is told he must not drink alcohol while taking the tablets.

The final part of the world-record challenge arrives: a large supply of cream crackers. The housemates are all hopeless at the task, coughing and spluttering and complaining of aching jaws as they struggle to eat three of the dry biscuits in record time. The only one who comes close to the record is Josh who, with practice, gets down to ten seconds outside the time limit. Dean patiently carries on perfecting his sugar-cube technique.

Liz is called to the Diary Room and tells Big Brother she's disappointed at how unadventurous the others are when it comes to staking money on the tasks. She says everyone is trying especially hard with this one, lured on by the thrill of setting a world record.

When Big Brother asks her what she is missing, she replies, 'Open fields, open space, going for walks, talking to people I know. Talking freely – there is so much in here that we can't talk about, like the nominations. So, what I miss is freedom of speech and freedom of movement.'

By contrast, when Helen goes in shortly afterwards and is asked the same question about what she misses, the answer is 'Chocolate, crisps, cake!'

The group while away the time waiting for the nomination results sunbathing and chatting. Josh tells a horrified Brian that he masturbated in the boys' room last night, but reassures Brian that he wasn't thinking about him. Dean and Bubble admit they've already done the same, but poor Brian, who says he is gagging for it, protests that, 'I'd feel vulgar. It's different at home, but I'm not going to do it when people at home could be watching me.'

He adds, 'When I get out of here, I'm going to control myself until I meet someone.'

He's not the only one suffering. Paul admits to being aroused when he, Helen and Brian discuss the problems of life without sex.

'I don't like talking sex stuff in here because you just want it so bad,' he says.

Helen, who has already announced that the jaw ache she suffered eating cream crackers reminded her of giving oral sex, now tells Paul to 'think of someone on their knees'. He tells her to 'leave it out' as she's turning him on.

They're distracted by the announcement of the nomination results, which Paul takes with now-familiar aplomb, smiling and hugging the others. Bubble, by his own admission, is 'gutted'. He looks really shocked, and limps into the boys' room for a cigarette. Brian and Dean follow him and console him. Bubble admits it is hard, especially as he is so determined to win. He guesses that even if he survives the public vote this week, he will be nominated again, and again and again, until he is evicted or until the end of the show.

Paul, who also has the threat of eviction hanging over him, takes time out to advise Bubble.

'It's not over yet – I'm the living proof of that. Even if you go, you're not going to lose your life, you're going to get to see everyone you love.'

Amma, who has spent many late nights having cosy chats with Bubble, is called to the Diary Room and says it is 'less of a surprise, more of a disappointment' to find Bubble nominated.

'For the first time I was genuinely upset when they read out the nominations. I really do hope Bubble doesn't go, because of the blokes in here he's one of two I get on with.'

Discussion on the patio takes a serious turn in the afternoon, with a debate about racism followed by one on the state of the environment, in which Greenpeace member Dean is irritated by Bubble's indifferent attitude. They quickly get back to a topic nearer to their own hearts: the eviction vote. Dean presciently tells Bubble that the *Sun* newspaper will be backing him. (It is.)

The housemates have to choose who is going to enter the world-record challenges, and it's an all-boy team: Dean will tackle the sugar cubes, Brian the bubble-blowing, Bubble the sweetcorn, and Josh the cream crackers.

In the Diary Room, Bubble tells Big Brother how he feels about being up for the public vote:

'People say you're a winner to get here, to get this far. It's nice, they're trying to make you feel better. But when your name comes up, you can't help but feel gutted. Half of me is surprised I got this far, because I'm one of those people you like or you don't. But the other half of me thought that once I got past the first three weeks there was a good chance of me going a lot further. But it was not to be. It's not as if anyone's died. I've come into a game show. You take it on the chin, pick your head up and get on with it.'

To let off steam, the housemates have an energetic game of volleyball, and Amma causes a stir with both Bubble and Liz when her left nipple keeps popping out of her low-cut top. Liz later describes it as 'the funniest moment in the house'. She and Amma compare boobs in the mirror, working out a strategy of using them to make sure they distract and beat the other volleyball team.

Paul, who has disguised any upset he is feeling about nomination from the others, is called to the Diary Room, pausing to change his top and do his hair before going in. He confesses that he is rather shaken to find himself up for the vote a third time, although not surprised.

'I've already won in my eyes. I'm chuffed with myself, I think I've done alright. There's no way I realistically thought I would win it. It makes the week go faster, and Friday slower. You enjoy it more, knowing it could be your last few days here. I wouldn't change anything I've done. I don't think I've done anything wrong or offended anyone. I'm so chuffed I've had this experience, I'll treasure it forever. It will be a landmark in my life.'

At midnight, they all sing Happy Birthday to Liz, who is twenty-seven. Brian gives her a pretty pink shawl that Narinder left for her. Bubble, to everyone's astonishment, gives her one of his hats, and she is visibly moved by this huge gesture. Helen gives her a T-shirt. Liz later tells Dean that she is 'overwhelmed by their kindness', but also feels a bit guilty, because the same people have irritated her at times.

Elizabeth stays awake until 3 a.m., talking to Dean, Bubble and Amma. Bubble opens up to them about the extent of his past drug taking.

Late into the night, while everyone else is asleep, Bubble (with his night-owl accomplice Amma) writes a poem for Liz in pebbles. Big Brother has refused to give him a pen and paper, but has allowed him to use the pebbles, as he is not attempting to communicate with the outside world.

Appropriately, Liz is the first up, and is very moved to see the message, which took Bubble most of the night to finish. It reads:

To Betty Boo, our marathon queen
Have caution, guys, do you know what I mean?
Lots of long words and a heart of gold
We doubt you'll forget being twenty-seven years old.
Lots a luv
The BBII

'That is so gorgeous,' Liz exclaims. 'Wow, that's so nice.' When Dean gets up he tells Liz that it was all Bubble's handiwork, and they talk about what a great guy he is. Liz hugs Bubble when he surfaces, but he plays down his effort.

Following house tradition, Liz is offered a choice of present from Big Brother. She can have a running machine in the house for a week, or a pampering party, complete with chocolates, champagne and loads of beauty products. Brian is disgusted that she hasn't been asked to hand over a precious possession (he is still smarting from having to give up Mr Cow and Mr Bear). After discussion with the others, Liz chooses the party. The running machine, they decide, would only be used by Dean and Josh anyway.

At half past twelve, Big Brother announces that they have one hour to go before the world-record challenge. Bubble is back in bed, and is so deeply asleep that neither Josh nor Brian can rouse him. Eventually Liz coaxes him awake. He refuses food, on the grounds that he will do the sweetcorn challenge better if he is hungry. Josh goes first with the cream crackers, but takes more than two minutes. They all know they are not on target for a record there, as he was competing against a time of 1 minute 22 seconds. Then Brian manages to blow a 10-cm bubble, but as the world record is 58.4 cm, he is even further out of record range.

Dean is given three hours to do the sugar-cube challenge, and sets to work steadily and calmly. The others leave him to get on with it. From time to time he has to rebuke them: Helen and Brian are ordered outside for noisily waltzing up and down around him. Dean breaks the record with ease, making a tower that is 1 metre 20.1 cm high, more than 18 cm higher than the existing world record. He even has a second go, as there is plenty of time left over, and manages an even taller tower, which collapses before it can be measured.

The final task falls to Bubble, the sweetcorn-eating king. High hopes are riding on him, as he has done so well in practice. But he suffers from nerves and blows the first attempt, much to his own annoyance. The second is better, and the third better still, but not good enough for a world record – he misses

WHAT THE EXPERTS SAY

DEAN

'Dean's leadership in the world-record breaking task is interesting. It could be decisive. It tells how he's come to terms with a dilemma that has been imposed on him. He has stated on a number of occasions that he doesn't want to be a leader. However, regardless of how he feels, the group has consistently shown they want him to be leader, and have treated him as such. The other housemates use Dean as a source of comfort and seek his reassurance. But if Dean doesn't want to be leader, why is the group forcing him to be?

'All groups need leaders to give a sense of direction and identity, and Dean has been selected for a number of reasons. In the Big Brother house, there are several qualities that are important in a leader. The notable ones in Dean are his good negotiating skills, his age, his intelligence, and his ability to remain calm in volatile situations. But being comforting is not the only thing that comes with a leadership job. At times the leader has to be an authority figure who tells people what to do and when to do it in no uncertain terms. Dean had to do this during the first-aid task.

'Therein lies the dilemma. This aspect of the job can be hugely unpopular, to seem to behave out of character and be interpreted by others as being ratty. Leadership is a high-risk role in the Big Brother house. Remember, both Penny and Stuart, who attempted to be leaders, have been voted out. How long can Dean survive with the potentially poisoned chalice of leadership? He's spending more and more time alone. Could this be his way of protecting himself?'

Dr Sandra Scott, Psychiatrist

out by only three kernels. But when, at half past ten in the evening, Big Brother announces the results, which have been independently adjudicated by Della Howes from Guinness World Records, he is thrilled to find that although he missed a world title, he is now the official UK champion for sweetcorn eating.

'Eating sweetcorn. That is so stupid, but it's made my day,' he says.

The others are all thrilled by Dean's achievement, although he takes his success in his usual laconic style. He admits his nieces and nephews will be pleased, and wonders whether being a world-record holder means he will be invited on to the Birmingham City pitch for the first game of the season.

There's a general feeling of regret that the group did not wager more shopping money on the task. They will have £61.60 to spend, a massive £5.60 is all they've earnt for their efforts.

In the Diary Room, Amma admits to Big Brother that she is 'flabbergasted, shocked and amazed' to find herself still in the house, as they are now past the halfway stage.

'I always believed myself to be a very chilled, tolerant individual, and then I came in here. Now I realize that in some areas of my life I am a control freak. Sometimes I resent the fact that I have to ask permission to do the silliest things, like writing a poem in the garden. You have to remind yourself that it is for a maximum of nine weeks, that it's not real, you're not really being told what to do, you've agreed. I am free to do what I want, and I choose to play the game.'

The party arrives, with soft towelling robes for every housemate and lashings of beauty treatments that have Helen squealing with delight. Dean, Bubble and Paul are a little bit concerned that it will become her party, not Liz's. Josh and Brian are up for all of it, and are rummaging among the creams and potions as enthusiastically as the girls.

The housemates are all so excited that they forget to prepare a meal. Dean has peeled lots of potatoes, which they mash and eat with leftover lasagne, their faces covered with different-coloured face masks. Despite Dean's worry that the pampering party isn't right for Liz because she's not a girlie girl, she gets into it and enjoys everything on offer, including a sensual neck and shoulder massage from Josh, which causes her to shout, 'I don't believe Josh is gay.' At the same time, Helen threatens to try to turn Brian on but, realizing she will have no luck there, announces that she finds Dean sexy in his sunglasses.

Some of the boys are initially reluctant to get involved in all the pampering. In typical laddish fashion, Paul and Josh pull up the hoods of their dressing gowns and pretend they are Jedi, having a sword fight with imaginary light sabres in the garden. Josh and Brian then spend a giddy five minutes chasing each other around, with Josh pulling Brian's dressing gown up to reveal him wearing nothing underneath, and Brian pulling Josh's tiny shorts down. Bubble is determined that he is not going to participate in the preening, painting, waxing and massaging that is going on all around him, but after he hears the news that he has won the UK sweetcorn record, he throws away his inhibitions and slaps fake tan all over his body. He doesn't read the instructions, and is horrified to learn that it doesn't wash off straightaway. He turns to Josh for help, 'I haven't asked anything of you in two weeks, will you fill in the bits I've missed?' When Bubble is completely covered, he's pleased with the result, describing himself as a 'new-age bronzing man'. He even agrees to a face mask and then paints Brian's nails.

The only housemate not drawn into the pampering frenzy is Dean, but he has his own contribution to make to the evening's fun – he has written a song for Elizabeth, which he performs to general acclaim. Liz makes him promise he will record it for her when they leave the house. The lyrics are:

Think today of the fells, not so far away
That when you shall be under blue skies
You'll fly by,

Riding bare, fingers laced through your horse's hair
Riding wild and free under blue skies
Fly by,

Betty, babe, we'd like to wish you Happy Birthday
Think of us under blue skies
Blue skies.

Despite having been nominated for eviction, Bubble tells the others that this is the best day he has spent in the house. And Paul, a veteran of the eviction vote, agrees with him.

The hot-water supply has been switched on for the evening as part of the birthday treat. At midnight, the other girls lead Liz, her eyes covered, into the bathroom, where the bath has been filled and around it Josh has written the initials EW and the number twenty-seven in candles. Within seconds, the three girls have dropped their dressing gowns and are bathing together, their legs intermingling in the foam. Brian and Josh wander in and out, to the exasperation of the other boys, who are amazed at what Brian in particular can get away with simply because he is gay.

Hearing this, the girls decide to show there is no favouritism, and call for Paul to join them, telling him that there are three naked women who want to play with him. He takes them tea and a cigarette for Amma, and describes himself as 'one of the luckiest blokes in Britain'. Liz tries to persuade him to join them in the tub, but he's not feeling that lucky.

When the girls emerge from the bath she and Liz have a kiss and cuddle on the sofa. They are immediately accused of being 'squiffy' by the others. Seconds later, Liz suddenly shouts, 'I don't want to be a fuck slave!' She covers her face with her hands while the others stare at her in stunned silence. Then she shouts again: 'I want to be a fuck master!'

Amma then asks, 'If I was to announce that I am, in fact, bisexual, would that bother you, having a bath with me?'

'Even if you said you were a lesbian it would not bother me,' Liz replies, her voice slurring. 'Even if you fancied me or didn't fancy me I wouldn't want to have nothing to do with you.'

Amma smiles contentedly and announces to the whole group, 'I quite happily sit here in this house, because I don't feel anything for any of you.'

Liz says, 'If it wasn't for the cameras and society, I would sit here naked with anyone.'

Amma agrees that that could be misinterpreted. 'It's the implications of it, even if it means nothing,' she explains.

The erotic conversation goes no further, as a discussion about discrimination takes over. At four o'clock in the morning, the housemates are all still up talking. Brian plunges into the hot tub naked, and Helen and Dean both crash out together and sleep under a blanket on the patio. Eventually Paul and Brian slope off to bed, but the others stay up singing hymns, school songs and a wide medley of pop songs until five in the morning, when all except Amma and Elizabeth retreat to their beds. The two girls carry on singing, and then start playing with the cosmetics again, which brings Josh, Brian and Bubble out of bed to join them. It is seven o'clock in the morning before they all finally settle down to sleep.

The contestants are so out of it that rousing them for the morning routine of changing the microphone batteries is difficult: the disembodied voice of Big Brother calls for someone to go to the Diary Room five times before Josh sleepily walks in. He, Helen and Liz manage to stagger temporarily out of bed to have hot showers before the water goes off.

It is nearly midday before there is any sign of life in the house again, with Amma and Liz first up. They make the most of the remaining beauty products and then start to clean up the mess from the party. Liz soon discovers that false nails look nice but are not very practical.

The boys find getting up hard to do. Dean says he feels as though he has traded his skull in for one a size smaller. Bubble's amazing tan surprises everyone – Liz nicknames him 'Tango man'. The day is spent clearing up, complaining about hangovers, and sleeping. Everyone, including Paul, is assuming that he will be evicted. In the Diary Room, he says that he has had a good time in the house, but wishes he could have been sharing it with his friends.

Dean goes to the Diary Room and complains of feeling his age after all the merry making last night, but says he is enjoying the house and has made some really good friends.

'All the people I have met have been really interesting, and I've made some real friends, some people I will definitely stay in touch with. It is priceless – how else would you ever meet people from different walks of life? I thought I might make only superficial acquaintances, and I was prepared to get through the whole thing as if it was a training camp. But although there are things, like missing my girlfriend, it's been a journey of discovery and I have enjoyed it more than I thought.'

Bubble is also called to the Diary Room. He says he is in very good spirits, and delighted to be a UK record holder.

'The thing that got me was the nerves, I've never suffered from them in my life. But I did a better showing than I thought, and when I get out I'm going to beat the world record.' He says he has had some great moments in the house, and runs through some of the highlights. But he adds that the whole experience has surprised him:

'You think you know what you are getting into, you think you can handle it, but it's a different ball game when you get here. The intensity, the ups and downs, the fake environment. If you get involved in a confrontation in here, it's like World War Three.'

After dinner, during a discussion about fighting, Paul, Bubble, Dean and Amma all reveal that they have exchanged blows at some time in their adult lives. Amma provokes some startled looks from the housemates when she says that, if her row with Stuart had continued, she would have picked up a big stone and hit him with it.

Brian is still plagued by bleeding gums and the antibiotics he is taking are making him feel sick every morning. He decides that he may be pregnant, and accuses Bubble of being the father.

Despite the sleep they lost last night, it is 2 a.m. when most of the group finally retreat to bed. Bubble, Liz and Brian stay up talking. At 4 a.m., Bubble tells the others that he is thinking of scaling the wall, rather than wait for tomorrow's eviction. He goes to the Diary Room to ask Big Brother about it, and is told not to do it. But afterwards he takes a sweater and a hat and goes to the den in the garden to sleep, so that when Brian wakes up he will think Bubble really has escaped. Bubble shakes Brian's hand in a final goodbye, and bets him a hundred pounds that he'll be gone in the morning. Just to be on the safe side, Big Brother steps up security around the building.

Friday starts slowly, with most of the housemates surfacing around lunch time. Amma is becoming increasingly irritable. Her tobacco has disappeared, and with the prospect of no more tobacco until the shopping is delivered on Monday, she's growing ever more desperate.

After the weekly spring clean in readiness for eviction night, Paul and Helen discuss the questions he will be asked when he leaves the house (they are all assuming he will be going this evening). He says he is worried that his breath smells of garlic, which won't be nice for Davina. He reckons he will be asked about his relationship with Helen, and she tells him to put the record straight. He teases her that he is going to tell Davina to buy a hat for the wedding.

Brian goes to the Diary Room to tell Big Brother he is feeling 'weird'.

'I'm having a really bad day. For the first time, I really want to go. Me and Paul get on OK because we're living here together, but if he goes I wouldn't feel as bad as if Bubble were to go.'

He says Narinder's departure has forced him to talk more to others in the group, which has been good for him. But it is hard to constantly be the joker – if he sits quietly, reading, people ask him what's wrong.

When the time for the announcement of the vote comes, the house is very subdued. Even the cheer when Davina's voice comes through is muted. Then the news comes, and it's a real bombshell for all of them: Bubble is leaving. Everyone looks stunned, none more so than Bubble himself, who pushes his lucky hat to the back of his head and shouts, 'I'm coming home, baby.' The others hug him, and then he wanders through to the boys' room on his own to pack. Liz follows him, and he breaks down.

'I've let my little girl down,' he cries. 'I only came in to win the money for her, all for her.'

Elizabeth hugs him and strokes his arm, reassuring him that his exposure in the *Big Brother* house will open up money-making opportunities for him, like being a television sports commentator. She bets him fifty pounds that he'll make more than the £70,000, and even offers to sell the hat he gave her. Bubble regains some of his normal ebullience and quips, 'It must be worth at least a tenner.'

Amma, too, is reduced to tears and Brian, who is losing yet another friend, looks stunned. For Paul, too, there is little celebration. He's as shocked as anyone.

'I'm well chuffed, but I was totally planning stuff and wanting to see people,' he says.

As well as packing, Bubble finds time to go to the Diary Room to talk to Big Brother.

WHAT THE EXPERTS SAY

BRIAN AFTER NARINDER'S EVICTION

'You might think that Brian is all alone now that Narinder has left. But in fact he was the very centre of a triangle of housemates – Narinder, Bubble and Josh – all of whom quite literally were fighting for his attention.

'Play fights have been a feature of the house from the very first week, but the day before Narinder's eviction they rose to a crescendo as she, Bubble and Josh all competed for Brian's attention. Play fights are a juvenile way of establishing and reinforcing social bonds. The way that people play fight provides important clues to the nature of their friendships.

'Bubble initiates more than eighty per cent of these fights with Brian. Bubble pursues Brian, roughs him up and shakes him, just like an animal would shake it's prey. Bubble continues until there is submission and he can claim victory. These fights are laddish and aggressive.

'Josh also initiates most of his play fights with Brian. In the early stages, they were exploratory. For example, most of his punches were cautious and testing. He chased Brian without quite managing to catch him. As Josh and Brian get to know each other better, the nature of their rough and tumbles changes. Like Bubble, Josh pins Brian down, but instead of shaking him, he tickles him. This is sensual, both of them are involved, both are amused and neither feels threatened.'

'We have also seen Brian beginning to get to grips with Helen. Could he be looking for a substitute Narinder? Survival in the *Big Brother* house is all about alliances, and it will be interesting to see who Brian tackles next.'

Dr Peter Collett, Experimental Psychologist

'I'm gutted,' he says. 'I prepared myself for it, but to be truly honest I didn't think I would go. But then obviously people see different things on the outside.'

Before he leaves, he pays warm tributes to his housemates, describing Helen as 'fantastic, lovely, I've never had a bad thought about you' and Elizabeth as 'a diamond'. It is for Brian that he reserves his highest praise:

'Brian, you are the funniest man I have ever met. You've made this a lot more bearable. I have been locked up in this house away from my family, my friends and my little girl, and you have made it easier for me.'

Tears spring to Brian's eyes. 'That is so sweet. Thank you,' he says.

After hugging everyone, Bubble leaves through the arch of arms. The housemates are still numb – there isn't any of the excitement and frenzied dancing that usually accompanies an eviction. They all have a big hug, and chant 'And then there were seven.'

When they go through to the boys' room, both Brian and Dean discover that Bubble has left them presents: a hat each. It makes Brian want to cry again. But the housemates do eventually get into the burst of music that is flooding the house – this is their one night of sounds from outside – and Helen causes eyes to pop by kicking her leg high above her head and then jumping in the air and landing in the splits.

Sitting in the garden, Dean, Liz and Brian despair about the public's voting. They agree that if Paul had gone it would not have affected the house much, whereas Bubble's loss will be keenly felt. Paul joins them, and, perhaps sensing the general feeling that he should have been evicted, announces defiantly:

'I don't care. I don't feel rejected by anyone in here. You are all strangers. As long as I have my family, I don't need to worry.'

Dean goes to the Diary Room to ask whether he will get a certificate or some Guinness for breaking the world record. (Outside in the real world, Bubble has already been presented with a framed certificate for his UK sweet-corn-eating record.) Dean tells Big Brother that he will miss Bubble the most:

'I feel a bit weird tonight, because I didn't think Bubble would go. I got on really well with him, he was the only person in here I could talk to about certain things like football. We had similar backgrounds, and I'll miss that. I will miss him more than anyone else.'

Amma is then summoned to the Diary Room to be told off by Big Brother. In her desperation for tobacco, she has been trying to smoke bamboo leaves. She says she is upset by Bubble's departure, but that this has otherwise been the best week in the house. Liz's birthday was the high point, because 'we had alcohol, we didn't argue, it was nice, it was friendly, we had a laugh, there was no negativity in the air'.

After a late supper of sausages (which Brian eats with strawberry jam), Dean plays Oasis and Crowded House songs on his guitar, and although Helen would like something more poppy, she happily belts out 'Wonderwall'.

VOTING

More than a million viewers registered their votes, with fifty-three per cent (534,574) voting for Bubble to be evicted and forty-seven per cent (470,059) for Paul. Of all the votes, sixty-one per cent were registered by phone, and the other thirty-nine per cent using interactive digital TV.

Viewing figures for the week were up to an average of 4.6 million, a twenty-four per cent share of the viewing public. An average of 378,000 people were watching the late-night live transmissions from the house on E4.

The website remains the biggest entertainment site in the UK, with users spending an average of 18.17 minutes connected to it. There have so far been eleven million downloads of the live video streaming on the net.

BT Cellnet has so far sent out 1,500,000 text messages to *Big Brother* fans across all mobile phone networks.

Afterwards, Dean improvizes his own music and makes up lyrics, including one very prophetic line: 'And he opened the box and inside was a small puppy.'

Josh and Liz talk about the impact the loss of Bubble will have on Brian. Liz, who nominated Brian, says he needs to be part of a duo, and he's lost Penny, Narinder and now Bubble. When everyone except Amma has gone to bed, a semblance of normality returns – the boys wind Brian up, which culminates in a half-hour play fight between him and Josh.

BUBBLE LOOKS BACK: THE EXCLUSIVE INTERVIEW

Bubble on the housemates

Penny: 'Penny struggled in the house. But I really liked her. I'll never forget when we told the stories of things that had changed our lives, and I got really choked up talking about my little girl Bryony. Then Penny told her story and I thought, "Why am I getting upset?" She's had a lot to cope with. Sometimes she tried too hard, she'd be too much in your space. It didn't bother me that she tried to run things, but there were times when I wanted her to step back – I told her that other people wanted to do some of the cooking. Also, when she pinned my photos on the wall, I was upset, but I just took them down and didn't say anything. She was unlucky that I nominated her – it wasn't because I don't like her.'

Stuart: 'If I'd met Stuart in the real world, we wouldn't have given each other the time of day. As soon as I saw him, I knew he came from a different walk of life to mine – he looked as though he was dripping in money, his clothes were all designer labels, and he was a lot older than me. He'd have thought I was a loud-mouth idiot, and I'd have dismissed him as someone who thinks he's the bees knees. Which shows how you shouldn't judge by first impressions, because living together in the house we had to get to know each other, and I really got on with him. He was the only other father in there, so although the others tried to comfort me when I was missing Bryony at the weekends, Stuart was the one who really understood. After he'd gone, I discovered that the girls didn't get on with him so well, but that surprised me.'

Narinder: 'She was my least favourite, but I hope she may be very different out in the real world. There were good points to her – she was bubbly, funny, lively. And Brian really liked her, which made me question my own judgement and try harder with her. But in a group like that you have to live together, and speaking your mind doesn't always help. It may be good to be yourself, but there are times when you have to bite your tongue – I bit mine many times. Narinder needs to engage her brain before opening her mouth, because she said things that were offensive to other people. I found out after she'd left it wasn't just me biting my tongue.'

Amma: 'With everyone else, my relationship was based on laughing and joking, but with Amma it was completely different. We were both late birds, both smokers, so we'd sit up through the night talking on a different, more serious level. I got to know about her brothers, about Ghana, where her family are from. Within the group, she had a habit of talking very quietly, which meant other people talked across her – I thought I'd offended her a couple of times by doing that, but I didn't mean it. I think the fact that she has worked as a stripper will go against her when she is up for eviction, although it shouldn't.'

Dean: 'Dean is fantastic, very funny, a soulmate for me in the house. He's so laid back he's in danger of falling over. We were both missing our ladies, so we had that in common. He'll be through to the final week. And I'm so glad he got the world record – I can say I know a world-record holder. He's one of the three housemates I'm really hoping I will keep in touch with for the rest of my life, a real friend.'

Elizabeth: 'I called her Betty. She really grew on me, and became one of the people I most liked. At first I was wary of her – she used long words, she'd got a degree in politics, I was scared off, reluctant to talk to her. But when she got drunk on Helen's birthday, I could see she was letting go a bit. And the night we talked of our life-changing experiences, she was sitting opposite me and she didn't move a limb but her face said it all – she really felt for me. Her birthday was the most enjoyable day in the house for me, even though I was up for eviction. I put a smile on her face with the little ditty I wrote with pebbles, then we had the world-records task, and then her party. I was upset because I didn't think it was a good choice of party for her. Helen's was tailored for her, my football party was tailored for me, but Betty's seemed more appropriate for Helen. But in the end, we all got into it and had great fun. She's another of the three people I want to keep in touch with.'

Josh: 'I like Josh, but not as much as the others. He's very materialistic – anyone who can spend £2500 on a pair of trousers does not need to win £70,000. He can be domineering, everything had to be done his way. When we had to choose our dance tunes, he insisted on having happy house, which would have suited me and probably a few of the others. The atmosphere changed when he came in. He made Brian unhappy, and I have such a soft spot for Brian. But they've put that behind them now. The more time I spent with Josh, the more I liked him.'

Helen: 'She's lovely, bubbly, very young. She reminds me of the way I was when I was about eighteen, before I'd had a few slaps in the face. Maybe something will go wrong in her life which she will have to cope with, but I hope she keeps the charming personality she has now. She needs a lot of reassurance, which can be irritating. On one occasion I said to her, "Helen, it wasn't your fault, and I am telling you that now, and I'm not spending the next half hour telling you over and over." She's very funny, naturally, without trying.'

Paul: 'I never disliked Paul, but I never really liked him. It's hard to put it into words. He said what he thought people wanted to hear, not what he felt. He was a reasonable guy, but not someone who would ever stimulate me in conversation. And he always had another story to top anything you told him. I suppose we should have had a lot in common – we were the two young, single, straight guys. He was the good looking one with the body and I was the one with a bit of charisma and stupidity. I think he was shocked when I was evicted, and he gave me his Oakley sunglasses, which are far more expensive than any sunglasses I've ever owned.'

Brian: 'He's the man. He's a great guy. I instantly clicked with him when we met at one of the auditions before the show, and I went home thinking, "I'll never get in, he's so much funnier than me." So when I got in I was confident he'd be there, and he was. He's very quick-witted, brilliant, just thinking about him puts a smile on my face. Whenever I was bored, I'd just go and harass Brian, and it would turn into fun. He made the whole experience bearable. He still thinks he's going to go back to work for an airline. I said to him, "You just don't get it, Skip – you're going to be a star." I really think that he will. He's one of the three I hope I never lose touch with.'

Bubble on life in the house

'I didn't expect to get in, but I thought I'd give it a go. All through the auditions there were lots of lucky coincidences: the second application form came with a date stamped across the front for return, and it was Bryony's birthday. And one of the production staff I met said she only knew one road in Surbiton, where a friend of hers lives – it was my road. I really felt that if I managed to get in, I could go all the way. I get on with most people, it's what I'm good at. Unfortunately, I know I can also be irritating and annoying if you get too much of me. I just wanted the money, to put in the bank for Bryony's future.

PEOPLE ON BUBBLE

Bubble's brother, Mark: 'Deciding to go into the house was a tough call, because he knew he'd miss Bryony. But he's doing it for her. He originally looked at it like a job advert for a short-term contract: food and board, nine weeks, £70,000. He's one of the characters in the house. He's a bit of comic relief, and he's doing it for the right reasons. He's been very much himself. When he got nominated he was honest and said 'I'm gutted'. But he's also shown his sensitive side. He's made friends, because of who he is.'

Bubble's mother, Anna: 'He was a bit over the top on the first day, with the excitement of it all. Then the combination of missing Bryony and having his injured leg meant he was down. But he perked up again, got back to himself.'

Bubble's father, Jimmy: 'We're very, very proud of him. He's brought fun and laughter to that house.'

Jamie, student: 'Bubble's arse – please put it away, mate.'

Jim, rock climber: 'The funniest thing I've seen was Bubble taking that fall when he was trying to get to the task. At least you got out of the task, mate.'

'I didn't know I was going in first on my own – that was amazing, mind-blowing. When I met the others, I knew it was going to be a lot harder than I'd imagined. The *Big Brother* team kept saying it would be tougher than last year, so I was waiting for bizarre things to happen. But I now realize that it is tougher because it is hard to nominate when everybody else is so good.

'Living in there is much harder than anyone outside can imagine. There is no structure to life, nothing to do, you have to fill all the hours. I slept quite a lot during the day, but I was up later than the others at night. Weekends were much the hardest time for me – I didn't mind giving up the other forty-six days in the whole run, but those eighteen Saturdays and Sundays were the killer. In the end, I only did ten of them. They were tough because those are the days I have Bryony. It meant I was always down at weekends, but I tried to make up Mondays to Fridays. Unfortunately, the nominations happened on Mondays, just after my low time.

'I always wore the same baseball cap at weekends. I took Bryony to Chessington World of Adventures, and I was buying her something in the shop and she said, "You buy something, Daddy. Buy a hat." She chose the baseball cap, but it wasn't the sort of hat I would normally wear and it was about nine pounds, so I said to her, "Daddy hasn't got enough money." She said "I'll buy it for you, Daddy" and she took out her little purse and gave me all the money in it – twenty-two pence. So I had to buy the hat, didn't I? And I wore it every weekend to feel close to her.

'I knew I would miss her very badly, and I wouldn't have done it if I felt it would have affected her badly. But I was reassured by the psychotherapist that it would not damage her, so the only question was whether I would cope. I thought I was strong enough, but it was harder than I imagined. I kept telling myself "You came in here to win her a future, Bubble. Nobody forced you to do this. One day she'll see the videos and know that you made a fool of yourself, with all the world watching, to give her a future."

'Apart from missing Bryony, I coped alright. I knew I would have to live without TV, music, endless cans of Coke. But it's the unexpected things you miss: the sound of a car door closing, footsteps on the pavement, going to the garage at 3 a.m. to buy Coke because you've run out, walking to the shop to buy a paper, going to the park.'

Bubble on Bubble

'All I want now is to live happily ever after, and I just hope I'm going to be able to do that. I've learned things about myself in the house. I'm more emotional than I realized. I just cover up a lot of the time, make a joke about things. But in there, with all the tension, stress and time on your hands, you can't cover up. It brought me closer to myself.

'Unlike some of the people in there, I didn't see it as a stepping stone to a career in show business. If I had a great talent, I would be using it, and I would not need to go into the *Big Brother* house to win money. On the other hand, if something comes up I'll certainly give it a go, because I love performing. And I gave up my job to go into the house, so I need something to pay the bills.

WEEK FIVE FACT FILE

Main task: Guinness world record attempts:
Building a sugar cube tower over 1.02m tall

PASS ☑ **FAIL** ☐

Blowing a bubble-gum bubble larger than 58.4mm across

PASS ☐ **FAIL** ☒

Picking up and eating more than 169 sweetcorn kernels in one minute with a tooth pick

PASS ☐ **FAIL** ☒

Treats: Elizabeth's birthday party, pampering products, champagne, chocolates.

Bets are on!
To win: Brian is still favourite to claim the £70,000.
To walk: Amma is favourite to be the next one evicted from the house, with odds of 5/4.
Evictee's tip: Bubble says: Brian will win, with Dean a close second. He thinks Paul will be the one to go out next week.

'I know I'm strong. I've had problems with drugs and alcohol, and I've been honest about them in the house – if just one kid thinks twice before trying drugs, or one driver who is over the limit doesn't get into his car because of me talking about it, I will have achieved something. I've put all that behind me, beaten my own demons. I didn't just talk about the problems, but also about how I solved them, and that's what I hope people will remember about me.

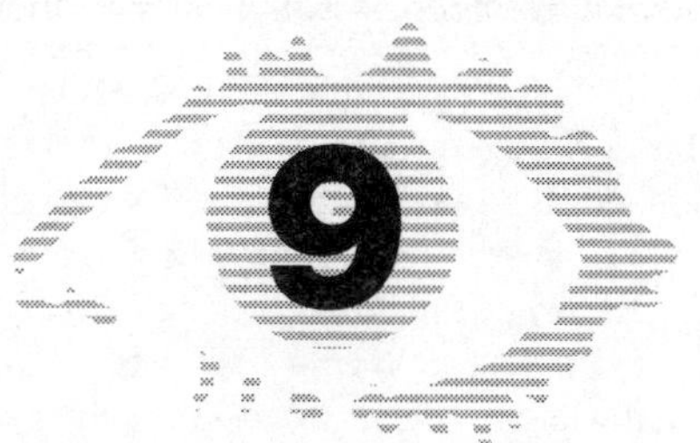

WEEK SIX

'That's just Helen living in Helen's little land.'
Helen

They have lost Bubble, but today a new housemate arrives: Paddy the dog. Paddy, a six-year-old Bichon Frise, will come into the house for four hours every day until Wednesday, and for this week's task, the housemates must prove that you can teach an old dog new tricks. They have to teach him eight tricks, and they will be tested on four of them, chosen at random. Feeling rash, the housemates decide to bet fifty per cent of their shopping money on succeeding with the training.

Paddy, a friendly little chap with a gentle and curious nature, arrives at 1.30 p.m. Josh, who is missing his own dog, collects him from the Diary Room, together with instructions for teaching Paddy his tricks. As the two of them emerge, Helen whispers her delight (she's under orders from Dean not to scream and frighten the dog). 'He's bloody gorgeous!' she says. She's been told she must not cut his hair, cover him in glitter or dress him up. She offers him a cup of tea and tells Paddy, 'I know your perm went wrong, but don't be upset.'

The group quickly divides into those who adore Paddy and those who are indifferent to him. Helen, Josh, Amma and Liz are thrilled with their new playmate, although Josh admits Paddy is a bit on the small side. But Paul describes him as 'a pathetic excuse for a dog', and Dean grumbles, 'This place is getting smaller every day. I could have done with something to keep my mind off it and that dog ain't it.' Brian describes Paddy as 'evil' and 'a demon'. When Helen comments that he's 'the kind of dog you see in Paris in people's handbags', Brian retorts, 'That's because they're taking them to be put down.'

Paul is called to the Diary Room to talk about his reaction to the eviction news. He stops at the nearest mirror to check his appearance first.

'I'm in a state of shock. I honestly thought I was going last night. I thought he [Bubble] would be the favourite for staying because he's a very funny guy. I'm expecting a big, big change because Bubble has gone. Bubble could possibly suppress other people's personalities, whether he did it knowingly or not.'

As he comes out of the Diary Room, Paul once again goes to the nearest mirror to gaze at himself. Resentment of Paul is simmering among all the housemates who wanted Bubble to stay, and they begin to pick on him. Amma tells him she has 'never seen a man who looks in a mirror so many times', adding that he is 'worse than any of the girls'.

It gets more heated a few moments later when Paul states that Anna Kournikova is his ideal woman. Elizabeth and the others challenge him about why he likes her, and suddenly the discussion turns bad-tempered, with Elizabeth forcefully telling him she doesn't agree with him. She later apologises, reflecting on the fact that Saturdays, the day after eviction night, are always hard for her.

Dean and Brian discuss how Paul fails to connect with the others in the house. When Brian says he feels sorry for him, Dean reminds him that Paul has survived three eviction votes, and may go on to win. In the evening, Amma openly tells Paul that she had been expecting Bubble to stay. Helen points out that the vote proves that inside the house they know 'jack shit' about how they are being portrayed on television.

Later, in the Diary Room, she talks about Paul.

'A few people in the house think the wrong person went yesterday, a few people are a little bit tense. I think he [Paul] is starting to irritate people, but I think, good on him. There's things I like about him but the others find irritating. If everyone was the same it would be boring.'

She then starts talking about what she's learned in the house, 'I have got to try not to look in the mirror so much. I've learned a lot about cooking from Liz, and I've learned I can't be so selfish and to be more tactful ... I don't want people to think I love myself.'

Brian livens the evening up by applying temporary tattoos to the girls' foreheads. The evening ends with Dean trying to teach Brian how to throw punches, and then telling him that he should run away, fast, if he ever gets involved in a real fight.

Paul talks in his sleep again, but none of the housemates wakes up at 5 a.m. to hear him say: 'Wouldn't you really? So important... absolutely.... thinks she's the bees knees, but she's not.'

Josh and Liz are the first up, and are able to have a few moments to themselves with Paddy when he arrives. The tricks are coming on well, but are not yet perfected – Paddy liked being bribed with pieces of chicken to perform, but he's not so happy about doing it without the incentive.

When the others emerge, Helen asks Paul if he will make his fish pie again – she's teasing him as his fish pie was not a success (Liz likened it to 'cement'). Paul doesn't realize and tells Big Brother how flattered he is. When he later discovers she was making fun, he pretends he knew all along, grateful that the housemates didn't hear what he said to Big Brother.

There are the usual Sunday-morning hassles over the shopping list, with Josh, Amma and Paul outvoting Liz, who would rather cut down on the cider in order to have more food.

Dean appears to be suffering from a mixture of boredom and cabin fever. His conversation all day revolves around how bored he is, and he talks of his

WHAT THE EXPERTS SAY

EVICTIONS AND BITCHING

'Bubble's eviction affected the house like no other. It was a bolt from the blue, and the housemates' shock was obvious. They sat motionless, unable to take it in. Liz removed her glasses as if to get a clearer view of the world. Up to this one, nominations and evictions have been predictable, and the reason for this is that there is a correlation between evictions and bitching.

'Bitching is talking negatively about someone behind their back. We've carried out a statistical analysis of the role it plays in the house. Each time so far, it has been the person bitched about the most or the person who has done most of the bitching who has been evicted. In the week before their evictions, Penny and Stuart were each the target of one third of the bitching. Narinder was responsible for almost two thirds of the bitching that occurred.

'Bitching has a function of spreading views around the house, and enabling the housemates to understand how everyone else feels. That's why, when it comes to nominations, there are usually no surprises.

'Bubble's nomination was very different. He rarely bitched and was rarely bitched about. Dean, for example, has never heard a single complaint about Bubble. Without bitching as a cue, those who didn't nominate Bubble just don't know why it happened. Their paranoia has been reinforced by the knowledge that the public don't want Bubble either. This was a key moment. For the first time, the housemates don't really know what's going to happen next. I predict that we are going to see an upsurge in bitching as the housemates try to come to terms with this confusion.'

Dr Peter Collett, Experimental Psychologist

urge to walk out. When Liz tells him about the problems they are having with the dog training, he seems totally uninterested. Briefly, he amuses himself by trying to teach Brian to roll over and fetch like Paddy. But like Paddy, who gets chicken as a reward, Brian wants vodka.

Just before 5 p.m., Josh is summoned to the Diary Room to be given the details of another, shorter task. Big Brother wants the group to create and perform a soap opera featuring all the housemates, past and present, but nobody is allowed to play themselves. They have to decide on a theme and then order the props they need. They decide on a *Dallas/Dynasty* theme. Dean is going to play Bubble and Narinder. Josh will be Brian and Paddy the dog. Brian will be Penny and Josh, and claims he needs 'huge fake tits', a Bible, a crucifix and a tight little top to play Penny, and a new body to play Josh. Liz and Amma will play each other, as will Paul and Helen. Paul says he wants 'massive jugs, loads of hair, big make-up'. Helen realizes that, as Paul, she will have to kiss Brian, who is playing Penny, and declares that she will not kiss Brian under any circumstances.

In the evening, Dean has a good old moan to Liz. Earlier in the day, the boys tested each other on general knowledge, and Dean was amazed by how little Brian knows. 'If the people who make this worthwhile weren't here, there wouldn't be any point for me,' he tells Liz. 'Even Brian – you can have a laugh with him, but when it comes to anything else ... For God's sake, he doesn't know the name of the first man on the moon! I don't want to talk about Destiny's Child. It's beneath me.'

Liz agrees, and says she struggles to talk about hair and makeup for hours on end with the other girls. 'I need some stimulus, something for my brain,' says Dean, and Liz replies that there is a limit to how long she can talk about 'sparkle, Posh and Becks and pop music'.

Later, in the Diary Room, Dean expounds on the theme:

'We are all going through what we have coined as "the wall", the hard part of the race. It feels like I'm not getting enough mental stimulation ... I'm having to downshift intellectually. It's alright for a bit, but after a while it gets difficult.

'Even though I can't vocalize what he [Bubble] did bring to the house, the fact that he's gone is a negative thing to me, at least, and as far as a couple of the others are concerned. It has not been a good weekend.'

His moan comes after the most dramatic event of the day, a row between Paul and Amma. Amma is still shaken by Bubble's departure, and Paul is still on the outside of the group. But his eviction survival seems to have given him a lot of confidence. He tells Amma that she talks down to him and to other people in the house.

'I could never have a conversation with you in here because my personality, someone like you, I would tear you to pieces.'

'Why don't you then?' says Amma.

He replies, 'It's not appropriate. My personality is actually very, very strong, I deal with different people in different ways.'

'I don't think I'm ever so horrible you need to shred me to pieces,' retorts Amma.

As Helen goes outside to tell the other housemates that 'there's a ding-dong going on', Paul warms to his theme of demolishing Amma:

'I would shred you to bits. I've allowed you to do everything you've done in here. I've allowed you. In here, I am the person in control of this house. What happens to me in here I can control.'

Amma, who remains cool and polite, agrees that Paul is in control of himself, but tells him that he cannot control her, or how she reacts.

'Yes I can, sweetheart. You're fake, and you think you have got one over on me, but you haven't.'

Amma refuses to rise to the bait, saying she would rather not argue with him. He tells her that she 'comes across in a psychologist kind of way' and that she is 'sarcastic'. Amma defuses the heated situation by saying she is going to make an effort to be less sarcastic. Paul admits he has enjoyed the whole discussion and thinks that must make him 'a bit of a sicko'.

'I get a kick out of mad circumstances, just like I get a kick out of being nominated,' he says.

At bedtime in the girls' room, Amma tells Liz that Paul's personality

WHAT THE EXPERTS SAY

AMMA

'Up until recently, Amma has been the quietest member of the group. Aside from her huge argument with Stuart, she is rarely a vocal presence in group events. Although a woman of few words, Amma's not a passive member of the group. Many of her attitudes and feelings towards the other housemates are forcefully expressed through silent, non-verbal behaviour. She builds intimate conversations with her eye contacts. She knows when to look to draw others in. She has built alliances with her fleeting patterns of eye gaze.

'Now things are changing, and we see Amma moving beyond her silent language and also committing herself verbally. Her disagreement with Paul is both an argument and a chance to view Amma's full capabilities. Amma repeatedly anticipates what Paul is going to say and overlaps her talk with his. She gains control of the floor. In contrast, Paul's attempts are much clumsier. He cuts into the middle of the conversation, which is much less effective, because Amma can defend by continuing to talk.

'The degree to which Amma is in control becomes apparent when Brian makes a number of his own points. Amma subsumes him into her turn without losing control. Even when Paul does get the floor, and expresses a view she disagrees with, Amma has one more non-verbal trick at her disposal. Her expression registers her rejection of his point and is made as he delivers the thrust of his argument. It's a risky strategy, unless she's confident of influencing the whole group. But it is a very effective strategy. It instantly communicates her reaction to the others before they have time to evaluate Paul's comments.

'Amma has always shown awareness and great skill in the silent language of the body. As her confidence in her alliances and her position in the house increases, she's bringing her verbal skills into play and is doubly effective.'

Professor Geoffrey Beattie, Psychologist

really annoys her. 'There's something about him that makes my sarcasm come out,' she says.

They all try to get to bed early – which, in *Big Brother* house terms, means before 2 a.m. Paddy will be arriving early in the morning, and they want to be fresh for his training session. In the boys' room, Josh and Brian agree that they will have their heads shaved if they are not nominated.

Sleeptalking seems to be infectious – tonight it is Dean's turn. He mumbles a lot, and then clearly shouts 'What the fuck's wrong with it?' followed by, 'Where the fuck is it?' Whatever it is, he seems to have found it, because his next utterance is more moderate: 'It's nice to see you. You didn't have to come all the way up.'

The next day, Paddy arrives at 9 a.m. He's bright and lively, but his trainers are not, and the session is not very successful. They are only allowed to train the dog for ten minutes in each four-hour session. After breakfast, Amma and Liz work with Paddy again, and this time he obediently performs all his tricks.

When Big Brother announces that the week's shopping is in the Store Room, Amma rushes in to claim her tobacco. She teaches Paul, who has the occasional cigarette, how to roll one, and takes the opportunity to make amends with him for yesterday's heated exchange. She tells him she wants to get on with him better, and asks him to bite back at her when she teases him. Paul appears to be bemused by her, but replies with his standard, 'That's cool.'

As they start rehearsals for the soap opera, Brian is called to the Diary Room.

'Everyone is feeling this thing where we're getting to the halfway point, everyone needs time out for a while,' he says.

He then admits that he doesn't get on as well with Paul as with the others, and says he's puzzled as to why the viewers outside the house don't see it the same way. When Big Brother asks him how he sees his own role in the house, Brian is at a loss.

'I don't have a particular role in the house. I can't do the shopping list, I don't have a head for that. I don't feel I give as much as other people do. All I've made is two pots of tea.'

As the nomination hour of 4 p.m. approaches, they hatch a plot to wear sunglasses and Liz's pink hat when they make their nominations. Big Brother warns the housemates that they must give full reasons for their choices. Despite this, they are all still trying to use Dean's formula, simply saying they get on with others better than with the nominee. However, under questioning from Big Brother, they are forced to be more forthcoming. This causes the stirrings of rebellion, as the housemates indulge in a long moaning session about the way Big Brother treats them.

To work off steam, they play volleyball, but the boys complain about the girls' team (of which Brian is a member), because they are not physical enough. When the girls' team manages to beat the boys, Dean accuses Brian of cheating, almost losing his temper.

Dean, who is still feeling down, then depresses both Brian and Helen by telling them that they will put on weight at twenty-seven and be fat by thirty unless they are very careful. Helen takes his warning to heart and tries on the dress she is saving for her eviction, only to find that it is tighter than it was when she came into the house. She announces that she will diet.

Dinner is served in the garden where the conversation turns to how sexually frustrated they all are, Josh confesses that he's had four wet dreams since he's been in the house.

The housemates spend the late evening in full dress rehearsal for their soap, which will incorporate highlights from life in the house, including Josh's arrival and Narinder's row with Helen. Some of them find it hard to get into character – Dean's attempts at a Geordie accent cause hilarity, and Liz and Amma struggle to impersonate each other. Josh minces around pretending to be Brian and then has to change into Paddy the dog, coming in with a string

WHO NOMINATES WHO

Amma nominates Paul and Josh
Brian nominates Paul and Amma
Dean nominates Paul and Amma
Elizabeth nominates Paul and Helen
Helen nominates Josh and Dean
Josh nominates Amma and Brian
Paul nominates Amma and Elizabeth

Amma	Brian	Dean	Elizabeth	Helen	Josh	Paul
Dean						Elizabeth
Josh						Dean
Brian					Helen	Brian
Paul	Josh	Helen	Paul	Elizabeth	Amma	Amma
4	1	1	1	1	2	4

Week 6 nominees: Amma and Paul with four nominations each.

Analysis
Brian has nominated both nominees. All housemates have at least one nomination. Unable to resolve the differences with Brian, Josh nominates him.

Reasons
Dean on Paul: 'We don't share the same interests, we've had different upbringings, and consequently we've not got much in common.'

Liz on Helen: 'She's a lovely person, but sometimes the decibel levels are just a bit high for me.'

Josh on Brian: 'It's been a struggle with Brian all along. I don't really think he gets on with me, and he hides it. Maybe I'm on his territory. I came in late, and I feel he just wishes I wasn't here.'

of sausages in his mouth. Helen draws a beard on her chin for her part as Dean. Brian playfully leaps on Helen, kissing her and proposing marriage to her, even offering her a ring.

'You know I love you. You are my life. Will you marry me?' he pleads.

'I sometimes wonder why you made me grow this beard.' says Helen.

If Paul is envious of Brian's physical closeness to Helen, he gets his own chance at bedtime. She springs out on him, her face covered in cream, as he is cleaning his teeth. They whisper briefly, then say goodnight – Paul kisses his hand and touches her with it.

Dean and Brian are the two late birds. Dean tells Brian how he felt angry with Amma during her argument with Paul, and how he has made an effort not to engage her in discussion because he does not like the way she debates. Josh is next to be dissected, and Brian says he feels uncomfortable around him. They also talk about Paul's unpopularity inside the house, compared with his survival in the public vote.

'People must relate to him. But what people?' wonders Brian. 'With all due respect, they must be ten years old, like *Star Wars* and be able to kick their legs really high.'

Next up for discussion is Liz, and they agree she seems to find the horse-play tiring, and that she is more comfortable having deep, meaningful conversations. Brian says he was unsure of her at first, but that he now likes her, although he feels she doesn't like him.

Eventually everyone is in bed, but the sleeptalking in the boys' room is spreading. Dean starts it off with 'Do not drink alcohol' and 'Don't talk about all the popular dogs in the world', followed by Paul muttering something unintelligible, and, two hours later, Josh saying, 'Stroke my hair, I'm gonna be famous.'

The dog trainers Josh, Amma, Liz and Helen are up early, because Paddy comes into the house at 7.30 a.m. to escape the heat of the day. When the hourly training time is up, he dozes with the housemates or follows Amma around as she cleans the kitchen. When Liz and Amma are the only two awake, Liz says she is certain she will be nominated. Amma reassures her:

'I can't honestly see it. The thing you have over everybody else is that you are a genuinely caring person, and it's very visible. Hurray, Elizabeth is capable of a bit of paranoia. We all do it.'

Liz makes eggy bread for breakfast, but Josh won't have any – he says he has noticed that he is getting fatter. When Paul gets up, he is surprised when Josh mentions that it is nomination-results day. He had completely forgotten, unlike the other housemates, who are beginning to get edgy about it.

When Helen is called to the Diary Room to collect more fish food, Big Brother asks if there is anything she would like to change about life in the house. The answer is pure Helen:

'I'd like more food, more chocolate, more alcohol, and being able to go out. That would be easier on everybody. Go to work, come back in, go back out, go out and teach dancing, come back in and have a hot tub. But that's just Helen living in Helen's little land.'

When she comes out, Brian goes in to ask when the dentist will be here to see him. He tells Big Brother that he is finding it hard to keep from losing his temper over trivial things.

'Sometimes you question your sanity, because in the outside world things wouldn't bother you, but in here if someone doesn't close the fridge you can fly off. Everyone's feeling the same, and everyone's so tense. You've got to keep smiling.'

It is after 3 p.m. when the nomination results are finally announced. Paul hardly reacts when his name is read out again. Amma, who has one hand over her face and the other clutching Josh's hand before the announcement, gives a huge smile and tells everyone she is cool about it. She comments, 'It's been a laugh. I've had so much fun, and I haven't worked for six weeks. Thank you Big Brother.'

There is a welcome distraction immediately after the announcement. Both Brian and Josh have said they will have their heads shaved if their names don't come up, and now they face the demon barber Dean, who gets to work with his clippers. Brian is quite pleased with his new look. Josh is less thrilled with the result. They all try to persuade Paul to have his done and he promises he will if he escapes eviction on Friday.

In the Diary Room Liz tells Big Brother that Bubble's eviction has affected her badly. But there are little characteristics of life in the Big Brother house that she enjoys: Josh's curry, home-made biscuits, seeing how the vegetables are growing, and finding out how many eggs have been laid.

The rest of the day is spent on rehearsals for the soap opera, *Ballas II*. Brian does a scarily good impersonation of Penny. Paul is consumed with giggles every time he has to attempt Helen's Welsh accent, and Dean complains that he's dressed as 'a transvestite killer Apache scout'. Liz has acquired huge breasts to play Amma, and Amma is sweltering in the heat under Liz's enormous fluffy pink jumper and pink hat.

At 7 p.m., the group perform their masterpiece, and manage to get through their five minutes without too many hiccups. When it's over, Paul, still convulsed with laughter, describes it as 'possibly one of the funniest things'. Josh is not sure whether anyone outside the house would find it so amusing, but Paul reckons they would.

Big Brother wastes no time in telling the housemates they have passed the test, but says that they will have to wait until the next day to know what their reward is. Jubilant, they retire to the garden, where they sit around discussing what they miss in the outside world.

Suddenly, the outside world comes to them – two youths scale the wall and drop down into the garden. Dean spots them first, and reacts in his usual laid-back way, telling the others to go inside the house. The two youths don't approach the housemates, but jump up and down in front of the cameras shouting, 'We're in the *Big Brother* house! We broke into the *Big Brother* house!' Almost immediately, Big Brother orders the housemates into a bedroom, while security men take the intruders out through the garden gate.

Soon afterwards, the housemates are given a reassuring message from Big

Brother, telling them that they are safe, and that their security is paramount. Helen is the most unsettled by the invasion. 'I was scared. I didn't like it one bit,' she says. The others all agree that it is disconcerting. They're slightly mollified when Big Brother gives them a bottle of wine and four cans of beer as a consolation, but complain that it isn't much compensation for what they've been through.

Afterwards they all relax in the garden, and Paul questions Brian and Josh about whether girls ever try to seduce gay men. They both agree it happens a lot. Josh admits that he last had sex with a girl less than a year ago, but that it was when he was drunk. Paul is unhappy – he believes Josh should not have been going in and out of the bathroom when the three girls were in the tub together naked. But the others remind him that the girls called him in there, too.

In the Diary Room, Paul tells Big Brother that it has been 'the most mental day' he has spent in the house so far. He says he wasn't surprised to be nominated, although he would have liked a week off from it. But he knows the public must like him to keep him in, and that makes him feel good. He reckons he brings level headedness to the house, and if he goes he hopes the group will miss this.

All the housemates, except Dean and Liz, go to bed early. In the quiet of the girls' bedroom Amma tells Helen for the first time about the boyfriend she was seeing for three weeks before she came into the house. She says she met him at a party and she plans to ring him as soon as she is out.

Outside in the garden, Liz and Dean settle down to a marathon three-and-a-half-hour chat, in which none of the other housemates escapes dissection. Liz is sad that another girl may be going at the end of the week, but is not surprised by Amma's nomination as she knows some of the boys have issues with her. She admits to being irritated by Amma too, but then proceeds to explain how she is irritated by everybody.

'I'm used to being able to get away from people I don't get on with. Sometimes I just need my space,' she moans.

She tells Dean that she does not think he has received any nominations, and that he is worshipped by Brian and Helen, both of whom treat him as 'Dean the god'. Dean is surprised by the inclusion of Helen, as he's unaware of her idolizing him. (In fact, Liz is misreading Helen, who nominated Dean, saying she didn't get on with him as well as Paul and Brian.)

They agree that Amma is argumentative, and Liz says she is beginning to wonder whether the row with Stuart was as one-sided as she initially thought. She can't work out Amma, who seems to have no role in the house, and suspects it is because Amma wants to seem mysterious.

But it is for Helen that Liz saves her real rant.

'I can't cope when Helen goes off. It's not her, it's the whole noise. A lot of them are so irrational and melodramatic and so not real. Get a grip. Even if you're bored, even if there is a big void in your life, keep a handle on reality. Why do you have to fucking yell about everything? Why do you have to speak over everybody? Why do you never listen? Why can't you be normal?

Why can't I smack you over the head? Why do you make me feel like this? Why am I going insane? You're making me feel like I've lost it. And that's what really fucks me off!'

After dissing the others – with the exception of Brian, who they believe has improved now that he has lost his mates Narinder and Bubble – Liz complains about her own image within the house. 'I'm like this spineless boffin who makes tea and keeps people calm,' she rants, explaining how she wants to do something that, although it would be in keeping with her real character, would be at odds with the way she is seen in the house and would shock the others.

As they discuss ways of coping with the pressures of the house, Dean tells Liz that for the last couple of days he has been wearing a special T-shirt. The message on it says 'The Gameford Files', which is part of a joke he shares with a friend about the old TV show *The Rockford Files*. When he wears the top, his friends know that he is finding it tough – and just letting them in on the stress makes him feel better.

On Wednesday morning, all the housemates are up early to greet Paddy – today is the day when he faces the test on the task. None of the housemates is very confident, as they know the dog can only do six of the eight tricks. They run through his training, and then the girls decide to have some fun at Brian's expense. He has had no involvement with Paddy, but they tell him Big Brother may select him to do the tricks with the dog. He's completely fooled, and has a practice session with Paddy, extracting the best performance of the morning from the little pooch. It's a very hot day – 30 degrees in the shade in the *Big Brother* garden – and they are all worried that Paddy will be hot and tired when he has to perform.

Brian and Josh are needling each other, with Brian issuing a stream of jokes at Josh's expense. Josh is called to the Diary Room and tells Big Brother that he is finding it harder than ever to get on with Brian:

'He's constantly digging at me. I daresay I might bite back sooner or later. He's very witty, very funny, a great sense of humour, but it can be constantly directed at myself and even other people keep asking me if he's having a go at me. I laugh it off most of the time, but it can be a bit wearing. If I say anything back, he says, "What's wrong with you? Are you in a mood?" He finds it easy to have a jibe at me being gay. I don't think there's a real resolution, because that's his character.'

Brian is chosen to pick from a box at random the tricks that Paddy must perform. The first one out is one of the two that the dog can't do: fetch. The other three are: 'play dead', 'stand on back legs', and 'lie down' – all tricks that he has mastered. Pessimism increases, as the housemates contemplate the fifty per cent of their shopping money that is riding on Paddy's tiny back. Amma has been selected to put Paddy through his paces, as she has worked well with him in the training. Predictably, he manages three of the tricks, but fails to fetch. Within minutes, the housemates are told by Big Brother that they will only have £24.50 for shopping next week – Amma who expects to leave on Friday tells the others, 'That's my parting gift: £24.50.'

They say goodbye to Paddy for the final time, an emotional moment for Helen and Amma, both of whom are very attached to the dog. Helen says Paddy failed the task for her, because he knows she wants to lose weight. Dean, however, complains about the task, describing it as 'frustrating, unrewarding, disappointing and horrible'. He doesn't blame the dog or the dog trainers, and says it isn't even the lack of food that's bothering him – he has a growing resentment of the control Big Brother has over their lives.

Called to the Diary Room, Paul is frank about his failure to gel with any of the other housemates, except Penny, Stuart and Helen. Meanwhile, Brian holds court in the garden, recounting tales of his time working for Ryanair, which he calls 'Brian Air'.

In the afternoon, the housemates' reward for passing the soap-opera task arrives – two ice-cream makers and a selection of ingredients, including choco-

WHAT THE EXPERTS SAY

ON PLAYGROUND BEHAVIOUR

'Over the past few weeks, the housemates have become increasingly childlike. This is a likely, but not inevitable, consequence of their environment. They have lost their normal routines, they have everything provided for them and very little to do. Beyond that, they are subject to a clear set of rules imposed on them by Big Brother. When they break them, they are called to the Diary Room, with all its echoes of the headteacher's study.

'It is hardly surprising that the particular period of childhood they have reverted to is primary school. Children in a school environment will either comply with or challenge authority, and in the Big Brother house, they divide along the same lines.

'There are the goodies. Helen is utterly compliant in the Diary Room. Brian is also a good boy in class. He's an upholder of rules and he's fearful of the consequences of breaking them.

'At the other end of the playground are the kids who rebel against authority. Dean always knew he was challenging Big Brother when he made a banana-skin cigarette. As he waits to hear whether it is against the rules or not, his body language is defiant and he does not try to reason as an adult would. Elizabeth also challenges Big Brother's authority. She's frequently critical.

'The division between the good kids and rebellious kids is apparent during the hypnotism trick. Again, as in the playground, there is usually an in-crowd and an out-crowd, and the in-crowd is led by the cool kids, the rebellious ones. This is no different to playground bullying. The in-crowd are playing a trick at the expense of Paul, Brian and Helen for their own amusement.

'But there is one kid in the playground who can play for either team: Josh. The housemates are roughly split down the middle. Josh's decision to join either gang permanently could well swing the balance of power.'

Dr Sonia Sharp, Educational Psychologist

late and strawberries. Paul joins the girls in making the first batches, and dubs himself the 'Ice-Cream King'. They are all disappointed when he finally reads the instructions properly and realizes the mixture has to be frozen overnight.

In the evening, Dean spends an hour talking to Big Brother in the Diary Room. He runs through all his grievances and worries about life in the house, especially the feeling of having no control over his own environment. He complains about the task, accusing Big Brother of moving the goalposts: they thought they were going to have four hours a day to train the dog, but because of the heat they could only train him for a small amount of time.

When he emerges, the others pretend not to recognize him, he has been gone so long. But he has emerged more cheerful than he went in, despite having his Gameford Files T-shirt confiscated because he was using it to communicate with the outside world. He tells the others to go in for a chat, because the Big Brother on duty is very good to talk to. Paul takes his advice, and spends forty-five minutes in there, going through his feelings about being nominated. He fears he has upset his housemates. But he is not worried about eviction night.

The bickering between Josh and Brian has been a counterpoint to all the day's activities, and the others are all very aware of it. Brian goes to the Diary Room and admits, 'I've said things to a certain person that didn't come out the right way, and made me look a bit of a twit, I suppose. At the start it was weird, because I felt I was being judged by another gay person. I felt that if my parents saw him and then saw me, he would portray himself as a gay man much better than I could.'

The Diary Room is in great demand, with Amma going in next. She takes issue with Big Brother over the reasons they are expected to provide for making nominations. When she is asked how she thinks the group will change if she is evicted, she replies:

'Not much. One or two people might miss me. I am a floater – I'm here, I'm there. You don't truly know how people perceive you, but I think they will manage perfectly well. They will take my shampoo and shower gel and I will be forgotten in a couple of days.'

Another game of volleyball follows. When Dean gives up after an hour and twenty minutes, Helen thinks it is her fault for not being good enough. She says the others never want her on their team, they think she's bad luck. 'I don't wanna be in this bloody house, I'm pissed off with it,' she exclaims, and then follows Dean into the house and bursts into tears. He and Amma comfort her, Dean assuring her that he gave up playing because he hurt his thumb, not because of her. Helen explains that she worries about playing the game in case the ball hits her face. 'I don't want to go out with a black eye,' she says. 'It would look common.' She adds that she knows she is too sensitive, and she says she's going to work on overcoming it, in the same way that she feels she has overcome the tact problems she had in the early days.

Brian and Josh have now resorted to bitching behind each other's backs to the rest of the housemates. Josh is getting a lot of support and sympathy from the others, who agree that Brian's relentless teasing can be difficult.

Dean agrees with Brian that the two of them should talk and clear the air. Josh, meanwhile, tells Amma that he feels Big Brother has betrayed his trust by telling Brian what he said about him in the Diary Room. He's wrong: Brian has simply picked up on how Josh is feeling.

Before the big air-clearing session can take place, Amma announces that some of the ice cream has been frozen for long enough, and although it's one o'clock in the morning, they all enjoy it. Their conversation is about a subject they have all been dwelling on – masturbation. Paul confesses to having indulged last week, and Brian says he did it early this morning. Helen asks:

'What do you do with the stuff?'

'Tissues, of course.' replies Brian.

Eventually, under pressure from the other housemates, Josh and Brian retire alone to the boys' room to try to sort out their differences. Their problems stem from Brian's attack on Josh soon after he entered the house, but now seem to centre around Josh's feeling that Brian oversteps the mark constantly with his humour, and that he doesn't like it when Josh ribs him back. Brian complains that Josh is condescending towards him. He also fears that there was an intention to match them up. 'I'm not going to let myself be matched with a guy in this house, who happens to be gay, for the amusement of half of England,' he asserts.

The discussion becomes heated, and the conclusion is that they are both misjudging the other. But there is no resolution to it. Brian says: 'I don't think you're ever going to get my character, and I don't think I'm ever going to understand you.' They do agree on one thing – they will not be keeping in touch with each other when their stay in the *Big Brother* house is over.

The next morning, Josh tells Liz that nothing was resolved because Brian is stubborn. 'He doesn't understand where I'm coming from.' But he adds that he's determined not to let the situation bother him.

Helen is called to the Diary Room and admits that she feels she let herself down after the volleyball match yesterday. 'In here the littlest things turn into the most humungous things.' She says she hasn't noticed any tensions in the house, but admits that could be because she's living 'in Helen's little land'.

She cooks pancakes for everybody for lunch, burning Paul's but disguising it with a generous dredging of sugar. She congratulates herself on making a meal for the house – although she then admits she didn't make the batter. Amma spends the afternoon embroidering the boob tube she is making as Liz's birthday present. It's a cut-down T-shirt, and she's using a sewing kit she brought in to add stars and crosses to it. She tells Josh she needs to finish it because she will soon be leaving, but he makes her correct herself: 'Well, I *might* be leaving on Friday.'

As they share a cigarette break, Paul asks Amma whether she is worried about going out because of the way the public may react to her being a stripper. Amma replies that she is Amma, and just happens to be a stripper. She and Paul jokingly adopt a moth which flutters down near them, calling it Monty and pretending to teach it to fetch and hold (the tricks Paddy failed to get to grips with).

The evening brings a diversion from the boredom that has set in – rain comes lashing down onto the garden in a huge thunderstorm. It is still warm, and Josh, Amma and Paul cavort outside.

The group play a game in which they have to guess the meaning of words. Brian stumps them with 'gash' (an airline word for rubbish). Paul is very dismissive of his effort, branding it a nonsense word, whereupon Brian defends it irritably. They are all ordered into the boys' room while Big Brother carries out repairs, and afterwards most of the group drift out, leaving Brian and Dean alone. Brian confesses that he doesn't believe he can make it through to the end.

'I'm getting on people's nerves lately, I'm a bit snappy. There's no way I can stay after week seven. I'll end up killing someone.'

Paul walks into the room as Brian is speaking, and tells him peremptorily: 'I was a bit pissed off when you snapped at me.' Brian points out that he snaps at everybody, and he has only snapped at Paul once in six weeks. Paul walks out, and whinges about Brian to Josh over a game of backgammon. Brian, in the meantime, moans about Paul to Dean, saying that he is resisting the temptation to have an argument with him.

Over dinner, the two camps remain entrenched, with Brian, Dean and Elizabeth eating outside, and Helen, Amma, Paul and Josh inside. Afterwards, Paul describes Brian as 'a selfish prat'. When Helen points out that it is hard for Brian after losing his friends Penny, Narinder and Bubble, Paul responds, 'Mate, there's eleven people in this house, not one.'

In the garden Brian is still letting off steam, telling the others how he nearly smashed a glass against the wall in frustration, and how he would now like to smash a plate. The others encourage him. He speaks into his mike:

'I'm going to break a plate because I'm angry. No, I can't. It's wrong. It's on television.'

Then, to cheers from the others, he does it anyway.

Liz goes to the Diary Room to collect oil of evening primrose tablets for her PMT, scissors for the kitchen and painkillers for Josh. She tells Big Brother she is relaxed and hopes they can all enjoy the last few weeks in the house.

'I'm a lot calmer. I'm tired, but that's probably down to getting up early for Paddy. I think Brian's feeling what I felt, but he can't put it down to PMT. I don't mind, because I like Brian, but I know that Paul and Josh find him immature.' Asked what she would like to change in the house, she comes up with a very practical list: she'd like a bigger oven, the hob replacing because only one side of it works, the plants are not getting enough sunlight, the garden should be bigger for volleyball, and the design of the garden table means everyone keeps stubbing their toes on it.

In the garden, Amma tells Paul and Helen about appearing in a music video which was shown on MTV. Only one part of Amma was on screen – her bum. She went along for a laugh with a friend who was auditioning for the job, and landed it. She gives her housemates a demonstration of the wiggles that won her the role.

Paul returns to one of his regular gripes: he is still banging on about Josh being bi-sexual rather than gay, as he slept with a woman less than a year ago. It still irks him that the two gay men in the house have been so trusted by the women, and says that if he discovered Brian was only pretending to be gay, he would 'knock his block off'. Amma tells him he would have no right to use physical violence, and a huge, heated discussion ensues. Brian eventually joins them, and the conversation becomes funny again as they quiz him on his domestic skills, which appear to be non-existent.

Late at night in the girls' room, Amma bares her soul about her eviction fears. She is worried about the public perception of her, as she feels she has not had a chance to be herself. She also thinks the house won't miss her, as she had no definable role. Helen falls asleep, but Liz and Amma talk until half past four in the morning.

Friday starts quietly. Amma gives herself a manicure, and tells Helen that the tension of waiting for the eviction results is bearable, but will probably be worse as the time gets nearer. Helen asks whether she thinks Davina will kiss her or shake her hand, and Amma accepts the assumption that she is going.

The two eviction nominees are each called to the Diary Room. Amma describes the *Big Brother* experience as 'being institutionalized in a nice prison'.

'In here, in a group, certain people assume responsibility and you let them get on with it. In the outside world I would be more forceful.'

Paul talks of feeling the usual mixture of nerves and excitement at the prospect of the evening. He says he feels he is a one-man band: 'I can't think of an occasion when I have had to talk to anyone about problems. I feel like I am in it on my own.' He adds that Brian is beginning to annoy people and describes him as 'a spoilt brat'.

'He smashed a plate, and if we all did that when we were a bit pissed off, we wouldn't have anything to eat off.'

Later, for the first time in his run of nominations for eviction, Paul packs his suitcase.

The housemates have a late lunch cooked by Liz and Josh, and afterwards begin their weekly cleaning session. Brian goes to the Diary Room and says:

'I feel I've changed a little bit. I'm thinking differently about certain things, talking about things, I'm willing to learn about different things. I've found out a few things about myself which aren't so good and that maybe I can change in years to come. Sometimes I'm oblivious to how others feel because I'm absorbed in myself. Josh told me that I think the world revolves around me, and I think he's right.'

It's time for the eviction announcement, and for the first time Big Brother tells the housemates they are allowed to sit around the garden table to hear the result. They hold hands, and Amma rests her head on Helen's shoulder. When the news that she is to go is announced she swears, before being hugged and kissed by the others. Big Brother has told them never to swear at this time as it is being broadcast live to the nation before the 9 p.m. watershed. Punishment for consistently doing so would be eviction!

Paul shakes a few hands and then goes into the garden on his own. 'What's going on, what is going on?' he asks, unable to believe his fourth week

VOTING

Amma received sixty-four per cent of the votes, a total of 947,946. Paul, on thirty-six per cent got 529,169 votes. The total vote of just under 1.5 million was the biggest cast so far. Sixty-eight per cent of the votes were made by phone. The rest were made through interactive digital television.

The average viewing figure for the week was 4.3 million, a twenty-four per cent share of the viewing public. An average of 378,000 viewers watched the live streaming on E4 at 11 p.m. every night, and an average of 327,000 watched the *Big Brother, Little Brother* magazine programme on E4. The website remains the number-one entertainment site in the UK, with users spending an average of more than eighteen minutes per session.

of luck. Once he's taken on board his survival, it gives him a surge of confidence, and he tells Dean that he now wants 'to go all the way'. The others think he has a good chance. Dean has, earlier in the week, told Brian that he thinks Paul could win, and Josh, commiserating with Amma, says Paul must have a big fan club outside the house. Amma agrees: 'He knows when he leaves he's got fuck all to worry about.'

Amma admits to the housemates that she is very nervous, and over an emotional dinner they all offer her advice, mostly to do with enjoying the moment and making the most of all things she will be able to enjoy – such as tequila and sex – when she is back in the real world. She makes a short speech, telling them all how much she will miss them.

'You're all fantastic and I've been really privileged to be here,' she says. She dresses in tight white trousers and a stunning white halter-neck top for her final goodbye to the house.

After Amma leaves, to hugs and kisses and shouts from Helen that she loves her and she must have 'a fab time', the others have a group hug and intone loudly in unison: 'And then there were six.' This refrain has now become a weekly post-eviction ritual. They remind each other that there are only three more weeks to go.

Out in the garden, they can hear the crowd shouting, despite the music being played by Big Brother. Brian thinks he hears voices shouting abuse about his sexuality, which unnerves him.

In an intimate chat, Paul tells Helen that a few years ago his run of success would have made his head swell, but that he is now mature enough not to be swayed by it. Helen tells him she is glad he is still there.

AMMA LOOKS BACK: THE EXCLUSIVE INTERVIEW

Amma on the housemates

Penny: 'She's a lovely woman who wants to share, look after people, care for them and give to them. She can be a bit too much in your face. She had her mad moments. But she's a big, wonderful character. She didn't cope very well with the *Big Brother* house, and that's why I nominated her – out of all the people I nominated, she's the only one where I did it for her sake, not because I didn't want her around. She was overtly sexual, she talked openly about her past love life and about terrible things that have happened to her – she's had a difficult life. But I'm sure she'll re-focus. My problems with her were all to do with me not being very good with authority. She tried to take control, and I resented her giving more food to the boys – I'm sure I eat as much as they do.'

Stuart: 'Contrary to popular belief, I think he's a good person, a wonderful father, a family man, and I'm sure he's very respected in his own circles. Again, like Penny, he tried to father everybody, and you can't do that in a house full of adults. When we had our row, I told him over and over again to leave it until the morning, because we'd both had a drink and the whole thing was drink-fuelled. I think it is easy for him to be seen as a bad character: he has money, he's very image conscious, a bit smug and competitive, and he rubs some people up the wrong way. But he left the house a couple of days after our row, and I'd have liked him to stay longer because, who knows? We might have become really good friends.'

Narinder: 'Narinder is Narinder. She made a lot of people feel uncomfortable. She was probably not quite as bitchy or offensive to us in the house as she was when talking in the Diary Room or since she came out, but she was bitchy, and I grew to respect her for that. I'd like to meet her, because I think outside the house I could see her in a more rounded way. She's bubbly, full of beans, and funny. But she thought everyone was boring. She wanted a house full of ten other Brians and Narinders, or full of her best mates. She wasn't interested in other people: she complained to me once that none of the blokes had made any effort to find out about her and her family. But if I'd asked her about my family, she would have known nothing, because she wasn't interested. She was able to dish it out but not so good at taking it.'

Bubble: 'Bubble was very honest about why he was in there: he wanted the money. Some of the others, like Narinder and Helen and Paul, thought this was wrong, and they were suspicious of him. I had a special relationship with him, and I was devastated when he left. He was the only bloke in there I had any kind of relationship with. He's open, warm, makes me laugh, a bit cheeky. Everyone else tiptoed around me, but he didn't bother. There aren't enough good things I can say about him, and I wish him good luck in everything he does. I know he'll do well.'

Paul: 'Paul could be irritating and annoying, but there's nothing about him that would make you not like him. He wants to be liked, which means he tries too hard, and his little sayings, which we heard over and over and over, got to me: "totally", "fair play to you", "mental", "cool", "wicked", "mate". He talks all the time about girls and drinking, girls and drinking. He's over-excitable, he talks over people and interrupts all the time. His mind is not open to other people's opinions. He accused me of talking down to him, and it's true, I did, but that's because I had no respect for him. I felt sorry for him, being nominated all the time, but he ended up believing he didn't need to talk to the rest of us, he had a "fuck all of you" attitude, as if he was saying, "They like me out there, and if you don't, tough." He has very little insight into the other people in there, or even into himself. He keeps telling us he's sensitive, but he's not. When he said he could control me, I thought that showed how little he knew about me or himself. And when I said I couldn't have an argument with him, that was not because he is so nice, but because there is nothing there to argue with. And what's with this thing of dressing up in women's clothes? I think it's to prove what a fun guy he is. One really irritating thing was his smoking. He tells people he only smokes occasionally, but he was getting as much tobacco as Bubble and me and smoking it faster, then using ours.'

Josh: 'He's the only one I would have no real desire to ever see again. He disappointed me. He nominated me, which is fair enough – we all have to do it, and I nominated him. But he spent the whole of my last week telling me how surprised he was that my name came up, and how I wouldn't be going. How two-faced are you? I don't mind if someone says nothing, or is just generally supportive. But to do what he did. He's a typical Londoner, there's a lot of facade, he says what people want to hear. He believes he's a fun bloke, but I'm not too sure – I expect it's only in the company of his own friends. In the house he's not fun, but neither was I. He claimed he would bring in fun and nudity – what we got was posing and backgammon. He's trying to be everybody's friend, he lacks confidence. He did come in late, but by now he should realize that people are willing to get to know him and give him a chance. The thing with Brian is not all one-sided: he gives as good as he gets and he's a lot more vindictive. Brian was genuinely upset. Josh was just a bit uncomfortable.'

Brian: 'He's the house comedian. He has a big heart, he's very funny, very naive, a bit immature sometimes, but he occasionally shows he has a serious side and bags of common sense. We didn't have much of a relationship, because we didn't have a lot in common. The only bad thing about him is that he can be a bit loud, but that is vastly outweighed by the times he made you roll around laughing. It's not fake, Brian's humour. It's non-stop. I've watched him get out of bed, bleary-eyed, and walk to the toilet, and he's still being funny. I think he's wicked. If he wins I'll be happy, because he's the best all-round character in there.'

Dean: 'I'm amazed to come out and find that the public think he is boring. He is not at all boring. He's extremely witty – he and Brian are the most entertaining people in there. It is such a shame if his dry humour does not come across. He's a very grounded bloke, intelligent, no nonsense, very caring. He's someone you listen to – when he opens his mouth you know something interesting or something funny is going to come out. I got on well enough with him, but I didn't have a deep relationship with him, and that's partly because I admire him and felt inadequate next to him. I felt that everything I said was nonsense and not worth listening to. The house would be very different without him. He keeps the peace.'

Elizabeth: 'She's smart, she can suss a person out. But she's lovely and very kind, and tries to see the good in people. She was the most willing to look into everybody, which is why I got close to her. I found it very hard with the people in there, but she made the effort to get to know me. She's a really special person. I know she's got a middle-class, horsey sort of image, but I hope that doesn't stop people realizing how nice she is. But I didn't fancy her and she didn't fancy me. We are just friends. It was a shock to come out and find that some people thought we were about to have a lesbian relationship. I don't even remember kissing her on her birthday.'

Helen: 'What you see is what you get: a bubbly little Welsh girl. She's warm and lovely. She can come across as a bimbo, and she knows this. She may not have a million GCSEs, but when you talk to her, she's got bags of common sense, life sense – more than people give her credit for. She's a big ball of fluff, glitter and warmth. She's very sensitive and reads a lot into things, sometimes too much. So it would do her the world of good to win, it would boost her confidence. She was a friend to me, and she needs to be told how wonderful she is.'

Amma on life in the house

'Some things were harder that I expected, some things were not nearly as hard. I found the day-to-day workings of the house easier than I thought they would be: the cameras on you all the time, getting undressed, going to the loo. The food, too, although we moaned about it, was pretty good – it's like moaning about school dinners. And I was really pleased with the mix of people. I expected to be stuck with people who really grated on me, and I thought there would be arguments straightaway.

'I was also expecting Big Brother to be nastier: it was actually a comfortable environment. And I thought I would get really wound up by the fact that I couldn't go anywhere, but it wasn't that bad. I knew I would be bored, and I was, but not nearly as much as I anticipated.

'On the down side, I didn't know I would get as upset as I did at times. Emotions are really heightened in there. And I didn't know it would be so hard to get my own personality across. In the real world, I am one of the louder, bubbly, happy people, not one of the surly, moody ones.

'I found the Diary Room difficult, talking to a stranger who just asks questions and doesn't give you any feedback. I hated nominations, even though you go in knowing you have to do it. The longer it went on, the harder it got. You feel so guilty doing it. And not being allowed to talk about it, to explain to the people you have nominated, is terrible. You feel two-faced, even though it's the rules of the game.

'I was a watcher in there: I enjoyed observing the others. Because I found it hard to speak my mind, I tended only to get heard when I had a problem,

PEOPLE ON AMMA

Amma's sister, Barbara: 'When she went into the house, she felt she would do well so long as she wasn't evicted the first week. So to do six weeks is brilliant. She was doing it for the experience. There's nothing we didn't know about her before she went in. Our mother didn't know what she did for a living, but I knew ... Amma likes to shock, but there's nothing she did in the house that we were surprised about or didn't agree with. She's got a beautiful voice – I'd like her to get into singing.'

Amma's mum, Juliana: 'I was really upset about her career, but she's promised me she won't go back to it. She's a very intelligent girl.'

Andy, travel agent: 'I couldn't believe my eyes – Liz, Helen and Amma in the bath tub together. Paul, you are NOT the luckiest guy in the world. Girls, do us a favour: cover up.'

Vanessa Feltz, TV presenter: 'Amma, what's with all this farting and burping? You know where the toilet is. Be a bit more ladylike, please.'

which isn't true to my character. Every day I woke up thinking: "Why can't you just be yourself, why can't you show the side of you that makes people love you, not the side that makes people distance themselves from you?"

'I didn't feel I had a role. I was a team player to the best of my abilities, but I didn't shout the odds when it came to making decisions, I just went along with everybody else.

'I think the amount of farting I did has been exaggerated, although I was the worst. The girls' room was foul – we all did it, except Penny. We were much worse than the boys. But mine were just noisy: they don't smell.'

Amma on Amma

'I've learned a lot about myself in there. I've learned to be more tolerant, how to live in a group with other people. I've learned that I need to put more faith in other people. There are aspects of my character that I'm going to look at and perhaps change. I know I was too guarded, stepped back too much, didn't confide in other people enough, or in the Diary Room. It's how I am all the time – I find it hard to express how I feel. But I'm better than I was at eighteen, and I'm going to work on being even better.

'One aim I had when I went in was to show the world that strippers are not a kind of *Jerry Springer* stereotype, and I hope I've achieved that. Table dancers are like everyone else in every occupation – there are clever ones, dumb ones, big ones, little ones, black ones, white ones, intelligent ones, funny ones. They are as diverse as the human race is.

'I've promised my mother that I won't go back to stripping, and I won't.

WEEK SIX FACT FILE

Main task: Train Paddy the dog to do eight tricks.

PASS ☐ FAIL ☒

Mini-task: Create a five-minute soap opera.

PASS ☑ FAIL ☐

Treats: Ice-cream makers. Wine and beer after the break-in.

Bets are on!
To win: Brian is still the favourite to win, at odds of 1/4. He is followed by Dean, Liz and Paul, all on 7/1.
To walk: The favourite to be the next out of the house is Josh, at 3/1.
Evictee's tip: Amma says, 'I'd like Helen to win, but I think it will be Brian or Dean. The next to go will, I hope, be Paul.'

But I don't know what I will do. I got into the job because I was bored. I was reading a newspaper with a friend and we saw an advert for an audition, so we went along for a laugh and I got the job.

'I didn't tell my mother because I didn't want to disappoint her. She's a true role model – I've never met anyone so selfless. She brought us all up on her own after my father was killed in a road crash when I was five. It certainly wasn't easy, but she gave us a happy childhood. She doesn't like me stripping, and she was shocked when I told her before I went into the *Big Brother* house. But she said, as she always has done, "I accept you and I love you and I want the best for you." I would now like to do something to make her proud of me.'

WEEK SEVEN

'I have lived my adult life like an international pop star.'
Paul

First up on Saturday morning is Josh, as usual. He soon spots some strange-looking pieces of equipment that have appeared in the garden. Helen joins him, and they decide it is an assault course. When Brian gets out of bed and sees it he gives a whimper and returns to bury himself under the duvet.

Over the course of the day, all the housemates will be called to the Diary Room to ask how they are feeling in the aftermath of another eviction. Helen is the first. She's sorry to see her friend Amma go, but cheers up when she realizes she will see her in three weeks. 'I'll miss her untidiness and her scooping her hair into a whip,' she says. Helen adds that she thinks Paul is unbeatable, because he's obviously very popular with the public.

Josh goes in next, and confesses that he feels guilty about nominating Amma.

'In my heart of hearts, I'd have liked her to stay, but this game makes you do strange things. I hope she didn't take it to heart. She was a really good ear to listen to me – her and Liz have been the main two. I've asked her to be there when I leave, and I hope she is.'

At 1 p.m. the housemates are given the details of the task. They have to transport a drum kit piece by piece across three obstacles: a spider's web, which they must get through without touching any part of it (with one housemate and one piece of kit only passing through each hole); a toxic swamp, across which all the pieces must be passed using ropes; and a wall, which the drum kit must be passed over and the housemates must crawl under. They then have to reassemble the kit and bang a cymbal. If a housemate or a piece of the kit touches the ground outside the course they will be given a fifteen-second penalty, and they must complete the whole task in less than eight minutes and fifteen seconds. Dean and Paul are excited about having something physical to concentrate on. They're split between wagering thirty per cent and forty per cent, and when Liz suggests thirty-five per cent, they realize that wagers don't have to be in round figures and settle, for a laugh, on thirty-six point four per cent.

The housemates spend the afternoon practising for the task, wearing the protective clothing (helmets and shoulder, knee and elbow pads) that Big Brother has provided. The drum kit arrives, and Dean quickly gets to grips with its assembly and disassembly.

Dean is next into the Diary Room and says that last night's was the most stress-free eviction so far. 'Whether by design or fluke, last night was a lot more housemate-friendly. It wasn't enjoyable, but it was as close as you are going to get, considering it's someone you like leaving.' He says he is not worried about leaving, and puts this down to the fact that 'my girlfriend and our life are pleasant and fulfilling, and all I want to do is get back to that'. He has cheered up since last week and says the whole *Big Brother* experience has been 'totally, one hundred per cent positive'.

An hour later, Paul is called in. He says the drum-kit task is the best they have had yet, and that it is nice being part of a smaller group. He is not surprised to have survived against Amma.

'It's quite obvious we didn't get on like a house on fire. She's convinced that when we get out we could be friends, but I don't think so. Six weeks in here and we haven't gelled.'

He adds that, although he is used to eviction nominations, the evening itself is stressful. 'Fifteen minutes before, I'm a nightmare. It would be nice to have a week off, but that isn't going to happen, because I'm left in the house with people I don't gel with, bar Helen, and I know I'll be up for nomination until the public vote me out. If Penny and Stuart were here, I wouldn't have been nominated so much.'

Because none of them were up early, the housemates have a late 'lunch' at 7 p.m. Afterwards, Big Brother gives them another mini-task: plates of cheese and crackers are delivered, and they are asked to guess which country and from which animal the cheese comes. Brian and Helen make a lot of noise about how horrible the cheese is, but fortunately the others are happy to get into the tasting. They get more than half of the answers right, which entitles

FAVOURITE SONGS/MUSIC

Amma: 'Cigarettes and Coffee' by Otis Redding
Brian: 'My Heart Will Go On' by Celine Dion
Bubble: 'Baby Girl Window' by Robbie Williams
Dean: Stevie Wonder
Elizabeth: Annie Lennox
Helen: 'Rhythm is a Dancer' by Snap
Josh: 'Promised Land' by Joe Cool
Narinder: 'Don't Call Me Baby' by Voice of the Beehive
Paul: 'Always' by Bon Jovi
Penny: 'Desert Rose' by Sting
Stuart: 'Underground Overground' by the Wombles ('my first ever purchase')

them to a cheese-and-wine party. Four bottles of wine and a lot more cheese and crackers are duly delivered.

Josh has been quietly working on a giant fan for a couple of days now. Brian is impressed. Although their head-to-head discussion last week did not seem to resolve anything, the pair are getting on better, and they have a quiet chat about their childhoods.

Liz is called to the Diary Room, and she thanks Big Brother for both tasks, which have brightened Saturday – usually her lowest day of the week. She admits that she does not connect with Paul, although she has a lot more respect for him now that there are fewer people in the house. She has also got to know Brian much better, and feels that the whole *Big Brother* experience is having a positive effect on him.

Brian is the sixth housemate to go into the Diary Room to talk about the eviction and its aftermath. He says that he is listening to other members of the group more, particularly Dean. He admits that when he first met Helen he thought she was immature, but says he would now like to be with her in the final week. He thinks he has grown up a lot:

'I'm thinking about reading more books and taking country walks. I've been quite ignorant. Initially, I'm going to be scared walking out of the house. It is going to be tough. I hope my friends still like me for who I am, and my family aren't too upset with how I've been perceived.' He says he's looking forward to going out and getting drunk, and that his long-term aim is to settle down, buy a dog and find the man of his dreams. 'But that's gonna be hard – I think I'll be like Bridget Jones.'

Paul tells the others about his taste in women – he likes 'girlie girls', but they also have to be intelligent. Helen says she has 'blown that one, then', and the others all rush to reassure her that there will be men queuing up for her when she leaves the house. Later, in the hot tub, Helen and Paul continue the discussion, but Paul gets side-tracked when Helen's bikini top springs open and he gets a good look at her boobs. She reminds him that he has seen them before.

With four bottles of wine downed, the housemates would love to carry on drinking. They try to persuade Big Brother to hand over more, with Brian sitting on Josh's lap in the Diary Room pleading that they need the booze to relieve the stress of not getting on with each other – they are told there will be no more alcohol that night. Brian takes a different tack and begins chatting up Big Brother, asking him, 'Are you single? Are you seeing Big Sister? Perhaps we could go out to dinner, either one of us – although I'm the obvious choice.'

Helen, Brian and Paul talk in the lounge about losing their virginity. Helen lost hers at eighteen, Paul at seventeen and Brian at twenty. In the garden, Dean and Liz have a long chat in which she tells Dean that she thinks Helen has lost her good qualities and is now rude, over-sensitive and paranoid. She adds that there are more people in the house she does not connect with than there are people she bonds with. Dean agrees, saying that he and Helen will never really get on.

Helen is alone in the girls' room, and Paul goes in to chat with her about her relationship with her boyfriend, Big G. Liz joins them, and Paul reverts to a favourite theme of his: Josh's sexuality and his annoyance with Josh for getting so close to the girls in the hot tub on Liz's birthday.

The boys wake up just before 9 a.m. on Sunday morning – much earlier than they intended. Paul is talking very loudly in his sleep. They all clearly hear him making an acceptance speech, as though he had won the *Big Brother* prize. 'Thank you for picking me, everybody that did – that's cool,' he says, and thanks those who voted for him. He is the last housemate to get up, not stirring until 1 p.m., and when he emerges from the bedroom he is greeted by a chorus of cheers and demands to hear his speech again. Dean jokes that they should all nominate him for his arrogance, but Brian says it would make no difference if they did. (They all believe, on the evidence of four eviction nights, that Paul has a massive fan club outside the house.) Later in the day, Paul confesses to Big Brother that he is embarrassed about his sleeptalking.

'I don't have a clue what I'm saying. The guys were winding me up, but that's not a cool thing to talk about. It sounds really arrogant,' he moans.

Three of the housemates, Dean, Elizabeth and Josh, have asked to have chats with the psychotherapist. Such meetings are the only time in the house when the contestants can talk without being recorded. All three of them are glad of the chance. Afterwards, Josh tells the others that during his session they discussed the fact that some of his family did not know about his sexuality until immediately before he came into the house. Liz says her encounter brought 'a touch of reality' into the strange *Big Brother* world. 'I feel a bit of a fuller person,' she says.

Despite her outburst against Helen last night, Liz teaches Helen how to make a flan. They practise the task while the flan is cooking, and then spend a quiet afternoon dozing and talking. Dean strums his guitar, and, with help from Josh and Dean, Brian begins improvizing the words of a song about the mood in the house. It goes:

'Here we sit
Wondering what's out there
We really don't know
We really don't care
We're probably hated
Everyone's wondering
Everyone's scared
Everyone's alone
If we trust each other
We'll get safely home
It takes a smile
A look in the eye
Everything will be fine
Everything, everything will be fine
All you do is think about me, me, me

▲ The housemates found the several mirrors disconcerting.

▲ Liz dressed as Amma, and Josh dressed as Brian for the soap opera.

▲ Liz vents her frustrations to Big Brother.

▲ With a moustache and beret, Liz reveals her artistic side.

▲ Liz in that pink jumper.

▲ Liz 'flirts' with an oblivious Stuart.

▲ Tiger eyes – Stuart terrifies the housemates.

▲ Stuart with his wife, Sian, after his eviction.

▲ Stuart can't resist a wink as he makes up with Penny.

▲ Stuart's ritual morning stomach crunches.

▲ Stuart perfects his golden tan.

▲ **Penny takes over the shopping list.**

▲ **Penny with 'her little love', Paul.**

▲ **A girlie chat for Penny and Narinder.**

▲ **Dressed in pyjamas, Penny gets to grips with the chickens.**

▲ **Bubble comforts Penny after her row with Stuart.**

▲ **Penny lays down the law about table manners.**

▲ **Josh is held in suspense before he joins the others.**

▲ **The shock arrival of Josh draws a crowd.**

▲ **Josh in the Diary Room.**

▲ **Josh put the housemates through their paces.**

▲ **Josh, who promised to bring fun, nudity and nocturnal naughtiness, settles for reading a book instead.**

▲ **Josh gets his revenge by winding Brian up on their romantic date.**

▲ **The housemates enjoy a sing-song while Dean plays guitar.**

▲ **Paddy, the twelfth housemate.**

▲ **The contestants put their finishing touches to their mural.**

▲ **Dean's in charge – here he reads out the details of the task to the others.**

▲ **Brian, Bubble and Narinder make a joint effort on the washing-up.**

▲ **The housemates practise for the drum kit task.**

▲ **Dean runs amok with a toy gun at the children's party.**

▲ **Liz and Stuart spent so much time playing tennis that the others began to gossip.**

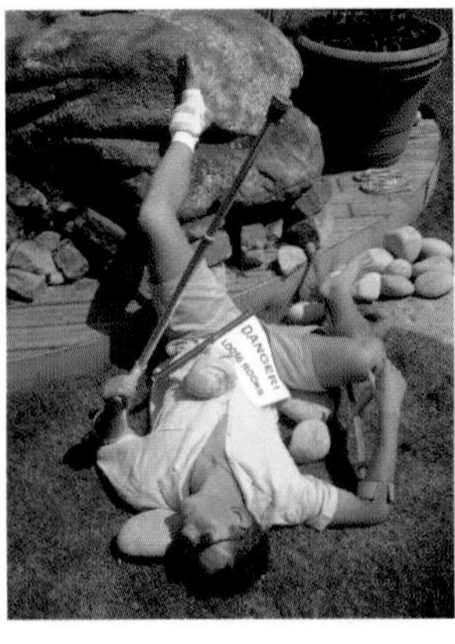

The contestants strike a pose for the calendar.

YOU MAKE
THE FINAL

▲ **A happy Liz reunited with partner Steve.**

▼ **Dean larges it for the cameras.**

▲ **After squealing all the way down the Walk of Shame, Helen finally gets her man.**

◀ **Brian celebrates winning with his friend Michelle.**

And I, I, I
Listen to the sound of claws
Clicking on the floor
That's lush, that's lush.'

Brian realizes that the next eviction will be taking place on Friday, 13 June, which he feels is a bad omen. He is convinced that he will be leaving the house on that day. The housemates all agree that if they survive the nomination process they should pay a forfeit. Brian initially says he will learn to play backgammon, but the others change this to wearing boxer shorts and safety gear for a whole day. Dean will dress in Brian's clothes. Liz will wear makeup and a dress and be girlie. A suggestion that Helen should speak as quietly as Amma for a day, with no screaming allowed, is overruled on the grounds of impossibility, and it is agreed she will learn some interesting facts from a trivia book they have. Paul has to wear Helen's Big G cap for a day.

In the Diary Room, Dean says how much he enjoyed talking with the psychotherapist, and how he is considering seeing a therapist when he leaves the house because 'this whole experience has been one of self-discovery, pushing myself this way and that, trying to unravel who I am'. He says that he is not going to nominate Paul, to give him a break.

Josh has a disappointment – after hours of work, he has finally finished his huge fan, but on its first use there is a loud crack as the framework snaps in half. Josh tries to laugh it off, but it's clear he is upset.

Brian is dismayed to find that since he has been inside the house his waist measurement has increased by two inches. In despair, he goes outside with Dean who puts him through 230 torturous sit-ups. When the boys go to bed Josh – who has been the butt of a great deal of humour from Brian – tells Brian that he has reinforced his bed.

The only three to get up before noon the next day are Josh, Helen and Elizabeth, but before too long, they head back to bed. At 1.05 p.m., when Big Brother announces that they will have to make nominations in one hour's time, all the housemates are asleep. They rouse themselves and eat porridge before the terrible naming of names. Josh gets four nominations and Helen three. Brian receives two nominations, as does Paul, who is off the eviction hook for a week. The housemates will not be told this until tomorrow. In the Diary Room, Dean explains his crucial decision not to choose Paul (if Dean had chosen Paul instead of Josh, there would have been three housemates up for the eviction vote, with Paul joining Josh and Helen).

'The chances are that I'd get on better with Josh on the outside than Paul. But the emotional decision I made this week was that Paul has had enough and has showed great character. Obviously it affects him, and obviously it hurts him, and for me it was time to show I appreciated the fact that he had been nominated four times and had reacted so well.'

The housemates put in some practice on the task, and seem to be getting the hang of it – although they incur penalty points, their time is well within the limit. Afterwards, Brian – who has been talking about how he craves

WHO NOMINATES WHO

Brian nominates Paul and Josh
Dean nominates Helen and Josh
Elizabeth nominates Paul and Helen
Helen nominates Dean and Josh
Josh nominates Brian and Helen
Paul nominates Brian and Josh

				Brian	
			Dean	Dean	
Josh			Elizabeth	Helen	Brian
Paul	Helen		Josh	Paul	Elizabeth
2	1	0	3	4	2
Brian	Dean	Elizabeth	Helen	Josh	Paul

Week 7 nominees: Josh with four nominations and Helen with three.

Analysis
For the first time in four weeks Paul is not up for eviction. Josh and Brian nominate each other. Elizabeth nominates Paul for the fifth time.

Reasons
Dean on Josh: 'He's been quite guarded, and I've found it difficult to make a real connection because of that.'
Elizabeth on Helen: 'She likes white, I like black; she likes sweet, I like savoury. Stupid reason, and I hate this because I can't find any good reasons.'
Paul on Josh: 'He's very, very competitive, and there's a bit of a poncey, slimy side to him.'

human contact – demands a hug from Helen. She obliges, even rolling around on the floor hugging him. Paul and she have been flirting for hours, and he would obviously love a hug, too, but the two of them manage to resist for an hour or so. In the kitchen later, when Helen initiates another conversation about hugging, they give in and fall into each other's arms. It's a long, affectionate hug, and Paul describes her as 'really very cuddly'. Brian says he can imagine the two of them together when they leave the house, driving each other insane. Helen rules out this possibility, because she lives in Wales and Paul lives in Reading. Brian jokingly describes her as a 'bit of a dirty bitch', who probably likes to 'be on top' when she makes love, to which Helen answers seriously: 'It's the only way to stop your hair getting messed up.'

If Paul and Helen are growing closer, so are Josh and Brian. Although, once again, the pair have nominated each other, they are engaging in lots of conversations. Josh tells Brian that the younger housemate has 'grown up a bit' since they first met. 'You're still funny, humorous Brian, but you're more sensible, you think before you say things, you're a bit kinder.' They agree that their paths would never have crossed in the outside world, and Brian tackles Josh about his failure to open up and be himself. Josh says he has held back, but would not have done so had he been in the house from the beginning.

'If you'd been here from the beginning we'd be as thick as thieves by now,' says Brian.

Josh agrees, 'We'd be a lot closer, more intimate.'

In the evening, Big Brother sets the group a time-travel topic for discussion. After initial confusion, Helen decides she would like to travel back to see the Beatles play live, or Elvis in concert in Las Vegas. She would also like to be around at the birth of disco, so she could dance like Olivia Newton John in *Grease*. Josh says he would like to be one of the knights of the Round Table, Liz would like to ride Red Rum to victory in the Grand National, or be a shaman in a native-American tribe (much to the confusion of Helen, who only knows of Shamen as in a pop band). Paul would like to travel to the future to discover what the human mind is capable of, and Dean would also like to leap forward to a time when colour, gender and sexuality don't matter, and everyone gets on with everyone else – 'a completely chilled-out place'. Brian would like to meet Mother Teresa or Princess Diana, or travel back to his parents' wedding day, and then his own birth. He also says he would like to be Queen Elizabeth I's right-hand man. 'I could fight, and be on my horse too. I've had gingivitis. I could help her,' he adds, bafflingly.

After midnight, the housemates recount stories of witchcraft and the occult, with Josh, Liz and Dean telling tales that terrify Brian and Helen. Liz admits she has a friend who is a witch, and Josh tells of his success at communicating with 'the other side' through a ouija board. He also owns up to an interest in devil worship, frightening the others by telling them of a belief that when you look in a mirror the devil is watching you from the other side. Brian has spent much of his time in the house being terrified by 'demons' behind the many mirrors, and now it appears that Josh is confirming his fears. He screams, long and loud.

It is only Dean's spooky tale that brings a chorus of approval. He talks of how he has twice had premonitions. Once, at Chicago airport, he felt a strong urge to tell a mother and two children to move, and as soon as they did shards of glass showered down on the place where they had been sitting. Brian calls him a hero. In another American incident, Dean was speeding along a freeway in San Francisco when something made him slow down, and seconds later a limo shot out in front, missing him by inches.

Later, as Liz and Helen settle down in the girls' room, they hear a lot of squealing and shrieking from the bedroom next door, as the boys, in total darkness, sneak up and terrify Brian. The two girls go in to join them, and Helen makes a beeline for Paul's bed. In the clamour and excitement of Brian-teasing, she and Paul lock fingers. They hold hands for a few seconds, before gently prising themselves apart.

Early in the morning, Paul again talks loudly in his sleep, mentioning Amma's name. The usual morning ritual ensues – Josh and Elizabeth are out of bed and have showers as soon as the hot water is on, followed this morning by Dean. Then they all go back to bed, and at 10.30 a.m., Big Brother wakes them with the news that they will get the nomination results in one hour.

As soon as Paul gets up, he hugs Helen. But it is with Josh she sits holding hands as the results are given, and it is she and Josh who are nominated. Paul gives a great whoop of delight and jumps in the air to celebrate not being included, and then apologizes to the nominees. Josh looks far more upset than Helen, who laughs it off, saying that all Paul's ten-year-old female fans will want her out so that she keeps her hands off him. They are all surprised that there are only two names up for voting – as the number of housemates decreases, the chance of there being more than two up for eviction increases.

The group have a practice run-through of the task, Liz and Helen wearing matching shorts that Liz has made for them, and they achieve a good time. Helen and Brian then closet themselves excitedly in the girls' room to discuss how Helen should wear her hair on Friday and to practise her eviction walk. The remaining housemates note how Helen is assuming that she will be the one to go.

In the Diary Room, Liz talks about how guilty she feels about nominating Helen, and wonders what it would be like to be the only girl in the house. Afterwards, Paul again discusses his lack of ease with Josh's sexuality. He says that if he discovers Josh is not gay he will have a serious issue with him, because he could have 'used the gay thing to compromise people's positions'. He's referring, yet again, to Liz's birthday party, when Josh and Brian may possibly have seen the girls naked. This really seems to bug Paul, despite the fact that he, too, was invited into the bathroom that night. Under attack from Josh and Liz, he denies that he is homophobic, insisting 'I just don't like lying'. Josh tries hard to step back from the argument and in the end tells Paul to let it drop.

In the Diary Room, Helen claims that she doesn't mind being nominated, saying she's surprised to have lasted as long as she has. Brian then goes to the Diary Room to say how surprised he was not to be nominated. He adds that

WHAT THE EXPERTS SAY

BRIAN AND JOSH

'From the day they met, the relationship between Brian and Josh has been fraught with tension. Last week, however, it appeared to hit the rocks. Subsequently relations have disintegrated even further. When the two squared up to talk about the tensions between them, Josh made it clear that much of the problem is Brian's sense of humour. Up until recently, humour has been Brian's strongest weapon, but critically it has depended on partners like Narinder and Bubble, who were prepared to play along with him. Taken out of context, many of the comments made by Brian, Narinder and Bubble could sound extremely spiteful, but none of them takes offence because they all understand the rules of the particular game they are playing, the ritual insult. Rule number one is that both parties have to signal a willingness to co-operate. They do this by maintaining high levels of eye contact throughout. Both parties must also exchange insults on a mutually agreed topic. They're a perfect comedy double act. But Narinder and Bubble have gone, leaving Brian without a partner, and now he has Josh in his sights. The rules of ritual insults mean that even the severest tease can be funny if reciprocated. But if someone doesn't play along, the insults cease to be funny and they're taken seriously. Although Josh says he's OK with it, his true feelings are revealed in a grimace. Furthermore, the group are picking up on Josh's discomfort.

'Can Brian be sufficiently sensitive to the responses of the remaining housemates to adapt his humour to the changed situation in the house?'

Professor Geoffrey Beattie, Psychologist

he has never thought about winning or even staying in the house to the end, as he doesn't want to build up his expectations and then get hurt.

Paul follows Brian in and expresses his relief at not being nominated, as he feels as though he doesn't know what it is like to live in the house without the threat of eviction. He says he thinks he may make it to the end of the show.

To relieve the boredom, both Liz and Josh have come up with new games. Using joss sticks and a plastic bottle, Liz has created a home-made version of Kerplunk!, which keeps Brian and Josh amused during the afternoon. In the evening, Josh gets the others playing a game called Ibble Dibble. This involves being branded on the face with the charcoal from a burnt cork, and then rapidly adding up the number of marks, or 'dibbles', on the faces of other contestants. Helen and Paul are both hopeless at it, which causes Helen much amusement:

'Me and Paul are the same mentality – and he designs car doors and I just cut hair!' she laughs. The game descends into chaos as she and Paul chase each other around and smudge each other's marks. 'They so need to shag each other stupid,' comments Brian. Josh remarks to Helen that when he first met her she talked about her boyfriend all the time, but now she hardly ever mentions him.

Sitting in the garden wrapped in blankets, Dean and Liz discuss their future within the house. Dean does not think he has much prospect of winning, because he comes across as quiet. He and Liz agree that they are not the most exciting characters to watch: Liz believes she must be seen outside as the most boring of the housemates. She says that, although she can have fun, she would rather ride a horse than 'go clubbing with stars on my nipples'. She admits that she finds it hard talking to Paul and Helen: 'I was talking to them and I could feel the shutters coming down, the plug coming out of the socket.'

Later, Dean goes into the Diary Room with his guitar. After singing hello to Big Brother, he says everyone is starting to think about the end of the show, and the more they think about the world outside the harder it is. 'Counting the days off is negative, and I've got to try to pull myself out of that. Everyone's focus has shifted from the present to the future.'

Brian questions Helen about her plans for when she leaves the *Big Brother* house. She's looking forward to having her hair done, a fake-tanning treatment, a facial, a manicure 'and everything', and then enjoying a night out in Cardiff with her friends. She does not mention Big G.

Josh persuades all the housemates to go to bed, so that they will be rested for the task in the morning. The evening ends with a pillow fight, which goes on much longer for Paul and Helen than for the others. Ironically, Josh gets up again after half an hour, unable to sleep. He goes to the Diary Room and talks about what he will miss if he leaves the house: 'I'll miss the mental struggle of getting through to the end, I'll miss the friends I've made. I'll miss everyone taking the piss out of Big Brother. I won't miss the food or the lack of exercise.'

He still isn't able to sleep, and Liz finds him reading in the lounge.

'Everything from the day is going through my head.' he says. 'I was a bit shaky up to 5 p.m., but now I'm through it. When I first heard my name I was gutted. There's a really weird feeling in your gut, you're trying to put a brave face on it, but you don't know how to react. It's really weird on your emotions. Crazy.'

Two hours later, when the housemates are all in bed, Paul starts to sleeptalk, saying 'I am top secret…' and sings a few notes. At the same time, as if they are in sync, Helen is muttering aloud in the girls' room.

It is very windy on Wednesday morning, and the wall that forms part of the task obstacle course blows over. More disconcertingly for Helen and Elizabeth – who are the only two out of bed at 11 a.m. – the door to the house blows open, and they catch a tantalizing glimpse of the young cameraman who closes it.

Shortly after noon, the housemates are tested on the drum-kit task. They perform it in a relaxed and ordered way, with Brian joining Dean as group leader, encouraging the others. The group reckon they made it in good time, but have to wait for two hours before Big Brother confirms that they completed the task in six minutes and forty-six seconds. With five penalty points, which cost fifteen seconds each, they have a final time of eight minutes and one second, scraping home fourteen seconds inside the limit. They are thrilled, and a loud shout of 'alcohol!' goes up as Big Brother tells them they have £57.29 to spend next week.

To while away the rest of the afternoon, Josh and Liz make an archery target. Dean improvizes a bow and arrow from garden canes and elastic, and everyone has fun having a go. Helen proves to be surprisingly good at it, but Brian struggles because he is left-handed. In the Diary Room, first Dean and then Helen appear cheerful: Dean says he thinks the task was a good one, because it brought the whole group together, and that he would like to stay in the house until the last day, which he thinks will be a lot of fun. Helen says that she would not mind leaving on Friday, but if she stays she is looking forward to another week and another task.

Brian takes Liz into the girls' room to do her hair and makeup: she has agreed to become a girlie girl for the day in return for not being nominated. Helen helps out, and when Liz emerges the other housemates compliment her. She's all dressed up and now she has a reason for it: as a treat, Big Brother announces that a gourmet dinner will be served at properly-laid tables for two. The housemates must divide into pairs and decide who is going to eat in the girls' room, the conservatory and the den. A huge cheer goes up when they hear that six bottles of wine are included in the treat. They can even choose from a menu: for starters, they can select roast-tomato tart with wild-rocket and balsamic dressing or Scottish smoked salmon with lemon; for the main course, there is pan-fried sea bass, stir-fried vegetables, *bok-choi* and chilli oil or rack of lamb with summer vegetables and port sauce; and for pudding, they can have either summer pudding or chocolate pot, with coffee to follow.

With this week's severely strained finances, the housemates' food supplies are running low and a free meal is very welcome. Helen squeals excitedly, bagging first Paul as her partner and then the den as her location, although, in the interests of fairness, the locations are eventually decided on the toss of a coin (they use Josh's American dime). Liz and Dean win and agree to eat in the conservatory. Helen and Paul come second and Helen gets her wish. Josh and Brian are relegated to the girls' room. As Helen delightedly fusses over the date, worrying about whether or not to wash her hair, Josh is called to the Diary Room to talk about his reaction to being nominated.

'Yesterday I was dwelling too much on who nominated me, different combinations of the votes. Up to about 6 p.m., my head was spinning with that. Now, I think, hey, it's out of my hands, the public are voting, so I've got to get on with the week, get the most out of it, enjoy it, and see if I'm still here on Saturday morning.'

Brian confides to Dean that he has no idea what he and Josh will talk to each other about for four hours during their dinner. Dean joins Liz in paying a forfeit for not being nominated – he dresses in Brian's clothes, but is extremely uncomfortable doing so.

When Paul asks Helen what the ground rules for their date are, she tells him there are none, and he should 'go with the flow'. Brian tells them that he could see them making a couple, and that they would be 'annoyingly in love'. He jokes about a *Big Brother* wedding.

The late afternoon and early evening fly by for Helen. While most of the others sleep, she gets down to the serious business of showering, putting her hair in rollers, buffing her nails and soaking her feet. Eventually, even she dozes off, and the housemates are all woken at 7 p.m. by an announcement from Big Brother that their meal will be with them shortly.

Josh and Brian pretend that they have never met before, and invent phoney pasts to enliven the over-dinner chat. Brian arrives first at the 'restaurant', and while he waits for Josh mutters nervously into his microphone: 'Which fork do I use? I feel like him in *Titanic* [Brian's all-time favourite film]. Work from the outside in, work from the outside in … '

Despite their misgivings, Brian and Josh manage to remain on civilized terms. Brian accuses Josh of trying to get him drunk, and Josh says that he is doing so because he wants to find the 'real Brian'. He even compliments Brian, and then forces his housemate to reciprocate. Brian tells Josh he has nice eyes, and that he thinks he is a 'really nice, sweet guy'. Josh quickly dispels this illusion by asking, 'So will you give me a blow job?' and by telling his dinner date, 'I don't do dates. I only do shags.' He then steals Brian's wine, which sets them off on their usual round of bickering.

For Dean and Elizabeth, the candle-lit meal loses one of its main ingredients when Paul and Helen steal their candle. Liz seems miffed, but Dean says he doesn't mind. She gives him a tip on wine etiquette, telling him always to leave an inch at the top of the glass. The pair chat about holidays and then, after drinking a toast to their absent partners, Vanessa and Steve, talk about relationships. Liz says that for her sex is 'a deep and heightened form of communication with someone' and that she can only have sex with someone she knows well. Dean says that he also thinks it is deep and meaningful, but that on another level it is possible to enjoy great sex with someone you don't know. They agree this is a male attitude.

The really exciting date is the one happening in the den, where Helen and Paul flirt outrageously all evening. Paul has raided the wardrobe of the house's fashion supremo, Josh, and is wearing a Gucci shirt. He tells Helen to eat all her asparagus, as it is an aphrodisiac, a word Helen has a problem repeating after two bottles of wine! She seems to be making the running – she tries to persuade Paul to spend the night with her in the den, she initiates hugs, and even tells him she loves him. For an instant, it seems that Paul is going to get carried away: he picks her up and puts her down on the cushions, kneeling next to her. But instead of following through with a kiss, he pulls away, saying, 'This is all getting out of hand. Down, boy!'

Despite the romantic setting, Paul is hardly Mr Smooth. He tells Helen that she's not beautiful (although he concedes she is pretty) and that she's not his cup of tea. He seems more interested in recounting a story about his problems with a dishwasher than in getting any closer to her. At one point he informs a bemused Helen:

'I've lived my adult life like an international pop star. I've always had fun.'

He also announces that Helen is not the 'clean-cut girl' he is waiting for, and that she wouldn't ever be able to trust him, to which she plaintively replies that she would trust him with her life.

The pair then emerge to pretend to the other housemates that they have snogged, although no-one believes them. But when Paul and Helen are back in the den, the rest of the group agree that there is a strong sexual chemistry between them, and that Paul is holding back because of Helen's relationship with Big G. They all discuss their sexual frustration, and Liz gives Brian some instructions on how to masturbate in bed, undetected by the cameras.

Paul and Helen try to persuade Brian that he should spend the night with them in the den as a chaperone, but he refuses. Back in the house with the others, the pair sit hand-in-hand drinking cider while all the housemates sing along to Dean's guitar playing. Perhaps fired up by the music, Brian does a series of cartwheels around the kitchen, and is so hyperactive that Dean gives him a dose of his herbal remedy, which is supposed to have a calming effect. Brian goes to bed, and when he says goodnight, Helen asks for a kiss. 'Here we go, tongues and everything,' he says, before swooping on her for a snog, and then declares that he is off to try out Liz's instructions. However, Brian's plans are thwarted when Helen and Paul join him in the boys' room, where he tries to get to the bottom of their feelings for one another. He discovers that Helen classes her relationship with her boyfriend as 'on-off', and that she does not think Paul should be inhibited by it. Paul says he has feelings for Helen, but is unsure whether it is because he has had no sex for seven weeks or whether he really likes her. He says they will not know until they are out of the house.

When Josh goes to bed he is surprised to find Brian asleep in it. Brian climbs out and goes into Bubble's vacant double bed, only to switch back to his own when Helen decides to sleep in the boys' room. It is 5 a.m. before the housemates are all asleep, and an hour later Paul is talking again. 'Why me?' he asks loudly.

The next morning, none of the housemates are pleased to be dragged from their beds at 10 a.m., when Big Brother orders them to return the tables and everything else that was provided for last night's meal. Brian manages to get up just as the others finish the clearing up, and he turns tail and follows them all straight back to bed, where Paul regales the other boys with stories of how he cut up Helen's food during their date and fed her like a baby. Brian is positively envious. Paul asks Josh to rate his date out of ten, and Josh gives Brian two – one for turning up and one for being able to talk. Brian appears to be hurt, but gives Josh four or five out of ten, as he was impressed that Josh looked good and made him talk. But the low marks, coupled with his hang-over, make the ebullient Brian unusually grumpy.

The housemates are given a new task, to be completed in one day. They have to paint a life-size portrait of the whole group. They decide to do a beach scene and assume a pose, with Helen in a deckchair, Paul sprawled at her feet, and the rest of the group ranged behind. Liz completes a preliminary sketch. Each housemate has to paint another. To help put them in an artistic mood, they are provided with berets and they paint moustaches on their faces. Liz suggests that Helen should wear her Big G hat, and Dean says that it should now be a Big P hat.

Dean paints Brian as Satan (as that is Brian's most frequently used description of almost anything). He gives his subject red horns, a tail and

WHAT THE EXPERTS SAY

PAUL AND MIRRORS

'Paul's relationship with the mirror has become increasingly important to him. Paul has always been the biggest user of mirrors in the house. He uses them five to ten times as much as anyone else. There are times when he simply can't help himself. Part of this is due to vanity, but mirrors are about much more. The way people use mirrors tells us a lot about their personality. In Paul's case, it provides important clues as to how he feels about himself and his changing situation within the house. In the early days, Paul's mirror watching was brief and functional, his concern was with his physical appearance. We can see this in the way he fiddles with the front of his hair, the part he assumes is the most visible to others.

'As the weeks have gone by, Paul has become increasingly confused. He knows the housemates are rejecting him, but doesn't know whether the public vote is for him or against his opponent. He's no longer sure how he's perceived. This has coincided with a fourfold increase in his mirror watching: he's now using the mirror to try to understand how other people see him. This is supported by the fact that most of his mirror use occurs at weekends, right after the eviction. In fact, on one Sunday he looked at himself about thirty times in half an hour.

'Paul is also isolated from the group, and because he's not getting any support or affection from the others, he has had to seek it elsewhere, and he's done this with the mirrors. Increasingly, we see him touching the top and back of his head. These are classic self-comforting gestures. Paul is actually doing to himself what he would like others to do to him.

'Recently, Paul has become much more confident, and we can see this reflected in the mirror. Shortly after Bubble's eviction, we see him rolling back his shoulders, puffing out his chest and stepping back to admire himself. His attention has shifted from his face to the more powerful muscles of his body. Our self-esteem is based largely on the positive reactions of others. Now Paul isn't getting this from the housemates, so resourcefully he's gone elsewhere. When he gets up in the morning, the first thing he does is look for himself in the mirror. It's only here he can get really close to someone, someone whose movements are perfectly synchronized with his own. If Paul's not careful, the most meaningful relationship he has in the house could be the one with his own image.'

Dr Peter Collett, Experimental Psychologist

cloven hooves, and surrounds him with flames, but adds a halo as an afterthought, to show Brian's angelic side. Dean then terrifies the impressionable Brian by telling him that in the night the Satan figure he has painted in the picture will come to life, leaving a hole in the canvas.

Brian announces that he has not had sex since December 1999. Despite this long period of celibacy, it is the time in the house which is proving the most difficult for him – he admits he is feeling hornier than he has ever felt in his life. Helen and Paul are still flirting madly, chasing each other around with paintbrushes in their hands, and soon Liz and Brian join in, daubing each other blue.

Paul paints 'I love sex' in bright yellow on Helen's back, then holds her close, trying to get the words on her back to imprint onto his bare chest. It doesn't work, but it gives the pair an excuse for even more bodily contact. She scrawls something on his leg, then he hugs her and strokes her arm, following her to one of the large cushions, where he puts his arm behind her.

In the Diary Room, Brian says he is painting Josh, and may miss his pecs out 'just to piss him off'. He says he will miss whichever of the nominees is evicted, but Helen more than Josh. Weekends are 'always crappy' he says, because normally he would be going out with his friends. 'But you can't go on feeling crappy, because you have to participate with the rest of the group, you have to give one hundred per cent and get on with it.'

It takes the group eleven hours to complete the painting. All very satisfied with their effort, which they describe as 'brilliant', they hand the finished masterpiece in just before midnight. Helen is grateful to Liz for painting her with nice boobs. Paul is less happy with Helen's depiction of him with orange hair and a deformed foot.

Josh and Brian, who are getting on better, have a serious conversation about the possibility of Josh leaving. They agree that, given time, they could get along well. Josh says he believes he will leave the house on Friday, as being gay will hinder his chances of staying. He says that he has enjoyed the last two days, and that he wants to stay in the house more than anything else. Their serious chat descends into farce when Josh discovers that Brian has hidden his book, and tickles him into a screaming frenzy until he reveals it. While the others listen to Brian describing how spoilt he was as a child, Paul and Helen enjoy a dip in the hot tub.

After the rest have drifted to bed, Dean, Paul and Helen chat in the conservatory. Helen is very impressed by Dean's tales of life in a band. Helen says she can see him on *Top of the Pops* when they leave, but Dean would prefer to appear on *Later with Jools Holland*. Paul and Helen share a hug before they go off to their separate bedrooms.

Friday morning is quiet, apart from a moment of panic when Elizabeth remembers that she forgot to take the cider out of the Store Room when it was open. This means they will not have alcohol for eviction night. Helen is treated to breakfast in bed – an omelette made for her by Paul. Brian is not so lucky – Paul throws a glass of water over him to wake him up. Later, when he is having a cold shower, Josh and Paul storm in and throw more water over him, with Josh saying it's holy water to 'purify' him.

As Paul and Helen continue to find any excuse to play together, Brian sums up the feelings of the other housemates when he says behind their backs: 'Shag, please, get it over with.' He and Dean agree that if the show were to last another ten weeks, Paul and Helen would be 'at it like rabbits'.

There's a serious moment in the afternoon when Dean challenges Brian's Catholicism, asking him how he can subscribe to a church which does not recognize his sexuality. Brian seems genuinely worried, and asks whether there are any churches that do accept homosexuality.

Liz goes on a house search for some missing black socks, and when Paul obligingly turns out his clothes to look for them he finds not the socks but a pair of her knickers. Helen reacts jealously, and insists on giving him a pair of hers. The two lovebirds spend the afternoon engrossed in each other, and Paul confesses to Helen that he will be 'gutted' if she leaves. They have a play fight, which climaxes with Paul wrestling Helen on to the bed and collapsing on top of her. Pinning her down, he makes her promise to be his slave for a day if she survives eviction.

Helen has already told Big Brother that she is not worried about the possibility of being evicted. In the Diary Room, Josh explains that he feels he cannot lose – he would love to stay in the house, but is also longing to see his family and friends.

The cider crisis is looming, as the group face a dry eviction night. Liz and Paul each go to the Diary Room to beg for the chance to retrieve the booze from the Store Room, but are turned down. They all start complaining, and contemplate whether they should refuse to co-operate with the eviction process. Dean says it would not be fair on Josh and Helen to spoil their last night. He, too, goes to the Diary Room – he is recalled shortly afterwards and emerges with the cider. Brian leads the others in a chant of 'Dean is a treasure, Vanessa is a lucky woman'.

When the news of the eviction comes through, the housemates are all sitting in the lounge, with Paul and Josh sitting either side of Helen, holding her hands. Liz and Brian cling to each other, and Dean sits on his own. When Davina announces that Josh is to go, he takes it well, telling the others, who queue to hug him, that he expected it. In the hour and a half he has to get ready, he tells them he is going to go straight home. He is dejected, feeling he did not get the chance to be himself.

In the Diary Room, Josh admits that he is 'scared, anxious, excited'.

'I'm just thinking of where I am going to be in a few hours. I think it will be an extraordinary emotional ride, going into the spotlight and then back to normal life. It's crazy, mad, unbelievable.'

Josh is too nervous to dance as the music plays into the house, but the others get into their usual frenzied Friday-night routine. Helen gives him messages for all her family and friends, including Big G, who she assumes will be there. In the quiet of the boys' room, Brian says a sad farewell to Josh, and then expounds to Dean the reason he believes that Josh never relaxed in the house.

'He never got the chance to be himself, coming in week two. And when

WHAT THE EXPERTS SAY

HELEN

'If the experience of being in the *Big Brother* house has made children of the group, Helen has carved out a more particular role for herself – she is the youngest child. She tends to use short, simple sentences, and often refers to herself in the third person, just as a child would. Her face is expressive and she frequently widens her eyes when she speaks. This makes her eyes look bigger, a baby-like quality which appeals to the other housemates. We are biologically tuned to nurture and care for the young, ensuring the survival of the species. Even the smallest child will care for a baby. This has advantages for both sides. For Helen, it means any weaknesses are tolerated and even indulged by the group. It also means she is not perceived as a threat to the others in this competitive environment.

'However, the role of the youngest child may only be successful in the short term. There is a down side to having a child in the house. Children need looking after – they don't always pull their weight or complete tasks. The costs of looking after her may outweigh the benefits of having her around. Already we see some signs of resentment creeping in. Unfortunately, one of Helen's most appealing assets could lead to her downfall.'

Dr Sonia Sharp, Educational Psychologist

he survived the first nomination round, he thought it was because he had been quiet, so he didn't want to change.'

The housemates form a shorter tunnel of hands every week, but it is a tradition and they do it for Josh, who leaves the house to be greeted enthusiastically by his eighty-nine-year-old grandmother, his brother, his sister-in-law and loads of friends. He doesn't wear his famous £2,500 trousers, much to Davina's disappointment – he tells her he decided to dress down.

Back in the house, Brian becomes tearful on his own in the boys' room, and Big Brother calls him to the Diary Room to talk about how he feels. He says he is feeling weepy, looking at pictures of his friends and family. He talks about feeling that he is the odd one out of the remaining five: Paul and Helen are a pair and Dean and Elizabeth get on very well. When he rejoins the others they are talking about superheroes. Liz reveals that she would love to ride around on a powerful motorbike wearing a bright orange catsuit, stiletto heels and with her hair dyed purple.

In the boys' room, when the lights are out, Dean advises Paul about his relationship with Helen. They all agree that Big G will not be pleased. 'I know that when I leave, he ain't gonna like me at all,' frets Paul. Dean tells him it is not his fault, and Paul says he has tried to cool the relationship 'but in the last couple of weeks it has been a bit bad'.

In the girls' room, Liz and Helen are discussing the same subject. Helen says she is unsure what is happening. She is sure Big G will be waiting for

VOTING

A massive 1,445,438 votes – the highest total so far – were cast, with eighty-four per cent of the voters choosing to evict Josh (1,219,834) and just sixteen per cent wanting Helen out (225,604). Sixty-six per cent of votes were made by phone and thirty-four per cent through interactive television. A million people logged on to the website on Friday. Average viewing figures for the Channel 4 programme were 4.3 million for the week, and the average for watching the live streaming from the house was 521,000, peaking at 626,000 on Wednesday night (the night of the romantic dinner dates). That same night hit a record for *Big Brother's Little Brother* on E4, with 560,000 viewers tuning in. More than three million text messages giving the latest news from the house have been sent out to mobile phones.

her when she leaves – it is a poignant statement, because outside in the real world, Big G has already announced that his relationship with Helen is over. He was not present in the studio to greet her if she had been evicted. Davina, who has spoken to him personally, told the nation on live television, 'Big G does not want to wash his dirty laundry in public, but, understandably, due to the circumstances over the last week or so, he does not want to go out with Helen any more. But he still thinks she is a lovely girl and hopes that she does well.'

JOSH LOOKS BACK: THE EXCLUSIVE INTERVIEW

Josh on the housemates

Stuart: 'Stuart is one of the few who made me feel very welcome. He started talking to me when the others were still holding back. He was up early in the morning like me, and he was into fitness, like me. I was deeply shocked when he was nominated. I don't think he knew much about gay people – he said he would not like to see a man kissing another man. That night I dreamt that he saw me kissing a guy – that's how paranoid I was. I was really pleased when everyone had to say one thing they disliked about another housemate and he chose my tan. It was all a joke, and it showed I was accepted. I wish I'd had longer with Stuart, I think we would have got on very well.'

Narinder: 'She was outspoken, which scared people a bit, and she was noisy, which some of the more sensible members of the group didn't like. She also clashed with Bubble, who was very popular in the house. So I wasn't surprised when she left. But I liked her, I didn't mind her sarcasm. She was very close to Brian, so I couldn't attempt to get to know her because he already felt threatened by me. She should have spent more time with the others. But Dean and Bubble would never have liked her.'

Bubble: 'I nominated him because he made several remarks that made me paranoid. When we were playing volleyball he said, "Josh is a bit competitive, like Stuart, and we all know what happened to him." Then he told me I should give others more time in the kitchen. I felt very guilty nominating him, but I was sure he'd walk it against Paul. He was brilliant in his last week – honest and emotional, which made me feel a real tosser for nominating him. When I saw him with tears in his eyes, I felt like Judas. I gave him some stuff for his skin to take out with him. It was just a small gesture. He'd been using it in the house and his skin had cleared up. When he went, everyone was so down, and we all believed that nobody could win against Paul.'

Amma: 'I want to keep in touch with Amma. I need to make amends with her for nominating her. I never got the chance to explain it to her, and I'm sure she was hurt by it. I really, really liked her. Like me, she wasn't being herself in the house. She's very quiet, and I think her frustration went inward. Then she'd say something that made her sound argumentative. It's a very loud group of people, you have to raise your voice above theirs, and neither she nor I were comfortable with that. I think she was intelligent, thoughtful, interesting. And I meant what I said when they asked me who I would sleep with – she's got a great body!'

Paul: 'He's getting better, and he coped very well with being nominated four times – I know how hard it is, and I admired him for that. But he's really cocky, talking in his sleep about winning. I don't think he truly cares for Helen. I think he's playing a game to win votes. He wants to be a free agent when he leaves – he's always talking about all the offers he'll have from girls. He's so boring.'

Brian: 'He's very juvenile, very funny, very spoilt. He believes the world revolves around him. He is liked inside the house, because he's so funny. I hated nominating him, because it is a very negative thing for a gay man to nominate another gay man. We are completely different people, though, and just because we are gay is no guarantee that we will hit it off. I'd like to meet up with him outside, but he's got so much talent that when he comes out I think he will be in a whirlwind, with lots happening for him. He's quite naive, so I hope he can cope with it all.'

Helen: 'She's great, the only really true person in the house, the only one who isn't playing a game. What you see is what you get – a loveable, sparkly person. She needs a lot of cradling and encouragement, you have to support her through the tasks, but it's all worth it to have her endearing personality around. I really don't want her to be hurt when she comes out, either by Paul or by the break-up of her relationship with Big G. Everybody who knows Helen would want to protect her from hurt.'

Elizabeth: 'She comes over outside as boring, not as exciting as the others. But she is a calming influence on the house, and you need that. She's a feminist, and into pursuits like hiking which some people probably don't understand, and which may make her seem boring. But she's level-headed, mature beyond her years. It was great to talk to her, because you could talk about things other than fashion and disco music. She took me under her wing

– she was the only one who noticed when I was distressed. I really hope I keep in touch with her.'

Dean: 'He's very cool for his age. I loved his guitar. I so missed music, and his guitar was the nearest thing we had to music. He's also level-headed and sensible, with a tremendous sense of equality – he's really opposed to prejudice about race or sexuality, which is very refreshing in a thirty-seven year old. He's got a downbeat humour, which he uses more to stoke the humour of others like Brian and Bubble. We all had a lot of respect for him, because he took no shit from Big Brother, and everybody else was a bit in awe of Big Brother. The only irritating thing is the way Brian is constantly praising him – "Dean's a treasure, Vanessa's so lucky" all the time.'

Josh on life in the house

'None of my true personality came over in the house. I came in as an outsider, and I stayed outside the group. They'd bonded so quickly – they'd been pushed to the limits by a couple of tough tasks, and by having so little food. They'd also had their evening of heart-rending revelations, so they all knew a lot about each other, and they were really close. They talked a lot about the day they all arrived. At first they thought I was a plant. It took three or four days for them to accept that I was another contestant. They were wary of me. And then, just a few days in, Brian launched into a very personal attack on

PEOPLE ON JOSH

Anne, who was up for election with Josh to go into the house: 'I don't think the people in the house allowed him to be himself. They seemed to be afraid of letting him take control and organize games. If they'd let him, they'd have found out what great fun he can be.'

Natasha, who was up for election with Josh to go into the house: 'We had a great laugh in Portugal, and you just haven't seen that side of Josh in the house. He's a great, fun guy, but he came in late and the others had their roles. Brian carries a lot of weight in there, he's loud and bubbly, and Josh was taken aback by it all.'

Josh's brother, Brett: 'He came in late and took a back seat. But when you remember the drinking game on Brian's birthday, it was the best entertainment on *Big Brother* and it was devised by my brother – it brought on the arguments between Brian and my brother and Amma and Stuart.'

Josh's friend, Julia: 'We haven't seen the Josh we know and love. He's not adapted well to life in there, and we haven't seen the real him. He's got so much more to give.'

Margherita Taylor, TV presenter: 'Look at that body!'

me. I was very upset. I was finding it difficult enough, and then one of the most popular members of the group really goes for me. So I took a big step back. Even without Brian, it would have been difficult. Bubble was so loud, such a centre-of-attention person, too.

'I felt like walking out for the whole of that first week. If I'd been there at the beginning it would have been fine. I went to Portugal with Natasha and Anne and we bonded straightaway, and had a great time. We didn't have to tiptoe around each other, but everyone in the house seemed to tiptoe around me. I know I did well to survive as long as I did, as newcomers are always voted out at the first opportunity. But I knew that as the numbers got smaller, I'd be the first to go. The sad thing is, I was beginning to relax. Dean said he was just beginning to get to know me.

'The whole experience was a challenge, and I have no regrets about doing it, and I'd do it again, but I'd want to go in at the beginning. I learned things about myself. I became paranoid in the first few days, thinking everyone disliked me. I've never experienced that kind of insecurity before – I've always been very confident. I knew Brian was mimicking other people, and I was sure he must be doing me behind my back.

'I also felt terribly guilty about nominations, especially Narinder and Amma. With Naz, I didn't really know her, and I just went with the flow of what others were saying. But I liked her, and I nominated her because of the feeling among the others, which was wrong. With Amma, I so regret it. I'd do it differently if I had the chance again.'

Josh on Josh

'Before I went into the house, I flew to Spain to see my parents and my grandmother, because I had to prepare them for everything they might find out about me. I'd told my mum I was gay eighteen months ago. She and my dad came to see me in London and she got drunk – I've never seen my mum drunk. She stayed the night with me, and my dad went back to the family home in Surrey. She said she knew, but she was upset. She made me promise not to tell my dad, and I respected that promise because it meant a lot to her. So before I went on the programme I rang and she told me she had told Dad six months earlier. We had a very emotional phone call, in which he said he still loved me. But then I had to fly out and tell my grandmother. She put her head in her hands and looked shocked, but the next morning she told me she loved me. You can't imagine how good it felt seeing her waiting for me outside the *Big Brother* house, with my brother and his wife. I really had to work hard at not crying.

'I didn't go into the house looking for a career in television or the media, although I'll be interested in anything that comes up. I'm about to become a director and partner in the accommodation agency where I work, which is for gays and lesbians. I was still in the closet when I started working there three years ago, and the first six months were a real learning curve as I found out from others their experiences of being gay. I was shocked about twelve times a day.

WEEK SEVEN FACT FILE

Main task: Transport a drum kit over three obstacles within a time limit.

PASS ☑ **FAIL** ☐

Mini-task: Cheese tasting: identify country and animal the cheese is from.

Mini-task: Complete life-size painting of housemates.

Treats: Cheese, crackers and four bottles of wine. Romantic dinners for two, with six bottles of wine and a gourmet menu.

Bets are on!
To win: Brian is way out ahead of the rest as favourite, at 1/4. Next comes Helen, at 4/1.
To walk: Favourite to leave the house next is Dean, followed by Liz.
Evictee's tip: Josh says, 'Brian or Helen will win. Paul will be the next out.'

'I wanted to create a positive image for gay people, and I hope I have been able to do that. It's great to be out and get my life back – I've got so many friends. And I spent two hours on my first night out just lying on the floor stroking Bailey, my dog. He's an Alsation–Greyhound cross, and I got him from a rescue home three years ago – I love him to bits.'

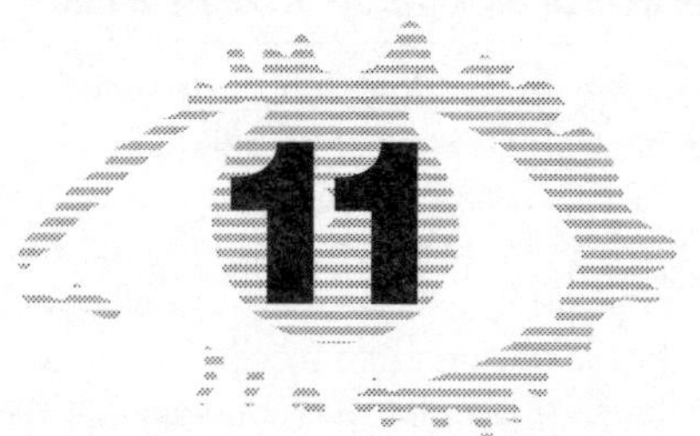

WEEK EIGHT

'I do fancy Helen. I fancy her personality completely.'
Paul

Saturday's usual flat, post-eviction feeling is alleviated by the incessant flirting that has gripped Paul and Helen. They can't get enough of each other. When they're not talking, they're playing games, or just gazing into each other's eyes. With a sleeping Brian as a chaperone, the pair have a frank discussion about Helen's boyfriend Big G. Helen's relationship with him is bothering Paul, who reckons Big G won't be happy watching their flirtation.

'We haven't done anything wrong. For all I know he could have another girlfriend by now,' Helen says.

'But what if he hasn't? What if he's missing you every day and waiting for you?'

'I'll say, "You don't understand what it's like to be in here. Me and Paul get on really well." And he's got female friends,' she replies, defensively.

Paul is not entirely reassured. 'It's really, really awkward. If I was your boyfriend I wouldn't be happy. It takes two to tango, and we're both tangoing. I'm being serious, I'm a bit worried – not about having my head smacked in.'

'He wouldn't hit you.'

'If he did hit me, I'd fucking hit him back. It's not to do with physical violence, it's to do with the fact that he's not happy.'

'Would our relationship be any different if I was single?' Helen asks. Paul nods his head.

They talk about their families and agree that they would all get on well. Helen tries to persuade Paul to spend the night with her in the den, but he resists, telling her they have to wait until they are outside to see what will happen between them. Helen says she will regret it if she doesn't do it, although she admits that she may also regret it if they do spend the night together. 'Would you rather regret doing it, or not doing it?' she asks. To which Paul replies, 'Of course I fucking want to do it. But in here is not the place to decide things for the future.'

Dean is summoned to talk to Big Brother. Asked who he thinks will be the winner, he predicts it will be close-run thing between Paul and Brian and that Paul will probably win. He says he would definitely like to make it to the last day. 'You're so close, you want to be in the last week. If you got to the last two, it would be a scary moment when you think you've got a fifty-fifty chance, and then you might allow yourself to think about winning.'

The main task for the week is announced. The housemates have to master four playground games: the hula hoop, the pogo stick, the space hopper and 'double-dutch' skipping (when two ropes are swung at once, in opposite directions). They decide to wager forty per cent of their £35 shopping money, and

WHAT THE EXPERTS SAY

PAUL AND HELEN

'Paul's declaration of "I love you" to Helen is a key moment in their developing relationship. He has the confidence to tell her "I love you" without looking back for reaction, and – significantly – she doesn't challenge it or comment. The two have finally reached the stage where they can be at ease with one another. Since the first week, they have been confronted by a series of impediments. One by one, these have disappeared. By statistical analysis, we can chart Paul's flirting history and identify a number of quite separate phases. To begin with, he flirted with Penny and to a lesser extent with Helen. Following Penny's eviction and his own nomination, he barely flirts at all. Paul's confidence is knocked by being nominated and then nominated again in subsequent weeks. However, as he successfully survives eviction, we see his flirting gradually increase again.

'If we look at Helen, we see that there was some flirting with Paul in the early days, but her flirting also tails off. She briefly rallied to flirt with Josh until she realized he was gay. Her flirting also shows a steady increase as Paul survives successive evictions.

'Paul and Helen have overcome a number of obstacles and gradually their flirting has become synchronized. However, up to this week, one huge impediment remains: Helen's relationship outside. Helen has been conscious of her boyfriend watching her throughout. But this week the way she spoke about him began to change. Helen has begun to suggest to Paul that her relationship with her boyfriend should not be construed as an obstacle. More tellingly, her behaviour after she survived eviction showed how her priorities are beginning to change. If we look back to week two, we can see she's tearful, says she's missing her boyfriend, and it is only one minute and twelve seconds before she asks for a message to be passed on to him.

'The second time, in week seven, her response is quite different. This time, forty-five seconds after the announcement her thoughts turn to an earlier promise to do anything for Paul. It is five minutes before she mentions her boyfriend.

'All impediments to Paul and Helen's relationship are at this point removed, and the only thing holding them back this week is themselves.'

Professor Geoffrey Beattie, Psychologist

agree that they can spend it all on alcohol and luxuries, as they will have enough staple food to last them until the end of their stay in the house. They are all thrilled with the task, except Brian, who says he will never be able to hula hoop. Helen, on the other hand, is confident that she will be able to do it, and is very disappointed when she finds it hard. Summoned to the Diary Room, she complains to Big Brother that she has lost her rhythm. Like Dean, she thinks Paul is the likely overall winner, but she also reckons Liz has a chance.

Brian follows Helen into the Diary Room, and sounds cheerfully resigned when he tells Big Brother about his shortcomings in the task.

'It's one of those tasks where, yet again, Brian is not too good. I'm having problems with the green ball. And this hula-hoop thing is not going to happen, plus the guys out there say that if you can't do the hula hoop it means you are crap in bed, so I'm crap in bed.'

He feels bad about Josh going, even though he nominated him. 'I didn't give him a chance, I was too worried about what people would think, which is crap really. Still, we've stolen his pillows already and I've taken his deodorant.'

The flirting is moving up a gear, as Paul and Helen roll around on the ground in the garden together in a very intimate play fight. Dean and Brian, observing them from the house, agree with Liz, who comments, 'If they'd just get on with it, that would be OK.' As they get up from the fight, Paul declares, almost casually and without looking at Helen, 'I love you.' She doesn't reply.

The inmates are definitely beginning to go stir crazy – in the early evening Paul, Dean and Brian stand on the garden table and shout across the fence. Dean starts by suggesting they make a break for it into the real world. All three chorus in unison 'Is there anybody there?' and Dean follows up with a plea for some beer. Brian then launches into one of his surreal monologues, claiming that the housemates are being held against their will. 'It looks like TV, but it's not. They make us smile for bread and water. My name's not even Brian. It's Simon O'Doherty. I'm just an actor.'

There is nothing but silence from the world across the fence.

In the Diary Room, Liz says she would have preferred Josh to stay as she gets on better with him, but she's glad to still have another girl in the bedroom. She reckons there is no sense of competition in the house.

'I never saw it as a competition. The people who were trying to be something they aren't are not here anymore.'

Later, the housemates are given a discussion topic by Big Brother, who wants each of them to reveal a secret from their past. Dean tells about being brought up as a Jehovah's Witness, without any birthday or Christmas celebrations. Paul admits that he and his sister once took part in a quiz on the *Live and Kicking* TV show. Helen is very concerned that her revelation will make the others think less of her, which whets their appetites for something spicy. She disappoints them – her secret is that she has a scar on her scalp where no hair grows. Brian provokes the biggest reaction, with the announcement that he was asked out by an ex- *EastEnders* cast member during one of his flights.

Eventually, Paul and Helen slope off to the den together, where they play snakes and ladders for an hour and a half. They lie together side by side, occasionally stroking each other's face and arms, but decide against sleeping there, and make their way to their separate bedrooms.

Once again, Paul talks in his sleep, saying 'I'm only human ... bloody game show. It's horrible.'

The Sunday morning ritual is the drawing up of the shopping list. As usual Liz takes charge, helped by Dean. Helen is called to the Diary Room, where she discusses how worried she is about the nominations – it is getting hard with so few people in the house. During the day, Dean talks to both Liz and Brian, reassuring them that he doesn't think they will go.

One of the chickens – a white one the housemates have called Princess Leia after the *Star Wars* character – is looking sickly. Liz bundles her into a cage and delivers her to the Diary Room so she can be taken to see a vet.

The afternoon livens up when Big Brother gives the group another task. They have to make two dozen sausages in two hours, with the help of a mincing machine and a sausage-stuffing machine. The housemates joke about using the sausage-measuring gauges – cards with circular holes to determine the thickness of the sausages – to measure the size of the boys' penises. Having lost ten minutes by failing to soak the sausage skins, the group ends up racing against time to finish the task. The last five minutes are fraught and tempers fray, but when Big Brother calls time they have made twenty-five sausages – one more than required. Big Brother tells Paul (who cuts his head on the Diary Room door in his rush to get them in) that he will let them know later whether or not the sausages are up to standard.

Paul spends more than half an hour in the Diary Room. He says all of the people left in the house are potential winners, but he doesn't think it will be him. He is worried about his relationship with Helen.

'I know that if I was her boyfriend and I saw two people fighting in the garden, I'd think, "What's going on there?" I don't want to hurt anyone. I'd be lying if I said I didn't have feelings for her, because I've grown fond of her, it works both ways. It's a weird scenario being in here. It's not an everyday thing, and you need to have fun with people to see you through.'

Afterwards, Paul has a long conversation with Helen, who argues that Big G is 'not really a boyfriend'. But Paul contradicts her:

'He is. You talked about nothing else when you came in. You've got photos all over your bed with love hearts between them.' Helen tells him that if anyone should worry, it is her. Paul agrees, but says:

'I'm slightly concerned, because I like you and care about you. You've got to go out in the real world and you've got to decide what you want from life. You've got to be happy.'

Big Brother announces that the housemates have passed the sausage task, and they are rewarded with a barbecue, their own sausages, lots of extra food and fifteen beers. While she's waiting for her meal to cook, Liz goes to the Diary Room and talks about the people who are left in the house. She also tells Big Brother what she misses about the outside world, listing 'light switches, floor mats and hot water'.

Brian later spends fifty minutes in the Diary Room talking about the impending nominations and how being in the house has affected him. He's surprised by the level of domesticity he has achieved (although it is doubtful whether any of the others would rate his contribution on the household front). At times, he says, he gets sick to death of not being able to go out and he envies the housemates who leave and get their lives back. But Brian's main worry is the nominations – he knows that he, effectively, holds the casting vote between the two pairs of allies: Dean and Liz and Paul and Helen. He has no real qualms about nominating Paul, but he is torn between the two girls, as he likes both of them.

As the evening draws on, the housemates discuss sex. Helen jokes that she and Brian can go out man-hunting together, and even share a man. Brian turns down her offer, as he wouldn't be interested in anyone who is bisexual. He astonishes the others by saying that he only has sex with the lights off and under the duvet. Liz wants to know what sex feels like from a man's point of view. 'Does it feel like putting it in a pot of warm jelly?' she asks. The only answer she gets is from Paul, who simply says, 'It's amazing.'

When they go to bed, the boys notice an awful sewage smell in their room. Unable to find the source, they decamp and sleep in the girls' room.

After her shower on Monday morning, Helen gazes at her pictures of Big G for twenty minutes. Her face remains expressionless – it's impossible to fathom what she is thinking.

Liz is the only member of the group who is beginning to get the hang of the skipping test. When she manages three jumps, she throws herself excitedly at Dean, wrapping her legs around him. Brian twists his ankle in his attempt to master skipping, and Paul immediately places a packet of frozen peas on it. Fortunately, it is a short-lived injury.

Just before three o'clock, the group are called to give their nominations. They are all aware that these will be their last ever nominations, and they launch into the unpleasant process with a group hug, during which Paul tells them, 'Whatever happens, we've all won anyway.'

By the time Brian, Dean and Elizabeth have all nominated Paul and Helen, it is clear that the remaining two sets of nominations will not affect the result. But the housemates don't know this, and as usual Big Brother tells them he will let them know the outcome later in the week.

They are distracted from the general gloom of nominations when Liz manages to skip properly, and this time she celebrates by hurling herself into Paul's arms and hugging Brian and Dean at the same time.

Sent to the boys' room, they discuss nicknames. Paul says he was known as 'wingnut', 'FA Cup' and 'trophy' at school because his ears stuck out. He says at work he is known as 'Posh Tubie', because computer monitors, with which he works, are known as tubes. The 'posh' bit was added when he referred to Twickenham as 'Twickers'. Brian says his mates call him Bambi, after a porn star. Liz was known at school as 'rubber duck' because of her surname, Woodcock. Dean is known as 'Stan' after footballer Stan Collymore, although he admits the name never stuck. Helen tells them she is known as 'gob head'.

Brian goes to the Diary Room for a chat. He reiterates that choosing

WHO NOMINATES WHO

Brian nominates Paul and Helen
Dean nominates Paul and Helen
Elizabeth nominates Paul and Helen
Helen nominates Dean and Elizabeth
Paul nominates Brian and Elizabeth

Brian	Dean	Elizabeth	Helen	Paul
1	1	2	3	3
Paul	Helen	Helen	Brian	Brian
		Paul	Dean	Dean
			Elizabeth	Elizabeth

Week 8 nominees: Helen and Paul are both up for eviction with three votes each.

Analysis
Brian had the casting vote. Had he nominated Dean and Elizabeth there could have been four housemates up for eviction. Elizabeth and Dean have once again both nominated Helen and Paul. Elizabeth completes a near-perfect run of nominating both evictees.

Reasons
Brian on Helen: 'My reason is because I have to. It's a shitty reason, a crappy reason, and probably not even a valid reason, but it's an honest reason.'
Helen on Liz: 'We do get on to a certain extent, but not as well as I thought we would, just me and her being the only two girls left. We don't connect that well.'
Paul on Brian: 'The spoilt factor. However, he has got better as time has gone on.'

between nominating Helen and Elizabeth was really tough. 'I'm doing it because I have to, but I do think Elizabeth deserves to be in the final four. She's done a lot for the group, she's always in the kitchen, always cooking, always putting other people first. It's silly because I do get on with Helen. It's very confusing, but you've got to decide what's best for the group, what's best for you, and who deserves to be here.' He adds that if he avoids being nominated this week he will feel slightly sad about having missed out on an essential part of the *Big Brother* experience (he has never been nominated).

In the early evening, the group is told that Princess Leia, the sick chicken, has died of a viral infection. Two more chickens are removed from the coop and taken to the Diary Room, as they show slight signs of suffering from the same infection. The housemates are given some medication for the other hens as a precautionary measure. It means that the group will no longer be able to eat the chickens' eggs, and instead Big Brother will supply them with shop-bought eggs. They are all upset, particularly Helen, who wails, 'We've killed a chicken!' The others reassure her that they are not to blame, but she thinks the remaining chickens look sad.

Paul and Helen clean out the chicken coop together. Prompted by the advice given to her by Brian to 'go with the flow', Helen twice tries to tell Paul how she feels about him. Twice he cuts her off, telling her to 'chill'. She seems hurt by his rejection, retorting that 'sometimes you have to chill so much you get to boiling point'. They both retreat to separate mirrors to groom themselves. But later in the afternoon, the tension between them melts when they curl up together in the garden and have a deep discussion about their situation.

Helen asks, 'Do you think about stuff? Stuff you're gonna do when you get out of here?'

'Yeah, you do think about stuff,' admits Paul. 'In here you want stuff so much, and it's cool that you can't have it, but when you get it, it's, like, cool stuff.'

To which Helen replies, 'You want stuff quite bad, but stuff ain't gonna happen in here, is it? But when you actually do get stuff, it could be breath-taking stuff.'

'Possibly,' says Paul, and goes on to discuss how Helen hasn't changed, but her situation has.

'If it's changed for good, that's cool, but you've got to sort it out. You've done the thinking, now you've gotta do the doing.'

They agree that it's 'shit' talking with cameras and microphones tracking them, but congratulate themselves on how good they are at talking in code. Perhaps Paul realizes that their attempts at using code are not too subtle, because he states openly, 'It's obvious you're breaking up with your boyfriend.' Helen is upset at his directness, and says she refuses to have 'this conversation' on national TV. But there's no coolness between them, and later on the pair discuss going away on a trip together when they are out of the house.

Big Brother sets the group an evening discussion topic on what they want to do before they die. Paul wants a lovely wife and a family. Brian wants to fall in love and settle down. He would also like to go to Ethiopia. 'I can't build an orphanage, but I could make the kids laugh and dress them and teach them something. I could get money for charity,' he says. Dean, too, would like to be able to help others.

Liz talks of establishing a Utopia where people 're-learn what it is to be human beings. There will be music, dancing, no alcohol, there may be some nudity, and certain rules like "do unto others as you would be done by", respect life. People need to be reminded of what's important, like living together harmoniously, smiling, love, health, nutrition, fresh air.' Under questioning from Brian, she adds that sex will only happen inside committed, loving relationships. He jokes that the place would be 'B-O-R-I-N-G'. It's left to Helen to bring the conversation back to a less philanthropic level – the things Helen would like before she dies include a Mercedes convertible, Gucci shoes and handbag and a trip to the Oscars.

After the discussion, Brian confides in Dean and Elizabeth that he wants to leave the house. 'If the door opened by mistake, I'd go,' he claims. In the Diary Room later, Dean explains that Brian is aware that he had the casting vote in the nominations, and it has weighed heavily on him.

Soon after midnight, Helen and Paul make another trip to the den to play snakes and ladders. The atmosphere is electric as they both struggle not to give in to the attraction between them. They each confess that they fancy the other. Eventually, after more than three hours in seclusion together, Paul announces that they must go to bed, and Helen launches herself into his arms under the blanket. They hold each other tightly, with the blanket pulled up over their heads. There is a lot of heavy breathing, and then the cockerel crows loudly and the mood breaks. Paul groans, 'It's a nightmare, isn't it? Come on, we've got to go to bed, have some sleep.'

The housemates all sleep in the girls' room again. On Tuesday morning, Liz goes to the Diary Room and tells Big Brother how hard nominations now are, and how she regrets excluding Helen a little bit.

Paul and Helen both seem to know and accept that they are the two up for eviction, and much of the talk during the day revolves around their relationship and the problems Paul may face if he goes out. He describes it as, '*West Side Story* – two groups of family and mates who don't know each other.' Dean does nothing to alleviate Paul's fears by saying that he knows plenty of blokes who, if they had seen their girlfriends behaving the way Helen has with Paul, would be 'coming down here, and not to meet the girlfriend'. Helen talks about how guilty she feels and how upset she will be if she sees Paul with a black eye. He retorts, 'If I've got a black eye, he'll have one.'

The nominations and the Helen–Paul relationship dominate the day, but there are other topics of conversation. Liz talks about going on a trip to France with her boyfriend, during which he paid the OAP rate and she paid the student price. The others probe her about the age difference.

The nomination results confirm what they all already know, and the two nominees are not the only ones who are upset. Dean goes out in the garden and stands for a few moments in a corner, facing the fence, until Paul goes to him, reassuring him and giving him a hug. Liz says that the three housemates who have not been nominated will be seen as 'the big baddies' by the outside world. Brian looks tearful, but he cheers up when Helen breezily announces that she doesn't blame anyone and gives him a big hug. Dean tells Paul that he will feel worse on Friday, when one of them leaves, than he will when he leaves the house himself.

In the Diary Room, Paul discusses how different it is, knowing who has made the nominations. 'It is an upset emotion for everyone. When you spend more and more time with people, you get to know them better. You grow fond of people, and that's what's happened, I've grown fond of Helen. Stuff just happens, I don't know why it happens, there's nothing you can do about it. On Friday it will be good that one of us goes.

'Whatever she's feeling, she's got a robust side to her. I don't want to call her simple, because that would not be a fair word, but she is simple in how she sees life, she takes it with a pinch of salt. She doesn't seem to have a care in the world, and isn't that a lovely approach to life?'

It has rained relentlessly for much of the day. After dinner, Elizabeth surprises all of them by producing a rain cape from her suitcase and going outside to clean the chicken coop. Paul and Helen while away the wet evening reading each other's palms, following a chart they find in a glossy magazine. According to Paul, Helen's heart line shows she will 'shy away from commitment and will be emotionally aloof'.

The boys speculate as to how they would have trained Paddy without the cameras present, and how the dog would, in Brian's words, have learned to do a lot more as a result: 'Not just fetch – he would have made me breakfast.' He sums Paddy up: 'He judged people. He was very materialistic. He reminded me of someone I know ... me.'

The day ends in quiet chat. Elizabeth quizzes Paul about his relationship with Helen, and Paul takes the opportunity to plead his case to the viewers, admitting that he regrets how far things have gone.

'I'm not prompting anything at all. It's all her. I am attracted to her, definitely. She's bubbly, doesn't take life seriously, has a laugh. She's completely my kind of girl. But that's it. Nothing is going to happen. I don't want it to. I'm gutted, because the last thing I wanted to do was feel I was wrecking something. But I'm not actually doing that. She's made the decision in her head. She's had time to think in here. Now we've got to draw the line, but it's critical people understand she's made that decision totally irrespective of me, because she's been in here and had time to think.'

He tells Liz that he and Helen both have to go out to their real lives, and in the future they can meet for a drink. He even admits, 'I've got interests in a couple of girls out there. You don't know what could happen.'

Paul and Helen have decided to have an early night, and go to bed at midnight. Liz is the only one who normally turns in this early, but tonight she stays up in the hot tub and tells Dean and Brian about her chat with Paul. She repeats his statement that it was always sixty per cent Helen doing the running and forty per cent him. 'He wants to cool things off. He is saying it is all her fault,' she tells them, adding that she has also talked to Helen. 'She really likes him and would like something to be going on.'

Brian is worried about Helen getting hurt. Dean's theory is that Paul may be backing off because he thinks there will be more women interested in him after he leaves the house.

Despite all this Paul-fuelled speculation about the end of the romance, in the bedroom Paul and Helen are still talking earnestly and intimately to each other. 'It's a nightmare,' moans Paul. 'Last night we were suddenly cuddling, and you liked it and I liked it and that's the deal. We've got to establish whether it's just because we're in here. We won't know until we are on the outside. Basically, you just fancy me.'

Helen asks, 'Do you fancy me?'

After teasing her that his answer is no, Paul says, 'Yeah, I do. We've got to just cool it, because it's rubbing salt in the wounds of someone in particular who is looking at me now.'

The housemates all sleep peacefully in the girls' room until quarter past five on Wednesday morning, when Paul disturbs them with more sleeptalking. He can clearly be heard saying, 'What are you doing? Smack. What are you actually doing there, Josh? I want to know. I'm being cool now.'

When they get up, the group concentrate on practising for the task, on which they will be tested at midday. They have some success: Brian finally masters the hula hoop, and he and Dean both manage the skipping for the first time. Helen, after many attempts, succeeds with the pogo stick. Nonetheless, when the time comes, the housemates fail the task. They all manage to complete fifteen seconds with the hula hoop and fifteen seconds of skipping, and succeed in the space-hopper relay. But the pogo stick is too much for Helen. Eventually, after forty-one attempts, she manages to stay on it for fifteen seconds, but by then the group has racked up an over-all time of nineteen minutes and thirty-four seconds, almost three times longer than the limit of six minutes and forty-five seconds. But there's no despondency – when Helen finally manages her fifteen seconds on the pogo stick, the others pick her up and carry her triumphantly round the garden.

Helen and Paul spend the afternoon in each other's company. Later, in the Diary Room, Paul reiterates his worries about the way his romance with Helen is being perceived outside the house, and what kind of reception he can expect when he leaves.

'It's pretty obvious that me and Helen have got quite close. It's cool, it has happened, but I kinda wish not in here, I wish things were a bit different. I wish she'd come here as a single girl ... From the first week I really didn't get on with her at all and then for some reason we clicked, we realized we had a bit in common, and then we became really good friends and then it goes a bit further than that as time goes on. We'll see what happens. It has made it more sensitive being in here. It has made it harder.'

At 6 p.m., Dean remembers that it is time to concentrate on his girlfriend Vanessa. Before he came into the house, they agreed on a time to concentrate their thoughts on each other, and Dean is really upset that he missed it last week. Liz turns her attention to customizing her eviction trousers for next week, and Paul and Helen indulge in their usual play fighting. They retire to

WHAT THE EXPERTS SAY

SLEEPTALKING

'Sleeptalking is perfectly normal and doesn't usually indicate any psychological problems. Paul sleeptalks on most nights. The propensity to sleeptalk is actually inherited, and about five per cent of all adults sleeptalk often. Coherent talking such as Paul's is quite frequent in sleeptalkers. Usually Paul will sleeptalk once or twice during the night, related to his social position in the house. Before the first time he is nominated, his sleeptalk reflects his worries about being evicted.'

Professor Dieter Wolke, Psychologist

'Recently, there's been a significant change in what Paul says in his sleep. Since surviving the public vote for the fourth time, the content of his talk has changed from resilience to confidence. His room mates have long since learned to sleep through his talking, but on this occasion (when Paul talks about winning), they all wake up. His confidence has subconsciously touched a nerve.

'Paul, however, is not the only sleeptalker in the house. As the weeks go by and the emotions and stress increase, the housemates not only sleep more, but we see Elizabeth, Dean and Helen all sleeptalking. It's fascinating and highly unusual that four out of the five remaining housemates have a propensity to sleeptalk. As we approach the finale, and the pressure in the house increases, their sleeptalking could provide an invaluable insight into their subconscious.'

Professor Geoffrey Beattie, Psychologist

the girls' room, where Paul pretends to sleepwalk over to Helen's bed, resulting in a lot of cuddling. Paul, as usual, is the one who calls a halt when things start to get steamy between them. He says they have to wait to know how they feel about each other in the outside world, and when Helen insists she will still like him, he says: 'But you don't know what's going to happen. There may be so much you're going to be doing or so much I'm going to be doing … ' Before he can finish, Helen plaintively says, using their code word, 'We could still fit in stuff.'

In the Diary Room, Liz describes the mood in the house.

'Everyone has a period when they are not feeling too good in the house. Mine was about week six or seven. Brian's hitting it now – he's finding it quite difficult, and Dean is really missing Vanessa, so they are wanting to go. They are all talking about life on the outside, what they will do, the countdown, and how boring it is. I don't like looking at it like that. But I've got to look at it as that's how they're coping. I'll do my thing, and hopefully we can meet in the middle.'

In the evening, Big Brother provides some henna kits, so that the housemates can give themselves temporary tattoos. Paul decides they should all have *Big Brother* tattoos, and tries to make a stencil of the eye logo. Elizabeth and Brian make a pact to tattoo each other's bums later in the evening.

For the first time in the history of the house, everyone helps to prepare dinner. During the meal, the housemates discuss unusual places where they have had sex. Liz confesses to doing it on a lawn under the bedroom window of the parents of the guy she was with; Brian owns up to an encounter in a night-club toilet (although he claims it wasn't sex); and Paul admits to managing it in the back row of a crowded cinema. Revealingly, Helen suggests that having sex on TV would be the strangest situation, and Paul quickly interjects 'I couldn't'.

After the meal a routine discussion about tomorrow's menu prompts another classic Helenism. 'Can you eat cock?' she asks, innocently – referring to the cockerel in the garden. Too stunned to laugh even, the others stare at her in disbelief, before she adds: 'Or is it turkey?' Brian clarifies matters for her.

The housemates get down to the tattooing, with Paul attempting to decorate Helen's ankle with a flower pattern. It comes out as a pink smudge, but Helen is loathe to criticize Paul's handiwork, and Liz puts her trust in him to do her palms. While they mess about with the tattoos, Dean and Brian gently tease Liz about her bossiness. Although she takes it in good part, she is clearly a little shocked by their assessment of her character.

The girls' room is now home to the whole group, and they settle down to sleep. As soon as the lights go out, Paul throws a pillow across the room at Helen, who retaliates in kind, hitting Paul so hard around the head that he complains it felt like a punch. While Brian storms around the room looking for 'demons' (the shadowy figures of the cameramen) in the mirrors, Helen rushes over to comfort Paul. She rocks him back and forth in her arms, kissing his ear and apologizing. Eventually, the housemates all settle into their own beds and peace descends for the next eight hours, broken only by a round of sleeptalking which involves everyone except Dean. Helen lets out a cry, Brian mutters unintelligibly, Liz smacks her lips and murmurs, later saying the word 'concentrate' quite clearly, and Paul – the sleeptalking master – shouts out 'Yes!' and then, 'But what can be weird is that people just don't get that I … ' They all sleep through their unconscious exchanges.

On Thursday morning, Paul and Helen clear up the kitchen, and he tells her that he wants her phone number. 'What for?' she asks. He asks her what people usually want phone numbers for. She says that if she leaves, she'll put a message on her phone answering service just for him, and says that if he leaves he must put a message on his for her.

Dean has meticulously cut a stencil of the *Big Brother* eye from the logo on their suitcases, and stencils it on to Paul's back. In the Diary Room, Big Brother asks Dean about the qualities of the remaining housemates. He replies that Helen has a good heart, Paul is honest, Elizabeth is resourceful and Brian is funny.

There's a security alert when a suspect plane flies over, and the housemates are confined in the boys' room. Helen and Paul discuss eviction outfits, while Dean and Liz talk about photographic exhibitions they have seen.

Helen later has a long chat with Big Brother. She says she feels she will be the one to leave tomorrow night, and that she will be excited and nervous, but happy. Paul will also be nervous and excited if he has to go, she reckons.

WHAT THE EXPERTS SAY

ELIZABETH

'Time and time again we see Elizabeth giving the housemates advice and support. She is dependable and resourceful and has assumed a key role at the centre of the house – that of the traditional mum. We see her displaying typical maternal qualities as she ensures that Brian gets his turn in the playground activities, and subsequently he becomes the sole focus of her attention. While she is in control, she is also reinforcing and praising everyone's accomplishments. The high pitch of her voice signifies her genuine delight in what Brian is doing. It's a similar noise to the one mothers make when they vicariously experience pleasure through the achievements of their children.

'Elizabeth's maternal behaviour ensures the house runs smoothly. She's often very mindful of the concerns and needs of the housemates. Like everyone else, she often feels resentment at the behaviour of the others, but she rarely raises these complaints with the rest of the "family", only with Dean, the father figure in the house.

'Most importantly, she's the main cook in the house. In the last week, she has been involved in practically every meal. Cooking allows her to meet the emotional and physical needs of the house. Significantly, her only real rival in the kitchen, Josh, has now gone. The nurturing and maternal aspects of Elizabeth's behaviour have made her appear increasingly indispensable to the housemates. The competition can only increase. This is not Happy Families they are playing. If Elizabeth is to survive, it could be that she needs to start putting herself first.'

Professor Geoffrey Beattie, Psychologist

'I think he's a little bit worried. If he goes, all my friends and family will be there. But he'll be alright. He's big enough to look after himself, Paul Clarke. But I've got the feeling I will go, because he's been up for nomination four times. They obviously all love him out there.'

Like Dean, Helen is asked to sum up the qualities of the others left in the house. She says Dean is very calming, Elizabeth is good at cooking and has taught her a lot, and that Brian was funny but has changed recently, which is upsetting her. She thinks he is worried about never having been nominated.

Helen then confesses that, when she first came into the house, she thought Paul was too much of a lad, but has since realized that he isn't. She also thought from the beginning that she and Liz would not get on, because they were from totally different walks of life. She thought they might grow closer when they were the only two girls left, but that hasn't happened.

Dean puts the eye tattoo on Liz's lower back. She and Helen then decide to forget about the cottage pie they were going to make, and instead concentrate on cooking puddings: Helen makes pancakes and her famous brioche, which she has now mastered, and Liz makes a chocolate pudding with sauce.

Paul talks hypothetically to Helen about living with her outside the house, and says the thing that would 'do his head in' would be her talking about Gucci shoes all the time. But they agree that any arguments would end up with them both laughing.

It's Liz's turn to go to the Diary Room to discuss her feelings about the last few days in the house. It transpires that she is brooding about the good-humoured comments made by Brian and Dean yesterday evening about her being over-efficient and dominant. She doesn't agree with them.

Over the past few weeks, the voices of the various producers who 'play' Big Brother have become familiar to the housemates, so they are shocked to hear a new one today. Unbeknown to them, it belongs to Dermot O'Leary, the presenter of the E4 magazine programme, *Big Brother's Little Brother*. He slips into the Big Brother role for a minute or two, but his voice freaks the housemates out – they dub him 'The Godfather', and speculate as to whether he is the 'real' Big Brother. Called to the Diary Room by this strange, new voice (which is, he reports back to the others, stern and serious), Paul is given a mini-task called Ten Green Bottles. The housemates are given three rubber balls. Thirteen wine bottles – ten empty ones and three containing wine – are lined up on a stand in the garden. Each housemate is allowed three throws in an attempt to knock down the empty bottles, and their reward will be to keep the full ones. They do very badly – Paul, Liz, Brian and Dean all manage to knock down one empty bottle, but Dean also demolishes a full one. Helen's girlie throws don't even reach the stand. Sadly, they hand back the remaining two full bottles.

Dinner is cooked by Brian who, as the house has emptied, has gradually become more and more involved in the daily round of chores which he so assiduously avoided during the first few weeks. Brian then has a singing lesson from Dean, which causes much amusement, as the tone-deaf Irishman lurches from wrong note to wrong note. 'I've never heard anyone who sings like you,' says Dean, and it's not a compliment. Brian, who is not easily offended, retorts that if he had a good voice he would be in Hear'say.

There's another security alarm when a football, with a note attached, is booted over the fence. The housemates have to take refuge in the bedroom. Big Brother rewards their cooperation with two bottles of wine.

Later, when all the housemates are together in the conservatory, Paul decides to tell them about his and Helen's feelings for one another. 'I do fancy Helen. I fancy her personality completely. When I walked in here, I didn't fancy her to look at, which is bizarre. I fancy her personality a lot. In a bar or a pub what attracts you is the way someone looks, but that's not what's happened here at all.'

Brian wants to know whether the pair have snogged yet. They tell him they haven't. 'Helen has a boyfriend. It's really, really difficult for both of us,' says Paul.

Liz says she thinks they will either get married or just be really good friends, and when Paul repeats to her how Helen has described her feelings for him ('I look in your eyes and all this stuff whizzes past me') Liz thinks it is beautiful. Helen seems to want acceptance from the group, and explains how she and Paul use their code word 'stuff' to denote sex.

When Paul and Helen retire to the den together, the other three discuss how relieved they both seemed after sharing their feelings with the group. Liz finds it amusing that the pair are on national television, with millions of viewers watching their relationship develop, and yet they are worried about the reaction of the other housemates. She is still worried that Paul will break Helen's heart.

Paul and Helen spend their last night together in the den playing snakes and ladders, which invariably leads to long cuddling sessions. There is a great deal of heavy breathing and limbs becoming entangled under the blankets until they eventually go to bed at 4 a.m.

Finally, after what seems to all of them like a long week, it is Friday – the day when the two lovers will be torn asunder. The day starts slowly, with only Dean and Liz emerging before lunchtime. They take up their usual places in the deckchairs and have a conversation about intelligence. Liz recalls a boyfriend at university telling her she was the most intelligent girlfriend he had ever had, and Dean says that his current girlfriend, Vanessa, is the first with whom he has felt completely intellectually comfortable.

Helen has more pressing things to think about – her beauty routine. Early in the afternoon, the two lovebirds are called, individually, to the Diary Room, where Paul admits he is worried about the prospect of meeting Big G, and Helen says she thinks the house will be quieter if she leaves.

In the kitchen, Liz cuts her finger opening a sardine tin, and she is bleeding profusely. Helen panics, but Brian remembers his airline first aid and bandages the wound. While they wait for the doctor (who eventually arrives in the Diary Room and puts one stitch in Liz's cut), the housemates discuss accidents they have been involved in. Dean tells of a car crash, Elizabeth of the time her parents' boat blew up.

It's cleaning day, and while Liz, Dean and Brian get on with the chores, Paul and Helen sneak a long cuddle. They lie like spoons on top of her bed, legs intertwined, talking about their situation. Helen comments that Paul's fourteen-year-old brother must be picking up some tips. 'Bad ones?' Paul asks. 'No, good ones,' she replies. Eventually, and after much hugging and tender whispering, Helen's guilt about not helping with the cleaning breaks up the session, but she promises Paul more hugs later.

Brian and Helen go to the Diary Room to tell Big Brother they are worried about the chickens (they have spotted blood in the birds' poo). They then retire together to the girls' room, where Brian helps Helen with her hair. After telling her he thinks she will be staying, he goes to chat with Big Brother, and elaborates on the same theme:

'I kinda feel that Helen might stay, purely because she's a loveable girl, she does no harm to anyone. She's the nice girl, the girl next door, the friendly hairdresser, funny, sweet, bubbly. She has flair and does things in a unique way. I know if I was watching, I'd probably get attached to her. She's quite humorous, quite colourful to watch.'

He adds that he is amused by the fact that Helen is more nervous about meeting Paul's parents than she is about leaving the house.

VOTING

A huge majority (eighty-four per cent of the 1,139,951 votes cast) were for Paul to leave the house. Only sixteen per cent (187,723) of the voters wanted to see Helen go. More than a third of the votes (thirty-eight per cent) were made via interactive televisions; the rest were made by phone. Viewing figures are soaring – an average of 4.8 million people watched *Big Brother* on Channel 4 this week. On Wednesday night, as the romantic action hotted up, 595,000 people were tuned in to the live streaming from the house on E4. Thursday saw a record number of four million page views on the internet site, and a record 3,951,296 live video streams from the net. More than three million *Big Brother* update text messages were sent out by BT Cellnet.

After a dinner of burnt barbecued chicken and sausages, Helen and Paul go to the boys' room and sit on the bed, holding hands. He asks her whether there is anything she wants to say to him – she says there isn't. Paul agrees it is all better left unsaid until they are in the outside world. Meanwhile, Dean and Brian discuss the exciting prospect of sex after they leave the house – Brian says he can't wait to get to first base with someone, and Dean says he's going to hit a home run. Brian – ever insecure – is worried that after seeing him in the house, nobody will want to date him.

As the moment for the eviction announcement approaches, the housemates all gather in the lounge. Paul admits he is now 'bricking it', while Helen feels the opposite – strangely calm and chilled. They all sing 'Lean On Me', except for Brian who is only allowed to mime the words because of his voice which Dean has described as sounding like 'a giant running his nails down a blackboard.' When the news comes, it is Paul who is going to leave. He leaps up and punches the air, delighted to have heard his dad's voice in the background to Davina's announcement. Everyone hugs both Paul and Helen, and Paul lifts Helen in his arms and bears her away to the boys' room, where he tells her he is so 'overwhelmed with emotion' he wants to cry. Helen says she feel guilty, as if she's kicked him out, and she asks him to tell her mother that she's alright.

The others quietly discuss how glad they are that it is Helen who is staying. Brian extols her 'personality, big heart, big smile. She's just got colour. You look at the girl and you can't help but smile.'

Just before he leaves, Paul gives Helen another prolonged hug. Then the remaining four form their traditional arches, with Helen at the front. She tries to grab Paul as he exits the house, but he does not look at her. Instead, he ploughs straight ahead to the manic reception the public, his family and his mates have in store for him.

The others have their routine post-eviction group hug, and chant, 'And then there were four.' They all hug and comfort Helen, who looks adrift without Paul. She wanders into the garden and goes to the den, their favourite canoodling place. 'This time I haven't got Paul Clarke with me,' she says plaintively to herself.

The remaining housemates gather in the lounge to drink cider. Helen talks about her feelings for Paul. She tells the others about 'stuff', which she has experienced with Paul, and which means the romantic, emotional part of a relationship, as opposed to 'Elvis', which in her code means the physical side. The housemates have a lengthy discussion about their relationships past and present, and whether they were based on 'stuff' or 'Elvis'. They agree that what they all want is a lover who combines 'stuff' and 'Elvis'. Brian says he gets lots of 'stuff' but not a lot of 'Elvis': 'With one person, the record wasn't even put on for eight months,' he says. They talk about 'fake stuff' and 'one-way stuff', and Helen sadly tells them that she has never felt 'stuff' before, and now she has been separated from it.

The housemates go on to discuss how they will all meet again at the *Big Brother* party after the programme finishes. Helen is worried that Paul might show up with another girl. When they finally go to bed, Helen gets into Paul's bed and noisily sniffs the pillows and duvet, pleased when she can smell his hair wax. She tells the others that this coming week she will work on 'the Welsh vote' by singing the Welsh national anthem while stripping. After Brian has done his obligatory round of demon-spotting – peering in the mirrors to try to glimpse the cameramen behind them – they all settle down to sleep.

PAUL LOOKS BACK: THE EXCLUSIVE INTERVIEW

Paul on the housemates

Penny: 'She was the most significant person when I walked in. We bonded immediately, I could have a laugh and a joke with her. She was very touchy-feely, an amazing character. She came in as one person, went through loads of changes – different dimensions that none of us understood – then went back to being the same person. On Bubble's birthday, I told her she should get back to being the cool person she was at first, and she did.

'But there was a midway point when she seemed to be losing the plot. She had a problem with Helen, probably because Helen was so cute and all that, and she obviously had feelings for me. She touched me a lot, held my hand a lot, pulled me in to her a lot, asked me if I'd be her friend after *Big Brother* – she asked me about five times in twenty minutes. She was very clingy to me. I didn't fancy her and I don't know whether she fancied me, she could just have been feeling lost. We had a brief snog, which I regretted instantly. She got on top of me and put her lips to mine and for some reason I put my tongue in, and she did too. I was gutted afterwards, but it was only a laugh. Although I liked her, I felt it was right that she should leave first, as she wasn't coping well.'

Stuart: 'I got on well with him. It helps to have something in common. Bubble and Brian knew each other from the auditions, and Stuart and I had a connection because my mum worked for the same firm as him, and I knew the names of some of his colleagues. He had a game plan: he would look into people's eyes and you knew he was wondering whether they were nominating him, working on his next move. He saw me as an ally – he winked at me after his big row with Penny. Occasionally I was embarrassed for him. He was so vain, a poser, he took the volleyball and other sports too seriously. He was there to win. But he never rubbed me up the wrong way. He missed his family a lot. When he left, he told us about his nine-acre farm – that's a line the rest of us will never forget. It was inappropriate.'

Narinder: 'She spent loads of time with Brian, but I didn't mind that. I didn't have a problem with her while she was in the house. There were a couple of occasions when I had to bite my arm to stop myself snapping at her: she said something on Brian's birthday which implied I wasn't pulling my weight, and I thought that was inappropriate. A couple of times I comforted her – once when I saw her crying in the lounge, and after the row with Helen, when I chatted to her to cool her down for the sake of the group. When she left, she delivered the most controversial line in the whole *Big Brother* experience: she told us we were all boring. After she'd gone, I found out things about her. She accused Bubble of being a shit-stirrer, but she was the biggest shit-stirrer of the lot.'

Bubble: 'He's a very funny guy, he came in with all guns blazing. I initially thought he would rub me up the wrong way. He went on and on and on. I felt he was selfish. He wanted to be the gag man. He'd cut you off in the middle of a story, he wouldn't listen. Dean was a bit the same. Maybe I was a bit boring at first. I was just finding my feet – I'm a guy who paces myself. But Bubble would walk away, or interrupt with a gag. There was a big incident when he and Amma accused me of failing the fire task. If I failed the task, I didn't know, because there's no way I would have let Helen take the blame. We'd decided we were a team, and they tried to destroy the team rules. As time went on, Bubble became quieter, he calmed down, and I realized he was a caring and emotional bloke because of his child. He was in it for the money, which I wasn't, but at least he was honest. I was sure he would beat me, and I was prepared in my head to go – it was a real shock. I gave him my Oakley sunglasses because he had lost his, and because I wanted to say to him that, although I nominated him, it was not because he's not a nice guy. He was just a little bit too loud for me.'

Amma: 'I got on least well with Amma. She always talked down to me, had no respect for me. She'd wait for a strong character like Bubble to pick a hole in me and then she'd add her two pennyworth. We'll never get on. Her line was that we could be friends. My line is, that ain't gonna happen. I had to tell her I was in control of the situation, and what I meant was that I was in control of myself and I wasn't allowing myself to slap her down. I didn't lash out at her for the sake of the peace of the house. When we were both nominated we got on a bit better, but she was still very confrontational. She thought she knew everything, she always had a point of view.'

Josh: 'I was the only bloke who didn't feel threatened by Josh, and I was the first to have a good conversation with him and make him feel welcome. We started on very good grounds. But as time went on and I got closer to Helen and the girls, I thought that he didn't put his cards on the table. He was gay, but there was a lot that led me to believe he was bisexual, not completely gay. I remember at Elizabeth's pampering party, he put on very tight boxer shorts so you could see his package and then massaged Amma's legs, looking at her – I thought there was a sexual thing there. I felt he was compromising the position of the girl I cared about and the other girls. I think they put trust in him because they thought he was gay. He was competitive, and he tried to take charge of things. When we had to draw the portrait, he took charge. He didn't realize it was my area of expertise, and it was me who eventually said we had better make a grid. He brought a very competitive edge to the volleyball, when it should have been fun. But I still like the guy.'

Elizabeth: 'I knew she would be there to the end. She fell into the oldest-girl role, she was a jack of all trades, and she pulled her weight massively. She was too serious and a bit dull. The key thing in my relationship with her was when she turned on me because I said I fancied Anna Kournikova: I did nothing wrong in that conversation, but she got stuck into me. She's a feminist, she made it hard for me. But she and Dean are like the Mummy and Daddy, and I knew she wouldn't get nominated.'

Dean: 'He never did anything to offend me, I never nominated him, and his music really touched me. When I started caring for Helen, he made it for me – when we were holding hands, his music made me go a bit funny. He kept the place alive with his music. He is a bit dull, a bit too serious. He's a father figure, especially for Bubble and Brian, which may have influenced the way Brian voted, which caused me and Helen to be nominated against each other. I'm a bit gutted by that, but it was a good thing for us to be separated.'

Brian: 'He's the funniest person I've ever met in my entire life. He's sharp, witty, funny. He always had a favourite, someone he could bounce his humour off. He's a very popular guy inside the house, because he's the light relief. There's no telly, but there is Brian. He's going to be a star. He's very selfish – it's me, me, me and I, I, I. He's a spoilt brat, very full of himself. I nominated him, but I never thought he would go. He got better as the house got smaller, but he's still very self-centred. I don't want him to win, because he will just spend the money on crap.'

Helen: 'When I walked in and saw her, I thought she was attractive, but not my type. I realized early on she was funny: there was her two-handed grip on the brioche, which made me and Dean laugh so much, and the incident when she stuffed her mouth with prawn crackers. But there were four reasons why I didn't really like her at first, and why I nominated her in the first round:

1. She was offered the Gucci shoes or a party, and it was like there was a decision. For me, they could have offered me anything and I would have taken the party.

2. She said that thing: "I'm blonde and sort of look OK-ish ... "
3. Dean said he would sleep with Elizabeth and she looked disgusted.
4. She told me she was the most popular girl at school and everyone fancied her.

'I thought she was up herself. And in fact, being nominated was the single best thing that could have happened to Helen, although she doesn't know it. Everyone gained respect for her with the way she handled it. I started looking at her in a different way, not a sexual way but a friendship way. I could see a lot of me in her – we are amazingly similar people. She talks about living in Helen's little world, and my mates have always joked that I live in Clarkie's world.

'The first real conversation we had she showed me all her photographs and she emphasized the size of Big G's shoulders a million times. She talked about him all the time in the first couple of weeks. When I jokingly picked her up and carried her to the den, she said "Big G is so going to kill you". I didn't mind at that stage, because there was nothing sexual between us. But I cared about her, and I gave her advice: I told her to be more tactful, and not to talk about Big G so much. I didn't at that stage have any plans about ending up with this girl, but I wanted her to be happy.

'Then I came up for nomination and she became the force that I needed. She looked after me big time. She fell for me, and I hope it wasn't just because she saw that I was popular outside the house, because she is a bit materialistic, what with the Gucci shoes and all that – I'm still worried about that. It was when I survived the first vote that I realized she liked me. She

PEOPLE ON PAUL

Paul's dad, Ken: 'Paul is a gentleman. He wanted to come out before Helen so he can lay his coat on the puddles for her to walk on.'

Paul's friend, Nicola: 'He's had a great experience. He's loved meeting new people. He's a strong character and he knew what he was getting into.'

Paul's mum, Jenny, on Paul and Helen: 'It's a brilliant relationship, absolutely brilliant. I know they'll always be the best of friends. I'm not surprised it's got more serious – she's such a great girl, who would not fall for her?'

Dom Joly, comedian: 'I don't like Paul, but I love to watch him.'

Stephanie, accounts handler: 'Paul, he thinks he's God. He's not.'

Paul, accountant: 'You said you wanted to have a family, Paul. It would be fabulous if there were little Pauls and Helens running around going "wicked" and "oh, my God"!'

looked at me in this unusual way, and said, "Is it bad that I really didn't want you to go?"

'We became closer and closer. As the weeks go on, and you are deprived of tender, loving care, and the numbers diminish, you get much closer to people. She gave me hugs, and even before I fancied her, whenever she touched me it did something to me. We fell for each other's personalities, not looks. In the real world, it starts with looks initially, but with us it was the other way round, it started with personality.

'It really got mad on the day of the romantic dinner date. I wanted to be with her so madly. There had been lots of flirty stuff before then, she touched me a lot, there were lots of innuendoes. It was her coming on to me – if she hadn't, it would never have happened, because I respected her position massively. I made a pact with myself that I would not snog her or have sex with her, however much I fell for her. I feel I have protected both of us.

'In the den with her on the romantic date I remember thinking, "I fancy the pants off you." My hatred for the cameras and microphones started then. I wanted to smash them. Something was happening to me that I wanted to be private, I didn't want everyone to know about it. Afterwards, we sat on the tyre chairs holding hands, Dean playing music, and that was me finished completely. She'd got me. After that, we couldn't get enough of each other, and every time I touched her it felt good. But at the back of it all was Big G. I was worried I'd wrecked her relationship. Helen didn't seem worried – her main concern was whether my parents would like her.

'It was a fairy-tale romance, and when I went into the house I said to the production staff that if I met someone I would like it to be a fairy tale. I don't think I am in love with her, because I need to see how we are in the real world before I can be in love. But no matter what happens, we will always be great friends. She will come out of the house to a huge reception, like I have, and we'll just have to see a few weeks down the line if I'm still thinking of her, if there's an issue going on in my head, then I'll phone her and we'll sort it out. If she dates a few other guys that would be good, then if she still wants to see me, it will be real.

'The girl is a work of art. How can you have someone so amazing, so gorgeous a personality, and then so naive? As I walked out of the house, I couldn't look at her. I'd have broken down if I'd looked into her face.'

Paul on life in the house

'I walked in as a normal guy, and I've walked out still the same guy, but to a different world, and it scares the shit out of me. I've had a unique experience within a unique experience – I survived four rounds of nominations, I twisted my ankle and was on crutches, I had all that stuff with Penny and then the big thing with Helen. I reckon it was more of a rollercoaster for me than anyone else in there.

'I had to learn to handle the feeling of everyone else wanting me out. I told myself I didn't feel rejected, because they were all strangers, and my mates and family were not rejecting me. I went into the house to learn about myself and about other people, and I've done that. I didn't go in for the money. After the fourth week, when I survived, I began to feel a bit invincible and I was thinking about winning, and I planned what I would do with the money: I would have divided it into eleven and given everyone a share, because it was the most amazing experience of my life and every single person in there contributed to it. I was praying I would win so people would see me dishing out the money.

'I accepted the cameras at the beginning. It's weird going for a poo and things like that, but you quickly get used to it. You can't ever completely relax, but I didn't mind that until I was close to Helen, then I hated it.

'The food in the house was fantastic, considering how little money we had. I've lost quite a lot of weight. I was the biggest person in there, in terms of height and weight, and I simply didn't get enough food. But what we had was fine.

'I missed my family and friends a helluva lot, and I didn't take enough photos in with me. I missed not being in control of my life, I missed the noise of traffic, I missed clean air – even in the garden it didn't feel clean. Sometimes I wanted to be with my mates so much I wanted to leave, but I would never have walked out. The worst time was after I beat Bubble, when I knew the others really wished he had stayed.

'I've done things I never thought I would do. I've slept in a room with two gay blokes and I've learned more tolerance of people in general. I've learned not to judge people from first impressions. I've learned to get on with people of different ages and from different walks of life. I'll keep in touch with some of them – I want to see Stuart, Penny, Bubble, Josh, Brian and Dean, as well as Helen, of course.'

Paul on Paul

'I don't know whether *Big Brother* will change my life permanently, but it has given me the most amazing memory of my life, and I'm grateful. I was successful in my job before, and I will possibly go back to that when all the mayhem has died down. I think I was the only person in the house who genuinely did not expect to make a new career out of it all.

'My life was fantastic before I went in – the risk I was taking was that I would lose what I had. But because I work freelance, I should be able to pick it up again. It will take a little while for this madness to calm down, but I know this may just be a flash in the pan, and I'll be happy whatever happens.

'I never saw myself as anyone very important, never the centre of attention, so all the interest in the programme, and in me and Helen in particular, has come as a real shock. I'm a guy who goes out a lot, gets off with a lot of girls, loves dating and chatting to girls, but doesn't really sleep around. I've slept with about fifteen girls in all, and I've had two long relationships. Before I went into the house, I was fond of a couple of girls, but they weren't girlfriends. Now I'll just wait and see where Helen and me go. I want to marry and have children one day. That's really important to me, but it will have to be the right girl.

'My family have been brilliant all the way through. We're a really strong

WEEK EIGHT FACT FILE

Main task: Playground skills.

PASS ☐ **FAIL** ☒

Mini-task: Sausage making.

Mini-task: Ten Green Bottles.

Treats: A barbecue with beer and loads of food for passing the sausage test. Two bottles of wine as a reward after two security breaches.

Bets are on!
To win: Brian is favourite to win at 1/5, with Helen next at 11/4, Dean at 25/l and Elizabeth at 33/1.
To walk: Elizabeth is the favourite to go on Thursday, at 1/5, followed by Dean at 3/1, Helen at 10/1 and Brian at 25/1.
Evictee's tip: Paul says, 'I want Helen to win, and I think she will, but it will be a close-run thing with Brian. Elizabeth will go on Thursday night, and Dean will go first on Friday.'

team. I use my favourite word – amazing – for Helen, but I also use it for my mum, who just is amazing, wicked, the best. And my dad too, and my sister and brother. I think this experience has bonded us all massively, and I think I have done my family proud.

'I've had a lump in my throat, wanting to cry, ever since I came out of the house. It has all been so emotional.'

HOUSEMATES' SELF-PORTRAITS

As part of the selection process each contestant was asked to draw a picture of themselves. These were analyzed by psychologists. It has got nothing to do with how good at drawing they are, but it can reveal a lot about someone's personality. Elizabeth did not submit a drawing.

Narinder

Hiya!

FAR TOO FLATTERING

Me in my Uniform

(Such a happy camper)

Brian

Bubble

THIS ONES ME !!

Mmm
Mmm !!

Paul

THATS WHAT I LOVE
ABOUT DRAWING YOURSELF
IT NEVER LOOKS ANYTHING
LIKE YA !

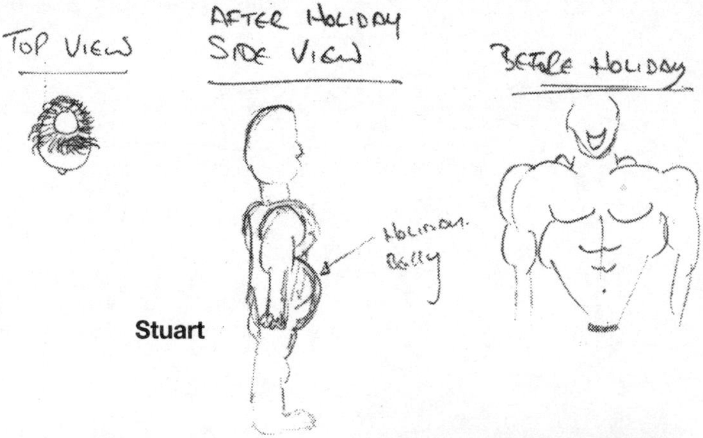

TOP VIEW

AFTER HOLIDAY SIDE VIEW

BEFORE HOLIDAY

HOLIDAY BELLY

Stuart

Amma

Dean

WEEK NINE

'I'd be dangerous with all that money.'
Helen

It's the final week, but if there is any added excitement among the housemates, they are keeping it firmly under wraps. Saturday starts with Dean and Elizabeth discussing the Middle-Eastern conflict, the Falklands war, the possibility of life in outer space, genetics and the meaning of life. Helen and Brian sleep through it.

Called to the Diary Room, Dean is asked who he thinks will win the *Big Brother* contest. He chooses Brian. 'If it's not him it will be Helen – she's got that shiny innocence and uncomplicated, genuine goodness about her.' He says he would be surprised if he won, and a little embarrassed.

The two youngsters, Brian and Helen, find the conversation more interesting when Dean and Elizabeth discuss magic mushrooms and hallucinogenic drugs. Dean tells a story about watching a friend's head morph into that of a goblin, 'just like science fiction'. His advice to Brian is that, with his vivid imagination, he should never risk experimenting with drugs.

Helen shocks Liz by claiming that she has been quieter inside the *Big Brother* house than she normally is. The others can't believe this is possible, and Liz admits she told Big Brother, when asked which of the other housemates' habits irritated her, that Helen 'stands right next to you and roars in your ear'. Helen giggles and says, 'Tell you what, I'm used to talking over hairdryers all the time.'

They are given their new task, which is a four-stage attempt to get to know the other housemates even better than they already do. Each stage will be rewarded with a treat, and there will be a party if they pass all four. The first part of the task involves the contestants splitting into pairs and learning about each other's childhoods. Dean and Liz pair off and Helen and Brian try to get to grips with remembering names of relatives and schools the other attended. Liz tells Dean she was captain of hockey, captain of netball, captain of athletics and deputy head girl at school, and she had her first kiss at the age of twelve in the metalwork room.

At every possible break in their practice, Helen talks about Paul and about how much she misses him. Brian, who is sympathetic, does his best to cheer her up.

Brian is called to the Diary Room and has to answer the same question that Dean faced about who he thinks will win. He hedges his bets, replying 'Helen or Dean, but it could be Liz'. He doesn't really want to win, he claims.

'It's weird, because if you were to win this it would be hard to go back to normal life. If someone wants to give me seventy grand, I'd take it, but I'm not sure that I want everything that goes with it – all the publicity. I think you would have a better chance coming fourth or third or second and adjusting back to normality quite quickly, going to the local shop and just being me. Having to win it would be kinda scary, hard. With coming first comes a lot of stuff harder than being in the *Big Brother* house and being recognized from that. If I was to sit here and say I didn't want seventy grand I'd be lying. But you have to think twice about it, to be honest.'

The housemates are tested on childhood memories: they each have to answer one question about their partner. They are thrilled to pass, especially as some of their answers are inspired guesses.

Helen is the next to be asked by Big Brother how she feels about the end of the contest. In the Diary Room, she talks about making it through to week nine. She was so sure that it would be her, not Paul, who would be leaving yesterday that she has not thought about the fact she is in the final week until now. She says it feels 'a bit funny' without Paul around, but that she's fine.

'I don't think I could win. I'd be too dangerous with all that money. I wouldn't know what to do with it. My bank would be going: what's going on? Why has she got all this money? It couldn't happen.'

The group's reward for passing the 'Knowing Me, Knowing You' test is a children's party. They're all very excited, although disappointed that there will be no booze. But the sight of Hula Hoops, fizzy pop, chocolate buttons, face paints and toy guns is enough to compensate. They enjoy themselves hugely, especially when Dean, with a silver-painted face, pretends to be a robot and pursues a demented Brian around the house. Liz and Helen make jelly and cakes, and Helen ices a 'P' for Paul on top of hers. Her face is painted purple with yellow spots, Brian has become the Satan he is always talking about, with a red face and horns, and Liz is a stylish-looking Geisha girl.

When the housemates are sitting quietly, Helen again chats to Brian about her romantic situation, telling him that she will ring Big G and break it off as soon as she is out of the house. Brian asks whether she was ever really thinking of marrying him.

'No way! It hasn't been a bed of roses. It was an on-off, on-off thing. When you're in this situation it makes you re-evaluate your life. It was going to be make or break ... it's break, isn't it?' She reckons that even if Big G and Paul have new girlfriends when she gets out of the house, she'll be OK. 'I don't expect anything from Paul, do I?'

They end the day singing together, to Dean's accompaniment. Brian wanders off key again. Dean tells him that he would have a voice good enough for Broadway if only he could sing in tune, but that as he's tone deaf no amount of training will help. Helen is still taking every opportunity to mention Paul, although she insists she's not lovesick, just pining for a friend. By 2 a.m., the small group are all tucked up in their beds in the girls' room.

The girls are up at a reasonable time on Sunday, and both have showers while the hot water is on. They do the shopping list together, managing out of their reduced budget of £21, to order five bottles of cider. Helen tells Liz how much she has gained from being in the house: 'I've learned not to be so sensitive, not to be so paranoid, to have more confidence, not to judge people, how to be around certain people, how to interact with people – loads of things.' Liz comments on how much Helen has grown up: 'In two months you've put on two years.'

Eventually Dean and Brian surface, and Dean retires to his favourite spot – a deckchair in the garden. While he's sitting there, he hears shouts from over the fence. Big Brother immediately plays crowd noises through the speakers, to drown out any attempts at contact. The other housemates are sure Dean has heard what was shouted – he eventually tells them it was 'Helen, we love you'. Later, he quietly he confesses to Elizabeth that what was actually shouted was

WHAT THE EXPERTS SAY

ON LOVE SICKNESS

'Helen is desperate to talk about Paul. She's showing classic signs of love sickness, a psychological condition which often afflicts those separated from their lover. There are a number of key symptoms which characterize the syndrome, and Helen is unwittingly displaying several of them. The first is re-enactment. A few hours after Paul is evicted, we find Helen going to the den alone, revisiting the scene where they had their most intimate moments. Helen is trying to recover some of the feelings that she experienced there with Paul.

'Helen chooses to sleep in Paul's bed. This is primitive superstitious behaviour, like keeping a lock of someone's hair. The closer you can get to something that belongs to your loved one, the closer you feel to them emotionally.

'It also enables her to take in his smell. Psychologists have discovered that of all the senses, smell is the most powerful stimulant to memory. By smelling Paul's pillow, Helen makes her memory of him all the more vivid and real.

'Paul dominates Helen's thoughts. The defining feature is the need to talk about and try to make sense of the relationship with the person who is absent. Crucially, it involves hearing what other people have to say. Importantly, she needs others to support her image of the relationship. Helen is clearly suffering from love sickness. She's likely to experience mood swings between elation and sadness. Sympathetic support from her housemates is going to be critical in helping her come to terms with her feelings for Paul.'

Dr Peter Collett, Experimental Psychologist

'Get your tits out, Helen'. Liz comments that she and Dean are the two housemates without fan clubs, and says that if people hate her when she leaves the house she will go to live in Spain. Dean predicts that the public feeling will not be hatred so much as indifference.

Brian is called to the Diary Room and talks about how he plans to spend his first day outside the house – shopping. He says the whole experience has changed him. 'But not too much, thankfully. I can still be silly at times. But I think I've changed for the best, definitely.'

Liz also goes to the Diary Room, to see the doctor and have the dressing on her finger changed. When she emerges, she looks curiously at Helen and remarks that her boobs look unusually large. Helen admits she is wearing a Wonderbra.

The second part of the task arrives – they must each create a three-dimensional clay model of another housemate's head. They have three hours in which to do it and must work from memory, separated in different rooms. Brian and Dean work on the two girls, and the girls do them. They create wire frames and then cover them with clay. The contestants are only allowed a margin of error of fifteen per cent on the size of the busts – luckily there is no such penalty margin on the artistic merits of their work. Dean's head representing Helen is good. The others are adequate enough to be marked as a pass.

In the Diary Room, Dean explains that the longing to see his friends and family is becoming more acute as the final days arrive. He says he is looking forward to doing normal things, like visiting his mum. 'Maybe when I leave here I'll start doing all the things I always say I'm going to do but never quite get round to. If I can leave here with that, that will be another bonus.'

The housemates unveil their sculptures to one another, making short speeches about each other's work and dissolving into helpless giggles. Brian reckons his makes him look like 'Mr Potato Head', while Helen exclaims, 'Oh my God, I look like my dad!' Dean says of Helen's attempt to recreate him: 'That is one ugly bastard. It looks like some kind of monster from the sea.' Liz is very pleased with Brian's version of her, although she does not think it looks like her. They're all delighted with their reward – champagne and canapés.

Called to the Diary Room, Liz tells Big Brother how good she thinks the task is. She describes the house as being a lot quieter. 'It seems a lot bigger, and seems like we're echoing around a bit. As we're getting to the end, the group is reverting back to individuals. Before, we were a group, but now the end is in sight we are all thinking about our own lives and families. It's quite relaxed. People are thinking more of Friday.'

Helen is still using Brian as her chief confidant and advisor on her troubled love life. She says she doesn't want her ex-boyfriend to greet her when she leaves the house. She asks Brian if that is wrong, and he tells her to stay as calm as possible, and just look forward to seeing Paul.

But Helen is still worried about meeting Big G. 'I just don't think I can face that, really. I would like to do that in Wales.' Brian points out that her life is not as simple as it was. But Helen's ebullience shines through and she soon cheers up – 'I just need to not worry about it too much and just get on with it, eh?'

Brian talks longingly about going shopping. He wants to buy a CD, find out who's been number one in the pop charts, and 'buy some hair'. He says his mouth is watering at the prospect of having a life again. It's nearly midnight, and the housemates realize that they have spent their final weekend in the *Big Brother* house. Brian and Helen agree that Friday night will be like Christmas. Helen goes to bed really early – before midnight – and the other three stay up, quietly reading. Liz eventually joins Dean in the garden, and expands on the theme of how they are no longer functioning as a group. It turns into a generalized bitch about the two younger housemates.

'I think at this stage your differences become so apparent. I look at them and think we have nothing in common with them,' says Liz. 'I can see Helen looking at me and thinking, "Who are you? You're different from me." I've been trying hard for so long, keeping face up. I'm now going "Oh, God".'

Elizabeth adds, 'It's like people are giving up. No one did the washing up. But that's not a criticism, it's an observation.'

Dean agrees. 'Brian and Helen are ready to stop now, but it's not over yet. You've got to put your energy into it.'

Brian finishes his book and joins them briefly in the garden before retiring to bed. Dean and Elizabeth follow soon afterwards. Perhaps because they are last to bed, they are also last to get up the next morning. In Dean's case, this is not surprising, as he has never been one of the early risers, but Liz can usually be relied upon to be up first, now that both Stuart and Josh have gone. Brian has a shower and goes back to bed, where he stays until midday. Helen makes porridge, which Dean quietly describes as 'like finishing plaster'.

Brian and Helen sunbathe while Dean and Elizabeth clean the house. The young pair have minor pangs of guilt for not helping, but suppress them because the sun is shining and they want to make the most of it. Once again, Helen brings the conversation around to the subject of Paul. Brian gently cautions her not to do anything rash over her relationship with Big G, as they may get back together again.

In the Diary Room, Big Brother asks Dean whether the house is more like a holiday camp or a prison camp. He can't decide.

'You'd think it would be easy lying in the sun, chilling out and reading a book. A lot of people would be envious, watching this from outside. But I'd love to do a day's work, anything. It's been a sort of mental prison. You've kept yourself in here on purpose, a sort of endurance test. There's a very oppressive edge to the cameras watching all the time, which you don't realize until week seven or eight. You start thinking, "God, I'd love those things not to be looking at me." I don't think I'll appreciate it until I'm out of here and in a room where I'm not being filmed. That will feel really, really good.'

Today's instalment of the 'Knowing Me, Knowing You' task arrives – they have to teach each other their skills. Brian must teach Liz to be an air stewardess and demonstrate an air-safety drill; Dean must teach Helen to play chords on the guitar for thirty seconds continuously; Liz, who has had flamenco lessons, must teach Brian to dance a few basic steps; and Dean must

WHAT THE EXPERTS SAY

ON WHO WILL WIN

'The Diary Room has always offered a unique insight into the thoughts and motivations of the housemates. It offers the best conditions not just to scrutinize what people say, but how they say it.

'In the last weekend in the house, each of the final four was asked a number of key questions in order to gauge their attitude to the competition and to each other as they entered the final week. The question about who would they like to win elicited some extremely revealing answers. Brian was very verbose, but never provided an answer. He was unable to select an individual housemate. The question provoked a physical response from Elizabeth. She quite literally bit her lip as she was thinking, and her leg (which she pulled up onto the chair) formed a defensive barrier. Dean touched his face, a sign of unease. At one point his hand even covered his mouth, obscuring what he was saying at a critical moment. But Helen went the furthest in stifling her response to the question.

'The housemates' failure to give a straightforward response to a straightforward question is telling. In fact, all the housemates said everybody should win. Assuming that it is very unlikely that they all viewed each other absolutely equally, we might have expected one or two names to be mentioned. But any answer could be viewed as an endorsement and thereby enhanced the chances of the person selected.

'They care deeply about the outcome, no matter what they say.'

Professor Geoffrey Beattie, Psychologist

learn to cut and style hair, under the tuition of hairdresser Helen. They are given some model heads for him to practise on.

The task is a hit with the housemates. Dean is astonished to find himself plaiting and French-pleating hair, but his surprise turns to horror when special clothes are delivered for each of them to wear. Liz gets a smart, blue airline uniform. Brian is supplied with a pink and lilac skirt, stockings, Cuban-heeled shoes and a lilac head-dress, which he wears with a pair of Helen's knickers. Helen becomes a rock chick in a black leather jacket. Dean is mortified when he has to put on the outfit that Helen and the other hairdressers at Classy Cutz wear: a skimpy, midriff-revealing white T-shirt with a glittery pink heart on the front and a pair of bright pink, three-quarter-length jeans. The others collapse in giggles.

Brian makes it worse by saying he likes Dean in his new gear.

'It's alright for you, Brian, you're gay. I'm straight. You don't understand what they've done to me. You haven't got friends like I've got. I'll never hear the end of this … I must admit, I didn't think I was going to have to dress like a homosexual.'

He then goes outside to assert his masculinity by kicking the football around.

When it's time for the task test, all the housemates do well. Dean plaits a blonde wig that Elizabeth wears for him. Brian sweeps and sashays around, following Liz's instructions to 'feel sexy, feel proud, enjoy it'. Liz, her hair up and her makeup perfected by Brian, is efficient and professional, and manages to avoid catching the giggling Brian's eye, as she informs the housemates where the safety exits are on the Boeing 707 bound for Bow.

After the group pass the test, Liz wears the blonde wig to do a Marilyn Monroe impression, singing 'Happy Birthday Mr President' to Brian. As a reward for their task success, the housemates are awarded one hour's pay each at £3.70 an hour – a total of £14.80 to spend on luxuries from a list which includes ice cream, chocolates, oysters and booze. They choose two bottles of Chardonnay, a four-pack of lager and one oyster, for Liz.

The housemates enjoy their treats with their meal of pizza. Afterwards, they mix their own supply of cider with the lager to make 'snakebite'. The girls probe the boys about how many times they have masturbated in the house. Brian says he has done it twice, adding that although he was dying to do it last night, has decided to try to hang on until he is out of the house. Dean admits to doing it six times.

Brian says he is looking forward to getting back to work at the airline, and seems perplexed when Dean says it will be impossible for him to go back to his old job after all this television exposure.

Liz is called to the Diary Room. She reports that she has really enjoyed the task, because she has spent half a day in Brian's company and she realizes she really didn't know him well. 'We've gone down a level further, in a kind of way. It was so much fun, I feel really relaxed.' She says Dean found it difficult because he was worried about losing his credibility.

Big Brother has told the housemates that they are now allowed to talk about nominations for the first time. There ensues a soul-baring session, in which each member of the group reveals whether they have ever nominated any of the other remaining housemates. Helen becomes very worried when she thinks that Paul nominated her last week (he didn't). Dean reassures her. Their talk is interrupted by fireworks, and they are ordered into the boys' bedroom, where Helen makes a beeline for Paul's bed.

They are all a bit the worse for wear, and when Helen says 'it pisses me off when people talk down about Paul Clarke when I really like him' the others, particularly Brian, snap. He tells her that she fancied Paul, which blinded her to his faults. She says she can't find anything wrong with him and Brian, standing up and waving his arms emphatically, shouts:

'Open your eyes, open your ears – you'll find a lot, I can assure you.'

'The things people don't like about Paul are the things I like. Paul talks shit and I talk shit and I like talking shit,' she retorts.

'He used to speak a lot of shit. Everything he said was completely hypocritical. He would say something and it would have no meaning,' Brian groans.

'That's what I like,' says Helen, vehemently.

The exchange becomes more heated, with Brian telling her to shut up and

Helen telling him that Paul is nicer than he is. Dean tries to placate Helen, but she warns the others: 'No one talk, or I'll punch them.'

But Helen's anger dissipates and her face crumples when Liz tells her how Paul said that she had done sixty per cent of the flirting and he had only done forty per cent. Helen looks devastated and is on the verge of tears. She wants to know when Paul said this. Liz tells her that it was during the conversation she had with him at the patio doors, when Paul also told her Helen had more to worry about than he did. Helen agrees with this bit, but says she thought the attraction was fifty–fifty. She seems completely defeated and miserable.

Brian reverts to the compassionate person who was so caring towards Helen earlier in the day. He explains to her that he thinks she put herself more on the line than Paul, and advises her not to put all her eggs in one basket. She asks Liz whether Paul said he fancied her, and although Liz replies that Paul was not sure, Helen rallies and declares that he is 'so nice', before adding, 'What an arse! Who knows what is going to happen. I'm not putting all my eggs in one basket.'

Allowed out of the bedroom, Dean and Brian embark on some drink-fuelled fun in the garden, lobbing empty cider and wine bottles and a couple of plates across the wall. Big Brother calls a halt to their smashing time. Brian goes to the Diary Room to apologize, and has a long, rambling, emotional, drunken conversation with Big Brother. He echoes what Liz said earlier – that it has been good for the two of them to spend time together, as they now know each other better. But teaching her his job made him think of all the happy times he had spent at work, and he is feeling homesick for his friends. With tears welling in his eyes, he tells Big Brother:

'I am scared about going home, scared about seeing my family and friends. It's weird for me, wondering what my family are thinking and how they're perceiving me for being gay or for being me. I'm looking forward to seeing my best friend, Richard. I miss Richard with all my heart. He'd tell me what to do and he'd give me a hug. That would make me feel safe.'

Big Brother asks him what advice Richard would give him, to which Brian replies:

'He would tell me to stop being such a fool, such a ponce, and to focus on the week ahead. He'd tell me he's proud of me, that my family are proud of me, and that he would always be my friend and he won't judge me. I should just concentrate on everything here.' He pauses, before adding, 'I should do that, I suppose. I should take his advice.'

While Brian is having his marathon session in the Diary Room, Helen continues to talk about Paul, and eventually Liz falls asleep listening to her. Helen wanders out into the garden and across to the den on her own. She snuggles down in the spot where she and Paul were so cosy together, but after a couple of minutes she goes back to the house, taking Paul's ashtray with her. She tells the others, 'It's not the same without Paul. It takes two to tango in that hut. With one, it's just not the same.'

Brian and Dean counsel her not to pin all her hopes on a romantic reunion with Paul. Brian again tells her that he didn't like Paul, but he says it much more quietly and rationally this time, pointing out that Paul was nominated so often that it is clear Brian was not alone in disliking him. Helen insists she just wants friendship from Paul.

The night ends comically, as Brian tries to shoo the hens back into their coop. The cockerel evades him, so he turns the hose pipe on the bird, which still refuses to go inside. When Brian turns away to talk to Helen, the cockerel calmly strolls in.

Elizabeth and Dean keep the sleeptalking habit going. She mutters something that Brian tells her sounded like 'flibiblob'. Dean says, loudly and clearly at 9 a.m., 'I hate you lot.'

Big Brother returns the heads the housemates sculpted of each other, and Dean arranges them round the conservatory. Their next part of the task is to get to grips with the politics and morality of the other housemates, so the day is spent in earnest discussion, which Brian brands as 'boring'. Dean describes Brian as a 'closet Communist' because he wants a Utopian world in which one political party represents everyone. Helen says she's not interested in politics, but Liz points out that politics affects her whether she likes it or not, citing the price of petrol and the price of a vodka and Coke as examples. Helen says she's still not interested because she knows no party will give her a free vodka and Coke. She admits that if she found a bag containing £40,000, and she knew that she wouldn't be caught, she wouldn't take it to the police. Instead, she would buy a Gucci handbag and give the rest to charity.

The fiercest debate is about the legalization of cannabis, with Dean and Liz for it and Brian and Helen against. Liz demolishes Helen's arguments. Called to the Diary Room, Helen bears no grudges and claims that being in the house has made her more 'mature and sensible' (and also a better cook).

The politics and morality debate rages on, with all the housemates agreeing that they would not shoplift, but they would change price stickers to get something cheaper. Helen admits she would be unfaithful, and Liz points out that after her romance with Paul she could hardly answer otherwise. Dean confesses that he once read a partner's diary 'and that's how I found out she was seeing someone else'. Brian and Dean both own up to peeing in the shower, and Brian accuses Liz of lying when she says she never has. She's indignant, and disgusted with them both. 'It stinks. Would you do it at home?' she demands.

They talk about pornography (Brian admits to being shocked when he saw a tape belonging to a boyfriend) and kinky sex, with Dean saying he can't get his head round why 'some blokes get prostitutes to tie them up and throw chocolate eclairs at their bollocks'.

Brian clears up the shattered remains of the bottles and plates he broke yesterday evening, and Helen pays a quick pilgrimage to the den, scene of her trysts with Paul. She and Brian agree that the week is passing faster and more easily than they expected.

In the Diary Room, Dean tells Big Brother that the task is interesting, especially because they are now talking about subjects 'we've purposely avoided for the past nine weeks'.

He says they are getting 'beyond the veneer of polite society'.

'I don't think British society is particularly good at opening up,' he adds. 'We feel much more comfortable having a cup of tea and polite chit-chat about nothing, rather than digging into the deep, meaningful things of life.'

The housemates are all called to the Diary Room one by one and their political and moral opinions are recorded. Dean admits that if he scraped the side of a Porsche late at night without being seen he wouldn't try to find the owner. Liz argues with Big Brother over the need to answer yes or no to whether fox hunting should be banned, but ultimately says yes, it should.

An hour later, they are each called in to answer three questions about the others' morality, one of which they must get right to pass the task. They are thrilled to make it, especially as Helen made her decision on Brian's opinions on the basis of 'he thinks a bit like me'. When she emerges from the Diary

WHAT THE EXPERTS SAY

THE FINAL FOUR

'Brian, Dean and Elizabeth survived to the last round because they never faced the public vote. They were always popular in the house. This is because they have all fulfilled essential roles: Dean is the leader, Elizabeth is the provider and Brian is the entertainer.

'Others have wanted these roles, but were never really successful. This is because, in their individual ways, Brian, Dean and Elizabeth were always best. They triumphed over the competition. Dean's rival was Stuart. As the two oldest people in the house, the group instinctively deferred to them and both could have been leader. Dean was happy to let Stuart take the lead in the early task. However, the group was not so happy. Stuart tended to overstep the mark, and his leadership focussed on correction and discipline. In stressful situations, Dean's focus tended to be on comfort rather than correction. He was confident enough to lead without dominating.

'Elizabeth's competition came from Penny. They were both seen as potential mother figures. The kitchen became disputed territory. When Penny was in there, she was seen as bossy and dictatorial. Elizabeth was able to take charge in the kitchen without antagonizing anyone. This was because she was able to encourage rather than dictate.

'Brian's competition came from Bubble. They are both very funny and they became good friends. Humour often relies on getting close to the bone. Brian is good at this, but Bubble sometimes goes too far and people don't always know when he's joking. Although they made a great comedy duo, Bubble ultimately realized who was the funnier man.

'Helen is different. Her main competition came from herself – it was her weaknesses that got her nominated, and her strengths that pulled her through and made her popular with the public. Her strengths are that she is irrepressible, very honest and she has always been just herself.'

Dr Sandra Scott, Psychiatrist

Room, they all pretend she failed, which she accepts unquestioningly, only to go mad with delight when she discovers that she answered two of her three questions correctly.

In the early evening, Liz and Dean are in their usual places on the patio, and Liz begins to get nostalgic about the *Big Brother* house, which they will all be leaving soon. 'I'm getting fond of this place. I like the way the fence curves round, the colour of the wall. If you could walk in and out of this place it would be fantastic.' Dean agrees that with a few modifications – such as the removal of a lot of mirrors with cameramen behind them – the place would make a comfortable home.

They both believe Helen will win, but they are worried about how Brian is seen by the world outside. 'It's either love him or hate him,' Liz reckons.

It's Brian's and Helen's turn to cook. They make shepherd's pie, using up all the carrots 'because we're not going to be needing them again'. Big Brother asks Brian to clean the mirror behind the sink, which launches Brian into a one-man show as he peers behind it searching for 'demons', and then engages in a running conversation with the fish.

The housemates are rewarded for passing the task with a bottle of champagne and a large wooden puzzle. They're delighted with the champagne, which they guzzle greedily, but unimpressed with the puzzle. Brian and Helen take no interest in it at all after Brian's initial shriek of disgust: 'It should be a treat!' He likens it to a teacher at school saying, 'For getting an A, Brian, you can write me an essay.' Dean and Liz have a go at the puzzle without any success. But they're all heartened to be told that they can have a party tomorrow night, and they choose a *Last of the Mohicans* theme. They also start planning their eviction outfits for what they have dubbed 'Final Friday'. Dean says he will do Helen's hair for her, as he is now an experienced hairdresser.

The news that the party will be tomorrow makes them start questioning the agenda for the rest of the week. Helen is ahead of the others when she points out that there may be an eviction before Friday (the housemates will not be told of the Thurday night's eviction until one and a half hours before one of them has to leave the house).

Called to the Diary Room, Liz is asked what she will remember about the house. She lists the garden, her birthday and the last week. 'Because there are fewer people it has been more special. I'll also remember the characters I've met, those who are here now and Bubble, who was a real character. It's been an amazing experience.'

Dean struggles on with the puzzle, vowing that he won't go to bed until he has cracked it. The two girls retire early – they're in bed before half past eleven. Brian follows them shortly afterwards, after a chat with Dean about how Helen will be 'a bit of a babe' when she leaves. Brian sees her appearing, clad in a bikini, on the cover of a magazine, adding that he will be on the cover of *Horse and Hound*. After describing the puzzle using Brian's favourite word – 'evil' – Dean eventually abandons the pile of planks. But he's not ready for bed: he starts packing for home. All his clothes are piled on the bed, and he even dives beneath the mattress to retrieve some forgotten T-shirts. He throws the clothes into his suitcase, and then wanders round the house picking up more of his belongings. He then starts to clean up, emptying all the bins, sweeping the carpet in the lounge and folding all the orange blankets. Finally, after playing a few tunes to himself on the guitar, he retires to bed on his own in the boys' room.

Dean sleeps through the drama of a smoke alarm going off loudly at 3 a.m. Although Brian, Liz and Helen are woken by it, it takes them quarter of an hour to take action, with Brian being dispatched to the Diary Room for reassurance. Fortunately, there is no emergency, just a faulty alarm. Lying in bed, he and Helen discuss whether the maintenance man who has been summoned to sort out the problem is good looking or not.

The first excitement on Wednesday is provided by two army helicopters flying overhead. Liz is barely dressed, but rushes out into the garden with Dean to wave at them. They are elated when the soldiers wave back. The two of them sit in the garden with Helen, eating porridge, and Liz says:

'One thing you realize in here – and this will sound really arty farty – is that you can't stop time. A while back it was Sunday and now it's Wednesday. Tomorrow comes after today, yesterday was behind. I've been brought up with this, but in here it's more exaggerated because you watch time more. You really notice how you can't hold on to it, you can't hold on to the moments.'

She and Dean discuss winning, and Liz says she would now like the money. For Dean, the most exciting prospect is seeing Vanessa. They have another half hour of concentrated effort with the giant wooden puzzle, without success.

Dean is delighted to be cleaning out the chickens for the final time (he won't be on the rota for the rest of the week). He collects eggs, which Brian describes as 'the embryos of Satan, developing as we speak'. Dean throws a couple of the eggs at Brian, who is looking forward to his final day on chicken-cleaning duties tomorrow. He promises to bid farewell to 'the demons' in style. 'You'll see feathers fly,' he threatens.

Helen is still having cookery lessons from Liz, who teaches her how to make an omelette for her lunch. Soon afterwards, Dean is called to the Diary Room and given a note from Big Brother. It congratulates them all on making it through to the final stage of the *Big Brother* experience and says they will be rewarded tomorrow with a gourmet meal of their choice. Helen doesn't know what 'gourmet' means, so Liz explains it as 'fancy'. They have to decide

WHAT THE EXPERTS SAY

INSTANT FAME

'The fact that the housemates have been out of touch with reality may help them. Instant fame is an unreal situation. They are going from one unreal situation into another unreal situation.'

Dr Sandra Scott, Psychiatrist

on a menu from several choices, and in the end plump for 'fancy' chicken with 'fancy' vegetables, followed by a Pavlova with chocolate sauce. The news about the meal allays their fears that there will be an eviction tomorrow, and they celebrate the fact that they are all going to be there until the last day.

The afternoon is spent sunbathing. Dean tries to solve the puzzle again, and even gets a bit tetchy with Elizabeth when he still fails to understand it. The others tell Helen that she has a white ring around her sunburned neck, and decide that it is caused by her talking too much. Dean comments that she has a tan on the inside of her mouth.

Helen and Brian discuss their plans for their first weekend of freedom: Brian wants to get drunk 'and pick my brains up the next morning'. They talk about relationships, and both seem unsure whether Paul saying he fancied Helen's personality means he really fancied her. Helen asks Brian if he would like to get back with his ex-boyfriend, and he says he would like to be friends with him, but he's not sure about anything more.

The housemates make a huge chain of balloons to decorate the lounge area for their party. Dean shaves his head for the last time in the house, and they all have cold showers and start to get ready for the party. Not for the first time, Dean realizes that he has overshot his 6 p.m. tryst with Vanessa – every Wednesday they both sit quietly and concentrate on each other. He goes to the den for a few quiet moments, and then says out loud, 'See you on Friday, babes.'

As Helen gets changed, Brian and Liz laugh at her white breasts: they agree she should have sunbathed naked. As one of the unmanned cameras whirrs round to record her nakedness, she exclaims, 'Oh my God! There goes the pervy camera again.'

The girls decide to serve a meal of lasagne, even though they may get more food for the *Last of the Mohicans* party. Over dinner in the garden, they discuss the best chefs in the house – Narinder and Josh get high marks, and they laugh at the memory of Paul's efforts. Brian confounds them all by offering to wash up.

Liz comments on how odd it is that they know so much about each other, but have never seen each other's handwriting. She says Josh's signature (on the painting) was too girlie for his personality. Brian disagrees, which prompts Liz to suggest he secretly fancies Josh. Brian jokes that he is going to meet up with him and they will double date with Paul and Helen.

The costumes for the party arrive, plus a lot of food for the barbecue, including authentic native-American delicacies such as venison, buffalo and dove. Dean is delighted to find a generous supply of beer among the goodies. The housemates pounce on the clothes gleefully. Dean dresses as a US cavalryman, Brian is the sheriff, Liz is an Indian chief with full war paint, and Helen is a squaw. Dean comments that, despite his macho clothes, Brian still looks gay. Brian terrifies himself when a cap gun makes a loud noise when he pulls the trigger.

It is just as well for Brian that the group have already eaten. He won't eat venison, 'because it would be like eating Bambi', and thinks his mum and sister would be upset if he ate dove. He refuses to try buffalo, despite Helen's reassurance: 'Buffalo is a bit like steak.' Dean tells her it is steak, and Liz patiently explains how buffalo is a relative of the cow. Helen then protests that she would not eat dove, asking 'Dove is a bird, isn't it?' Liz tells her it is, a white bird. As they chat over their second dinner of the night, Helen asks them to imagine what it would have been like if she had been evicted instead of Penny. Liz says she would have left if there had been any outbursts.

They discuss who they would have liked as housemates. Dean thinks a policeman or a soldier would have been good, but they decide a policeman would have been voted out in the first round. Dean also thinks it would have been fun if there had been someone very rightwing among them. Brian suggest someone homophobic.

In the Diary Room, Liz tells Big Brother that it has been interesting for her to meet people from different cultures and religions. She adds, 'Just thinking about Helen and Brian – we've had such different upbringings. Everyone can teach you something, you've got to have an open mind.'

Following the conversation in the garden about who they would have liked to meet in the house, Liz is asked to describe the perfect *Big Brother* contestant. She says, 'A general all-round perfect person. But if there was one person, they would probably be sickening, and everyone would want to fault them.' She adds, 'They might be called "over-efficient",' in reference to the light-hearted criticism that Dean and Brian made of her.

Dressed appropriately, they end the evening telling campfire tales. Despite Liz recounting a terrifying experience of being lost in the jungle in Chile, Helen is adamant that she wants to go camping. 'H, you don't. You really don't. There's no bathroom,' Dean tells her.

Dean is the first up on Thursday, and he's worrying about leaving the *Big Brother* house in a clean and tidy state. He asks Big Brother if they can have the hot water on longer tomorrow for cleaning purposes. They can't have more hot water, comes the reply, but they can have it on later in the day, between 4 p.m. and 5 p.m., instead of in the morning. Dean goes off to consult the others.

Chatting in the garden, Helen astonishes Dean by saying that given the choice between winning the £70,000 and zapping the spot on her lip, she'd zap the zit every time. When Brian gets up, she involves him in the spot debate – he assures her he can't see it. They sunbathe and chat, and about once an hour Helen brings up the subject of her spot until the others amiably tell her to shut up. Elizabeth is called to the Diary Room to have the stitch in her finger removed, and reports back that it hurt.

Helen's tan lines amuse the others. She has been wearing her shorts so much that she has a white strip from her waist to her thighs. Helen sings the Welsh National Anthem in Welsh. Then she wanders off to spend more than an hour getting ready for the gourmet dinner, which makes the others wonder how long she will need to prepare for leaving the house – they decide that two and a half hours will be the minimum.

The dinner arrives at quarter to seven. The housemates regard this as suspiciously early and speculate on what Big Brother may have in store for them. Nevertheless, they enjoy their last supper together: there is a starter of rocket, basil and tomato, followed by Thai chicken and then a strawberry pavlova with chocolate sauce, all washed down with a vintage wine that Elizabeth thinks is delicious and Brian describes as 'evil'. Helen says she has learned one important thing in the house – she likes red wine. She says the meal is 'stonking', but Brian is suspicious about the unknown ingredients.

The housemates enjoy a relaxed and comfortable discussion after the meal, with Brian and Helen ganging up against Dean, who complains about the number of tasks which have involved dressing up. The two youngsters have loved those tasks, and attack him for his lack of fun. Before he can reply, they are all surprised to hear the voice of Davina being broadcast into the house. She announces that one of the group will be leaving this evening. Helen is the first to react, screaming 'My hair! My hair! My hair!' Davina tells Helen her hair looks fine, and Brian tells her to be quiet for a minute.

'Before you entered the *Big Brother* house,' continues Davina, 'Big Brother told you to expect the unexpected. This is your final surprise. The public has been voting all week to elect the winner. Tonight we will evict the person with the least votes.'

Helen continues to run around shouting about her hair – she and Brian are both convinced they will be the one to go. But when Davina's voice is heard again, she informs the group that it is Elizabeth who will be packing her case. Helen is still shrieking, and Brian takes hold of her and quietens her, out of respect for Liz. Helen's main concern is the limited amount of time she has to do her hair and makeup for the live eviction programme – she seems to forget that she's on camera all the time. Both Liz and Dean take the news quietly and retire to the girls' room. In the garden, Brian reminds Helen that they may have been tactless, and says he is furious with Big Brother for springing this on Liz. Meanwhile, Liz tells Dean that she's glad they weren't given more warning and she's happy to be going. She has a few quiet moments saying goodbye to the chickens, and then talks to Dean about whether she will cry when she sees her friends and family. Dean, ever practical, suggests that she doesn't wear mascara. He paints her fingernails for her.

Helen and Brian are delighted to do Liz's hair for her, but she refuses to allow them to do her makeup, as she feels they were too liberal with the blusher when they turned her into an air stewardess. They insist she makes the traditional goodbye speech. She tells the others how much she has enjoyed their company, thanking Brian for being so funny, Helen for being so loud and bubbly and Dean for being there for her throughout. Brian suggests the other three make a break for freedom when the door opens, but Dean tells him there's no point as they are so near the end. Brian admits he just wants to break the rules.

When it's time to go, there are lots of hugs and kisses, and Brian tells Liz

VOTING

By the time of Elizabeth's eviction, 3.6 million viewers had voted on who they wanted to win. Of these, 73,482 – just two per cent of the total – chose Elizabeth. A third of all Elizabeth's votes were made via interactive TV; the rest were made by telephone.

he expects her to be waiting at the gate with the drinks when they leave tomorrow. When she has gone the others all look dejected. Dean suggests they get drunk. They decide they will all sleep in the boys' room, and Helen will have Paul's bed.

Brian has found the whole evening very stressful, and Helen borrows Paul's phrase when she tells him to 'chill your boots' as they bicker in the kitchen. She goes to the Diary Room and tells Big Brother that she has been trying to give Brian advice, as she has more experience of facing eviction, but she feels he is taking the night badly. In the garden, Brian and Dean agree that Helen's preoccupation with her hair has irritated them, because something more important – an eviction – was happening. Brian opens up to Dean and confronts some of his fears. He is terrified that his parents will not be there for him when he leaves, which he would regard as a rejection of his sexuality.

Big Brother calls Brian to the Diary Room to discuss his worries. While he is in there, it is Helen's turn to open up to Dean about her relationship with Big G, repeating that it was 'on and off'. She describes how Big G told her life would change completely after *Big Brother*. 'I thought it would make or break us,' she adds, 'and it definitely broke us.' She says she is looking forward to seeing Paul again, and claims she is a new and improved Helen – more mature and adult, and ready to lead her own life without relying on other people, like her mum and Big G, to do her thinking for her.

When Brian rejoins them, he and Helen badger Dean to play their favourite of all the songs he has written, 'De-luxe'. It reminds Helen of romantic moments holding Paul's hand, and those thoughts probably spur her into making a last nostalgic trip to the den. She looks around in silence and then says, 'Hmmmm, Mr Clarke. Paul Clarke. Just think about the stuff we were doing in here last Thursday – not a lot but it could have been more.' Brian, who has always been scared of the den, agrees to spend ten seconds in there on his own. The other two ambush him as he comes out.

As 2 a.m. approaches, Brian finds the energy to prance around on top of the coffee table, singing 'New York, New York'. Then he and Dean take two pins and run around bursting balloons. Dean calms down with a Tai Chi session and waters the garden. When he finally comes to bed, the other two are asleep. It is Helen's turn to talk in her sleep. She says 'Paul ... Paul. Shit, you're not Paul, you're Brian. Who do you think is gonna go first?'

ELIZABETH LOOKS BACK: THE EXCLUSIVE INTERVIEW

Elizabeth on the housemates

Penny: 'I don't think she coped with it very well at all. I remember her getting there and saying, "Let's go and unpack our bags now. I'll make up your bed and put your pictures up." That was a bit much, but that was her way of coping. She wanted to take care of everybody, mother everybody, be loved by everybody. In that situation it didn't work – you had to give people their space. For me, there were rules, and personal space was very important. You were sharing a confined space with so many people, so you need to keep your personal space, and Penny came into it too much. She was very tactile – she tried to kiss you and even when she looked at you she came too close. She had a heart of gold, meant well, I just don't think *Big Brother* was right for her. I want to get to know her outside. When I see her, I want to start from scratch. I think I would be able to get on with her, because she's a lovely, genuine person.'

Stuart: 'I've been told people thought I was flirting with Stuart – I certainly wasn't. Stuart was quite silent, and it must have been difficult for him, being the father of a family and being a managing director, to then come in with people a lot younger than him. Although he was only in his thirties and younger than Dean, he seemed by far the oldest member of the group, because he was used to being in a position of authority. But you have to strip all of that away: it's a meritocracy of personalities, which he may have found odd because he was used to being given respect because of his position. He's never had to depend on a personality thing. He never let the mask down, probably in the same way I didn't. And because of that we both came across as scheming. He's a genuine man, but probably a bit competitive. It was strange when I saw video clips of him in the Diary Room – he sprawled across the chair like Mr Confident, which wasn't how I'd seen him in the house.'

Narinder: 'I liked Naz – she was very energetic, bubbly, maybe a bit too sensitive. I can understand everything she said both inside and outside the house. There are times when you sit there and think, "God, you are boring", because it gets boring in there, and sometimes I felt I was the most boring person in the world. You need external stimulus. She's right – we were boring, but she shouldn't have said it. She clung too closely to Brian, which didn't allow her own humour to come through. Towards the end, she started to say some very funny things about Newcastle and about her upbringing. She was also perhaps a bit hung up on being the only Asian girl. She was very feisty. The week I nominated Stuart it was, for me, between her and him. I wanted to keep in the intelligent people, the people I could have a discussion with, and Naz was one of those. We talked about third-world debt. And there was also something cheeky and very loveable about her. I wanted to tell her to stop mouthing off, because she's such a nice person. She needs someone to put a hand over her mouth.'

Bubble: 'I remember Bubble from the first few moments. I was the last person in and I saw this throng of people and there was lots of screaming, and I felt so black (I was wearing black) and so normal. People were so high, you couldn't talk to them. Bubble was so sweet, and I thought he looked small and young and he had a funny hat on, and he introduced himself in a chirpy way. From that moment, I thought he was a really nice bloke, really genuine. He could be really loud sometimes, and when he got into that stream he didn't listen to people. I didn't mind that, because I also knew his quiet side, his intelligent and witty side. He is very sharp and perceptive. It's a shame that some of the others just saw him as someone who slept a lot and shouted. I don't have a bad thing to say about him. What you see is what you get, there's no pretence there. He was not into designer clothes or beauty preparations, and we had that in common, because there's only so long I can talk about clothes and hair for without it doing my head in. We could talk about real things.'

Amma: 'She never really came out. She knew she hadn't done herself justice. She felt she couldn't be herself, she couldn't understand what role she played. I think she felt like a bit of a nobody. I kept telling her she was beautiful, lovely, animated. It was hard to hear her, and she'd fade off at the end of sentences. She walked around in flip-flops, making a shushing noise on the floor, and did everything slowly – that was just how she was. When I said it about her, it was used to make me seem two-faced, but I actually said it to her face. She kept a different body clock to everyone except Bubble, staying up very late, which didn't help her get involved. She told me she was analyzing everything and I told her to get out of it, because from everything she told me – from her job and from looking at her – I believe outside she probably is a vibrant, life-and-soul person. I want to spend time with her and get to know her again.'

Josh: 'It was very hard for him, coming in after two weeks. I remember first seeing him and he looked so clean and shiny and new, and he had freshly-laundered clothes. It was really funny: he was wearing a T-shirt and I thought he had ripped it, and he had to explain to me that they were designer rips. He was very into his image, with his fashion, his £11 toothpaste, so I didn't expect to get on with him. But he was actually really, really nice. He didn't have a good introduction to the house, especially because of the row with Brian. He said we all had in-jokes. By the time he arrived, we had our roles. He had a lot of energy, lots of ideas for games, but he didn't get a fair break. But I think Josh is a robust character and he handled it well.'

Paul: 'I feel I haven't done him justice, and I feel so guilty for constantly nominating him. I just didn't connect with him. He spent the first couple of weeks rolling around on the floor with Penny, and with Brian and Narinder on the edge of that group. I'm not the kind of person to push myself in. It's so intense in there, it's twenty-four hours. I think it's wrong to have exclusive relationships in the *Big Brother* house, because you become dependent on that person, who might leave. Other people notice it and resent it, because it's a group thing. And as well as that, every time I did hear him speak, he was talking about having rampant sex with rubber-clad nurses or about cars or something – real lad stuff. That's just not me. I don't think he's met a girl like me, and he accused me of being a feminist. He was honest, straightforward and as excited as a little boy. He spat a lot at the beginning, but he did stop, which proves he listened to what others said to him. And when he had the week off from being nominated he did relax and I think he would have been a different person if he hadn't been constantly nominated. When he first got together with Helen, we thought they were doing it for a laugh, because it was boring and we'd joke about doing it for the ratings. Then it became obvious that there was more to it. We just didn't want him to hurt Helen. He said the Penny thing was all because she came on to him, and then he said the Helen thing was sixty–forty, but it takes two to tango. But just the week before he left, it seems as though he really did care about her. He's a kind of hapless hero who walks along smiling, but leaves a trail of havoc behind him. I can see him and Helen as really good mates, but I somehow don't see them staying together.'

Helen: 'I don't think I could meet anyone more different from me, in looks, character, everything. Do I have anything in common with H? I don't think so, other than that we are both genuine, straightforward people – although I know that's not how the public see me. There were no real common grounds for talking. I think about what I'm going to say – she opens her mouth and it all comes out. And she's very loud. Even though she's standing next to you she still yells. I remember seeing her the day we all arrived – she was so pink and glittery and she was bouncing about like she had springs on her feet. She's such a sensitive little flower, always beating herself up if she thought she'd done anything wrong. Everyone felt very protective towards Helen, and that's something that really pissed Narinder off. Helen's like a child, vulnerable and in need of protection, but, like a child, you sometimes want to give her a clout round the ear. She's not stupid – she's very perceptive and has a lot of common sense. I know she is dyslexic, and as my mum works teaching kids with dyslexia, I felt even more protective towards her. When I had my outburst against her, which was shown on TV, it was during my really low weeks, and it was the night the two boys broke into the garden, which

PEOPLE ON ELIZABETH

Elizabeth's partner, Steve: 'She has no game plan, she just wanted to enjoy the first couple of weeks in the house. I'm baffled by what people think of her. She's portrayed as scheming, but she's the most straightforward person. I think she should win – she'd do exciting things with the money. The show will go on – she'll get on a horse and ride to China.'

Dom Joly, comedian: 'She has weird moments when she puts on shades and her hat and starts slagging everyone off. She thinks she's incredibly more mature than anyone else. She's a nightmare.'

Richard, music producer: 'I really want Elizabeth to win. She's by far the most intelligent person in the house. Rooting for you, Elizabeth!'

made Helen shriek and shout for ages. And again, I wasn't being two-faced, because I told Helen that there were times when she was too noisy for me. We were very concerned about the way the relationship with Paul was affecting her. We all care about her and we didn't want to see her get hurt.'

Brian: 'I've been accused of having more faces than Big Ben. Brian's got about ten Big Bens. I don't think I spoke to him until about the third week. It took me a couple of weeks to get his humour, which is very caustic and sometimes seems very close to the edge, although he seems to sense who to do it to. Then, when he was rotten to Josh at his birthday party, I thought he was spoilt, vindictive, the centre of his own universe, with no consideration for anyone else's feelings. But the thing about Brian is he knows it is all me, me, me and I, I, I and he jokes about it. It's like when he sings: he sings his own tune, his own note, his own key, and that's a bit how he was with his personality at the beginning – doing it all his way regardless of everyone else. But after he lost Narinder and Bubble he started listening a bit, and I realized I like him. He began to look at me as though I was a real person with real thoughts. It was as if he opened his eyes and stopped concentrating on himself. He's funny, charming, innocent, and if he can keep his head together, not be a prima donna, and not get fazed or exploited, he'll have a great career. It's funny that in the last couple of weeks he got very possessive about the kitchen, keeping it clean and doing all the washing up – at the beginning he did very little housework.'

Dean: 'He's a lovely guy, someone I really got on with. It was inevitable that he would come across as boring, because he's steady and level, and does what he wants and knows who he is. It's like, "This is me, if you like it, great, but if you don't, I'm not bothered." He laughed a lot more in the early weeks, when he had Bubble to spark off. He was really important to me – he was my Diary Room, because I can't talk to a camera. He was my sanity, my rock. I wouldn't have gone bonkers without him, and perhaps if he hadn't been there I might have been forced to have been more outgoing, spontaneous, jumping around. He provided a peaceful space which was easy to go into. I'm glad he was there. I didn't fancy him and I never flirted with him.'

Elizabeth on life in the house

'The hardest thing was the nominations. I thought before I went in it was a game show, there would be ten people and there would be no problem. But it was so difficult. One of the reasons people think I'm boring is that I really did get on with everybody, and I could never find a good reason for nominating them. I did it because I had to, but *Big Brother* wanted a reason, like they wanted me to come up with some character defect for them. I felt I didn't have the right to make judgements, having known them for such a short time. Perhaps I was too serious about it. If I did it again, I'd lighten up and not try to be so balanced. I'd say things like, "I'm nominating him because I don't like his hair colour."

'Getting on with the people in there was easier than I expected. They told me before I came in not to worry, that everyone was nice. And I thought,

"Yeah, ten nice people, how boring." I really didn't think they would all be so genuinely nice and liberal and amiable. But they were, and it worked.

'I didn't mind the cameras, but I felt more inhibited by the microphones. Whatever I said was going into this thing on my chest and I resented it and wanted to rip it off. It took away my freedom of speech. I didn't want to say anything I could be judged on, taken out of context, blown up. I didn't mind the cameras in the showers and loos – I'm comfortable with my body, everybody's got what I've got. It was a bit odd sitting on the toilet knowing people were looking at you. Towards the end, I heard voices in the camera run talking while I was on the loo, and there was one night when I was trying tops on and off, and when I switched off the light to go to bed I realized there was someone behind the mirror. That felt different from it being shown to the nation through the eye of a camera, which somehow cleanses it and neutralizes it.

'The food was fine. I didn't have too many expectations about it and I'm easy to please. I missed hot water, the freedom to pop to the shops just to get an ingredient for the cooking or something. But I didn't miss too much because I switched off in there, put a protective shield around myself. I'm still trying to work out why I was the way I was in there. In the Diary Room, they said, "Do you miss people on the outside?" and I said, "This is my reality. I'm making this work. And if I pine for people it won't work for me." They said, "Is that your plan, your scheme, your strategy?" But it's just how I am. To get through it, you have to be it. You can't think of missing people on the outside. Who in their right minds wants to stay in a house with strangers for nine weeks? So I did that with everything, so that I didn't really miss anything much. I've been brought up to be resourceful, to work with what I have and not think about what I can't have.

'The other strange thing was the powerlessness. I wasn't in control of my own life. So I sort of switched off and relaxed into letting Big Brother run everything for me.'

Elizabeth on Elizabeth

'I don't think I did myself justice in there. I thought about it too much and that serious part of my character was emphasized too much. I wanted to come across as I am – an open, genuine person who takes people as I find them. But I may have done that too much and forgotten about the funny, laughing side of me. I'm the frivolous one outside, the wild one. My friends are all getting married and taking out mortgages and I'm the one saying "let's go to Mongolia this summer". I wasn't seen as exciting, but if your idea of exciting is jumping up and down and making a lot of noise, that's not me anyway. I think I was seen as scheming because I think before I speak.

'I didn't go into *Big Brother* in order to change my life, but to have a new experience. I wasn't looking for a show-business career out of it. I like to do challenging things, and I work to make money for the next adventure. I suppose I should be thinking about security and a career, but at the moment I've never found anything that I want to do for years and years. I was thinking

WEEK NINE FACT FILE

Main task: 'Knowing Me, Knowing You'.

PASS ☑ **FAIL** ☐

Treats: A children's party; champagne and canapés; £14.80 to spend on treats (they choose wine, beer and one oyster); champagne and a wooden puzzle; a *Last of the Mohicans* party; and a gourmet dinner.

Bets are on!
To win: Brian remains steady as odds-on favourite, still on 1/5. Helen is still in second place, but her odds have improved to 2/1. Dean is an outsider at 25/1. Before she was evicted, Elizabeth was on 33/1.

about doing a law degree and I may take up that option again. I've designed a few websites, but only for friends. It's not a profession.

'I'm looking forward to going back to Edinburgh with my partner Steve. He's been described as a millionaire, but he's not. He works as a transport planning consultant. We get on extremely well, and although he's twenty-six years older than me, the age difference poses no problems. We won't get married because I'm not into marriage, I don't think it's necessary, but we're happy.

'I know outside there were suggestions that I flirted with Stuart, Dean and even Amma – and I'm supposed to be the boring one! But Steve had no doubts, he knew I didn't flirt. I just got on well with them.

'As for my famous pink jumper: it cost £5 from a charity shop. I bought it because it was so disgusting I had to have it. I only stuck it into my case at the last minute as an afterthought, because it is mohair and very warm. It came in useful, and I can't believe it's become such a famous piece of clothing. I think some of the others thought it was a style competition – in which case I came last!'

THE RESULT

The final day dawns hot and humid. It is Friday, 27 July 2001, or Day 64 on the *Big Brother* calendar, a day that the three remaining housemates will never forget. They wake earlier than usual – by 9 a.m. they are lying in their beds chatting. Brian says he has had a very disturbed, sleepless night. He is too tired to share the excitement of Dean and Helen when the suitcases arrive and the reality of going home begins to sink in. Dean's happiness explodes into song, and he sings for most of the day, only pausing to talk and eat.

For Helen, the timetable for the day revolves around beauty treatments: when the boys reckoned she would need two and a half hours to get ready they grossly underestimated the amount of body maintenance that would go on. She cleans her teeth seven times before she leaves the house. She has three major worries: the spot on her lip, a fear of her hair going fluffy and concern about how she will walk over the metal grille outside the house in her high heels. Brian and Dean help her perfect an elegant way of carrying her shoes. Brian also rehearses his exit, practising towing his suitcase around. Dean tells him it would look more macho if he carried it.

In the afternoon, Big Brother asks one of the housemates to go to the Diary Room. Dean goes cheerfully, and emerges to tease the others with news that they have been given another task. Brian promptly says he'll refuse to do it. In fact, they are given a treat – lemonade, Coca Cola, ice lollies, strawberries and cream and a swingball set. They manage to put the swingball post into the decking, and Helen and Brian enjoy an hour or so of hitting the ball at each other. They stop as soon as Dean reminds them that they don't want to walk out with a black eye.

Without Elizabeth, they are all at a loss when it comes to cooking. It falls to Brian and Helen to rustle up sausages wrapped in bacon. After nine weeks in the house, they have to get the instructions out to find out how to switch the cooker on.

From 4 p.m. onwards, Helen's hair is in rollers and she's wandering around in a black bra and with an orange towel around her waist (she does not want to mess up her fabulous eviction dress). Brian is worried that his white shirt has shrunk because he washed it by hand. He wants an iron, but Big Brother refuses to give him one. The three contestants reassure each other constantly that no matter what order they leave in, they are all winners and will always be good friends.

The housemates have to be packed and ready by 8.30 p.m., as the announcement of who will be the first to leave will give them just sixty seconds' warning. They are not the only ones getting ready – massive preparations have been under way outside throughout the day. A huge podium has been erected, seats have been installed for the three housemates' families and friends and barricades have been put in place to hold back the crowds. People have been queuing from lunchtime to be among the lucky 1,200 who are allowed in to wave their banners and scream and cheer for their favourites. Many more turn up and fail to get in. The atmosphere is electric, and every time one of the housemates appears on the giant screens there are screams, cheers and the frenzied blowing of horns. There are lots of banners: 'Go, Glitter Girl'; 'Brian for Queen'; 'Dean, take life less seriously – pink suits you'; 'Play it cool'; 'Brian Bless-ed'; 'Evil Demons'; 'Brian, your mother is so proud of you'; 'Helen UR a Star'; 'I want Stuff'; 'We love to blink, too'.

The crowd goes wild when the heavily pregnant Davina appears, wearing a T-shirt inscribed BIG MUTHA. The cheers reach a deafening crescendo as, two by two, all the ex-housemates appear and take their seats alongside the stage. They all look amazing: Stuart is wearing a lilac-coloured suit; Narinder and Amma each have sexy, tight white dresses on; Bubble has donned his trademark hat. Liz, who only left the house yesterday, is wearing a stunning blue dress that her boyfriend bought for her earlier in the day (she had no dresses with her in the house).

At last, the moment arrives, and Davina's voice is greeted with great excitement by the housemates. Then they hold hands in a circle. Davina makes the announcement she has already made eight times so far: 'The ninth person to leave the *Big Brother* house will be … ' As ever, she leaves a long pause, during which Brian silently mouths his own name. But when Davina speaks again she says Dean's name. He cheers and shouts and hugs the others. Despite the music that is being pumped into the house, they can hear the crowd chanting D-E-A-N and the last two housemates take it up. In the few seconds he has left, Dean – as ever – is worried about Helen and Brian, and tells them to make sure the cooker is switched off and to stop drinking cider.

Dean walks out to the tune of 'I'd Like to Teach the World to Sing' (the final-night tunes have been voted for by *Big Brother* web-users). He walks until he spots Vanessa, and then runs towards her and locks his arms around her. It is a long, passionate greeting. Davina eventually pulls them apart and whisks Dean off to the studio to meet friends and family and talk about his time in the house.

For Brian and Helen, the hardest one and a half hours of the day start now. Helen comments that the pair of them are 'like two children when the babysitter has left'. They sing one of Dean's songs, 'De-Luxe', perhaps to reassure themselves. They check each other's clothes and appearance endlessly. They are each called to the Diary Room, and warned that their chat with Big Brother is being broadcast live to the nation. Brian says:

'I'm very nervous. I'm shocked to be here, overwhelmed by everything. It's such an achievement to get this far. I've excelled myself and I hope my friends and family are dead proud. I'm just waiting to go next. If my smile explains anything, it's that I'm dead chuffed, so happy. I cannot wait to leave this house to see everybody. I love all my family and friends, my mum and dad most of all, and my mum has overcome her fear of flying to be here. The world probably sees me as a fool who's afraid of chickens and dogs. I just hope everyone sees me as an honest guy who enjoys going out and having fun, laughing and joking and being who I am.'

When it's Helen's turn, she says she can't wait to leave the house. 'It's going to be fantastic, I'm so excited. I'm very, very, very shocked that I'm still here. It's going to be lush. I want to see my mum and my friends Rhoda and Paul and my brother. There must be so much dancing gossip to catch up with, it's going to be amazing.'

She reckons the world probably sees her as 'loud, I scream a lot, I like glittering things, I like pink, I'm a girlie sort of girl who's chatty and worries about her hair a lot and the way I look. Just Helen things.'

Afterwards, she and Brian while away the time planning a whole series of shopping trips they are going to make next week.

They both look startled when Davina's voice finally comes through, although they have been waiting all evening for it. They hold hands and look into each other's eyes as she tells them that she is about to announce the name of the *Big Brother* winner. There is the usual long pause. Brian shouts, 'Come on, Davina!' Then she gives the name – it is his. He puts his hands in the air and steps back, then he and Helen have a long hug. Davina tells them that she is coming for Helen, and that Brian should make himself a cup of tea and stay calm. 'I am *not* calm!' he replies, adding half-jokingly that when the door opens for Helen he's going with her, because he doesn't want to stay there on his own.

All Helen's plans to walk elegantly out of the house go out of the window as soon as she senses the atmosphere outside. Although she cannot see her family from the door, she knows they are there, and breaks into a run. She's wearing a shimmering, one-shoulder, pale-turquoise dress encrusted with sequins, as glittering as her whole image, with her blonde hair piled high on her head. The music chosen for her exit is Dolly Parton's 'Stand by Your Man', but she doesn't hear it above the roar of the crowd. She runs straight into the arms of her mum and friends, but quickly realizes there is someone

VOTING

At the time of his eviction, Dean had four per cent of the total of 269,489 votes cast. Almost another two million votes came in during the final hour and a half, bringing the total to 7,255,094. Helen had thirty-seven per cent of the votes, with 2,680,463. Brian had fifty-eight per cent, with 4,231,660 votes. Eighteen per cent of the votes were made via interactive TV screens.

else waiting for her at the gate – Paul Clarke. He takes her into his arms and whispers, 'I've missed you so much, you would not believe.'

Then it is her turn to be whisked away by Davina. Helen exclaims with delight when she sees the presenter's T-shirt, and then it's across the bridge to pose excitedly for the massed ranks of press photographers, a quick wave at the other eight housemates, and into the studio.

Brian, on his own in the house that had seemed so crowded nine weeks ago, stares out of the patio door at the garden, lost in his own thoughts. Called to the Diary Room, he stutters over the realization that more than four million people have voted for him. He pleads with the anonymous cameraman to show his face, just once, but the *Big Brother* experience stays true to the end.

If Brian seems sad, his spirits revive instantly when Davina's voice comes through, and he yells greetings to all his friends and family. The door swings open to the tune of Janet Jackson's 'Nasty Boy', to which he and Narinder danced their famous routine. As Brian moves down the walkway, silver fountains of fireworks spring up in his wake, and then he's in the arms of his mother and sister, hugging his father and his best friend, Richard. Then Davina and Brian cross the bridge, pausing to see a staggering display of rockets blasting into the night sky. But the light of the fireworks is matched by the huge explosion of camera flashes that greets him on the other side. As he reaches the podium, Narinder rushes forward into Brian's arms, flinging her feet round his waist. Penny follows to hug him.

Davina attempts to interview Brian on the podium, but it is hard for him to concentrate with so many friends and family in the crowd. Someone throws a pair of knickers at him, and Bubble comes on stage to dance the last waltz with him and return Mr Cow and Mr Bear. In front of the nation's eyes, the prize money of £70,000 is transferred into Brian's bank account on a huge screen. The crowd is going wild – horns are blaring and the whistling, cheering and screaming is deafening. More fireworks erupt, and laser lights rake the darkening sky.

On the other side of the bridge, the *Big Brother* house looks strangely lifeless. The lights flicker and go off. The show is over for another year – but for Brian, the show is just beginning ...

DEAN LOOKS BACK: THE EXCLUSIVE INTERVIEW

Dean on the housemates

Penny: 'She was interesting, lovely, really caring, very maternal. But the maternal impulse was misplaced in that environment. Everyone was quite strong, and in the early days they were vying for position. There was no room for the character she was. She found it more difficult to fit in than anyone else did.'

Stuart: 'I got on well with Stuart. After he left, the others said he was competitive, but I didn't see that in a big way. I thought he was competitive, but so were lots of people in there. I could relate to him because he was nearer my age. It was good being able to talk to him about grown-up things. I was surprised when he left.'

Narinder: 'She was the least compromising person in the house, and you need to compromise in there in order to survive. She didn't seem to make allowances for people and the situation. She seemed to get easily irritated. She was close to Brian, and I don't think exclusive relationships are a good idea in there, but they got on so well, it would have been silly of them not to spend time together. She's very funny, she really made me laugh a few times.'

Bubble: 'It shocked me a lot when he went. He's a diamond. I've come out of the house with the bonus of two really good friends, Bubble and Brian. Bubble was a godsend, he kept me sane for a lot of weeks. He was loud, but that was cool – loud isn't necessarily a bad adjective.'

Amma: 'I felt she struggled. She wasn't being herself, she couldn't relax completely. It was hard to get to know her. I told her a couple of times that her voice was too quiet – in there, people were competing for attention, and if you didn't assert yourself you got lost in the traffic. She's very intelligent and had some really interesting things to say. Just because she didn't say them loud enough, they didn't get heard.'

Josh: 'Without a shadow of doubt he had the hardest mission. It was very unfair for him to be brought in after two weeks. It was hard to get to know him. He didn't feel he could be himself. It's so intense in there that every feeling is amplified. If someone is not relaxed you can really sense it. It would have been the easy option to nominate him, but I wanted to give him a chance, because it would have been unfair to nominate him too early. I think we could have got on really well. When he was nominated, he relaxed and his personality came to the fore.'

Paul: 'I like Paul and I know that we'll go out for a drink and become mates and do boys' things. But I feel the environment didn't suit him and we didn't connect. Because I was committed to my system of nominations, which meant I looked at the housemates like a bus queue ranging from the ones I got on best with to the other end, and I simply nominated the two who were at the end. It never felt good nominating Paul, but I was committed to the system. It was never going to work in there for me and him, but I think outside we can be boys, swearing and talking about girls' bums and whatever boys do. I've got mates like that and we have a great time, but the house wasn't the right place.'

Elizabeth: 'I really connected with her on an intellectual level. She was the only person in there, certainly in the later weeks, I could talk to about things on a higher plane, things a little bit more taxing on the brain, which was really important to me. I needed it. She helped me through, she was my outlet for serious conversation and it would have been really hard to survive without that outlet. I didn't notice if she was flirting with me, I didn't see it. My mind was firmly fixed on getting out and getting back to Vanessa.'

Helen: 'The first week, she was spectacularly annoying. She was so loud I thought there was no way I could share the same space as her, and I think a few people thought that. But once she was nominated and survived, she really changed and relaxed. She's got the best heart. She handled the nomination with dignity. I did nominate her again, just because my system came into play. But I never felt right saying her name. She's so good. What you see on the screen, the naivety and innocence, is absolutely genuine. We were worried that Paul was a bit of a ladies' man and she was so innocent. But I would always tell the other two that you can't tell what's happening between two people and what it looks like from the outside might be quite different to what they see. So we let them get on with it, we didn't interfere. I felt massively protective towards her – I felt like her dad. I was worried about her and Brian being left in there at the end, and one of them having to come out. I think I'll always feel protective towards Brian and Helen, probably for the rest of my life.'

Brian: 'Where do I start? He's got no ego, which is really rare in someone like him, he's such an extraordinary person. He's perceptive, which is amazing, because he seems to have lived in a box for twenty-three years and have missed so much of everything that you kind of think, "Were you made in a lab and introduced last year?" While it's astonishing ignorance, it's charming and Brian really appreciated that he was ignorant of things and really tried to change it. Having his eyes opened, he realized that he'd missed a lot and wanted to broaden his horizons. Both he and Helen became more sensitive to other people's thoughts and feelings.

'I hope winning doesn't change him too much, and that it doesn't become too much for him, and he has the chance to sort himself out. He needs to work out where he's going. He's a new Brian, with a new haircut and new parents, because they now know he's gay, and he needs to deal with all those personal issues before he becomes a commodity. I watched him in there and thought, "If he's half as funny out there as he is in here, he'll be massive." When I saw some of the clips of him, I thought, "Oh my God, I know someone who is going to be famous." He is without doubt the funniest man I've ever met, and he's also a really nice person.'

Dean on life in the house

'I thought it would be really hard, being with nine strangers in a confined space. I thought I would argue with people and people would annoy me. I thought I'd find it hard to make the compromises and concessions necessary. But it was much easier than I expected. I grew up with four sisters in quite a small house, on top of each other, so I suppose that was good grounding. You know when to give people space and respect their feelings.

'I was missing Vanessa inordinate amounts. That was the only thing that would have made me come out. I was very close to walking out in the first week. It seemed like whatever I was going to get out of it was not going to be worth the separation. But I managed to stick it out. I didn't turn to anyone, I sorted it in my head. I put my photos up as soon as I got in there, but every time I looked at them I was getting upset, so I took them down. But I found that didn't turn it off, so I put them back up again.

'The other difficult thing was that it was all very young, apart from Elizabeth and Stuart. There were no adult activities, and I missed being a grown up, making decisions about things like what I would do tomorrow. I started to feel like a child, and I felt parts of my brain were closing off and I wasn't being challenged enough. Because I didn't appear to be thirty-seven, the others forgot how old I was. But there were times when I was painfully thirty-seven. Sometimes I felt fifty-seven. I kept longing for little things, like putting keys in my pocket.

'The week after Bubble left was really hard. Brian and I couldn't understand what was going on. Nothing against Paul, we just couldn't work out why Bubble had been voted out. We felt Paul was going to win.

'I lost a lot of weight at first, partly because it was all very stressful, it was hot and you didn't feel like eating, and the food was badly managed at first. You didn't feel you could just go and eat whenever you felt like it, because food was a precious resource. And you were conscious in the early weeks of not wanting to give anyone a reason to want you out of the house. After that week when we had very little money there was always plenty of food. I didn't take charge of it, but the people who did – mainly Elizabeth and Josh – did really well.

'I did the garden, the boring old man again. It's amazing. If you ask Vanessa, the only thing I do in the garden at home is play football, but in there you grab something to do, an activity was so precious. There were long, barren stretches of time with nothing happening. Anything we did have to do became so important. Nominations took about forty minutes, but the whole day was known as Nominations Day and was geared around it.

'Some tasks were very good, for us, and others were possibly better to watch. I really liked the drum-kit one, the first-aid task and the memory test

PEOPLE ON DEAN

Dean's fiancée, Vanessa: 'We saw the whole, rounded Dean on television, but very much scaled down. There were lots of really good, funny bits that I saw on the live coverage which didn't get into the Channel 4 shows – all we saw on those was Dean being very chilled out and laid back, not when he was geeing people up and getting on with things. I think his maturity showed. He had the ability to deal with situations, which others didn't have – he was a really calming influence. When all that hysteria was going on around Amma, he knew it was important to take her away, to defuse the situation. I'm really proud of him.'

Dean's sister, Mandy: 'Dean is sensitive, an all-rounder and a great musician.'

Dean's mate, Dave: 'He looked quite fetching in pink, but I don't think he'll wear that outfit to a Birmingham City match. It will haunt him to his grave. His friends will never let him forget it.'

Tara Palmer-Tomkinson: 'I fancy Dean. He has that *je ne sais quoi*. He looks like quite a few people I know.'

John, copywriter: 'Dean's a winner: he holds the world record for the highest stack of sugar cubes.'

we did in the early weeks. I hated Paddy the dog – Paddy the human, the nasty little boy in a dog outfit. All the other tasks we were succeeding or failing on our own merit, and then there was this other little being there who would just please himself, who wasn't interested in doing things, and you couldn't kick him up the arse and make him. In a comical way, we focussed our resentment on the dog, but it was really the task which I felt was unfair. Also, it excluded some of us, you couldn't all get involved with him. It annoyed the life out of me, and that was the worst task. I wasn't too keen on the dancing, either. There was always a sense of foreboding when tasks came round. It was great to have something to do, but after a couple of tasks we didn't like, we were always worried.

'I accepted the cameras in the loo and the shower. The decision was: I need to go to the toilet and I can shit myself or I can go to the loo and be on camera. After the first time it was no problem. But it was very draining, having cameras on you the whole time. I remember one night in the garden when I realized none of the cameras were following me, which felt so good. After I'd been there about two minutes I sighed, and as soon as I made a noise they turned towards me, but the respite was very, very nice.

'We were all a bit paranoid, and we lost the sense of anything happening by chance. If anything went wrong in the house, like the hot water not coming on or something, we thought it was done on purpose. Since I came out, the production team have told me about things that went wrong. We felt it was a controlled environment and that nothing could go wrong, so it was all planned. That shows how your powers of understanding and feeling responsible for yourself are stripped away in a controlled environment.

'I saw Big Brother as an adversary, until I had a really good talk with one Big Brother, which cleared up a lot of things. I kept thinking it was a TV show and they're going to jerk you around, make you jump through hoops, and the discomfort was deliberate. But she explained that they only needed twenty-four minutes of television for the evening show, and they didn't want us to feel bad the whole time. After that, things changed for me and it became easier.

'I never opened up in the Diary Room. I didn't need to, but also talking to a camera and lights in a very small room is no different to talking to myself in my head, so what was the point? They never gave any answers, they just listened. Often they told us to go and talk to other members of the group. I know some of them found it very useful, but I didn't.'

Dean on Dean

'I'm looking forward to getting my life back. Seeing Vanessa again was like we'd only been apart for three hours, because we're rock solid, and I knew that wouldn't be a problem. But it will take a while to get used to all the mad things that are going on.

'I'd like to see where my music goes. I've had a few offers. It's really cool to know that the others appreciated my music. Brian used to say "put 'De-Luxe' on" as though it was a record. The music helped me more than anything else, and I've always had music in my life, so whatever happens that won't change. There are other things I'd like to do, like writing.

'Most of all, I want to spend hours talking to Vanessa, catching up on everything that's happened. She knows what's been happening in my world for nine weeks. I want to find out what's been happening outside.

'We are going to get married, and I hope it can all be arranged for August. I always knew we would, and I feel married anyway. We were going to do it last year, but we moved house. But being in there crystallized my feeling that I want to get on with it. It never really excited me before, but now it has taken on a whole new meaning.

'I don't resent the fact that I was described as boring. Next to Helen and Brian, what do you expect? But also, if people perceive me as boring, I'll wear that, because when they meet me they will be surprised to find I'm not. It's better than the other way round, thinking someone's fantastic and then finding they're boring.

'I'm glad I made it to the end, because I felt I had to finish it. But I never expected to win against Brian – I thought from a long time ago that he was a winner. I'm really glad I've done it. It has been the most amazing experience.'

HELEN LOOKS BACK: THE EXCLUSIVE INTERVIEW

Helen on the housemates

Penny: 'She's a really nice person, but she could be a bit too much sometimes. She generally wanted to do too much for people. I think she left at the right time, although that might sound horrible, because I was up for eviction against her. A few people didn't like the way she kissed people on the lips, but she was just very touchy feely. I was cool about it. I'm looking forward to having a really good chat with her.'

Stuart: 'I got on with him, he'd been to Wales and knew lots of the places I know. When he walked in, I thought he was an owner of a nightclub or something. I think he found it hard. He was used to being a father figure and I think he found it a bit difficult to adapt. I think so many of us were young and he perhaps found us irritating. He missed his children. He's such a good family man.'

Narinder: 'Our personalities did clash a bit, but she's a nice girl. At the end of the day I liked her. She's always right about most things. I think we were a bit similar. Every little feeling in that house is blown up by a hundred, which means the smallest little row becomes very big, and you can't get away from people. I've seen Narinder already and we've had a chat and I'm looking forward to seeing her more. We're fine, there's no bad feeling.'

Bubble: 'He's such a funny geezer. There were a few times when I was a bit scared of him, because I didn't always know when he was joking. He was very good at playing practical jokes. The more I knew him, the more I liked him. I probably didn't ever have a serious conversation with him, but that doesn't make any difference. I tried to persuade him to have a tan, which worked a little bit. A really nice, cool guy. He adored his daughter, and he told me his little girl would love me because I'm so blonde and pink and sparkly.'

Amma: 'We got on from day one. We walked in together, which gave us a bit of a special thing, and we were both girlie girls. We were always there for each other. I think she's gonna become a really good friend for the rest of my life. We had a really good laugh. I feel it was a shame she felt she couldn't really be herself in the house. We just got on, we both knew where we were coming from, we could talk about anything.'

Josh: 'He had a tough time, coming in late, which was unfair on him. He didn't really become himself until he was up for nomination, when he relaxed more. I found I could talk to him and we could have a good laugh together. He didn't think I was any good at volleyball, but he knew I couldn't do things like that. He took games a bit seriously, but he didn't seem to mind that I didn't. I only heard about his row with Brian from the others, because I was asleep, but I felt sorry for him. He went through a lot to come into the house, and then he got a tough time.'

Paul: 'Where do we start with Mr Clarke? He's the nicest, kindest, most honest man I've ever met. Even if he hadn't bought me Gucci stuff, I would have said that anyway. When he walked into the house, I thought he was a nice-looking bloke, but I thought he was a bit of a lad and it was, "Oh my God, I'm not going to get on with him." But as I got to know his personality we found the same things funny. If something was going to happen it was going to happen to me or Paul, because we're accident prone, and we both just took it, like, whatever. I didn't fancy him from the start. Penny was all over him and that didn't bother me. By week three, it was Paul's a really nice guy, Paul's this, Paul's that, then the stuff started developing and the more I got to know him, the more I liked him. We just connected more and it was weird the way we got on so well, and we spent more and more time together. I was a bit worried, because I wanted to be with him, but I thought we should be more with the group. I was upset when he kept being nominated. I never nominated him once. I thought he was a really cool guy and I couldn't understand why the others nominated him. I don't think the others saw the true Paul Clarke I knew. When he left in week eight it was upsetting. I didn't know what life would be like in the *Big Brother* house without Mr Clarke. I stuck up for him when the others said things about him. He hasn't got a nasty bone in his body, he's truthful, he's ... words fail me, there's so many nice things to say about him, my mind's gone blank.

'Stuff is when I look at him and I see these lights and everything, and I think he likes me, but I didn't know if he saw the stuff, in the eyes. I was thinking about that all the last week, so worried that he would be with another girl when I came out. It was good that he went when he did, because it would have been hard being there. We don't do Elvis, me and Mr Clarke, but it was hard, what with all the stuff. And then he was there at the gate when I came out. He looked so different, so polished – breath-taking! When you're in the *Big Brother* house you don't look your best – not that he didn't look good in there – but he just looked amazing when I saw him again. It was really something that he bought me all the Gucci stuff, my head was spinning. Who knows what will happen now? But we'll be meeting up and spending some time together, that's for sure.'

Elizabeth: 'She's very kind, she looked after everybody, she taught me a lot about cooking. We are worlds apart, but we did get on. We are so different – my most expensive item is a dress, hers is a pair of walking boots. But we did get on. I thought it would be better when we were just two girls, but it was OK, it was cool, we just were too different to be really close. I screamed a bit too much in her ear, I was a bit too loud for her, but she told me that. She was honest. She was never going to be a girlie girl. Me and Brian tried to transform her, but if it's not in you to be a girlie girl you never will. I thought she was a librarian when she walked in.'

Dean: 'One thing I've learned from him is not to get stressed out, to chill, relax. He'd tell me to stop practising the task and just take it easy. He's a really good guitar player and that was so important, he gave us our songs. He instilled confidence in me and Brian. No way was he boring in any way, shape or form. He's a guy with lots of experience, lots of stories to tell, and we've both learned a lot from him about life. He made us think a bit, he opened us up to things outside Brian's and Helen's little world. He's really cool, and Vanessa's very beautiful – great hair!'

Brian: 'The two babies were left in the house together. He's a very funny, funny guy. We can talk about anything, me and Brian – fashion, pigginess, chicness, tanning lines, you name it we can talk about it. I don't think there was a day when he didn't make me laugh. He went through a lot to come into the house and he deserved to win and I'm so happy for him. I'm always going to see him, go shopping with him. That last hour and a half, we just knew what each other was feeling. We were getting ready, putting bronzer on and Vaseline on each other's cheekbones, and Brian helping me into my dress, not talking a lot. I'm so comfortable with Brian. We went round the house looking at everything, but we weren't allowed out to shut the chickens in, so I couldn't look at the den. Brian's just fantastic, he's great, I want everything good in the world to happen for him.'

Helen on life in the house

'When I walked in, I kept telling myself to just be myself, but I wasn't myself at all in that first week and perhaps even the second week. You were in this house with nine people you don't know and you've got to get along with, and it's, "Oh, my God, how am I going to deal with all this?" It's the maddest and most fantastic thing that's ever happened to me, the best experience of my whole life. I had a fabulous time. I never regret one minute of it and it's the maddest experience I will probably ever have in my life.

'At first I liked the microphones and cameras, I thought it was like being Cat Deeley. I was pinching myself, thinking, "I'm in the *Big Brother* house!" Then there's a point where you get totally used to it, and in the end you want to throw the microphones over the wall and trash the cameras. When I was with Paul, we wanted to talk about things. And not just with him, because we weren't allowed to talk about nominations, and if you talked about anybody in the house you knew they might see it on television, so you really felt you had to be careful all the time and it drove you mad. It was really frustrating. One of the best things about coming out was ripping the microphone off.

PEOPLE ON HELEN

Helen's mum, Liz: 'I told her to go in there and have fun, and fun's what she's had. I don't know whether she'll keep the relationship with Paul in the real world, but when you saw them in the house, their eyes just followed each other everywhere.'

Helen's brother, Mark: 'She's got big hair, a big mouth, a big arse, and I wish I could turn the volume down. But she has become more mature and confident, and she's doing more in the kitchen than I've ever seen.'

Cerys Matthews, singer: 'Helen's so endearing, so Welsh, so lovely.'

Anna, brand manager: 'Helen's my favourite. She's the only housemate who came in without any strategy whatsoever. It's a wonderful achievement – she's just been Helen all the time.'

Jerry, bookie: 'Helen's the only fanciable girl in the house. She looks lovely in her bikini. Wear the bikini more, Helen.'

'You get used to the cameras being in the toilet and shower. It's not that nice, but you get used to it. My mum told me there was a picture of me with snot hanging from my nose and I think, "So what? I've been filmed in the toilet."

'We were so hungry. I longed for chocolate, sweets, crisps and chips from the chip shop. My mum's not happy because I licked my plate, but in there, if you had something you liked you wanted every bit of it, because you knew you wouldn't eat again until porridge in the morning. We got so used to eating porridge made with water that when I made it with milk in the last week it was too rich for us all.

'I missed going out of a door and closing it and coming back in, the choice. I missed my family and friends and Ruby, my dog. There were phases when I missed them more. The weekends were hard. During the week, I could look at the clock and I knew what my mum was doing, I knew when my friends Rhoda and Paul were teaching dancing, but at the weekends they could have been doing anything and I didn't know.

'Having Paddy helped me with missing Ruby, because Paddy was lush. I loved that task, and the dancing task. I hated the pogo stick, that's the only one I didn't like. Thanks to Brian teaching first aid, I could save someone's life.

'I've learned loads in there. I've changed for the better. My friends told me I had to be more tactful, and I think I am. I've learned not to be so sensitive, so paranoid, and I've learned to relax more. And I've learned to cook.'

Helen on Helen

'Right now, I just want to have a good time. I may go back to cutting hair and dancing – that's what I was put on this earth to do, they're my life and my passion. But I want to have a laugh, a good time, without hurting anyone's feelings, and take my time getting back to normal. I'll take the whole experience with me for the rest of my life, but I don't know whether it will change how I live my life.

'You find out who your really good friends are when you go in the *Big Brother* house. I've had such good support, especially from my mum and my brother and my best friends Rhoda and Paul [her friend from home]. Paul made my eviction dress – his own design, brilliant. And now I've come out, he's made me sparkly jeans, tops and three more dresses. He doesn't do it for a business, but he should.

'It was funny when I tried my dress on and Brian said it was a bit tight on my bum, so I started eating smaller portions and by week nine I tried it on again and Brian said it was perfect. I couldn't wait to get that dress on my back.

'I felt relieved when Davina said Big G had dumped me. That's all for the best and it would have happened anyway. I think I talked about him so much at the beginning because when you first go in there you just cling to the things on the outside. You feel lonely, so you clutch at your memories. Then you think about things and re-evaluate your life, and I felt I wanted to go forward and concentrate on myself, which might sound a bit selfish, but I think you have to do it. It was an on-off relationship anyway, and it was on again before I came in. But it was for the best that I didn't know in there that it was over, because perhaps things would have happened with Mr Clarke that shouldn't have happened. When Davina told me, I thought: "Whatever, there's worse that can happen at sea." Davina could have hit me with anything and it wouldn't have phased me, I was enjoying the moment so much.

'I don't honestly know what will happen with Paul Clarke. I think we just need time to sort out how we feel, outside in the real world. Like Big Brother says, "I'll get back to you on that one."'

BRIAN LOOKS BACK: THE EXCLUSIVE INTERVIEW

Brian on the housemates

Penny: 'I love Penny. We hit it off. She had the same wacky humour as me. We walked in together and she seemed a bit quiet, and for the first day or two I was a bit wary of her. But on the second day we were sunbathing and she gave me a back massage, and from then on we were as thick as thieves. She's a lovely girl and we've got lots to catch up with each other about. I was gutted when she left. I felt really shitty when the door closed and she was gone. I cried.'

Stuart: 'He's a real nice guy, but we didn't get the chance to bond. There was a bit of an age difference and we didn't have that much in common. But I could speak to him in a serious kind of way, my Brian-the-Air-Steward way, because I don't think he really found me as funny as the rest. But we did share some laughs in the house. I didn't think he was as relaxed as the rest about me being gay, but not because he was prejudiced, he just wasn't used to people like me. But he handled it well.'

Narinder: 'I can't wait to see her. I missed her the most of everyone who went. Me and her, from day one, we got on so well. She made me laugh. I admired her because she spoke her mind. She took no crap from anyone, she said what she felt. At times it was maybe a bit harsh, but she was honest to herself. I told her to be nice when she was up for eviction, so that she could leave with her head held high and not have people bitch about her. But Narinder wanted to go out in style and she went out with guns blazing. Then, as she left, I knocked on the door and so did she, and I think *Big Brother* thought one of us was caught, so they opened the door again. It was great to see her little face and I gave her another hug. I can see us being friends forever and keeping in contact when all this is over.'

Bubble: 'We met at the auditions and we clicked off together really well. He's a really nice guy. Me and Bubble are so different: different backgrounds, different upbringings, different views on life, but yet we had a lot in common because we had the same sense of humour. At times we'd push each other to the edge, but we'd bring it back before it turned nasty. I could always turn to Bubble if I was upset. He's had a hard life, but he's honest, sensible and fair and I hope we're going to stay in contact.'

Amma: 'She's lovely, but we never really got to know each other. She was there for six weeks and we never really clicked. We could have conversations and we could share a laugh and a joke, but we didn't get close. She said she didn't know who she was and that she didn't have a role in the house, but none of us had assigned roles. I think outside she's probably loud and wacky, but in there she saw the likes of me, Helen, Narinder and Bubble and she toned herself down. It was a shame, and I just don't think we got the chance to get close. She lives in London, so I'm sure I'll see her.'

Josh: 'This is a tough one. Initially, coming into the house as a gay guy, I was afraid of what the other guys would think, but they were all relaxed, it was no big deal. But then Josh came in and I felt I wasn't being judged by the straight guys, but I was being judged by the gay guy. I felt Josh had been there, done it all, and I felt people would be comparing me with Josh and thinking I would never be like him. Josh had the physique, I had the love handles. I was suddenly more conscious of the outside world when Josh came in. I had my family to think of. I presumed people would try to pair us off. But it never kicked off, I never looked at Josh in that kind of way. If he had been there from day one, who knows, we would probably have been OK. There were times when we were fooling around, laughing and joking, and sometimes I'd look at him and realize he's fun. But at the same time, the only thing we had in common was that we were gay. The dinner date was awkward. When I sat down, I thought, "this is going to be nasty" and he was sweet, he put a flower in my glass. But I'm glad we did have the meal because we found out things about me. He still thinks I'm spoilt and self-orientated. I don't think he'll ever change his views on me, but we are going for a meal and I'm paying. It was hard for him, he always felt he was never part of the group. Our row was unfortunate. I was feeling touchy because I'd had to give up my teddy bears and I was missing my friends on my birthday and worrying about my sister being pregnant. I needed to talk, and I had the pressure of talking about it on national television, and I had the pressure of worrying about my parents and how they felt about me being gay. Josh said to me, "You've disliked me from day one," and I unleashed. I snapped at Bubble and Narinder as well that night, but they knew me well enough to know I was just down. I went into the Diary Room and cried my eyes out.'

Paul: 'We got on, in a sense, but we had nothing in common. We had almost the same sense of humour. His stories were long-winded. But I could take the piss out of Paul and he always took it in jest, he didn't mind. I got him into a regime of cleansing, toning and eye gel. Of everyone in the house, he's the one who should have a real sense of achievement, he was up for nomination so much. He came across as confident, but he was honest and he had it hard because of how he felt about Helen. I was worried about Helen, because of the way he talked about girls, really laddy. I thought he might break her heart. With Penny, he tries to make out that it was all her, but his arms were wrapped around her, and it takes two. But outside the house everything is very different, and I may find I really get on with him. As the days went by, I think we realized he did care about Helen, and I'm glad they were there for each other.'

Elizabeth: 'We never really clicked, and I only got to know her in the last two or three weeks. We could have a laugh and a joke. The last nominations were tough for me, because I knew I was probably deciding it. I looked at Elizabeth and felt she deserved to be in – she cooked, cleaned, did the budget, everything. I could always go to her with a problem. She's a very strong, independent woman. I've never met someone like her. I looked at her big sweater at the beginning and that sort of put me off. I'm used to girlie girls. Dean and I agreed she was overly-efficient and a bit bossy, but we'd all have been lost without her.'

Dean: 'Dean scared me at first, with his faces. I thought he looked like a monk, with his sandals and shaven head. I don't think I really clicked with him until week three, but after Narinder and Bubble were gone, we really clicked in. We were doing sit-ups together, we were laughing and joking, talking about relationships. He is so liberal and open-minded. I used to say, "Vanessa is such a lucky girl. Dean is a treasure." Dean really knows me. I plan to go to Birmingham to see him, and I think we'll always stay in touch.'

Helen: 'The first two weeks I was very unsure of her. She was sensitive and immature – although that's the pot calling the kettle black, because me and Helen are two of a kind. I wasn't sure where she was coming from, but when she was up for eviction she became mature, focussed, level-headed, and when she stayed, it was like we got a new Helen. After that we got on so well. When I nominated her the second time it was just me being a wimp, because I still didn't know who to nominate. I'm so glad she didn't go. We could laugh, take the piss. She's so sensitive to other people's needs. I know I'm loud, but she is louder. I never thought I would meet someone who is louder than me. We had such good times, I'd do her hair, her makeup, we lived in our own Brian's and Helen's world. When people were talking intelligently, we'd deliberately start talking about Posh Spice's dress. Last night I helped pour her into her dress, I just really love her, and I always knew after the first few weeks she'd get to the end. She's a fantastic person, and I hope Paul doesn't hurt her, because the guy that gets Helen is so lucky. We are so alike – we both want the fairy-tale romance, we both want to see "the stuff". I've never seen the stuff, but she's seen the stuff with Paul, and I just hope it's Helen stuff, not *Big Brother* stuff. I think I'll always know her. We'll go out and laugh and joke. We'll still be going shopping together in fifteen years' time. I keep using her expressions: "Love him, bless his little cotton socks", "fan-bloody-tastic", "Oh, my God". We've shared something that only Craig and Anna from last year really know about – those last few hours in the house.'

Brian on life in the house

'Before I went in, I never thought about cooking and how we would eat. I never thought of the boredom, how down I would feel. I didn't realize there were things I wouldn't be allowed to talk about. I didn't realize you had to be so non-judgemental. I watched it last year and thought it looked easy. I couldn't see why making nominations would be hard, because they were all strangers. But I liked them all and it was terrible to have to say their names.

'Every day, I woke up and looked around and couldn't believe I was in there. At first I couldn't stop looking at the cameras, which we were told not to do. At first I was on a high, thrilled to be in there, on television. Then, by the second or third week, you think, "What am I doing?" You are told what you can do, when you can have your showers, how much you can spend on food. I've never had a problem with authority, but I've never had people

PEOPLE ON BRIAN

Brian's mum, Rosie: 'There's no problem about Brian being gay. I love him and I'm very proud of him.'

Brian's sister, Michelle: 'He's found it stressful. He had his down moments, when he lost Narinder and Bubble, and his argumentative moments, when he went head to head with Josh, but overall he's made some fantastic friends and he'll cherish the whole *Big Brother* experience.'

Jerome, company director: 'I think Brian should win. Even if he doesn't, he should run for Prime Minister. He'd be a brilliant Conservative leader. He'd have a huge party, it would be Planet Camp, it would be brilliant.'

Chris Moyles, Radio One DJ: 'Brian's dancing has been spectacular. He brings a butchness to the programme, he's such a laddy lad, likes the girls. He's my favourite.'

Nicola, advertising manager: 'The person I like most is Brian. He's incredibly extrovert, incredibly OTT. He plays up the gay, camp man brilliantly. He has moments when he gets moody, but he's great.'

dictating to me like that. The Diary Room isn't private. I felt I couldn't open up, although there were times when I got emotional in there.

'Being in the house is a unique experience. I got used to the cameras in the loo quite quickly, although the first time I peed sitting down. The first time I had a poo, I forgot and stood up to wipe my bum, then sat down quickly. I actually got into the toilet more easily than the showers, because I knew the shower might be shown on television, and I knew friends would be looking at me saying, "There's his willy." I never really cleaned myself that well, I just danced in and out. My worst mistake was running around naked after a cold shower, when it went tiny.

'Food was very good, I gained weight. I started doing sit-ups, but I've been told I was doing them wrong. I never ate as well as that, veg-wise. It was healthier than I normally eat. The week we had very little money, week two, was tough. But after that we were resourceful and we worked out our betting on the tasks well. Lunch was always very late, and me and Helen would be starving, but we couldn't do it ourselves, so we had to wait.

'I found sharing a room difficult because I've never shared in my life. I wasn't used to all that farting. One thing was really great – I've never had such a close relationship with a bunch of guys. They let me into their group. Then I had to move, and the girls were wonderful. Helen said she liked to see my face in the morning. Amma used to tuck my feet in when she came to bed.

'I enjoyed most of the tasks, even though I wasn't that good at some of them. I didn't enjoy Paddy because we weren't all involved. He was sent by Satan, that dog. The world records were good, but again they didn't involve everybody. I liked the first-aid task and the dance task – me and Helen loved that. The skipping was evil.

'My worst week in the house was week eight. It's strange, but after Amma and Josh left I felt low, even though they weren't people I was close to. I think I felt bad because I had never been nominated. I wanted the feedback of a nomination. I wanted to know what people were thinking of me, if my mum and dad and sister were OK. Dean, Helen and Paul all realized in week eight that I wanted to go, and they all persuaded me not to. Dean said he'd fling himself across the door if I tried. And he saved me, then, by paying me the greatest compliment anyone could have given me, which just made me feel it was all OK. I was so worried about my parents, and he said, "If I was your dad, I'd be very proud of you."

Brian on Brian

'I can't believe I've won yet, I'm overwhelmed, I'm so happy. It's so amazing that people gave me a chance, put my sexuality aside and saw me for the person I am, the person I've always longed to be – a confident, secure, down-to-earth, nice guy. That's all I am, that's all I want to be.

'I came on the show for me, to be me, and I didn't expect to win. I wanted to get confidence and abolish my insecurities and see that people can accept me.

'I won in week six or seven when I found out things about myself that seventy grand could not buy. I found out that I was quite ignorant of things around me and my eyes were closed to lots of things. I'm not racist, but the first black person I've spoken to is Amma, the first Asian is Narinder. My life has been narrow. Dean opened me up to lots of things, even to listening to different kinds of music. He made me think about the church and my sexuality, and that's something I've got to deal with.

'Now I need time just to be me. I want to start meeting people, dating, going out, get a social life back. I can afford not to work for a while, have a holiday, take stock of what I'm going to do. I still think I'm going back to work, but everyone tells me that I can't.

'I hugged my father for the first time last night when I came out of the house, and being in there has made me realize just how much I love my family. It is so wonderful that they love me no matter what. I was a wimp when I told them about my sexuality, because I told them and ran away back to England. It was hard for them, but my sister Michelle told me I had to tell them. Most of my sisters knew, and my school friends. But I ran away and let them handle the backlash, and it's proved to me how strong my family are. They're taking it in their stride. I'm getting approval from people I've wanted it from all my life. I am Brian, I am judged on that and not on being gay. I'll never be able to hide the fact that I'm gay again, but that's a relief.

'I think society is changing, for a gay, camp air steward to become the winner, but I don't want to be a gay role model, I want to be me. But if me winning *Big Brother* helps someone else tell their parents, that's great. But I'm never going to milk my gayness.

'I had made a resolution to tell my parents this year, and getting into *Big Brother* gave me the push I needed. I'd needed to do it since I was nineteen. Now Mum and Dad know I've got the support of over four million people. My mum's first reaction was to say, "Are you trying to be fashionable? Is it just a phase?" But then she straightaway said, "Are you being careful?", so in ten seconds she was back to normality, worrying about if I'm alright.

'I hope through this I can support my family, and I'm really looking forward to my sister's baby being born. I've been worried about my sister, because I only found out about a month before I came in. I want to go home and see her before she has the baby.

'People keep saying I'm going to have a career in show business, but I really don't know. I want to keep calm and take my time and work out what's best for me. This has been the most fabulous, fantastic experience, and I'm still trying to catch my breath and take it in. Thank you, *Big Brother*.'

CONCLUSION

It's been nine frantic, fabulous weeks. For sixty-four days, we've all been riveted by the goings-on in the surreal *Big Brother* environment, where eleven strangers have laughed together, cried together and done their best to survive together. Four of them made it to the final week, three of them to the very last day. For all of them, without exception, it has been an amazing experience. They have learned a great deal about themselves, and the rest of us have learned not just lots about them, but also about human nature in general. We've been looking at the housemates through the eyes of thirty-one unforgiving cameras – we have seen them at their best and also at their worst. And we've been hooked, not just on the high drama and the tension, not just on the tender, romantic moments, but on the low-key, everyday fabric of their existence in the *Big Brother* goldfish bowl.

Although the success of the first series and of the week-long *Celebrity Big Brother* meant the production team knew they had a winning formula, nobody anticipated that the second series would be as big as it has been. Controller of Entertainment for Endemol UK, Ruth Wrigley believes that, apart from the fact that the contestants were such a strong group, the secret was 'that it was a bigger proposition for the audience. This time, there was even more: eighteen hours a day live streaming on E4, the interactive element with voting through your remote control, *Big Brother's Little Brother*, a fantastic fanzine show that lots of people engaged with. It all made the viewers so much more involved.' The first series ran through the summer holidays, when newspapers are famously short of stories to print. This year's series ended before the 'silly season', yet it was constantly featured on the front pages of every tabloid newspaper. The housemates' friends, family, ex-boyfriends and ex-girlfriends, colleagues and mere acquaintances found themselves under siege from journalists, all wanting any snippet of news about the overnight celebrities.

The second series of *Big Brother* took place at the same time as a general election and a Tory-party leadership battle, but it was Penny's and Bubble's fates that choked us with emotion, not William Hague's. The programme ran through the time of year when students and schoolchildren were busy with their exams, yet they found time to break off from the revision and tune in and chill out in the house in Bow.

Not only were there day-by-day diaries of life in the house to follow on Channel 4, but the E4 digital channel gave the audience the chance to monitor the happenings in the house live, a strangely compulsive occupation that had viewers tuning in over breakfast to watch the housemates doing nothing more than sleeping. The fact that the action was live – happening in front of our eyes, unscripted and totally real – meant that there was no need for high drama to make it addictive viewing. These eleven people became as much a part of our lives as members of our own families, and even the duller moments in the house were compelling.

Executive producer Conrad Green is delighted by the success of the series, not least because it didn't have the dramatic peak of the Nasty Nick affair last year. 'It's been remarkable. What I love about this series is that it was gentle. Nothing amazing happened. The people in the house opened up really gently, and the public has warmed to them. They are a very likeable bunch by and large, and particularly Brian and Helen seem to have really captured the viewers. That's why it was such a tense showdown.

'The love story between Paul and Helen was also very important, very tender and touching. When the series launched, everyone was talking about sex on TV, as if that is what it was about. But it's not sex at all – it's people falling in love, and only *Big Brother* can show that happening at real pace. You would never have predicted that would happen with those two people, yet to watch it unfold has just been quite charming.

'It's been a very harmonious house – the housemates have tried to support each other through it all. What is fascinating is the simplicity and honesty of it. It's like a soap opera, without the murders, kidnaps and plane crashes. A soap opera with real people, happening in real time in front of our eyes.

'The contestants in this series were a very balanced lot. Part of the appeal is that everyone knows people like them.'

Conrad believes that any of the eleven, and particularly any of the final four, would have made a worthy winner.

'They all brought something special to the house, all of them. But those who were still there in the final week showed extra-special qualities. Elizabeth was enormously important for keeping the house together. She was very giving in the house, in that she's always bitten her tongue when she was irritated by things. She has always been very diplomatic when dealing with the different personalities in there. She also taught them all to cook! She's been the glue for the house, one of the rocks that they've all relied on.

'Dean has played a similar role. His dry humour provided a commentary for the house. Everyone looked up to him, both as a father figure and as someone who could make sense of some of the unknowns of the house. He helped calm people a lot, because he himself is calm and paces himself very well. He isn't fazed by things. He was like a fun uncle – they relied on him in a paternalistic way, and yet at the same time he was a good laugh, good fun to have around. He also brought one very vital ingredient into the house: his music. They all found it very calming. Music is one of the things they missed most, and the fact that Dean could bring it to the group made him invaluable.

'Helen contributed incredible exuberance, enthusiasm and honesty to the house. She's a really loveable girl, direct and uncomplicated in the best possible way. She's totally charming, a very nice person to have around. She made the others laugh, usually unwittingly. If Dean and Elizabeth fell into the roles of the mother and father of the group, Helen was the naughty schoolgirl.

'And Brian was the naughty schoolboy. He was the house comic – it was his wit that carried him through a long way. But he was also very caring within the group, very good at listening and opening them up. He provided a very important bridge between the boys and the girls, a buffer between both camps which stopped there being a boy–girl divide within the house as there was last year. He also bridged the gap between the older, more mature members of the group and the youngsters. He provided great entertainment, but at the same time he was part of the glue that held them all together.'

Brian's immense popularity with viewers was reflected in the number of e-mails that flooded into the *Big Brother* website for him – a total of five thousand by the end of the nine-week run. That's more than double the amount that Helen, the next most popular housemate, received. Bubble got 1,700 e-mails, and Paul and Narinder both received well over a thousand, with Josh close behind them.

Because of the live streaming on E4, the number of people watching the action live on the internet was down on last year, but there was an increase in the number of people visiting the website for news updates, competitions, polls and background information on the housemates. Yet again, it was the biggest entertainment website in Britain. Users stayed logged on for an average of twenty minutes – ten times the usual length of a web visit.

Digital viewers with E4 soon got the hang of voting from their television screen. By the end of the run, almost forty per cent of all votes were being made on screen rather than by phone. Interactive viewers were also able to choose their favourite housemate of the day, and a camera would follow the person with the most votes for a full twenty-four hours. Brian, predictably, was the most followed, but when the affair between Paul and Helen hotted up, she took over as the one we all wanted to see more of.

And there were some people who couldn't bear to miss out on what was happening in the house when they were away from their television or computer screens. More than 200,000 people registered to receive news updates on their mobile phones, which BT Cellnet were sending out to all networks: they sent out more than five million text messages to house addicts during the nine-week run. All in all, it seemed that the second series was even bigger than the first, 'I was pleased that it all worked,' said Ruth Wrigley. ' It was such a difficult thing to pull off, to make the biggest thing in TV bigger. But we did it.'

The house itself caused almost as much interest as the contestants, with loads of enquiries flooding in about where viewers could buy the duvet covers or the orange blankets. The solar panel that provided such a wonderful backdrop to the eviction walk was also able to provide the housemates' electricity throughout the nine weeks. There was even enough power left over to support the electricity-guzzling floodlights in the compound. (The amount of electricity produced would have kept a standard three-bedroomed house going for eight months.) A charity auction of the contents of the house caused such excitement that on the first day of a ten-day auction, bidding for the orange blankets was up to £350 each and offers for the self-portrait painted by the housemates were already running to thousands of pounds. It seemed as if people wanted a memento to remind them of the eleven housemates. There is certainly no shortage of memories to choose from.

Who will ever forget the tantrums in the hot tub, when Brian turned on Josh, and Amma and Stuart laid into each other? Or Penny's manic moments both in and out of the kitchen? Or her row with Stuart, and the way he winked at Paul when they made up? Or the look on the girls' faces when gorgeous Josh walked in – and their expressions when they found out he was gay? What about Narinder's and Brian's amazing routines – and Josh and Dean's even funnier take-off of them during the soap-opera task? Or Bubble's spectacular trip over the coffee table. The birthday parties and the squabble between Helen and Narinder about 'crappy cuts'. What about the tender, burgeoning romance between Paul and Helen? And the constant bickering between Brian and Josh? And Dean's guitar music, Elizabeth's famous jumper? Whatever your favourite moment, the series provided an unlimited supply of comedy, romance and drama.

Now it's over, we can all reclaim the lives we led before (although it's hard to know what can replace a Friday evening spent watching an emotional eviction).

It may only be telly, but it's for real – and it's just about as good as it gets.